The Story of Don McClure
ADVENTURE IN AFRICA

CHARLES PARTEE

Zondervan Publishing House

Academic and Professional Books

Grand Rapids, Michigan

A Division of HarperCollinsPublishers

ADVENTURE IN AFRICA
Copyright © 1990 by Charles Partee

Requests for information should be addressed to:
Zondervan Publishing House,
Academic and Professional Books
1415 Lake Drive, S.E.
Grand Rapids, Michigan 49506.

Edited by Martha Manikas-Foster and James E. Ruark
Cover Design and Interior Design by Rachel Hostetter

Library of Congress Cataloging in Publication Data

Partee, Charles.
    Adventure in Africa : the story of Don McClure / Charles
Partee.
        p.   cm.
    ISBN 0-310-51971-3
1. McClure, W. Donald, 1906–1977. 2. Missionaries—Ethiopia–
Biography. 3. Missionaries—Sudan—Biography.
4. Missionaries—United States—Biography. I. Title.
BV3562.M38P37   1990
266′.0092—dc20   90-5717
[B]   CIP

Printed in the United States of America

91 92 93 94 95 / AM / 10 9 8 7 6 5 4 3 2

ADVENTURE IN AFRICA

To
GLENN P. REED
Missionary, friend, administrator,
"by all odds the ablest man in Africa"

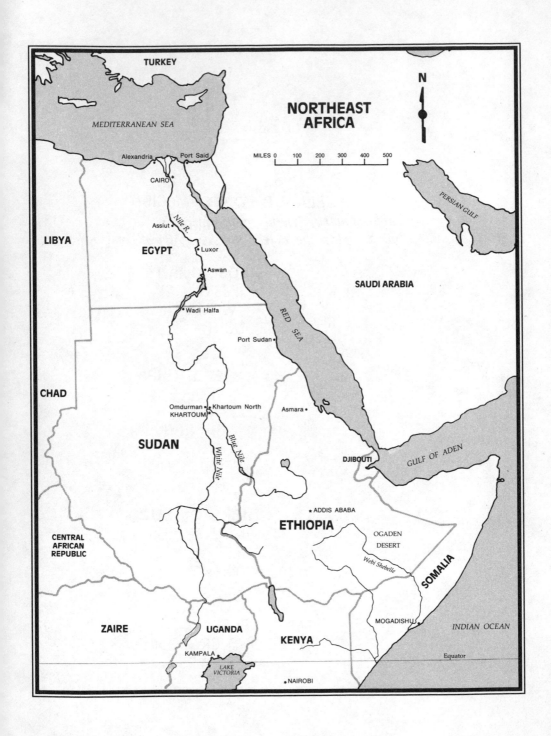

▼CONTENTS

WILLIAM DONALD McCLURE

b. Blairsville, PA, 28 Apr. 1906 to Robert Elmer McClure and Margaret McNaugher; public schools Blairsville; B.A. Westminster College (PA) 1928; teacher (short-term) Am. Mission, Khartoum, Sudan 1928–31; B.D. Pittsburgh Theological Seminary 1934; pastor Murrysville, PA 1932–4; m. Lyda Lake Boyd 20 Aug. 1932; children: Margaret Jean, W. Don, Jr., Lyda Lake; missionary: Am. Mission Doleib Hill, Sudan 1934–8, Akobo 1938–50, Pokwo, Ethiopia 1950–60, Gilo 1960–2, Gode 1970–7; Field Secretary Am. Mission, Addis Ababa 1962–70; D.D. Westminster College 1947; d. Gode 27 Mar. 1977.

▼ INTRODUCTION
▼ AFRICAN GUERRILLAS

THE SHARP BLADE of a guerrilla's bayonet ripping through the wire screen of an open window was the first dark portent that a life devoted to Africa was about to be cut down. As is true everywhere, the most dangerous animal in Africa is the savage beast called man. For all kinds of reasons, and for no reason, this cruel predator will attack those who intend him no harm, bear him no malice, and pose him no threat. This animal will kill even those of his own species who desire only his happiness and wish for nothing more than the opportunity to love and serve him.

On that day, 27 March 1977, the Reverend Dr. W. Donald McClure was gunned down in the Ogaden desert near Ethiopia's Somali border after nearly a half century of joyful service in Africa. Don was in that hostile region because he had given his word to His Imperial Majesty, Haile Selassie I, that he would direct a settlement project at Gode (*GO-dee*) to bring peace and prosperity to the area. But Don had lived in Africa long enough for his hair to change from bright red to snow white. At the end, his blood mingled with the earth in that land where he had long labored with unselfish enthusiasm.

By 1977 it was painfully evident that Don's great dream to establish a settlement for the nomads of the Ogaden desert was failing and would soon end. Marauding bands of Somali guerrillas, armed with modern weapons, continued to forage across the disputed border and steal whatever of value they could find. When viewed in retrospect, the fall of Haile Selassie in 1974 was the beginning of the end for this project; no other Ethiopian had the interest or power to support the plan to build a city that would be a haven for the often-starving desert nomads.

Officially retired, Don's two three-year volunteer terms had run out, and the denominational authorities were not disposed to appoint him to another. Nevertheless, Don had struggled on with great persistence and some success, but he was now seventy-one years old. If occasionally he wryly confessed that he did not possess the same strength as in earlier days, yet his energy was undiminished and he could still outwork most younger men. With years of experience and the accumulated wisdom that comes from accomplishment, Don's desire for a Christian Africa flamed as fiercely as ever. Closed behind him were the fruitful years with the Shulla and the Anuak peoples, and closing before him were the projected years with the Somalis. It became necessary to leave Gode for good—or ill.

Africa was Don's home. It was the land he knew best and loved most. Don was two years overdue on keeping his promise to his wife to return to America when she was seventy, but he was not yet ready to return to a leisurely life in rural Pennsylvania where he had grown up. Don had not expected to complete the Gode project, but he had anticipated soundly establishing it. Now the dangerous political reality of the border situation—which he could neither control nor direct—had overtaken the dream for Gode. A permanent mission there now seemed impossible. Abandoning a job undone and a challenge unmet was contrary to Don's nature. Don was not happy as he prepared to leave, but he threw himself into this task with as much resolute cheerfulness as he could muster. It was not a task he had chosen, but one he would perform.

On Monday, 21 March, Don was informed that a plane chartered from Addis Ababa to Gode had three vacant seats. He and his wife, Lyda, were eager to get to Gode so that they might retrieve some personal belongings, including a Toyota truck. Their son, Don, Jr., also a missionary, agreed to go along to help them drive the six hundred arduous miles between Gode and Addis Ababa. Although the road had been closed because of guerrilla activity, Don heard that it was now open; individuals were organizing a convoy of trucks to travel the road together. Don thought that if he was able to get to Gode he could join the convoy.

Early Tuesday morning Don, Lyda, and Don, Jr. drove to the airfield in Addis Ababa. After they entered the plane and the engine was warmed up, the run-up completed, clearance to taxi given by the tower, and the brakes released, the manager of the charter service came running alongside the plane. He banged on the door and informed the pilot that a previously paid charter customer had arrived and that his seat must be made available to him. The family decided that Lyda would remain in Addis Ababa and the two Dons would go on to Gode.

When they arrived in Gode, the McClures discovered that the road to Addis Ababa had never been open. Even if it were, there was no gasoline available. Therefore Don radioed to Lyda that it was impossible to drive out and asked her to arrange for a plane to come for them. Don knew that he could not get out immediately because the charter services were busy and flights required government clearance. Moreover, even after his flight was booked and cleared, there would be a forty-eight-hour waiting period, since Gode was a restricted military airport because it was the last military outpost between Ethiopia and Somalia. The two men spent the remainder of Tuesday and Wednesday doing routine jobs around the mission station with the hope of leaving by the weekend.

Earlier, the group at Gode—which included the Graeme Smith family, two Ethiopian nurses, an irrigation engineer from England, and two German builders—had heard by radio that the border town of Callafo had been attacked by guerrillas. The Callafo missionaries asked those at Gode to relay their request for emergency evacuation to Addis Ababa. The guerrillas had stripped the seven missionaries living in Callafo of everything except the clothing they wore. On Friday the Callafo refugees landed briefly in Gode and recounted their harrowing experiences. The Gode folk were quite concerned about this information and discussed the possibility of immediate evacuation for Pam Smith and her four children, but they made no decision. The group ate dinner together on Saturday, and though uneasy, they enjoyed their fellowship, discussed the recent events, and sought to discern God's will for each of them. After a period of prayer, Pam admitted that she was frightened by the closeness of the border troubles, but since none of the Callafo missionaries had been harmed physically, she was convinced that she should stay with her husband and cook for the group. In short, the situation in that part of the world was quite serious, but it did not seem foolhardy to remain at assigned tasks. Earlier Pam had asked Don what he would do if guerrillas appeared in Gode. "I don't think they will come here," he replied, "but if they do, I will give them everything I own rather than shoot one of them."

Since the McClures could not drive out of Gode, Don, Sr. decided that he should get back to Addis Ababa as soon as possible to finish some business with the military government. Don, Jr. wanted to return to his own work at Surma in southwestern Ethiopia. Thus they continued to prepare for the airplane trip to Addis Ababa.

About 9:00 P.M. on that last Saturday a fierce dust storm blew in. Before the McClures could close all the windows, the storm had covered everything in the house with a sixteenth of an inch of dust. Don and his son spent the rest of the evening discussing the incomprehensible magnitude of God's creation, the mysteries of the solar system, and the enormous distances of the galaxies. At one point, Don, Sr. said that he was curious about how much he would understand once he got to heaven—would he be able to comprehend the mysteries of creation and God's providence for it?

About midnight the two men were ready to sleep, but the storm was still blowing. It was very hot and sultry and the beds were covered with dust. They lay down on the rugs in the living room and drifted off to sleep. Half an hour later they awoke to discover that the storm had ended. They arose, took showers, cleaned off the beds, opened the windows, and went to sleep again.

About 1:30 Don, Jr. was startled awake by strange noises in the other bedroom, and his mind immediately leaped to the border troubles of Thursday. When he hurried into his dad's room he saw rifle barrels sticking through the screens. Guerrillas had cut the screens with their bayonets and at gunpoint demanded that the door be unlocked. As they entered the house, one of the guerrillas jabbed Don, Jr. in the leg with a bayonet and another ordered him outside. Don, Sr. was compelled to remain inside to open the safe and to show the guerrillas where things were stored.

Some fifty yards away, Graeme Smith also heard noise and began walking over to the McClures' house to get a gun for protection. Graeme was immediately apprehended and forced to join Don, Jr. standing on the porch along with guerrilla guards. The two men thought they might seize an opportunity to escape into the darkness, especially since Graeme wanted to get back to his house to offer his family what protection he could. However, they decided instead to cooperate with the guerrillas because their escape might well imperil Don, Sr., who was still inside the house. Furthermore, Don, Jr. surmised that because he had only been bayoneted and not shot, the guerrillas' intention was simply robbery.

Looting the house took about thirty minutes. Don, Sr. had never owned anything that he was unwilling to give away, although he had always tried to share with others in an orderly and productive way. When he was brought out of the house, the bandits, speaking Somali, demanded more money from him and from Graeme by name. Obviously the guerrillas knew them both, but the missionaries had no more money to give. The captives were then marched about thirty yards toward Graeme's office. Although language was a problem, Don, Sr. tried to joke with the guerrillas. He was not afraid, and it was clear that he bore no malice toward them. The guerrillas halted the procession, and after a quick exchange in Arabic and Somali, one of them pointed to Graeme's feet. He assumed they wanted his shoes and bent to untie them. However, at the sound of a command from the leader of the guerrillas, Graeme straightened up. He was standing at Don, Jr.'s left shoulder with Don, Sr. on his other side. Facing them were three guerrillas with rifles leveled. The command was questioned in Somali and quickly repeated: "Shoot them."

Immediately one of the rifles fired. In the instant he saw the muzzle blast engulfing his dad's chest, Don, Jr. realized the guerrillas intended to kill them all. And in that flash of gunpowder a heart that had metaphorically bled for the pain of Africa for half a century began to bleed in actuality. Then it stopped forever.

Seeing his father fall, Don, Jr. was instantly overpowered by the instinct to survive. In the split second he took to turn to run for his life, Don saw another muzzle blast, the flame this time engulfing Graeme. He saw Graeme's body jerk from the bullet's impact as he fell. The guerrillas also shot at Don—still at point-blank range—and Graeme, who had miraculously fallen to the ground unhurt, saw the blast surround Don, Jr. and was certain that he was hit and dying.

The guerrillas continued firing, and as Don, Jr. ran, he fully expected to feel the burning pain of a bullet. Diving under some vehicles, he spent a few seconds getting oriented so that he would not blunder into another group of guerrillas. Then he saw a clear path out through the gate and across the airfield. Knowing that a garrison of Ethiopian soldiers guarded the bridge over the Webi Shebelle River, Don ran toward the crossing to get help.

The rough terrain across which Don ran was full of erosion ditches formed by water running into the nearby river—some of them with sheer drops of twelve feet. Fortunately, he did not fall into any of them, but he did slide down banks and through thornbushes. Part of his mind registered that thorns were ripping into his skin, that his leg was bleeding, that he was surrounded by scorpions, that he was barefoot and dressed only in a pair of shorts; but in the main he was conscious of the great need to escape, the terrific noise he was making, and the oppressive feeling that he was being followed.

When he was halfway between the mission and the bridge, the Ethiopian soldiers opened fire. Don knew that there were night patrols around the bridge. He assumed he had stumbled toward one of them, which was shooting in the direction of the unexplained noise. He flattened out in an erosion ditch and watched tracers flying toward the mission. He heard return fire. When the shooting ended, Don realized that he was unable to see well enough to make plans. He determined to move to the top of a small hill, hoping to survey the situation by climbing a tree, but since there were no trees on the hill, he was forced to dig a hole under a large bush to conceal his position. At least he could now see the bridge, the town, and the mission.

In this manner he crouched, awaiting the dawn, struggling with the dark thoughts of the massacre in which he was the only survivor. The guerrillas' intention was clearly to loot and then to kill. Since the mission was completely defenseless and he had heard many rounds of ammunition fired, Don could not imagine that anyone else was still alive. He felt an especially heavy guilt for the death of Graeme Smith, because he had urged Graeme not to attempt to escape.

The darkest agony of all concerned his dad. Don not only bore his father's name, but carried his hope for a continued family presence in Christian mission in Africa. For many years they had worked together, often playfully attempting to surpass the other. Standing side by side for the last time, the elder Don had fallen to an assassin's bullet and the younger had lived to escape. Now that instinct had time to give way for reflection, Don thought it might have been better to die face forward rather than to be alive in hiding. Had he failed his dad? What else could he have done?

As daylight neared, Don tried to discover whether the guerrillas were still in the area. He could see Somalis on the bridge, but not Ethiopian troops. The fearful events of the night colored his perceptions, and Don did not recognize that the people he saw were villagers crossing the bridge to cultivate their fields before the heat of the day became too intense. Don also watched the mission compound. Very early a truck full of people pulled out, but he could not determine who they were. He did not dare to move, so he prepared to spend several days hiding in the hole he had dug. He knew that he could get water from the river at night. If the government forces did not soon regain control, he determined to walk directly into Somalia, avoiding the area of guerrilla activity, in the hope of finding responsible people who would help him.

About an hour after the first truck had left the mission, another vehicle appeared. Don recognized Abdi Nur, a Somali Christian, by his remarkable height and bright clothes. Don crawled out of the hole and asked, "Abdi, what has happened?" He was told, "The guerrillas have gone. No one is seriously injured, but your father—your father is dead." Don thought Abdi Nur was trying to protect him from the terrible truth that all were dead, but in fact the town was secure and all the mission personnel had been taken to the hospital.

During the time that the guerrillas were holding the McClures and Graeme Smith, a second band of guerrillas about fifty yards away had rounded up the other missionaries, including Pam Smith and the four small children, and had taken them out on the lawn. The guerrillas were preparing to shoot them when they heard the gunfire near the McClure house. This second group of guerrillas became confused, perhaps thinking that soldiers had arrived or that armed resistance had begun among the missionaries. In any case, the second band began shooting in the direction of the first, who returned their fire. In the resulting melee, both groups had fled, but not before one guerrilla fired a random shot that hit Pam's knee. Fortunately, the bullet did not sever a tendon or break a bone, but she received a painful wound, to which the Ethiopian nurses applied a tourniquet.

Thus the gunfire that caused Don's death created sufficient confusion to spare the lives of all the others. Don McClure was always ready to lay down his life for his friends, but never more so than in March 1977, when his last and greatest dream was fading away.[1]

Because of the impact of the gun blast, Graeme Smith lay numb and stunned on the ground near Don. He assumed that his own life was draining away. As the guerrillas broke and ran, one man hurried past him but then halted for a second. Graeme thought he would be shot or bayoneted, but the guerrilla moved on. When things were quiet, Graeme got up and hurried to join his family. They were all safe, and only his wife had been injured. The whole group spent the rest of the night hiding in the house.

Don's body lay on the ground where he had fallen, until the morning when Graeme returned and covered the body with a sheet. One of the Smith children came to say good-bye, but her father told her that "Uncle Don" was not there anymore—he had gone home to God, and only his body remained.

▼▲▼

According to his family, Don's death was not a tragedy, but the triumphal conclusion of a wonderful life. Don McClure was a man of boundless enthusiasm and relentless energy. Because of his faith and his zest for adventure, he was absolutely fearless. His unnerving cheerfulness was combined with such a total dedication to his task that it took a bullet to stop him.

Don McClure had spent his first African years in Khartoum, the capital of Sudan. Later he went south to live with the Shulla people at Doleib Hill. When he found his unique mission in life, he moved among the Anuak people first at Akobo, Sudan, and then closer to the heart of the tribe at Pokwo and again at Gilo in Ethiopia. As the pioneering phase of the Anuak project came to an end, Don was persuaded to work for a while as an executive in Addis Ababa, but he longed to get away from the desk and back to the field. A personal request from, and a promise to, the emperor of Ethiopia brought Don to his last frontier in Gode. And there he died.

This narrative is based on Don's letters home, always written in haste, but carefully preserved by his mother. After her death, the letters were transferred from box to box. Some of them are crumbling with age, some are faded and difficult to read; some reflect family occasions—birthdays, anniversaries, and so forth—but all in all this collection of letters offers a remarkable record of the adventure of a pioneer Christian missionary among the primitive people of East Africa in the middle decades of the twentieth century.[2]

William Donald McClure,
1928

Lyda Lake Boyd, 1926

KHARTOUM
FIRST STEPS IN AFRICA
1928–1934

▼ First Impressions

DON McCLURE'S African adventure began on 4 September 1928 when he stepped aboard the SS *City of Harvard* bound for that great continent[3] where, in time, he would discover that he was called to Christian service as a missionary.

When Don completed his studies at Westminster College in New Wilmington, Pennsylvania, he was still uncertain about the direction of his life and thought that a few years in the Sudan would give him time and space to decide what to do with himself. Like many young men he appreciated the support of a close-knit family, but he also needed the freedom to become an independent person. Although he never allowed his ties with home to snap while he was alive, he stretched them across half the earth.

During the years Don spent in and around Khartoum he worked as a teacher, an agriculturist, and an unlicensed—and untrained—physician (the title of "doctor" would come later in the form of an honorary degree). He was also a veterinarian, a part-time evangelist, a big game hunter, and a full-time handyman. Performing such a wide variety of tasks served Don well when he found his proper goal in life, but until he had completed exploring himself and Africa, this unfocused usefulness frustrated him. He wanted a sustained challenge. He was never content as a caretaker; he was by nature a pioneer.

Don was twenty-three years old when he stepped aboard ship anticipating both his journey and its goal. The American denomina-

21

tion to which the McClures belonged had been sending missionaries to Africa since 1854. Because the church was small, its members knew nearly all the missionaries by name and prayed regularly for them. Thus it was not entirely a voyage into the unknown.[4] Don expected to see some familiar faces in Africa.

Don was leaving behind three brothers and three sisters, a father he loved and greatly respected, and a mother he loved and deeply admired. As the American coastline faded from view, Don, as he would do all his life, took a few minutes at his typewriter and with his one-finger typing style cast lines back across the sea. Thus he addressed his mother:

> Last night as I watched you and Father disappear down the deck, the first realization of my leaving came to me. It hurt to leave, Mother dear, but now that feeling is all gone as I see the wonders of the ocean and enjoy the salty breezes. I sat up late and watched the lights of New York and then those of the Jersey shore fade from sight, and as the last of the beacons sank into the sea, I waved a farewell kiss to dear old America and all of you who have filled my life these last years. They have been great years, and I will always try to live so that people who come in contact with me will realize what a wonderful mother and father I have had.

Turning from the past to the present, Don expressed his delight in ocean travel. There were plenty of barefoot stewards (called "boys" whether they were aged twenty or sixty) to provide everything a traveler could desire. Don would be awakened at six in the morning when a steward brought some very strong tea, toast, apples, pears or oranges. He followed this little breakfast with a saltwater bath (in which the soap would not lather) and a freshwater rinse. Don was inordinately proud of the fact that, while other passengers had experienced a very rough day at sea and a rougher night, he had not shown the slightest sign of seasickness, not even a quake or a qualm. He admitted, however, that in order not to hurt the steward's feelings, he had indeed used the porthole to add to the level of the Atlantic Ocean—one cup of undrinkable tea.

In addition to his lifelong pleasure in food, Don loved games and was delighted to participate in his first game of deck tennis. The game, he explained, is much the same as regular tennis except the players use a ring of heavy rope, which they toss underhanded back and forth until it hits the deck. Don played with some missionaries and must have looked promising, because the captain asked Don to be his partner against two of the other officers of the ship. According to Don, the captain was so skillful that they won the match. Games of dominoes and checkers filled the afternoon hours. Don also discovered some chess players whom he intended to challenge.

Don's first real twinge of homesickness hit on the third day at sea, a Sunday. He missed worshiping with his family at home. He attended a simple service for the passengers on deck, but confessed that his thoughts were not on the sermon. He did enjoy the hymns, however, and thought that the people poured their hearts into the singing because they too were feeling lonely for those left behind.

Singing sounds so different out on the ocean. The immensity of space seems to carry the sound off into infinity, and yet I feel a keen sense of God's presence and the conviction that God really does brood over the deep.

While Don's singing voice fell *far* short of reaching operatic quality, he sang with good volume and great enthusiasm. Thus he was chosen to lead the singing on the second Sunday at sea. He explained to his mother that he had organized a fine quartet of male voices for the occasion and assured her that he would not place himself among them.

Of the forty-two passengers on the ship in Don's group, about a half dozen were his age. Twenty-two, representing three denominations, were going to India as missionaries. Don made friends with all of them, but was surprised at two young men, about twenty-five years old, who were going to India as insurance salesmen. Don said that apparently they felt they were already too old to do anything except play bridge and checkers. Don always had trouble understanding the sedentary life, and he spent the voyage setting up tennis and quoit tournaments and organizing the weekly entertainment festivities. As it developed, he had to reschedule the skits arranged for Saturday night, because some of the older missionaries thought such levity the night before the Sabbath would be inappropriate. Don respected their conviction, but found it hard to see their viewpoint. When he explained the situation to the captain, the latter threw up his hands and said, "My God, I surely hope the Lord will reward his faithful." This schedule change meant that Don had to go through all his preparations again. He felt that it would have been more considerate for those missionaries to make known their personal feelings and beliefs some time before the morning of the scheduled event!

On the eleventh day at sea, the ship passed through the straits of Gibraltar into the Mediterranean Sea. The African coast to the south looked just as barren and uninviting as the Spanish, but seemed somehow more vast and more mysterious. Don thought the blue of the Mediterranean out-blued all other blues of blue water. He reflected on the battles that had been fought in that place and all the romance connected with the Spanish courts and Spanish ladies with their dark-eyed Romeos (casually transporting Romeo from Shakespeare's Italy to Don's Spain).

Every day we see flying fish, and one of the greatest sights of all is to see the large porpoises swim along with the ship and in great, graceful dives leap ten feet out of the water and then repeat their stunt.

The porpoises seemed to jump just for the pure joy of living. And so did Don McClure. It was great to be young and starting an adventure in Africa.

▼▲▼

The American Mission to which Don McClure belonged had been working along the lower Nile in Egypt for several decades prior to a request in the early 1880s to create a Christian outpost deep in the Sudan. However, the terrible blood-letting of the revolution (1881–85) led by the Mahdi, or "the Divinely Guided One" (whose coming is prophesied in the Koran), had already begun. Its purpose was to overthrow the Egyptian rulers of Sudan in order to purify the Islamic faith by destroying those who had defiled it. By the end of 1883 the Mahdi's forces had slaughtered three Egyptian armies and were moving on Khartoum. Thus, when General Charles Gordon passed through Assiut in 1884 on his way to defend Khartoum and to meet his heroic death, the Reverend J. Kelly Giffen[5] of the American Mission was one of those who assembled to shake his hand and wish him Godspeed. After heroically resisting siege for 321 days, Khartoum fell on 26 January 1885, and Gordon's severed head was carried to the Mahdi and onto the world's outraged conscience.[6]

Later, when General Horatio Herbert Kitchener, accompanied by a young Winston Churchill, liberated Omdurman (the Mahdi's capital on the Nile opposite Khartoum) on 3 September 1898, the American Mission was prepared to move into Sudan. Indeed, the time span between these stirring events was so relatively short that Giffen was ending his long and distinguished missionary career in Sudan as Don McClure began his.[7]

Before beginning work in Sudan, the American Mission had devoted nearly a half century to work among Muslim people. Therefore the American missionaries already spoke Arabic. They were prepared to establish work among the Muslim tribes of north Sudan, but the British government, fearing political unrest, decreed that there could be no discussion of religion with Sudanese Muslims. So Giffen sought to work among the pagan, black tribes farther south. The mission was granted two hundred acres on the Sobat River in Shulla territory, some six hundred miles south of Khartoum, but when permission to live there was withdrawn, the missionaries settled in Khartoum. There they began a school where they could wait silently and witness to their faith by their example until the government made its final decision about the south.

When permission was finally granted, Giffen, his wife, and a medical couple began a Christian mission among the Shulla people and built a station that they called Doleib Hill. Actually it was not a hill at all, but a slight elevation on the riverbank where numerous Doleib palm trees (*Borassus Aethiopum*) grew. The first Christian services at Doleib Hill were held on 15 May 1903. By 1905, both pioneer families had returned to work in the north Sudan, but the missionary left in charge at Doleib Hill had managed to make a tour farther up the river, preaching through an interpreter to the Dinka and Nuer tribes.[8]

▼▲▼

Don began his work in Sudan at Khartoum (which means "Elephant's Trunk" in Arabic), where the Blue Nile and the White Nile join and where the colors remain separate for a while until they finally become mixed on their common journey to the sea. His first assignment was to teach at the Boys' School, which had sixty-nine boys who were boarders and one hundred others who came in for the day. His schedule involved waking at 5:30 A.M., breakfasting at 6:15, reading and praying for a time, and then teaching from 7:15 A.M. to 1:15 P.M. His class was like a small League of Nations, with Jews, Armenians, Greeks, Egyptians, Sudanese, Abyssinians, and Arabs. The Copts (a native Egyptian Christian minority) would have nothing to do with the Muslims, whom they considered beneath them, and both despised the Sudanese as a slave race. In addition to managing these tensions, Don had to work hard to keep ahead of the class, especially in English grammar and arithmetic.

The difficulty is that the arithmetic problems are given in English money and the metric system and do not look at all as they would appear in a sensible language.

Don thought too many of his students were listless in pursuing their studies and suggested that the climate made the people sluggish. But then he wryly admitted that he probably knew everything about Africa since he had only been there for a few weeks and was still experiencing culture shock. Therefore it was quite likely that the more he actually learned about Africa, the less he would think he knew. In any case, life seemed cheap. It was dismaying to see thousands of kids playing by the canals with no one around to watch them. If a child drowned, the attitude seemed to be that there was one less mouth to feed. He noted that a family took greater care of its goats.

Don was frustrated that he could not learn to speak Arabic faster, because without the language, he could not get to know non–English-speaking people. The mission did not pay for language study for those who were appointed to the field for a short term. So Don paid for his own Arabic lessons at fifty cents per hour, but he also had to spend twenty cents for a bridge toll and make a twenty-mile bike ride. He thought it was a serious hardship to ride that far to study an hour of "this fool language." On one occasion he told his parents that there were three types of Arabic:

The everyday language, the middle style into which the Bible was translated and which those with a good education could understand, and finally the classical style used by preachers in prayers and on special occasions—including those in which they were unprepared to speak and did not want anyone to recognize the fact. With the native people I am communicating by signs and wonders. That is, I make a sign, and they wonder what I mean.

Don was learning to love the Sudan.

I like the days and nights of cloudless skies. I even like the miles and miles of sand through which the life-giving Nile flows. Without water, everything is burned brown by the merciless African sun, but the soil must be rich. It has been tested and no seeds are found. Yet when the rains come and the Nile overflows, what was formerly desert becomes a vast meadow. Today it is 112 degrees in the shade, and the wind off the desert is like the breath of a furnace. The other day a sandstorm, or haboob, struck us. It would be hard to imagine the magnificence of the tremendous cloud that enshrouded everything. It looked as if a genie had opened a magic jar and released red and amber smoke. We saw a solid wall of sand about three hundred feet high and ten miles wide. The first part soared over our heads, and then we were struck by all its fury. We could feel the house quiver as sand blasted against it. The air was so fiery hot that doors had to be left open. Our hair was stiff, breathing was difficult, and ears and mouths were filled. Now I know what it means to get a *taste* of the country.

I love the Sudan. It is easy to see why so many missionaries call this their *real* home. Here life, and each day, demands everything you have. I was discouraged at first because the need is so great that meeting it seems hopeless. Missionaries here are not overworked by heavy duties, but are overwhelmed by innumerable trifles. I am usually disgusted with what I have been able to accomplish, but it is a joy to give my all. Everything we do is really appreciated. My students have begun to comb their hair on the same side as I do and, as much as they are able, to dress like me. One of them asked if it cost a lot to dye my hair red. I said it was very costly, and rolling up my trousers, I told him it was even more expensive to make the hair on my legs the right color!

On another occasion Don wrote,

It is very difficult for me to picture in any vivid manner the physical features of the Sudan, because we have nothing in America with which to compare it. The Sudan is situated in central Africa, immediately south of Egypt and northeast of Abyssinia and bordering on the Red Sea. It is a bit larger than one-third the size of the United States. Try to picture the United States from the Mississippi River to the Atlantic Ocean, from Canada to Mexico, and you have the size of the Sudan. Then, with a ruthless hand tear from it all the marvelous glories of our surpassingly beautiful land. Take away the flowing rivers, the pastured valleys, the superb forests of pine and oak; the hills would have to be robbed of all their charm and wealth, and then as if with a giant scraper, cut off the tops of mountains and dump them into the valleys, blot out the cities, and drive away 79 of our 85 million people. Then pour sand all over the vast plain, plant a few thornbushes and some scrubby trees, and set a merciless sun high in the heavens. In the midst of all this desolation, place the life-giving River Nile and you have some idea of the Sudan.[9]

Dwelling places in the Sudan are of several types. I can see out in the middle of this vast desert, burning under the sun, a pitched tent made of goat skins. It is merely a shelter to protect the Arab and his family from the heat of the sun. The sand is his bed, the heavens his canopy, goats' milk and dates his food, sensuality his amusement, idleness his occupation, and Mohammed his prophet. Again, I see another hut built by the riverside; this house is made of grass and cornstalks. There is one low door and no windows, no furniture; two large gourds hollowed out and cut in half serve as their only utensils.

Not long ago I visited the village house of a well-to-do Sudanese, a friend of mine, Hadj el Khider, whose low mud house is set in the middle of a small mud-enclosed courtyard. As I entered the gate, Hadj el Khider came to meet me. He is a fine-looking, dark-skinned Arab with flashing black eyes. He kicked back the dogs with curses and then led me into his front yard. There were four oxen, a horse, and about a dozen sheep and goats all nosing about the filth of that yard. He asked me if I would care to sit inside or outside. Looking about and at the same time pushing a goat out of my path, I said, "Let's go inside." But as we stooped to enter the house I wanted to recall my suggestion. As we pushed our way into that blackness from the bright sunlight, I heard a squawk and dodged aside just in time to avoid the chicken as it flew out the door. Then several others ran between my legs. After I had helped my friend throw a lazy goat off the only piece of furniture in the house—the bed, which was made of ropes stretched across a wooden frame and set up on legs—I decided that it would be very nice outside. As we skirted the bed, a hen that had been setting ran out, screaming her protest. She had been nesting under the bed in the midst of all their dishes. Under the bed is the only place the people have to keep their things—clothes, dishes, food—and when the floor is swept, that is where the sweepings go.

When one is visiting, it is absolutely necessary to drink something. It may be coffee or tea or perhaps only sweetened water with a little perfume in it in your honor, but something must pass your lips while there. So shortly the slave girl went into the room, drove the old hen out again, and came out carrying two small glasses. As she came into the light and held out the glasses for inspection, I could see the accumulation of years of dirt. The glasses had never been properly washed. So she shook the dust and dirt out of them and then, to do me great honor, took the hem of her utterly hopeless dress, which she had been dragging in the worst conceivable filth and which had not been changed for months, and with it she wiped out my glass. Such is a Sudanese house. Not a picture, nor a table, nor a carpet except the thick dust and animal dirt that cover everything; nothing of beauty—just mud walls and filth—filth and mud walls.

But these are externals. In all the Arabic language there is no word for *home* as we understand that word. They have a word *bait* that means "house," but nothing to express the love, tenderness, and happiness that we associate with "home." Hadj el Khider himself has never known a happy moment in all his life. He has three wives, whom I have never seen because they would not dare to show themselves to a guest. They never even eat their meals with him. He eats alone. There is never the slightest sign of affection between them. He has them for only two reasons: to work for him and to satisfy his lust. There are no sounds of children's voices around the house. It has been rumored that Hadj has had six baby girls, but they always disappeared the first day. If there had been a boy, he would have lived. Hadj is now seeking a wife who will give him a son and heir. His wives are treated worse than he treats his cattle and goats; indeed, he would rather have the cattle, for they bring him some income.

Of the people, the vast majority are black Sudanese or Arabs, who have enslaved large numbers of the Sudanese, or people of mixed races. They do not need our education or civilization or even our religion. What they need is the love of God and man. I have heard Dr. Giffen say more than once, when he had a houseful of guests who were talking and laughing around the table, that he has seen Sudanese steal up to the windows and gaze in wistfully. It was not the food they desired, for they do not like our food; they longed for acceptance and human fellowship in the context of fellowship with a loving God.

The plight of women especially will break your heart. One day a small group of women and children stood at the door of the clinic at Gereif, our station near Khartoum. They had come to be treated for colds, for eyes and wounds to be dressed, or for salve for their terrible running sores; but as they filed in, I saw an old woman off in one corner of the yard with her cloth draped over her head. I knew from the sound of her cry that it was not from physical pain, but rather a broken heart. I left her as I hurried and finished with the others, and then after they had all gone, I went out. Lifting up her head, I saw that she was covered with dried blood, and a deep gash in her head was filled with sand and dirt. I helped her in and washed and bandaged her, and she told me her story. The evening before, she had not been well and was too weak to prepare the evening meal for her husband, who was not only much younger than she but had married another young girl. This old woman was only married to do the housework. The younger wife refused to help with the meal, so when the husband came home and found no food, he cursed the old woman, knocked her down, and then, picking her up, hurled her out through the door and shouted after her three times, "I divorce you." Under the Islamic law that is sufficient to put her away forever.

This country has no character because it has several characters. Five thousand years of freedom, except for hungry lions and snakes; followed by five hundred years of Christianity[10]— and it is a certainty that the Christianity of Ethiopia was that of the Sudan, for we still have their ruined temples, and the old city of Soba mentioned in the Old Testament is just five miles from Omdurman, or rather Khartoum; followed by five hundred years of Muslim rule of the most vicious order; followed by a few years of Egyptian despotism when nearly all were made slaves; followed by thirty years of British iron rule, supposedly

Christian but dominantly mercenary—all this leaves no room for, and in no way creates, one distinct characteristic. So the Sudan has no language, customs, or laws of its own now.

Sudanese culture was very different from home. Therefore, according to Don,

I have been doing some heavy reflection on "speed" and "scale." The motto of the people here is "never do anything today that can be done tomorrow or later." The most-used word in the language is *bukkra*, meaning "tomorrow," or *badain*, translated "after a little" or "when I get rested." The leisurely pace of life out here makes our ideas of what can be done and should be done in a day's work appear unseemly. Is that a feature of climate, diet, race?

The second axiom is "never do anything yourself that you can order someone else to do." These people have the most interesting system of servants of any country in the world. Of course every white man or family has at least two or three servants and usually more. If the garden is large, there must be still more. But the unique part about it all is, there is no limit to the degree of lowliness of servants and they can go down to a slave of a slave, meaning that even the lowest slave can have his personal butler. It is like this in an ordinary cross-section (of course I could start still higher and make the numbers greater), but picture for yourself the average household of four people. In the house proper, there are three servants: the cook, *tabbah*, and he is the king of the roost. His magnificent salary of fifteen dollars a month (if he is a good one), demands, and gets, the respect of all others on the compound. He is boss of all inside the house and some outside. Next in order comes the serving boy and bottle washer, *sufraggi*, and he must be the cleanest and quickest, for he serves at the table. He may be paid five dollars a month after he has had some training. The third boy, or *haddam*, is just a servant, and he has to do all the cleaning and bed-making.

Outside, the number is largely governed by the size of the garden. Here we have two gardeners with their wives, and all of them work. Some places there is also another man, who does not have a thing to do but sit at the front gate and sleep there all night, a *bowwab*. He is necessary because a visitor coming to your house never walks to the front door, but stops at the gate and claps his hands until someone comes and opens it for him. Then of course there is the washing woman and ironing man, neither of whom are full-time servants.

But to me the home life of our servants is the most interesting. They have followed in the footsteps of the white man, and they too must have their servants. The servants have their own homes, and since they are working for us from five in the morning until nine at night, there must be someone at home to take care of the house, so our servants will very often have their own servants, always a black of some lower tribe. And if the work is at all tiring, any of these servants of servants will have a slave that he has bought someplace for a few cents. And strangest of all, the slave will have his own slave, which is always a female whom he has somehow browbeaten into being his own property. This woman is usually rented to his friends who are less fortunate than he.

Such is the structure of Sudanese society. Every man in this country is the servant of someone. Even the big sheikhs are at the beck and call of British officials. There are lots of young blacks working in the government offices or commercial houses, and as a rule, as soon as they get a position they leave the house of father and mother and set up their own establishment with their own servants. Imagine a young fellow at home making thirty dollars a month, owning his house, and having servants!

Last night I borrowed a tuxedo and strutted off to the governor's reception at the palace for the Right Honorable Lord Lloyd, High Commissioner of Egypt. Lord Lloyd has been in south Sudan on a sightseeing tour, and he returned to Khartoum yesterday morning—I expect just to meet us at the palace garden. I have never attended anything so elaborate in all my life. It would be too long a story to attempt to describe the gorgeous beauty of the decorations and costumes. Of course it was outside, and all the garden was marvelously arrayed in myriads of colored lights. Every tree and shrub had taken on the appearance of a Christmas tree, shining with the tiny bulbs and huge, fantastic lanterns of all conceivable shades. The palm trees had beautiful clusters and nests of lights most cleverly arranged. The flowers in the artfully designed beds were all lighted with their own individual lamps of multi-colors.

In keeping with the anything but overdone or amateurish dressing of the grounds were the gentlemen and ladies. All the officers of the various regiments, departments, and divisions were dressed differently and in all the shades of the rainbow; some in scarlet with gold braid, blue and gold, black and red and white; and wonderful plumed hats. Of course the ladies had to dress even more spectacularly. Some marvelous works of dressmaking were displayed with bare arms and naked backs. (The reason I cannot describe the *dresses* with more accuracy is that I kept forgetting to look at them!) To amuse us and furnish inspiration for dancing in various parts of the garden, there were three fancy-dressed and well-trained bands playing popular and classical airs. To keep us happy and well fed there were impossible quantities of fruit cocktail, cake, punch, whiskey, champagne and wine, and so on and so on.

Of a quite different dinner, Don wrote:

The other night several of us had dinner with a Sudanese family. We were seated on mats covered with filth. The mother was carrying twin babies on her hip while she prepared dinner. As soon as the father came home, we started with our dinner. And what a dinner! The number of courses would rival the finest hotel at home, and with the exception of an excess garlic supply, the food was as good as anything I have eaten since I left home. We started with a thick chicken broth and an excellent salad, all served in rather dilapidated crockery and eaten with a single spoon. Next came a splendid roast and rice, and I ate as if it were the end; but as soon as our plates were emptied, a huge steaming leg of mutton was presented with macaroni and cheese. The roast and leg of mutton were served by the father with the help of his fork and strong fingers. I shoved down some mutton and was waiting for the dessert and hoping it was light, when a tray piled high with stuffed pigeons was carried in by the black slave. I was ready to quit. One pigeon disposed of, I made the inane remark that it was very fine, and immediately the father grabbed his half-eaten bird and plopped it down on my plate; such is an Eastern custom and it cannot be refused. My belt was entirely loose and I was uncomfortable, but my misery was not yet over. The plate of roasted chicken with stuffed peppers found me praying for increased capacity. The chicken concealed, I insisted to the host that I could not eat another bite, but he only laughed at my discomfort and made me eat my share of the pineapple, mangoes, and bananas, and then we went to the other room to have the Eastern coffee served.

I am sure that never in my life have I eaten so much, and yet he then apologized for not having more, because the Islamic feast had drained the market. I was extremely grateful for the feasting Muslims. The mats on which we sat were not only filthy, but also inhabited by a number of playful creatures who were also having dinner. It is a strange experience to eat and be eaten at the same time.

▼▲▼

While Don's schoolboys were not very enthusiastic about academics, they thoroughly enjoyed games. Don was amused when he was demonstrating the manly art of boxing and a large student decided that the time had come to teach the teacher a thing or two. Don responded quickly and chortled later that the big fellow had taken a good punch to the head and would doubtless have a black eye if his skin were not already black.

Don declared that he did not desire to make Western boys of his students, because "theirs is an old civilization and has elements of nobility in it." On the other hand, he was not ashamed of his Christian faith, and while he did not often talk about Christianity in class, he was trying to live a model Christian life. Don thought he might be having a positive effect when two of his students asked the senior missionary for instruction in the Christian faith. One of the Muslim boys said to Don, "You are a true Christian." When Don asked why, the boy replied, "You are always thinking of us, and you are always happy." Don thought that was a good definition of a true Christian and wished the definition could be more accurately applied to him.

I am filled with an undying ambition to do something worthwhile in the great land of Africa. I often wonder if I am worth enough to the Lord to give up all the joys of family and friends in America. If I cannot demonstrate my worth in the next five years as one of the Lord's harvest hands, I will not encumber the African vineyard any longer.

Don's fascination with Sudan was endless.

Today I walked over the ruins of Omdurman. It is hard to realize that it was once a city of a million inhabitants under the Mahdi,[11] with fortifications, dungeons, barracks, and an arsenal. I saw where Gordon fell. He is one of my heroes. For God and for duty he stayed at his post until the end. I went to Omdurman to visit the Government Industrial School upon invitation from Mr. Stirk, the superintendent. He took me around to show me his potters, plumbers, builders, stonecarvers, carpenters, and smiths. I saw enough to make me believe that he is doing the most practical work in the Sudan. Mr. Stirk himself is most interesting. An Oxford graduate and fluent in German, Italian, French, and Greek, he is a prodigious reader and worker in languages. Yesterday when I walked into his office, he started to put away a Bible and a notebook into which he was writing; I asked him what he was doing, and he said, "Oh, just putting in a little time translating the Bible into Italian." He lives alone in a beautiful house along the Nile, and during other spare hours he writes poetry in Arabic. I have played tennis and golf with him several times and have been invited to take dinner with him in the near future; that is, as soon as Ramadan is over and his Muslim cooks can work again. This is the Ramadan season when all the Muslims fast during the day and feast at night. Our cook does not sleep at night and does not have much time to do so in the daytime. He is so religious in his fasting that he will not swallow his saliva, but must walk outside every ten minutes to spit.

I had a delightful ride last night. I read until I was too tired to read anymore. Then I turned on the single eye of my two-wheeled "iron horse" and started for the Nile. The new moon was a quarter full, and as it sank down behind the tall, graceful date palms on its way to America, it was a scene of indescribable beauty. A few days ago I rode five miles on my bike in the hot sun for a prayer meeting. I would not feel the heat so much if I were on the way to a tennis match. Dr. Sowash, one of our missionaries, says that playing with the ladies is *not* tennis, but a separate game called "hit and giggle."

Since the country was governed by England, British customs were faithfully observed in Sudan. The long arm of the British empire often held a tea cup in its hand, and Don found himself learning to enjoy afternoon tea. On the occasion of the approaching marriage of one of the missionary women, a collection had been taken to buy a rug as a wedding present. Since Don contributed to the fund, he went to the tea determined to recoup some of his contribution. Don also took up golf, spending his first month's salary on golf clubs. The governor general of Sudan was president of the Omdurman Club, and Don thought it might be helpful to know him. Don also played tennis with three government officials—all of them Cambridge University men and, in his opinion, splendid fellows except for their extreme conceit. One of them had been in Sudan for twenty-one years. This man's life consisted of office work, reading, drinking whiskey, and playing tennis. Don was this man's doubles partner and they lost the first set, 6–1, and the second, 6–4. Then they won the last three: 7–5, 6–3, 6–0. Don felt that his use of an unfamiliar British racquet might explain his poor play in the first two sets, but was pleased that his game improved quickly. He thought some of the other players were as good as he, but none was obviously superior. "The English were chagrined," he said, "since they are extremely proud of two things: their manners and their tennis."

▼ The Right Woman

Don's LARGE FAMILY always celebrated Christmas in an extraordinarily festive manner. All the brothers and sisters, uncles, aunts, and cousins exchanged numerous gifts, and everyone tried to add a special touch in order to be noticed. The family ritual included the decoration of the tree on Christmas Eve by adults and older children who were not required to go off early to bed. Thus, for a child to attain the age for "decorating the tree" was a significant rite of passage to adulthood. On Christmas Day all were able to open their stocking presents immediately (as a kindness to the very little ones, whose anticipation was so strong) and then eat a splendid breakfast and wash, dry, and put away the dishes (as a kindness to the mother). The family then gathered around the tree; Don's father read Luke's account of the birth of Christ and prayed. The youngest child who was able to read distributed the gifts to all, and they were opened one by one around the circle from the youngest to the oldest.

In Africa, Don missed most the Christmas celebration at home. As the end of 1928 approached, he wrote,

Last year I little realized that this Christmas I would be seven thousand miles from home. You will be trying to keep warm and I will be trying to keep cool. Actually, the temperature gets down to fifty-six degrees at night, but when the sun comes up it is ninety degrees. I will not be able to celebrate Christmas with a snowball fight, but you cannot have a tennis match either. Christmas week started with a bird hunt up the White Nile. It was mostly "hunt" because I got only one bird and that was on the way home. On Tuesday I was Santa Claus (or Abu Krimsas) for 150 young girls, many of whom were badly frightened, thinking old Santa was an evil spirit. The next time I played

37

Santa we invited the village boys and girls. We told the Christmas story and then distributed dolls to the girls, balls to the boys, and candy to everyone. Santa's pack included a trick coin purse for me, which was a sly joke at my always being broke.

Don was amazed to discover that personality conflicts made deciding the location of the big Christmas dinner difficult. Some missionaries were barely speaking to other missionaries and would not enter their houses. "Life here is not one grand united effort to bring Muslims to the new life in Christ. We are all too human." Nonetheless Don received a lot of attention from the various missionary families. "I guess I was not able to conceal my Christmas-time homesickness very well."

▼▲▼

Taking his role as older brother seriously, Don felt it was his duty to give his sister some advice about men! "Remember," he wrote, "talk is cheap. I know, because I have been an expert in that expenditure." Single and carefree, Don thought it was marvelous to hear of girls he had once dated getting married. He claimed that he had given them a good start in such a direction. Yet he himself remained proudly unattached, happily so, he asserted—such pride going before a mighty fall, for about this time Don met Lyda Boyd.

Lyda, a slender, dark-haired, dark-eyed graduate of Muskingum College, was teaching mathematics in Wheeling, West Virginia, when she applied for short-term service in Egypt, where many of her aunts and uncles were already working. In the summer of 1928 she was asked to teach in Sudan, but declined, since she had already signed a teaching contract (which included a nice raise) and she had not saved enough money to go to Africa. However, a letter from a Sudan missionary implored her to reconsider, since hers was the only application that had been processed and approved and she was needed in the Khartoum North School. Lyda asked the president of the Wheeling school board for a three-year leave of absence, and twelve days after she received the letter from Sudan she was on a boat for Africa, where she would spend the rest of her life.

Don McClure had gone to Sudan in part to put some distance between himself and a certain young woman who was thinking seriously about a wedding—his. Like many young men who have not found the right woman, Don spent a lot of time assuring and reassuring himself that he was not ready for marriage. But when he saw Lyda, "something inside me said, 'Yours.'" The first mention of Lyda in a letter home was laconic and quaint, "I attended Miss Boyd." Don thought she was quite attractive and a good sport.

After supper, I sought for a companion to walk home, and being turned down by all the overstuffed men of the mission, I finally found an amiable companion in Miss Boyd, a niece of Dr. Jim Boyd. We walked the eight miles back to Khartoum North through the sand, and it was great fun.

Don later told his family that Lyda seemed to be interested in an Englishman who was not at all worthy of her. Don offered the opinion that she would get over this interest. Apparently he was right, since two years later she married Don. He thought, "She is too pretty and clever to pay any attention to me," but with his remarkable persuasive powers he convinced her otherwise. In March 1930, Don was at some pains to explain to his parents that this attraction was not that of two lonesome children who were much thrown together in the exotic and romantic East, but the love of a man for a wonderful woman. "She is perfect for me. She is adorable to the last degree, and you will like her immensely. It will take about fifty years for me to get over this." So close was their relationship that they later became famous in Africa as a couple who required only one regular-sized sleeping bag.

Don had very little money to apply toward an engagement ring, but in a small jewelry store in Khartoum he found a white gold ring with three tiny diamonds that he could afford. It was not very expensive, because one of the diamonds was chipped. When Don and Lyda announced their engagement in October 1930, Don complained that all their friends "felt quite safe and even enthusiastic in congratulating me and telling me that she is too good for me; they are not nearly so fervent in their congratulations *to her.*"

Last week we had a wonderful boat trip that included Jim and Minnie McKnight[12] and Lyda. The time of sailing was set for three o'clock on Friday. I was ready with the boat at the appointed time and place and only had to wait an hour and a half for the others to show up with all their gear: pots, pans, chairs, tables, beds, food, and water jugs. We had a crew of five boatmen who were to handle the sail when the wind was blowing in the right direction and to pull the boat when the wind was against us. As we started downstream, the boatmen had to pull, and we could hear their low chant by which they kept step. That looked like fun, so I kicked off my shoes and waded out to the bank to help. The boatmen protested strenuously that I should not work with them because they were poor men and unfit to work with me. Nevertheless, I drew one of the shoulder straps over my head and started out at the head of the gang. Our crowd on the boat shouted a lot of useless advice. The boatmen were silent for a time, and then they began their chant again. The sun had set, and the full moon looked like a newly minted coin. The glories of a Sudanese full moon are unequaled anywhere. The light is bright enough to read by. I felt that I would enjoy pulling that boat all the rest of my life.

All kinds of challenges presented themselves, including on-the-job medical experience.

My medical skills are improving, although my fees are not keeping pace. Still, I think it shows a lamentable lack of gratitude for a charity patient to attempt to take a bite out of the surgeon. One of our new camels has a bad abscess on the front of his hump that was lanced and treated in Khartoum. However, since we need this camel working on the farm, I decided to finish the treatment myself. I had the camel brought in and tied down, and set a man to hold a rope around his powerful jaws. Well, the first thing we veteran veterinarians do with an abscess is to irrigate it. Thus I asked my nurse to hand me the garden hose, which I inserted into the wound for the purpose of letting the water carry away all the decayed matter through a drain provided at the back of the hump.

I ran the water for some time, and no doubt Mr. Camel was experiencing some discomfort. When I shut off the water and squirted some disinfectant into the raw sore, the patient objected to the procedure with such vigor that the man holding his jaws was thrown off his feet and the camel swung his wicked teeth around to seek redress from the source of his misery. I had my back to his head, but fortunately I was wearing a broad belt. The camel caught me on the belt, squeezing it together sufficiently to give me a mighty pinch and driving with such force that he knocked me clear over his hump to the opposite side. I grabbed the squirt gun and gave him such a mouthful of the miserable disinfectant that he will be spitting for weeks to come. I almost bit him back, but I decided such conduct might embarrass the medical profession of which I am now a proud, if very junior, member.

▼▲▼

Always eager for new experiences, Don wanted to use his first vacation for a European tour with Mack, a missionary friend who also had very little money. The two men planned to meet in Cairo. Don was pleased that he and Mack

Are the same size and can wear each other's clothes, including shoes, so in good biblical fashion we will have all things in common. Each of us packed two pair of khaki shorts, two pair of golf socks, shaving stuff (which we do not intend to use), handkerchiefs, notebooks, diary, and half a tent. Mack will carry the Old Testament, and I will carry the New. I cheated by sneaking in a copy of Goethe's *Faust*. Mack likes detective stories, so I imagine he will smuggle a couple of them.

Don assured his parents that he would remember all the good advice that they had given him, but he did not promise to follow it.

Last Wednesday, with Lyda and Miss Wilson of our mission, I left Khartoum for Cairo, the capital of Africa to Egyptians and missionaries. I was traveling second class in a compartment already occupied by two Syrian men of elephantine proportions and an enormous amount of luggage. I did not mind during the daylight hours, because I could eat, play cards, and read in the women's compartment. But at nine o'clock I went back to my own car to check the sleeping arrangements. That was already settled, because those two huge, sweating, stinking men were stretched out on the two seats, looking for all the world like twin hippos and sounding like twin sawmills. The floor space was covered by their baskets and clothes. Finally, I threw most of their stuff out in the hall and spread my one blanket on the floor. The next difficulty seized me with such force that I almost gave up the thought of sleeping. I had a choice between breathing feet or garlic all night. The feet were strong and likely to get stronger; the garlic, I thought, might wane, so I chose their heads. Anyway, the windows were open, and while sand blew in, I hoped the smell would waft out. Such a night I have never before experienced.

Since Mack and Don could not afford a cabin, they booked deck passage across the Mediterranean Sea for $20.00. Their tour of Italy included eating delicious fruit at Messina and seeing Mount Etna in Sicily from the boat on the way to Rome. Don thought the churches in Rome were both marvelous and "marble-ous." He and Mack found a room for 30 lira, or $1.50, which included beds, water, towels, and— at no extra cost—bugs and flies. They also visited Capri and, ignoring the prohibition, swam in the waters of the beautiful Blue Grotto. The trip to Pompeii included a visit to Vesuvius, the volcano that destroyed the city. The men got up in the middle of the night intending to reach the crater by sunrise, waking the snoring proprietor to return their passports. Equipped with a bag of raisins and dates, they set out. Soon they were lost in the darkness, but continued to push upward. Mack became so tired that Don took off his belt and spent some time pulling Mack along with it. However, when Mack finally sat down and put his head between his knees, Don realized that his friend was too exhausted to continue. Don was not tired and went on to the top to greet the sunrise.

In Florence, Don and Mack found a room for $1.00 that was wonderfully clean and had a balcony that looked out over a small fountain and flower garden from which they could watch the artists at work. For lunch they ate a quart basket of red cherries, which cost 5 cents. While there, the young men were invited by some wealthy Americans to a fancy dinner. Don thought the most interesting feature of the meal was when Mack mistook a glass of white wine for water. The thirst caused by the hot Italian summer led to a sizable swallow of wine, but Mack was not prepared for the result—which was not unlike the earlier eruption of Vesuvius.

On 4 July the men arrived in Geneva and found a hotel room that cost 52 cents. Lunch that day consisted of two eggs, lots of bread, and a quart of milk, all for 7 cents. Don and Mack were eager to get to the American Express office, because they had been out of touch with their families since they left Africa at the end of May. Don was delighted to receive eighteen letters from home.

In order to conserve our small supply of money we have eaten a lot of fruit that is both filling and cheap. However, I ate too many strawberries and have a bad case of hives. I have skipped the last six meals because I did not feel well. The strawberries are heavy on my stomach, and I cannot convince the stupid things to go out of my system either way.

Leaving Geneva, the tourists visited the famous castle of Chillon. Excitedly, Don wrote home that he had seen the famous dungeon and touched the very pillar to which Byron had been chained. Don would have been amused to learn that the prisoner of Chillon was *not* Lord Byron (1788–1824), but François Bonnivard (1498–1570), who was chained to a pillar for four years because of his opposition to political developments in sixteenth-century Geneva. The unconventional Byron was so impressed by Bonnivard's suffering in the cause of freedom that he scratched the name "Byron" on another pillar some three hundred years later and wrote the passionate poem in tribute to Bonnivard that begins, "Eternal Spirit of the chainless mind."

After Switzerland, Don and Mack went to Paris. Don was impressed by the romance of Paris and by all the couples who were "saying or rather *doing*" good night. He was afraid that if anyone bumped into them, they would lose some teeth. The young missionaries were denied their desire to see and hear the Paris Opera, because their knickers were not considered proper attire.

When we left Paris we counted our money, and it came out to 20 Egyptian pounds, or $100.00. Calculating on the same rates we paid to get to Europe, we figured $50.00 would be ample for the train to Marseilles and deck passage to Alexandria. So we went to Barcelona, found a cheap hotel, took in a bullfight, and then decided we had better buy our tickets. We left Cook's Steamship Travel Agency dazed, because the cheapest possible passage back was $90.00. In addition, our hotel added a twenty-five percent tariff to our bill to defray the costs of some local exhibition. We paid half the hotel bill, and I left my camera as security for the rest, which I will send back to them from Egypt.

So here we are with $4.80 to cover lodging for the three days until our boat sails and food for those three days plus the four days on the sea. Right now we are camping in a hidden valley about ten miles from Marseilles. We tried to camp and cook our meals in a public park, but we were asked to leave. We are near

a spring that provides good water, and we bought 10 cents'
worth of beefsteak and two large potatoes. Mack is not much of
a cook, so I found a heavy piece of wire and prepared a spit on
which I cooked the meat to a nice brown. Actually it was mostly
black, since I was using a pine fire. France is a delightful
country, but no place to be broke. I am hardboiling a dozen eggs
to last us the four days on the ship.

On the way back to Africa, Don met forty Oxford University
theology students who were traveling to Israel. "Most of them," he
confided to his mother, "live closer to Christ than I have been able to
approach. I have never known a group of men so united in spirit and
with one tremendous purpose to preach the gospel of Jesus Christ."
By now Don had recognized that his future required a theological
education, and he was restless to begin seminary study. Many other
young people headed for a career of Christian service have experienced what he confessed: "It is terrible to have the desire to preach
the gospel and yet have nothing to say." He requested of his family,

Do not forget to remember me in your prayers as I try to plan for
next year. I have great visions if I can only carry them out. I
often wonder what would happen in a human life that was
totally dedicated to the service of God. I want to leave Africa
dead tired and worn out. My college track coach always
complained that I looked too fresh at the end of a long race. In
the race of life, I want to go all out, all the way until I am
completely exhausted in his service.

The great regret of that year was Don's loss of his brown felt hat.
A man's hat can be a very personal and cherished possession. Don
admitted that some persons would judge his hat tattered and even
disreputable, but the crown was in good shape and the hat had
character. Don remembered putting his hat on the carrier of his
bicycle, but his mind was so occupied by meeting Miss Boyd that he
forgot to secure it, and the hat must have fallen off somewhere.

Don was never very attached to material things. It was his practice
to give immediately whatever was admired to the person who liked it.
This included countless sets of cuff links, and later, a great deal of his
wife's jewelry. A friend once remarked that he most sincerely and
fervently hoped no one ever admired Don's trousers![13] However, his
brown felt hat was an exception. Don had worn it in Europe, and it

had been his faithful companion for many years. Striking an attitude that originated with our father Adam in the Garden of Eden, Don blamed the woman. "Clearly," he wrote home, tongue-in-cheek, "it's *her* fault that I lost my hat."

Dark Thoughts

DON THOUGHT a mission conference in Khartoum had been a huge success, including the recreation hour. Some of the preachers had never been so outrageously frivolous, and it did them a world of good. Because the conference had ended and because he knew the personalities of his friends Glenn Reed[14] and Lowrie Anderson, Don expected some kind of continuation of the fun. Thus, after closing up the last New Year's party, he made his way carefully and safely to his bed on the roof through a maze of buckets of water set on the tops of doors, pots and pans on the stairs, ropes across the floor, and a bed fixed to collapse under his weight. He could not sleep, however, with the thought of Glenn and Lowrie getting off scot-free; so he climbed out of bed, gathered two long ropes, and crept down to the beds where they were sleeping on the lawn.

Don tied a rope to each bed, climbed back up on the roof, and pulled the beds up. Glenn and Lowrie woke up in the New Year to find their beds trundling across the lawn and, before they were fully conscious, discovered that the beds had begun to climb the walls of the house. The two young missionaries were dumped unceremoniously on the ground and swearing a mighty vengeance. Don then tied the suspended beds fast and went to sleep. Glenn and Lowrie, of course, tried to get at Don, but he had thoughtfully locked the door that led to the roof.

Besides planning fun, Don used his time to reflect on his purpose in Africa.

I have already made some terrible mistakes in Africa, but all of them have served to make me better than I was before, and now I would not have had those experiences other than they were. I am sure there have been countless opportunities that I have

46

missed; some because of lack of inclination and zeal; some I did not have the energy to meet because I had spent my strength selfishly; at other times I lacked the courage, but more often I found myself handicapped because I had no preparation either in the Arabic or theology necessary to meet the situation. One such case presented itself as recently as last Friday. Sheik Tayib called to inquire for me, thinking I was still ill. I was teaching at the time, but when I came out to greet him, he poured out upon me more than the usual number of greetings and looked upon me as one back from the dead. We talked a bit about sickness, and then he said, "We believe that when a man sins, God visits upon him some sickness as a punishment for that sin and always a man is punished for his deeds here and now. If the man makes only a little sin, he is just a little sick, but if the sin is grievous, he will surely die. If God wills," he said, "I hope your punishment is now finished and the sin requited." That is a literal translation of what he said; I could not quite get it all. If I had only been able to command the Arabic sufficient to tell him what we think of forgiveness by grace through Christ, I am sure Sheik Tayib would never have forgotten that lesson; but all I could reply was, "Through the grace of God I am better." If God allows that someday I am able to return to Sudan, before I come, I will surely spend a year of language study in Cairo. Then I will be prepared to meet every situation from the very beginning.

▼▲▼

Don always hated to see potential unrealized. The religion of the young Muslim men among whom he was living did not permit the consumption of beer or whiskey, but a great many wasted their potential by sitting around all day drinking in coffee houses that were "rotten holes." To do his part to improve the situation, Don was paying for the school expenses of three boys, saying that he could not spend money on himself with so much need among the Sudanese people. He was also helping a black boy who was intelligent but possessed absolutely nothing except one filthy shirt. The boy's poverty-stricken mother had consented for her son to come to the school, but she could not help him with his fees.

Don was especially interested in a young man named Ahmed Nagi. Ahmed had nearly died of appendicitis, and Don often visited him and prayed with him. One day Ahmed closed his prayer in the name of Christ. He seemed open to the Christian faith until his uncles found out and threatened either to kill him or send him away to a distant province. Don wanted Ahmed to have the opportunity to continue his education at Assiut College in Egypt. Since the yearly cost was $150, Don asked all his family to forego Christmas presents to him in 1930 and instead send the money they would have spent so that Ahmed could go to college. Don's idea was to establish the "Assiut College Revolving Fund," with each student paying back the money as he was able so that another student could continue his education.

Last week in a scrap at the school, one of the boys laid open Mohammed Ali's head quite badly. Jim McKnight and I took him to the government hospital in Khartoum and left him in the care of a Sudanese orderly. The next day as we returned to Khartoum to check on him, we met Mohammed starting to walk back to the school. The wound had never been treated, and the poor kid had not been given any food or water for eighteen hours. Jim and I took him immediately to the English mission hospital in Omdurman, and now the doctor is having a battle for the boy's life. We do not yet know whether the skull is fractured, but infection has set in and has affected his eyes so he is almost blind. Jim is entering a charge of criminal neglect against the civil doctors. I almost feel like a real doctor today. I have treated a little girl about two years old who fell into a fire and received a horrible burn; a boy with mumps; another with malaria; a third with a bad cold; washed and dressed two small wounds; fed some Epsom salts and doled out Vaseline for chapped hands. If I do not treat these people, no one will.

Not long ago, I went down to the village called El Gala to doctor an old woman who was supposed to have a devil in her head. A devil in the stomach is not so serious, because the application of a few pieces of red-hot wire will drive him out, but these head devils are stubborn fellows. She had been burned on both temples and then a string wrapped round and round as tight as a man could wrap it in an effort to squeeze the devil out. All these efforts had failed, so the "golden doctor" (my red hair) was called. I soon cut the strings and put some salve on the festering sores. It was easy enough to see that she was suffering from neuralgia, for she had caught cold in her right eye and ear.

I gave her a good dose of aspirin and rubbed some menthol oil into her head and neck. I went down again about two o'clock in the afternoon and ordered them to send me word when she was better. About an hour later, a step-son came along to tell me the devil had disappeared. If they have a sick donkey or sheep within the next week, I will be called upon to continue my cure until the devil decides to take up abode with some other family. Perhaps that family will come in for treatment, and thus it goes—I chase one persistent evil spirit all over the village. The devil and I certainly get well acquainted.

Just now I have two other patients who have given me considerable concern. One, a young girl who was knocked into the fire by her husband and whose arm was treated with a native red dye before they brought her in. Another is a little girl about four who pulled a pot of boiling coffee over on her head. Her hair was so thickly matted with dirt and grease and the blisters were so large that I could not cut the hair all off, and now her head is one mass of infection. And if I try to cut out the hair, it will take off all the skin and flesh with it. She should be in the hospital, but because she is a female they would never even carry her across the street to be treated. Instead they cover their sores with a paste of oil and chicken dung and leave that on until the infection runs itself out. Out here in this hot sun an infection does not often turn into blood poisoning unless it is covered air-tight and away from the sun. If it were not for the purifying rays of the sun, these people would die off in a few months, because they live in utter filth.

Don continued to write about the medical situation—and about faith.

We received some great encouragement out at Gereif this week. Glenn Reed has a special concern for a boy named Shareef, who was not expected to live more than a year, but his illness has become mysteriously healed and the doctor says he cannot explain it. We can, because we were praying for Shareef to be healed. For some time Shareef has shown more than a common interest in the Sunday school class and has been asking searching questions. Last Monday we were talking about the Trinity in Bible class, and he said if he could understand this he would become a Christian. The other boys in the class seemed to freeze, and the air became quite tense. I made no attempt to explain to them what my conception of this mystery was. I had tried that before and failed, but I told them it was one of those things we had to accept in faith and our faith grew through prayer.

To my surprise, Shareef asked me to pray with him. So that night after the study hour, we went for a walk out in the date orchard and sat down to talk it all over. Shareef was already a Christian in his heart, but he needed the strength to make a public confession. He has had special training under Glenn and others, so he did not need to be instructed further. I talked to him, and then we prayed together and talked again, and finally he said that he was ready to take the forward step and make a public acknowledgment of his belief in Christ. I never before knew the joy that at once filled my heart and seemed to fill his as well. We went in and woke up Jim McKnight and told him about it. It is hard for Americans to realize just what this step means to Shareef and others like him, because he now will be turned out of his home, and his friends will spurn him and try to turn him away from his newfound faith. Shareef is one of the finest products of our mission schools, and there is a great future before him, but his way will be very hard.

On 28 April 1929, his twenty-third birthday, Don was asked to preach his first sermon. He thought it was wise to place him toward the end of the year's schedule so as not to drive too many people away. Don worked very hard on this sermon, writing it out word for word and sending a copy home. The title was "Change," and the text was John 21:1–17. He focused on the words, "I will make you fishers of men," but his major thrust was an attack on habits. According to Don, fishermen in the East are still accustomed to casting their nets from the left side. Thus, when Jesus told his disciples to cast from the right side, he was demanding new methods and new approaches. Obviously this was a young man's sermon expressing his impatience with the old ways.

Don's sermon was quite a modest effort because he was imitating the didactic, sermonic style of his father. Even later, Don's written sermons were not outstanding, because the written word could not capture the winsomeness of his compelling sincerity or the unbounded joyfulness of his personality. His love for all aspects of what he was doing was finally irresistible. Indeed, countless men and women were first attracted to Christian service by hearing him describe the work in which he was engaged.

Don later found that a rather unorthodox style of sermon preparation suited him: some quiet time, often lying on the floor as if asleep, a few notes on a piece of paper that he left in his notebook, and an opportunity to warm up by talking to someone. His first sermon concluded with a story Don had often heard from his father's pulpit. Because the illustration made such an impression on the boy, it reveals a great deal about the daring of the man.

During a terrible storm off the coast of Maine, a ship was stranded not far from a small village. Time after time the rescuers went out into the increasing gale and brought sailors safely to shore. At last all but one man was safe, and the exhausted crew refused to go back to what was almost certain death. It was entirely too dangerous to risk the lives of eight men to save one. The small knot of villagers huddled on the shore could see in the gathering darkness the last man still clinging to the mast as the waves tore at the boat beneath him. Finally one strong young man, John Holden by name, stepped forth from the crowd and said, "I will go for him. Are there seven others who will go with me?" Eight men climbed into a boat, but a gray-haired woman ran out from the group and, throwing her arms around John, pleaded with him, "John, don't go, don't go! Three years ago your father was lost at sea; one year ago your brother, Will, went to sea and we have never heard from him. Doubtless he too found a watery grave. You are all I have left." Gently he lifted her arms from his neck and said, "Mother, a man will die out there. I must try to rescue him." Soon they were lost to sight, and the only sound was the roaring wind and the wild dash of the waves. As the group waited on shore, someone heard an oar and called out, "John, John Holden, did you save the man?" And high above the sound of wind and wave came the answer, "Yes, and tell Mother we have found brother Will." Don McClure intended likewise to be "one strong young man stepping forth."

Later Don wrote to his mother,

The burdens of life are resting heavily on the shoulders of your second son tonight. It started this morning when I nearly fell off the top of a sixty-foot windmill that I had climbed in order to readjust it and apply its yearly dose of oil. My hands were covered with oil, and so was my perch. When an extra gust of wind hit me, I lost my footing, and as I started backward, it was a miracle that my fingers closed around a last strut. I felt the Lord's presence very close as my slippery fingers held fast, and there came upon me a strong conviction that surely God had some great task for me to complete before I passed out of the picture. Otherwise I would have been killed long ago. Secondly, we had a prayer meeting in which we prayed for success in our work of reaching non-Christians. I was struck by the fact that we had done the same thing a year ago and had so little to show for our efforts. Our missionaries have been working here in Khartoum for thirty years, and we do not have even one *outstanding* convert who can attract others to the Christian faith. Thirdly, I was being worked on by a Syrian dentist who is a skeptic and believes that if there is a God at all, he is not concerned about us. I could not say anything with his hands in my mouth, but I have been thinking. The last shock came when Glenn asked me what I would be willing to do for Christ. My immediate response was "Anything!" But I am not so sure.

I am convinced the fault lies in us. We have not been led by God's Spirit. Second, our methods are wrong. The apostle Paul preached, converted, and then taught. We, on the other hand, teach a lot of classes, then preach some, but no one is converted. I used to believe that the head is the gateway to the heart, but no more. I think the time is ripe to preach the gospel in all its power. We teach well in our schools, but we are too cautious and dispassionate in our Christian proclamation. I believe that we could go on like this for a thousand years and never cause a moment's worry to Islamic leaders. We are ineffectual. I realize that the government forbids public preaching, but I think we should defy the government and proclaim our faith. Oh well, perhaps tomorrow I will be able to enjoy my work and my religion in quiet and peace, but for tonight I am really discouraged.

▼▲▼

Don always found that a good, brisk hunt lifted his spirits.

Friday morning we had some very good sport. A group of us went hunting up the Blue Nile for sand grouse. The sand grouse is something like a cross between our pheasant or grouse and the quail. It flies just as fast as either, but they keep bunched together and do not settle for long. The best place and time to get them is up along the Blue Nile rather close to the water and early in the morning. We left here a little before six and drove, with a party of six Englishmen and women, and walked for half an hour out across the desert. In hunting the grouse there is no tramping about through the bush, but instead we scatter out over a large territory and take a position and just wait until the grouse fly over. They fly out over the river and then back to the bush, where they settle for a minute or so, and then they rise again, being frightened by the other guns. I was using a fine Ithaca gun not unlike Dad's; Dr. Sowash[15] has a twin to it, and Jeff Sowash has a fine English gun, all twelve gauge. Ronnie Sowash had to be satisfied with his .22. We took our stands wherever we thought best, and as I had never before been out, it was pretty much of a guess with me, but I waded down through the mud (the Nile is lowering) to the edge of the water.

The men back in the bush began to shoot first, and I heard a tremendous barrage even before I saw a bird. One fellow had a pump gun, and I thought he must have cornered an elephant and was trying to see how much shot he could pour into the beast before it realized that it was hit. My first five shots were at long range and evidently just teased them, for no birds bothered to stop. Then I began to get the knack of it and waited until I could see the whites of their eyes. The shooting was fine, and lots of times I had to watch birds fly past as I fumbled to reload. Ronnie had condescended to stay with me, and I made the poor kid take off his shoes and socks and become a retriever. He was so excited that he was glad to do it. I had only taken twenty-five shells with me, and soon they were all gone, and the birds were coming thicker than ever. The men back in the inland parts were firing away at a great rate. I sent Ronnie back to his dad for more shells. While Ronnie was gone, I used the .22 with little effect, getting one bird far out on an island and too far to retrieve. Soon Ronnie came back and reported only three shells left. So for the next half-hour all I could do was listen to the others and pick up my birds. When I got them all, I found twelve had fallen within reach and two more out on the water we could not get.

On going back to the car with my bag I was almost embarrassed to show it, because I felt sure the others would have at least twice as many. But only Mr. Lawson the police commissioner and Mr. Williams the health officer could show more; they each had thirteen birds and thought it was a big morning. Dr. Sowash picked off six; and Jeff, one. The other Englishers, one with the pump gun, came in and said *they* had six (three each), but added that they lost a lot more. So did I, and we are going back next week to get some of the ones we lost. It is rare sport and promises to add much to winter's enjoyment.

In 1931, Don's father and mother came to Africa. Such a trip was still an adventure, although their son and many friends were waiting for them. Don's dad, Elmer, was an enthusiastic hunter (his last Canadian deer hunt was undertaken when he was ninety-four years old) and a great admirer of Theodore Roosevelt. In fact, he looked a bit like Teddy and had the same bluff and hearty manner. He was eager to replicate the African big game hunt that Teddy Roosevelt had undertaken in 1909–10,[16] including shooting a rare Lady Grey antelope, which is found only on a certain island in that area of the upper Nile. Although there is now international concern to conserve the once magnificent animal populations of East Africa, in those days Africa still teemed with game. Don teased that he and his dad would shoot all the elephants, lions, water buffaloes, *and* mosquitoes!

The two men took a launch from Doleib Hill and went south up the Nile accompanied by both Shulla and Anuak bearers. Their destination was Lake No in the land of the Nuers, where the vast swamp called the sudd begins and the Nile meanders through thick vegetation. In the late 1920s, the Anuaks were regarded as the finest builders of canoes in the upper Nile region. They were related to the Shullas and sold their canoes among neighboring tribes such as the Nuer and Dinka.[17] Don was impressed by the Anuak people and dismayed by the fact that no Christian missionary had ever lived and worked among them. Here was a large African tribe that was entirely untouched by the gospel.

During these weeks of hunting, whenever an animal was sighted, Don's dad shouted, "Ho Don!" which the Anuaks assumed was Don's name (since the names of their male children begin with "O").

Ever after they called him "Odon." Don's dad was a superb shot and brought home a leopard, a Cape buffalo, and a couple of Lady Grey antelope and was able to celebrate his seventieth birthday by bringing down an elephant.

After the big game hunt, Don and his fiancée returned to America with his parents. Don was the travel agent because of his ability to get things done. After leaving Egypt he arranged an automobile trip from Jerusalem to Nazareth, Damascus, Baalbek, and Beirut. The driver and the owner of the car discussed and then doubled the cost of the trip, unaware that by now Don could follow the Arabic conversation. The owner was rather dismayed to find that he was constrained to quote a reasonable price.

Somehow along the trip, the McClures picked up a professor of New Testament from New Zealand who was eager to accompany them. This open-handedness and open-heartedness was typical of Don's lifestyle. Lyda thoroughly enjoyed traveling through the land of the Bible with three knowledgeable students of Scripture. The professor complained for some days about the rank odor that permeated the car. Finally he located the smell emanating from a beautiful, amber-colored hippopotamus-hide cane which Don's dad was packing home and of which he was especially fond.

From Beirut the group went to Istanbul and then to Italy. In Istanbul, Don and Lyda saw a pair of brass candlesticks that they very much wanted to purchase, but neither had sufficient money. They solved the problem by each buying one. This transaction—an unmarried man and woman buying a matched set of candlesticks with the clear implication that they would someday stand side by side— scandalized Don's mother. Don and Lyda were rather amused by this, because they were not overly concerned about appearances before a suspicious world. They knew their own minds and were never bound by what seemed to them to be inappropriate conventions.

Somewhere along the way, the New Zealander left the party and disappeared from Don's life forever. There would be many like him over the years—warmly accepted and affectionately treated, but released to their own future without a backward glance or thought. Don always enjoyed the present too much to hoard the past. He appreciated the current moment and looked excitedly toward the future.

When the group reached England, Lyda ran out of money and left for home. She got her old teaching job back in Wheeling, and Don entered Pittsburgh Theological Seminary. Neither did a very good job of concentrating during that year apart, and when Don found a church that would pay him seventy dollars a month, they decided to get married. At the time this was an unconventional decision. The normal pattern was for a seminary student to postpone marriage until after he had completed his education. Don's father was certain that the young couple would be unable to manage financially. Don's uncle, Dr. John McNaugher, professor of New Testament and president of the seminary, was the outstanding scholar of his church and was affectionately called "the Pope." He hoped that Don would follow in his footsteps. A wife, he thought, would distract the young scholar. Not only did he think an early marriage was ill-advised, he also thought Don's decision to be a missionary was unwise. Dr. McNaugher held the sometimes unfortunately apt—but for a Christian, strange—view that "only failures and misfits go to the mission field." Don had such promising potential that a wealthy Pittsburgh businessman offered him a huge salary in the hope that he would stay and work in America. But Don had a vision for Africa, and nothing would deter him.

In any case, Don was not cut out for the life of scholarship; he was not the academic type. Don always found people more interesting than books. He read a good deal for devotion, for relaxation, and to learn how to do things, yet his gift was not in pursuing ideas but in implementing them. A great part of his learning took place in conversations with more scholarly friends, especially Glenn Reed, during which he exercised his judgment on what he could glean that was useful. His graduate studies were wide-ranging, which is to say his grades ranged from "A" to "C." There was no apparent pattern of special interest and ability in any one theological area. In three years he even received a "D" in one of his preaching courses. Apparently no one paid the slightest attention to this spotty academic record, because once Don found his proper subject he became one of the most sought-after preachers in his church.

About this subject Don once explained,

I do not go out to raise funds and never ever ask any person or group to give money. My sole purpose is to arouse interest in Christian mission at home and abroad. I try to thrill hearts about what the Lord is doing in Africa and especially in the Anuak tribe. It is not necessary to ask churches to take up an offering, nor to give me anything for expenses. If someone wants to make a contribution, I never refuse because I recognize that giving is an expression of love and concern, and I would not hinder people from giving anymore than I would try to stop them from praying. I am always delighted to tell the Anuak story at any time to anyone in any place. I do not care whether it is a Women's Missionary Society, a youth meeting, a children's Sunday school class, a few people gathered in a home, or a church service.

When he spoke to groups, Don's subject was always "What the Lord Is Doing in Africa Today." He described the Lord's activity with infectious joy and enthusiasm. He reported it all with deep delight in God's goodness, but without a trace of personal pride. Don's audience always felt that it would be wonderful if they too could serve God in Africa, and they wanted to help. Don's judgment was sharp and sensitive, but it did not include self-reflective pride. He heard and understood compliments and recognized work well done, but he enjoyed his accomplishments without reflecting on them for his own satisfaction. Don was just as capable of preparing a meal as of preaching a sermon, and he enjoyed doing both. He pitched into whatever work was before him, including teaching his wife to cook. Toward the end of the first year of marriage Don's mother, a fine cook, came to dinner. With his ebullient and mischievous good humor, Don told his wife that her biscuits were *almost* as good as his mother's—to his delight embarrassing both women at one time.

In the summers Don was the manager of the New Wilmington Missionary Conference. He promoted the conference by traveling around to various churches, thereby meeting many of those people who would support his work in Africa. He was also in great demand as a speaker on big game hunting.

Although Don was running a missionary conference in America, his great desire to be a missionary in Africa was well-known. During the conference in the summer of 1934—depression time when nobody had much money—the young delegates decided to carry glass jars everywhere they went. Whatever money they had for candy, chewing gum, or ice cream went into the jars. The money they raised was sufficient to send the McClures back to Africa—this time together, and for the rest of their lives. Many of those jar-carrying kids continued to support them for all those years in Africa.

On the boat to Africa, the McClures traveled with Dr. W. B. Anderson,[18] the secretary of the Foreign Mission Board. One day at sea he looked sternly at Lyda and said, "Remember, you are *not* the missionary; you are the missionary's wife!" Doubtless he recognized in her a zeal, a competence, and an independence equal to Don's and thought he should make her place in the scheme of things quite clear. Don's and Lyda's gifts were quite different, but her willingness to stand very firmly and competently at his shoulder both protected and impelled him in their common quest of service to the kingdom's cause in Africa. She forced him to temper some of his rashness by making him promise *not* to go into high grass after a wounded lion! Don was willing to observe some elementary caution, but he believed with an absolute conviction that until his work for God on earth was finished, he was immortal and invincible.

By this time Don had completed his years of exploration. Now he knew that he wanted to devote the rest of his life to service as a missionary in Africa. He had found his calling and his best and most faithful companion—his wife, Lyda. His three years in and around Khartoum, his theological degree, and his experience as the pastor of an American congregation readied him for the years of apprenticeship among the Shulla people in the south Sudan at Doleib Hill.

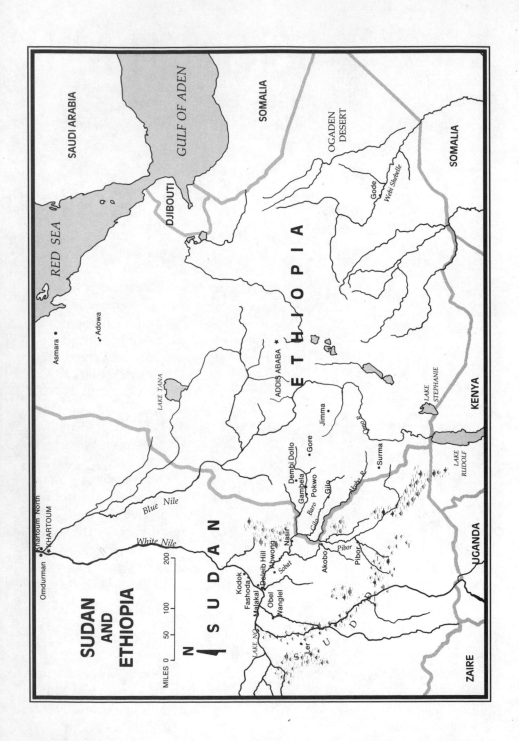

II DOLEIB HILL
AMONG THE SHULLAS
1934–1938

▼ The Shulla People

WHEN DON RETURNED to Africa in 1934, he discovered that he was still remembered as one whose blood flowed in the veins of a camel. The camel on which he had performed a surgical procedure five years earlier was still alive, while four of its fellows had died. "The Sudanese," said Don, "think this camel will not die until I do. I certainly wish him good health and long life."

In those days, missionaries were assigned only to a field, and the entire mission was required to vote on the specific location within the field. The Sudan mission was divided into work among Muslim people in the north, where Don had been, and work among black tribes in the south, where he wanted to go. Both areas always needed more personnel, but the McClures felt called to live in the south among the Shulla people,[19] and it was not at all certain that their wishes would be respected or even regarded. According to Don, the line was narrow between being jealous for one's own work and being zealous for it. Perhaps the northern missionaries, who had the voting majority, recognized that Don and Lyda were prepared to return to America if they were not allowed to go south. In any case the McClures were assigned to Doleib Hill, fifteen miles south of Malakal on the north bank of the Sobat River.

Don was now where he would be happiest, in a frontier outpost where every day was a challenge in every direction. True, it was not his own frontier in the same way that Akobo, Pokwo, and Gode would be, because at Doleib Hill he was joining a mission that was

61

already established and had programs in progress. Still, at Doleib Hill Don had the opportunity to be innovative, and he used every skill he possessed. He threw himself into the work with delight. This was his first sustained engagement with primitive, black Africa, and during this time he recognized his calling to be a pioneer missionary among primitive people.

The senior missionary at Doleib Hill[20] was the Reverend J. Alfred Heasty, D.D., who had lived there since 1921 and was regarded as an outstanding expert on the Shulla people. Indeed, Don thought Heasty spoke the Shulla tonal language better than the Shulla themselves.[21] However, Heasty did not always see eye to eye with Glenn Reed and Don, the "young Turks"—or better, the "young Christians"—who were eager to try doing things differently. Doubtless, in the nature of things those who are older and more experienced must often appear staid and unimaginative to their juniors. Gleefully and without malice, Don and Glenn used Heasty's often repeated words to put an end to arguments between themselves: "When you know the Shulla mind as well as I do, you won't think that!"

As long as Heasty was more or less alone at Doleib Hill he directed most of his energy toward maintaining the mission station and continuing the work that could be best done there. Don and Glenn, on the other hand, were on fire to mount an extensive evangelistic tour in the surrounding area. The danger was always present that missionaries would become so involved in maintaining buildings, gardens, and station programs that evangelism would fall into the background. Don once wrote that Glenn

Is trying to find some money in the budget to buy a large pump for irrigation. I hope he fails, because I am afraid if we get into farming and farm machinery in a big way, it will take too much time away from evangelism. I did not come to Africa to raise eggplant and cabbage, and neither did he.

The Shullas were primarily herdsmen, not farmers, who molded their hair into fantastic shapes. They could often be seen watching their cattle for hours while standing on one leg with the suspended foot resting on the other knee.[22] Shulla wealth and social position was reckoned by the number of cows a person owned. The condition of the animal did not matter. This was quite evident when various Shullas begged to buy the mission's blind and useless sixteen-year-old cow, which was going to be eaten. If a cow died, then the family was allowed to eat it, but killing a cow was regarded as wrong. Shulla fathers would even let their children die rather than kill cattle to feed them, and many families starved to death while their cows remained healthy.[23]

In Shulla territory a cow was considered a very delicate creature to be treated with due respect. There were no milk *maids*, because no female was allowed to touch a cow out of the conviction that the cow would cease to give milk and soon die. Moreover, among women only nursing mothers were allowed to drink milk. The Shullas believed that otherwise the cow would not calf again. A married man could herd cattle, but not milk them. Only young boys, who had not begun to notice girls, were allowed to milk, and they did that in the dark to keep the flies away.

The boys milked the cows by allowing a calf to suck while the boy-milker proceeded to wash his hands and arms in cow urine, which was collected by another boy whose sole job was to run behind the cattle carrying a gourd to collect it. The milk-boy then dried his hands on the cow. Next, another boy pushed the calf away and the milk-boy milked the cow. However, if no milk came, the boy went behind the cow and "blew her up." This meant that he placed his mouth directly over the cow's rear aperture and filled her with air. The increased pressure and discomfort made the cow release the milk. Don mused that this would never have been a very popular practice back home on the range.

▼▲▼

The Shullas traced their ancestry directly to Jwok, their god, who made the whole world and the Shulla people as his first creation. In the 1930s the Shullas were still one of the greatest tribes in central Africa, estimated then at 300,000 and at least twice that number before the slave traders decimated their ranks.[24] The Shullas were independent people; each family attempted to raise enough grain, cotton, and pumpkins to keep them through the year. But it was a precarious life. During the dry season, when it was impossible to grow crops, the Shullas hunted and fished. If there was not enough rain to bring a crop, then hundreds of old people died and the non-suckling babies tried to live on the roots and grass seeds their mothers found. Often mothers gathered weeds and cooked them as greens. In any event, if the small children managed to live through the period of starvation, their growth would be stunted for several years. Adults, except for the very old, did not suffer as severely because they had learned to exist on the grass seeds and water lilies that grew abundantly. According to Don,

Our primary task among these people is to lead them to a saving knowledge of Jesus Christ, but hand in hand with that program we must teach them to improve their social and economic standard of living. At the present time durra, a hard, unpalatable grain like the American kaffir corn and very weak in nutritive value, is their only food. After babies are weaned they are started immediately on this miserable, almost indigestible, diet and in a short time what had once been a fine-looking baby turns into a little creature who is all eyes and stomach. The hard food makes their stomachs swell and get so big, one would think they were going to burst. Their bodies become poor, legs begin to bow, and their eyes seem to pop out of their heads. This goes on for two or three years until their stomachs learn to handle the food forced into them. I want to teach the Shullas to raise not only their durra, but also wheat, corn, barley, and oats during the rainy season and then in the dry months to start gardens on the riverbank that can be irrigated by water wheels turned by oxen.

The use of oxen as beasts of burden is a great sore point with all the Shulla people. Since coming here, I have broken two teams of bulls to a plow and as a result have lost respect with all the people around the place. Never before have oxen been so disgraced in Shullaland, for "did I not know that cows and bulls were to be used only for buying wives, and therefore to work a bull in the plow was like working your wife?" I did not see the similarity, since I would not be willing to sell my wife for all the bulls in Shulla country, but I saw no objection to making bulls earn their keep. So I put them to work. It was difficult getting anyone to work with bulls at first, but now the schoolboys seem eager to learn, and one of the teachers says that he is going to train two of his bulls. That is a big step forward, a very big step, for never before has a Shulla ever worked his bulls so much as an hour. All this may seem nonessential, but in reality it is of utmost importance. We can never break down the barbarous customs of the Shullas unless we start at some point on which they are less fanatical than others and then work toward the heart and center of their paganism. If we are able to break down one custom and superstition, we will be more easily able to break down others.

Along with our desire to teach them to plant crops other than durra, we are making every effort to teach them to raise small vegetables. We are erecting several lifts for getting water from the river and pouring it out on the fields close to the riverbank, and now we are going to try to persuade them to grow things on the banks. If they will raise vegetables and bring them in to us, we will market the vegetables for them in Malakal, the capital of Upper Nile Province. In this way the Shullas will not only learn how to raise vegetables, but will create an appetite for them.

The north Sudan is indeed bleak and barren, as I have said before, but the south Sudan is different, because of one of God's most satisfying gifts—rain. We get it, and the north does not. Khartoum receives an annual rainfall of two inches. At Doleib Hill we get forty-five inches of rain, which transforms this land into a Garden of Eden. During the rainy season the dry plains become a beautiful pastureland of thousands of square miles. We could feed millions of cattle at our back door and not crowd out the sheep. The grass will soon be shoulder high, and that is wonderful except as a place to meet a hungry lion.

I am now a lord of land with 300 acres to look after and keep in shape (I'm not telling anyone that 250 acres of it is pasture and needs no attention), and I always have fifty to sixty workers to keep busy. Of course, fifty of these are schoolboys who only work in the afternoons, but I will keep that a secret too, so that the world will think that I am an important man. I really have been busy since the rains started. I have gotten in about 8 acres of durra and 2 of corn, and I plowed several more for peanuts and sesame. Another good rain, and I will get all the cotton and the rest of the durra in and then be finished except for the actual hoeing and harvesting—if there is to be a harvest. We are getting very fearful for all our grain crops because, apparently out of nowhere, great hordes of rats have appeared. Six weeks ago we scarcely saw a rat, and now I see a hundred in a day and they are increasing by leaps and bounds. I killed four this morning with a stick and saw a man carrying twenty or thirty by their tails.

I used to think that only the Chinese ate rats and that it was a sign of terrible depravity. But during these last six weeks I have seen hundreds of rats eaten with great relish. (Actually, the Shullas eat them without relish, since they do not have a relish to put on their ratburgers.) The Shullas say we are crazy for not eating rats. According to them, the meat is sweeter than chicken. I will take their word for it! As soon as they catch a half-dozen or so, they will build a fire and throw the whole rat in, not even bothering to skin or clean it, and then after a few minutes in the hot coals the rat will be dragged out, and in one pull all his skin is off and there in your hand is the nicest piece of white meat you ever saw. I must say it looks tempting, but I will try to be satisfied with my chickens. The schoolboys are reveling in luxury these days as they dig the rats out and have picnics using *rats* instead of *hot dogs;* but they have little choice and think we are queer people to prefer a dirty hog to a nice, clean rat.

Recently I have been selling cattle, and to date I have sold twenty head, for which I received the magnificent sum of a little over two hundred dollars, or something over ten dollars per head. You could scarcely make money on cattle at that price in the States, but when you consider that we do not have a cent of expense for feed and only about six dollars per month for "cowboys," with no other expense, then any money is clear profit for the mission. But as a mission here we have almost spoiled our chances to reach the people in this vicinity, because during all the past years our time and attention has been occupied in making money for the mission instead of converts for the kingdom of God.

The rains are really on. We have had only two big rains, one of four inches and the other two inches, but we have had enough small rains coming frequently enough to keep things wet and muddy. I worked all one day extricating an old Arab and his dilapidated Ford from a mudpuddle just at the edge of our compound. I only got him out because I did not want him to camp there for the next four months until the rains are over. And in doing so, I did him no kindness, because I am certain he could not possibly make it to Malakal, however sanguine he was about it. I know that at this very minute he is sitting someplace between here and Malakal in one of the waterways and entirely at the mercy of the lions which roam that country when the road is shut off. He would take no warning and insisted on pushing on. Still, I hope his blood remains in his own veins and is not mingled with some lion's beard.

On another occasion Don wrote,

These Shullas are the most improvident people I have ever seen. No man ever considers storing grain for the next year when his crop might fail. If he did, he would be considered stingy by all his fellow villagers, and that is the last thing a Shulla wants to be called. Indeed, they are so generous that a stranger coming into a village can find shelter in *any* house, and he might stay on for a month and his host will never say a word about payment or the fast-diminishing grain. If the stranger were asked to move on, it would be a slur on the host's hospitality. So now, when grain is plentiful, they are trying to outdo each other in giving the biggest party. The only regulator of their drinking of beer is the amount of grain they have to make drink.

The Shullas make beer in two ways. The most common and the kind that everyone drinks every day is a very mild and almost non-alcoholic drink made of sour grain. The grain is permitted to sour for only one day, and they grind it very fine into a sort of pasty meal. This meal is then mixed with water and drunk. I have tasted the stuff, and aside from being very unpleasant and sour it has no injurious qualities.

However, there is a second kind that is strong enough to take the hair off your head, or at least to make it grow on your chest. It is made of fermented grain and is very high in alcohol content. This beer is commonly made for all big dances and festivals of any kind. Often people drink too much of it, and then a good spear fight can be expected. They all know the danger of the spear fights when they are drunk and have made a very sensible provision for it—if it worked. They have a rule that when a certain group of young bucks goes to a dance, there will always be one of their number who does not drink. Then if the others get excited, he will be able to ward off any fighting. If the designated non-drinkers played their part faithfully, this custom would serve a very important need. But few of them are willing to stay away from drinking entirely. As a rule they plan to take just one drink and then sit down and watch. But drink has a habit of destroying a man's good intentions.

Last week we witnessed a true spectacular. It was the big event of the Shulla social season, which is called "the Dance of the Skin." Yes, there is also a lot of female skin in evidence, but the skin referred to is gazelle, which is donated by some lucky hunter and will be awarded to the young lady winning the most approval. This is the "Miss Shulla" beauty contest that has been a ceremony for generations. The girls are dressed in their very best, which does not mean they are *clothed*, but rather *painted* in dancing stripes of red, white, green, blue, and yellow. They wear all the beads they can manage, all sorts of feathers are stuck in the hair, and their arms and legs are decorated with woven palm fibers.

In all other Shulla dances—rain, death, war, cattle—the men invariably lead and the women stand around the outside and clap their hands or stamp their feet. In this dance the roles are reversed. The young women do the dancing, and the young men stand around and discuss the points of beauty and strength on display. The choice does not always end in agreement, but a stubborn chap holding out for his favorite can usually be made to vote with the majority after being threatened with a club or spear.

The unmarried girls dance all afternoon and into the night. The lucky winner is considered the prize catch of the year, and the fellows will vie for her. The father of this girl will receive a double dowry. The usual dowry is ten cows, thirty sheep, five or six spearheads, and a few dollars. However, to be a twelve-cow wife is far more prestigious than being a ten-cow wife. Obviously a twenty-cow wife is a high society lady.

The Shullas use several kinds of drums, and each has a special place in their lives. The first type is small, about the size of two tambourines fastened together and eight inches across. The body is wood, and the head is tightly stretched gazelle skin. This drum is used just for making a noise or in dances where a number of unmarried girls sit together and beat out a rhythm. These drums can be beaten by anyone. The second type is usually a little larger and sometimes is stretched over half a gourd because it makes a deeper, hollow sound. Again gazelle skin is used. These drums are used exclusively for mournings and beaten by members of the family—usually women, though not always. If used at a funeral, the drums are sometimes buried with the body. A third type is the signal drum, which is merely a hollow log about three feet long and ten inches thick with open ends. This one is always beaten by an experienced man, who uses the same drum for all signaling except war—that is, for announcing a birth or even a death to a distant village. It is used to call others to a dance or a hunt. The war drum is used only for that purpose and beaten only by men. There might be several such drums in a village. They are about the size of a snare drum, with heavy cowhide heads on either end of a hollow log and built to withstand wear and abuse. A man sits with one of these between his legs and pounds it as hard as he can with a smooth-knobbed stick, beating out a staccato alarm. A fifth type is used at the induction of a chief or new king. The body of this drum is usually of foreign wood, possibly mahogany from Ethiopia, and only the bladder or stomach of an animal is used for the head. This drum is beaten as the chief wishes and are heirlooms that have been in the possession of the family for generations. The first, second, and fifth drums are usually beaten by hand, the others with a club.

The boys are having a dance tonight. This will require that some of the boys sit on the ground singing their dancing songs; two others pound the drum while the rest of them, about sixty in all, dance around in a circle stiff-legged. One might wonder how anyone dances with stiff legs, but it is most graceful. The boys jump up and down with their legs rigid, swaying only from the waists and hopping forward about six inches with each jump. For one person to dance alone would be ludicrous, but when they all jump and hop at the same time they look like some huge beast slowly weaving around in a circle—and that is the desired effect.

Each boy has decorated himself with brick dust, stuck feathers in his hair, made armlets and leglets from palm branches and palm fibers that reach from wrist to elbow or knee to ankle, all nicely woven. Each has gathered all the spears and clubs he can borrow for the occasion. None of the boys is permitted to have a spear in school because of accidental cuts that constantly occur when small boys play with them, but they all manage to find two or three to brandish in a dance. Strange to say, they seldom cut themselves while dancing. The secret of it is that every boy knows exactly what the other is going to do, and if one gets out of step he is banished from the dance. It is most musical and restful as we listen and watch them dance.

Don also related some other after-dark activities.

I am feeling lousy today. I have a bad cold and a touch of the flu. I ache in every joint, and my head feels like a barrel. I blame the whole thing on Glenn! The reason is that we are in the middle of the tuga nut season.[25] That is, we have hundreds of tuga nut trees full of yellow fruit, and when the fruit drops off, you hear the crash and then the pounding of twenty or thirty pairs of feet as the Shullas run to find the nut. Some weeks ago while I was away (or I would have told him to save his breath), Glenn issued orders that no one was permitted on the mission compound after nine o'clock at night. I am working on all our fences, but they have been in a terrible state of disrepair for years, so we have no real barriers to keep anyone away.

At nine o'clock Glenn goes out and in a loud voice orders everyone off the place and then makes a patrol to see that his command is being carried out. All is quiet for a few minutes after he gets in the house, and then, crash, thud—a tuga nut falls, and simultaneously with the thud there is the patter of scores of feet as the Shullas dash out of hiding to get the nut. In a few minutes all is quiet again. Such activity does not trouble me in the least because my childhood days are not far away, but Glenn simply gets furious and wants to tear the Shullas limb from limb. As I say, it is at its worst just now, and people are in here all night long. Glenn has found that it is impossible to catch them single-handed, so for the last three nights, long after I have gone to bed, he has come over and routed me out to help him chase them off. He cannot sleep if he hears a single Shulla running around.

So for three nights I piled out in my pajamas and gave chase under full sail. Last night was the climax. We cornered six fellows down along the riverbank about one in the morning and were closing in on them. Seeing that they were about to be caught, they threw their spears into the river and dived in after them. Now, it is one thing to swim near the shore of the Sobat River, but it it quite another to swim across. I would not want to try it. However, as they jumped in, one chap was a little more timid than the others and he tarried a bit; but just as I was about to grab him, he too tossed in his spear and jumped. Having gotten that close, I was not for letting him go, so pajamas and all I dived in after him. I was gaining on him for the first fifty feet, but then I started thinking about the crocodiles that I knew to be in the Sobat, and I considered they might have a preference for white meat so I lost my nerve and started back.

Glenn, who was a bit behind me in the running and cannot swim a stroke, was on the point of throwing a fit and tearing his hair out. Anyway, I climbed out, and we watched those fellows swim across the river, fearing every moment that one or more of them would be taken by a crocodile or drown. However, they landed safely, laughed at us, and told us that they would be back. It is all a game to them (and I guess to me, too), but now I am paying for my swim in the service of Glenn's chase.

Don was fascinated with Shulla customs and related to his mother how Shullas plan their marriages.

The Shullas around here are lovably unsophisticated. For example, the Heastys have a certain "watergirl" whose husband died three years ago, leaving her alone with two small children. Ordinarily five or six men would stand ready to inherit her because they were related to her husband. However, her husband had died during a famine year when men were deserting their wives and going off on their own. No one would take her, and being left to starve, she came to the mission for help. The Heastys hired her for 5 cents a day, and she has been a faithful worker ever since. On her monthly salary of $1.50, she has raised her two children, built a house, bought two cows, and invested(!) some of her savings in expensive beads.

Now, of course, she has become wealthy and therefore a desirable wife, and several men have come forward to claim her. The prior claim fell to an uncle. So Heasty talked to the uncle and in the presence of the young woman asked the fellow why he only now wanted to marry her—expecting that the uncle would offer some lies about feeling sorry for her living without a husband, how he had struggled with his conscience and decided it was his duty to take her as a wife, and so on. Then Heasty could confront him with the truth and have some grounds for refusing to let her go. However, the uncle said, "I want her because she has land, cattle, valuable possessions, two children, and is young enough to give me more." The other men standing around nodded gravely and said, "That's true." Such simple guilelessness is extremely disconcerting. The watergirl does not want to leave the mission, because the work is easier here than it would be in some man's house. Heasty sent them to the chief of the tribe.

Shulla marriage customs are very interesting. Divorce is almost unknown, because it takes an ordinary fellow two to five years to arrange a marriage. Normally it goes like this: A chap of about sixteen years observes a young girl of about fourteen and decides that she would make a nice wife in about five years. Having made his selection, he then chooses two go-betweens— each from a different village and unrelated to him or the girl— who go to the girl's father and offer him a sheep. If the father accepts the sheep, it is an indication that he is willing to consider the suitor. Then after a decent interval, during which the lad must find a couple more sheep, he chooses two more go-betweens to take his gifts to the prospective father-in-law and to arrange a time when the young man can appear in person and find out what the girl is going to cost him.

When all this protocol has been observed and after several months have passed, the chap, who has not yet spoken to his intended, will go with two friends, all leaving their clubs and spears behind but taking two more sheep as an offering, and will bow themselves into the presence of the father, who has the village chief and one other witness on hand. Then the negotiation begins. The father will sing the praises of his wonderful daughter—how well she can hoe the durra and gather wood; how much water she can carry on her head; how well she can make rope and weave baskets; what fine beer and food she can prepare; how well she can build and repair the house; and on and on until the lad has a picture of himself sitting under a shade tree all the day long and never having to work at all.

After all this talk, the bride price is quoted. It is a set custom that a man must pay ten head of cattle and about thirty sheep for his wife, and then as much in money, spears, and chickens as the father-in-law can wheedle out of him. My poor friend, whose name is Kyeny, was a poor bargainer. He agreed to give eleven cows, thirty-five sheep, a dozen spearheads, five dollars in money, and as many chickens as he could scrape up. The funny part is that he is proud of the fact that he is paying so much. If a fellow gets a wife cheap, he feels that he has a cheap wife. The prospective groom does not try to reduce the bride price, because his lips are sealed; it is the responsibility of his two friends to try to drive a fair bargain for him. But before the groom starts to gather cows, he must first obtain the girl's consent. The father does not make the entire decision. Thus, if a girl refuses to marry a man, there is no forcing her. Usually the girl accepts, especially if she is to be the first wife, since there are more girls than boys in Shullaland. They all have a horror of being left unmarried and then having to marry a man who already has several wives.

At sixteen Kyeny is facing a huge debt to obtain a wife. However, wives are an economic investment since they represent wealth, and he must work on the details. If Kyeny had to buy all those cattle, he would never marry, because the best possible wage he could earn is ten cents a day and that would never buy what is demanded of him. If the groom has an older sister who has already married, his problem is solved. He will use the cattle that his father received for the marriage of his sister. If his immediate family has not received a dowry, he will make a wider circle, going to uncles, grandfathers, and other relatives. From each he will beg an ox or a cow or some sheep. They seldom refuse his requests, because they know that they in turn can send their sons to him later on to make the same request. He will also go to the old men in the village and ask them to furnish a spear or a sheep, and they will be provided if at all possible. The only exception is if the groom is an irresponsible rascal without credit in his family and village circle. Then the men of property will not help him, and he will be forced to collect a group of his rowdy friends, and they will make a raid on some Dinka or Anuak cattle pens.

These arrangements take time in a country where no one hurries and tomorrow is always better than today simply because it is tomorrow. So after two or three years the chap has paid eight or nine cattle, twenty sheep, and all the money. He will then have the engagement confirmed by a big dance and beer drink. Everyone will gather in and drink to the couple's health and wish them happiness. This ceremony is almost considered marriage because they are permitted marriage relationships, although the girl is not allowed to leave her father's house until all the cattle are paid. If, in the meantime, she bears a child, she becomes of greater value, and the price is raised five head of cattle and several sheep. The poor groom gets it going and coming. Moreover, if any of the cattle die before the marriage, he must replace them. On the other hand, if the girl changes her mind about him or dies, then all his cattle are returned.

For a divorce proceeding, the same transactions are repeated, only backward. There are few divorces among the Shullas. It takes too much time and effort.

▼ Big Game Hunting

Don McCLURE always loved to hunt. With energy to burn, a midnight tramp over the African plains in search of animals of prey or vermin was his idea of relaxation. Such activity, he thought, rested him and kept his system tuned to the right pitch. Thus, at Doleib Hill, in addition to his regular hunting for food, he took up night hunting for sport because he thought more thrills and adventure could be packed into an hour after dark than in five hours of daylight. After a hard day's work outside and a long evening at his desk, he was both too tired and too keyed up to sleep. So he took his rifle and flashlight and hiked for an hour to shoot jackals and small wild cats.

I have heard that there is an immense elephant some miles downriver. He is supposed to be so large that his tusks touch the ground and so old that the other elephants push him along or take branches and whip him to keep him going. I was also told that his tusks were so heavy that he rested them on the back of a smaller elephant in front as they walked. Who knows, maybe I will run across him someday.

About hunting Don wrote,

Last Friday night we had supper with the Reeds and afterward played a few games. On the way home with Lyda, I spotted a jackal in our backyard. Now, those insolent curs have never learned to respect my ability with a rifle and flashlight, even though I have shot dozens of them, and the sight of one always does something to my insides that can only be satisfied with a shot or a good chase. So I grabbed my gun and started out. Some of the jackals have learned that behind my light there is

75

something not to be taken lightly and give me a respectful right of way. Such was the case with this chap. As soon as I would spot him with my light, he would turn tail and run. But when I shut off the light, he would stop and yap at me. I gave chase for about half an hour. If I had had my shotgun I could have shot him a dozen times, but with a .22 rifle, a moving target at night is risky and difficult. Just as I was about to give up, promising him a different story someday, I caught the reflection of a brilliant pair of eyes about five hundred yards away.

I am beginning to claim a unique ability to discriminate among the eyes of different animals at night even though some distance away. So I know just by the color of the eye, or the swing of the head, or the reaction to the light, exactly what kind of animal I am looking at even when I cannot discern a single body-mark or size. A jackal has reddish-yellow eyes and a jerky swing; a wild cat has deep yellow eyes and no swinging of the head as it walks, with an occasional stop to sniff the breeze; a hyena has bright blue eyes as big as cups; a leopard has brilliant yellow, piercing eyes that look steadily at the light as if to see what is behind; while the eyes of all game animals are blue and soft and always swing up and down as the animal walks.

The eyes that I saw while chasing the jackal were brilliant and at once sent a thrill up and down my spine, because I knew they belonged to some unusual animal. At first I thought it was a leopard and began to consider what I should do. I was not particularly eager to tackle a leopard with a .22 rifle, especially at night when he has all the advantage. I debated whether to retreat and concede him the field or sit tight and await developments. Actually I had no notion of letting him get away.

However, he took the matter out of my hands by walking directly down the path and right into the light. I held the light on him and did not dare shut if off, lest he see me in the starlight and I would not be able to see him. On and on he came, apparently oblivious that I existed and that there was anything unusual going on. Animals do not seem to sense the meaning of a flashlight at all and will walk right up to me if the wind is right and I have not made any noise. When the eyes came within fifty yards of where I stood, I began to make out the outline of the animal, which I thought was a small leopard. It was spotted like a leopard and had the long legs and thin body of that family. By that time I had decided to take a chance on a close shot, trusting my eye and hand to finish him off with the first shot. So when he kept coming slowly and gracefully, I carefully knelt down on one knee (not to pray, but to steady my rifle—the time for praying would come if I missed him) and took careful aim. As I lined my sights up with the light, my flashlight clicked on the gunbarrel, and instantly the animal became a mere shadow. It stopped with one front paw in the air, threw its head high looking right at me, and its body became almost as thin as a sheet of paper. I knew I had only a second before it would leap off into the grass and disappear, so I lined up on its neck just above the chest and pulled the trigger. With the crack of the gun the animal gave a tremendous leap into the air and came down on its back, snarling and writhing. I ran up and put a second shot through its head to finish the story.

It only took me a second to see that I had gotten a fine, big cheetah. Of course, the cheetah is of the leopard family with very similar spots and markings, but much smaller. I was deceived at first into thinking it might be a leopard by misjudging its distance from me. It was actually much closer than I thought and therefore correspondingly larger. But that did not prevent me from having the scare of my life in thinking I was going to meet a leopard with only a .22 rifle in my hands.

▼▲▼

In 1935 the McClures' first child was born at the Civil Hospital in Khartoum. She was named "Margaret" after both grandmothers, but as a child was called "Marghi"—with a hard *g* rather than the softer *g* of "Margie." She had red hair like her father, and according to Don, while the birth took a normal course, it was obviously of international, and maybe even cosmic, significance. Don got to hold her for an hour at 5:00 each afternoon.

I spend a lot of time playing with her. A baby is almost as much fun as a puppy! She has the lovely disposition that everyone knows goes with red hair. Marghi is a splendid baby. She is really beautiful. Those who see her always remark on her beauty, then they look at me and suggest that she must favor her mother. She is also very intelligent. I know that, because she laughs every time she sees me. The Shullas call her "Nyawela," which means "one born on a journey." This is a rather common name around here, because the scientific understanding of pregnancy is nonexistent and not a few babies are born away from home.

▼▲▼

Don wrote about another invigorating experience: a hippo hunt.

I have just come in from a hippo hunt, and my hand still shakes from the excitement of a close chase. During a chase I never have a tremor, but when quarters are as close as they were tonight, I usually have a queer feeling inside after it is all over. This was not the mild kind of a hippo hunt when one stands in a motor launch and shoots from a hundred yards. Granted, it takes a bit of shooting to put a bullet in a hippo's ear at one hundred yards, but after all, it is like shooting a cow. I have just returned from a two-hour chase through a great swamp with our only light being an uncertain quarter moon and my large flashlight.

The story starts some weeks ago when a big bull hippo began to come in here at night. He only came to the mission one night and tried to get into the garden, but he has given the village people no end of trouble. Nearly every day a delegation would come in to plead with me to go out and shoot the brute. But that was easier said than done, for during the day he always returned to the river and only came in at night. Finally I consented to have a try and went up to the swamp where he fed. On two successive nights I braved the mosquitoes and crocodiles and snakes, wading around in the swamp, trying to get a shot at him. But he was wary, and I could not get my light on him long enough to shoot. So I gave up that kind of hunting.

However, today another group came in and said that last night the hippo had destroyed a year's supply of grain by eating and tramping down a whole field. And they said that when they went out to drive him off, he snorted and stamped so loudly they were afraid to get close enough to throw a spear. Then tonight as I worked here in my study, the bunch came in again and said the hippo was in their fields. I hurriedly changed clothes and, loading up the Winchester .405, took my light and started out. We ran to the swamp at a dogtrot, hoping to get the beast before he went back into the water. When we arrived, he was just moving off into the deep water, and I was ready to give up. But the Shullas asked me just to shoot my gun at him and scare him away. I did not want to throw shells away and decided to get a bit closer before I had a try at him. So the chase was on.

We waded in behind the hippo and, walking as quietly as possible through the deepening water, I got up close enough that I could see his eyes with my light. I took a crack at him, but misjudged the distance in the dark and shot too low. The bullet hit the water and ricocheted off, singing into the night. The hippo plunged and wallowed around in the water until the boys thought he was hit; but the light was confusing him, and instead of swimming off to the river, as I expected, he turned to the left into a deeper part of the swamp. We followed, but when my feet would not touch bottom, I gave up and started to turn back. The group urged me to wait and they would bring a boat. So I waited. Soon they came back with a small native canoe and two long poles. The canoe was so small I could hardly get my hips into it, and with four of us on board, the water lapped at the gunwales. Being of an optimistic nature, I let them take me on.

Now the fun started. It was one thing to follow a hippo on foot, even though I was shoulder high in water, but it was quite another thing to chase him into the deep water in a small canoe that a breath would upset. At least we now had the advantage of speed, since the two boys poling could move faster than the hippo. I was not sure that speed was such an advantage, for we rapidly closed in on the hippo and things began to get pretty tense.

The water was about eight feet deep, but the hippo would swim underwater for some distance, and we could only see where he was by the movement of the grass that stuck up about a foot through the water. Then after a few minutes' swimming, the hippo would burst through the surface with a great snort and a deep-throated grunt that fairly shook the boat. Each time he broke water, the boys poling would sit down and steady the boat while I scrambled to my feet and tried to get my light on the hippo or pick up his eyes. But the grass made this difficult, and time after time, even when he was within thirty yards, I could not get a shot at him before he went down again. Then too, the third chap in the canoe, whose task it was to look after the eight or ten spears they had brought along, would stand up to see what there was to see. I came near falling out several times as the boat rocked under us, until I made that chap believe that I would throw him out if he got up again.

My boys were becoming exasperated that I did not shoot and at the same time a little braver because the hippo was moving away instead of showing fight. So they pushed on faster and faster. Finally we got within fifty feet of where I could see the grass moving and knew the hippo was. I stood up and waited for him to show his head. Soon he came up and blew water in all directions. I had my light and gun ready, and as his dark head showed in a bit of moonlight I turned my light on, and getting my sights lined up on his head, I pulled the trigger. With the crack of the rifle the boat started to go over, for the impact was too heavy for me to absorb. Simultaneously the three men jumped up to see what was happening. That was too much for the little boat, and over I went backward—gun, light, and all— into the filthy, black water. I managed to get my feet under me and struggle to the surface, almost expecting the hippo to be on top of me when I opened my eyes. But it turned out that he was scared worse than I was and had plunged off again.

The other chaps in the boat had managed to hang on and so kept their skins dry even though they were naked. I looked a sight and smelled like a stale goldfish bowl. The other fellows had managed to stay in the boat because their hands were free and they had not quite gotten to their feet. They grabbed my gun and light and pulled me in. I still expected the hippo to be upon us, but when I rubbed the water out of my eyes and the swamp scum off my face, I heard the hippo pushing off still farther to the left.

By that time I had had enough, but the Shullas thought the chase was only started. They assured me I had hit him that time, but I knew better, for I felt the boat rock under my feet just as the gun cracked; though I did not see where the bullet hit, yet I knew it was a miss. Without consulting my feelings or asking my desires, the Shullas poled me on and, in spite of myself, I was in for more. This time it might not be so fortunate for either me or the hippo.

The hippo was wild and excited and did not seem to know what he was doing (I am not sure I did either, or I would have been home safe in bed). First he would tread water directly ahead of us, and as we headed for that spot he would come through on the left and snort and grunt. Turning that way, our boat would rock with the waves he made. In three or four minutes we would fairly jump out of our skins as he came up close on the right. All this happened so quickly that I could not get to my feet before he was gone again, and all the time he was moving on ahead. I knew that if we kept going, he soon would be driven to shallow water and then I would have him at my mercy or be at his mercy. At any rate, there would be no mercy shown on either side.

Time after time as we pushed through the grass, not knowing whether the hippo would come up to the left or right under the canoe, I would feel the hair rise up on the back of my neck. I guess it must have been from the cold bath I had, because I did not feel the least bit scared—only very excited and eager to push on.

Finally we came to a bit of open water, and I had the boys stop and hold the canoe steady. I stood up and played my light around over the water, and when he came through, I was ready. I took careful aim and let drive. This time I heard the satisfying thud of a bullet going home, and I knew he was hit. But the funny part about it was, the hippo did not seem to have the same knowledge. He did, however, thrash around in the water and make waves like a storm at sea and then finally at full steam ahead started for the river, which was only a hundred yards off. We followed and when he left the deep water to climb the low bank before plunging into the river, I had the satisfaction of hearing another bullet plunk into his side. But he went on. The question now is, will we find him tomorrow bottom-side up floating down the river? I am dubious, for I fear I did not get a vital spot.

Don finished the story sometime later.

I found out the next day that I did not get the hippo. He was seen swimming down the river. He was badly hit, for his submarine apparatus seemed to be out of commission. He was not able to stay under the water, although he would plunge and plunge, trying to stay down. I would have gone after him again to put him out of his misery, but he was swimming too fast and would have been out of the country before I could get ready. He will undoubtedly die down the river some place. I have shot hyenas, leopards, and lots of large animals and hunted lions at night, but of them all, the hippo furnishes the most excitement. I have had enough to last me a long time, too.

Sometime earlier a rogue hippo had been wrecking gardens and driving fishermen off the river. It disappeared for some months, but later came back to Doleib Hill and started again. Don was in a boat returning from hunting for meat down near the mouth of the Sobat when he saw the hippo come up for air. Don put a bullet in the hippo's head, expecting that the carcass would float to the surface, but even after some time he could not locate it. He thought some villagers had stolen the hippo and had tried to hide it, but on the second day a Shulla with a keen nose located the hippo, which had plunged down under a lot of grass and water weeds. The carcass was so bloated that it looked like a huge sausage balloon. In high glee the Shullas cut it up and distributed the meat to two or three hundred people. The smell was so overwhelming that each piece of meat seemed ready to walk away on its own. That made it even more desirable. Don thought one bite would kill an American, but the Shullas claimed it was deliciously sweet and tender. At least it was tender.

Don occasionally worried that his reputation as a man with a gun was more widespread among the Shullas than his reputation as a man with a Bible. However, his shooting prowess had saved many Africans from wild animals, and the Shullas were grateful. If his rifle, "the magic spear," could be used to protect people from harm, it was just another gift to be employed for God's glory. Besides, the great animals of Africa were a challenge and a thrill.[26]

Early (five o'clock) on the morning of 27 July, while I was still dreaming of shooting lions as big as battleships, I was awakened by La Amoleker excitedly calling me from outside. "*Jaldwong, Jaldwong* (Old man, old man), come quickly with your gun. A lion has come into the village." Well before the chap had "village" out of his mouth, I was rushing for some clothes and my rifle. Grabbing a box of shells, I handed La my rifle and I dressed as we ran for the village. The whole place was in an uproar, with women screaming and carrying crying, half-awake children on their hips and with the men running about for their spears and shields. No one knew just what the trouble was, nor where the animal could be found. It seemed that two women had gone to the river for water, and they had sent out a wild cry for help. Immediately everyone took it up, and the word went around that the women were being attacked by lions. We ran for the river and, getting beyond the village, we saw far up the bank about a half-mile from the mission a herd of six huge elephants. The elephants were as much frightened as the women, and both were doing some horrible screaming.

It was little wonder the women were frightened to death, for it was the first time they had ever seen elephants, nor had they ever seen a lion alive. To them these terrible creatures were some kind of monster lions intent on devouring them. Elephants have not been seen in this neighborhood for forty years, though there are lots of them less than twenty miles away across the Sobat River.

On seeing the elephants I lost all interest in shooting, because it costs seventy-five dollars for a special elephant license. The seventy-five dollars looked bigger to me than even six elephants. However, I followed the crowd to watch the fun. In half an hour the word had traveled all over the villages in the vicinity, and the Shullas came pouring in by the hundreds, absolutely naked but armed with every spear to be found. Even our schoolboys and their teachers lost all traces of civilization and education as they ran like savages after the lumbering herd. Had some of my American friends or seminary professors seen a certain red-headed savage running wildly with the rest, gun in hand and eyes alight, and even outrunning his black companions, I doubt not but some of them would stop to ponder the worth of academic training or its ability to change the hunter inherent in us all.

The elephants were running all together in a ponderous, lumbering gallop upriver and keeping very close to the bank. The grass was so high that at times they were lost to sight, and then as the grass thinned out they bobbed into view again; each time they did so, the Shullas would increase their speed and throw their spears wildly. No one knew the technique of killing elephants, for not even in the memory of the oldest man had any been killed in that area. But everyone knew that the first thing was to keep out of the elephants' way. After a three-mile run the elephants came to a large village on the riverbank. There they stopped to look the situation over, milling about in the middle of the grain field until it looked like a hog wallow. Some of the more adventurous Shullas crept under cover of the high grass to the edge of the field and threw their spears. One or two spears found their mark, and with a shrill squeal the injured elephants turned and with uplifted trunks and widespread ears charged right at the hundreds of Shullas closing in.

If Jesse Owens had been on hand that moment, he would have learned something about speed of foot.[27] I never saw such running in all my life, or so much of it. Hundreds of men broke and ran pell-mell for their lives regardless of whom they knocked down or cut with their spears. I was standing in the midst of them and feared for my life, not from the charging elephants, but from flying spears. I managed to step behind a large thornbush and was thus spared. I also spared my breath, for the charge of the elephants was only a bluff. As soon as the men ran, the two charging beasts stopped and with loud trumpetings backed up to where their companions quietly stood eating grain.

As soon as the men realized that they were not being followed, they began to close in again, and then the fun began. The men soon divided themselves into two groups, and when one bunch kept the elephants occupied in front, the others would creep in behind and throw their spears. On being speared, the elephants would scream in pain and pull the spears out with their trunks, tossing them high into the air or trampling them to splinters and bent iron beneath their feet. Time after time, one or two of the elephants would charge the mob, and then it was a wild helter-skelter and every man for himself. In their mad flight the Shullas slashed and lashed each other with spears and spear handles until they were almost as badly cut as the elephants. But nothing would stop that mob!

I soon discovered that the elephants' charge was short, never for more than two hundred yards, and that they always charged in a straight line at the crowd rather than at one person. So if I was not in a direct line of charge I held my ground, crouching low in the grass to escape detection. Time after time I found myself all alone with a trumpeting elephant within thirty yards of me. My gun was always ready and my trigger finger itched, and I almost prayed for the elephant to find and charge me. Then I would have a good excuse for shooting. How I would have explained to the game warden my presence in the neighborhood of charging elephants did not occur to me. But the elephants always preferred running men to a standing one.

All that time the Shullas were pleading with me to shoot, but I kept telling them that I could only shoot to save my life or to save one of them. My time almost came before I realized it. The elephants had again started downstream toward the mission, and hundreds of Shullas kept closing in behind them and from the cover of high grass threw their spears, usually with little effect. I was watching from a slight elevation when suddenly two elephants charged from different directions. One of our teachers, Pakwan (the young man who always accompanies me on my hunts), and a schoolboy were in the direct line of one elephant. I never saw a man run so fast as did Pakwan, but even so the apparently slow-moving elephant was gaining on him. Suddenly Pakwan dodged off into the grass one way, and the schoolboy followed suit in the other direction. Neither of them had seen the second elephant. Nor had I at the first moment of charge. Then I was too late, for the schoolboy, running blindly through the high grass, which was well over his head, ran headlong into the second elephant. He was struck by the flying trunk and knocked twelve or fifteen feet to the left of the beast. I covered the elephant and was just about to shoot at the close range of forty yards when he stopped in his charge and slowly backed up again to the river. I do not believe he even knew he had hit the boy. Pakwan made good his escape. The boy, however, was so badly scared that he lost his reason and for days afterward would sit as in a stupor and then suddenly spring up and run for his life, screaming at the top of his voice that the elephants were after him. He gradually got over it and a few days ago returned to school, apparently normal.

A few minutes later, the Shullas cornered one bull elephant and cut him off from the rest. Then they began to hack him to pieces. Individually the spears did little damage and never pierced his vitals, nor could they hamstring him, as they tried to do again and again. But there were hundreds of spear wounds, and blood poured from every wound, so eventually if they could keep the elephant from getting away, he would bleed to death. This bull was getting more and more frantic as he tried to break through and again join the herd. First he would charge in one direction, and then the men behind would rush in and throw their spears. Whirling around, he would charge at them while the others rushed in. It was the greatest sight of brutality, savagery, and bloodthirstiness I have ever seen. All the while the elephant was madly trumpeting and screaming (and what a terrible scream they have); it could be heard for miles. Suddenly he charged directly toward the spot where I was standing. As the Shullas rushed past in headlong flight, I again took refuge behind a small bush and covered the charging beast. There was a small water course about thirty yards in front of me, and I determined that if he started to cross that, I would shoot. Suddenly I heard someone behind me yelling in terror at the top of his voice. Quickly glancing around, I saw a young chap by the name of Ajungdit squirming on the ground and yelling in pain. He had fallen into a hole and broken his leg. That settled the question, so I turned to shoot. The elephant, however, had stopped and was then just at the edge of the water course and wildly waving his trunk. I slowly backed up to where the boy was vainly trying to get up and run, and I told him to lie still and keep quiet. Strange to say, he obeyed and the elephant, in his nearsightedness, missed us and soon was charging in the opposite direction.

My decision changed, however, as I saw that the Shullas would never leave the elephants until some or all of them had been killed, and in doing so, some of the Shullas would get killed, too. Their spears were running short, and they were getting more and more desperate and bold. At the same time, the elephants were becoming more frantic and more deadly in their charge. So government or no government, license or no license, I decided to put an end to this butchery and to save my friends from self-destruction.

How it happened I do not know, but when I left the house that morning in the semi-darkness, I had grabbed a box of shells from my gun case and, as luck would have it, I got the single box that had steel-jacket bullets. I only had four such bullets left, since all the others had been used up on crocodiles. What I might have done if I had met a lion instead of elephants, I do not know, but I would not care to try to stop a lion with a steel bullet. Unless he were hit in the head, a lion would never stop. Nor would I want to shoot at an elephant with a soft-nose bullet, for my later experience proved that it has no effect on him.

So I looked to my rifle and began to close in on this big bull that was so badly cut to pieces. Suddenly he turned, and just when he lifted his trunk to charge, I took a bead on his open mouth. His head was tilted at such an angle that the bullet pierced the roof of his mouth and entered the brain. With a great lunge he plunged forward and dug his tusks into the ground and lay still. With a loud cry of triumph, hundreds of Shullas dashed forward, and every man threw his spear into the quivering hulk until it was just a forest of spear handles. They took as much pride in the kill as if they had done it themselves.

Suddenly there was a cry, and instantly everyone of those chaps who had been so brave a few seconds before turned tail and, leaving their spears stuck in the dead elephant, fled empty-handed. They had good reason to run, for bearing down on us like an express train was another big elephant. I could not shoot through the mass of spear handles, but as soon as I could move without being knocked down by black feet, I stepped out from behind the dead elephant and let drive at the approaching mountain of flesh. I shot straight for the forehead. With the smack of the bullet, he stumbled to his knees, and then as he tried to get up again, I shot again and he rolled over on his side and gave a few feeble kicks. My first shot was a bit high and only stunned him. I marveled that I hit him at all, for I was scared stiff. Again the cheering Shullas ran back and claimed a great victory and proceeded to establish it by hacking the second brute to pieces by spear thrusts.

I had had enough for one day and tried to persuade the people to leave the remaining elephants alone. This they would have done had not the elephants placed themselves in the Shullas' hands. The remaining four elephants took to the water and tried to swim across the Sobat. I had never before seen an elephant in the water, and it was a queer sight. They swim entirely submerged except for their trunks, which they hold above water like a periscope, only they are used for breathing and not seeing. Occasionally the elephant would bob up and have a look around and then again go down like a whale.

But they were only running into trouble instead of getting away from it, because across the river there were scores of men with their spears who were just waiting for such a chance. When the elephants started up the opposite bank, they were met with a solid phalanx of spears. Immediately the poor elephants turned and came back to our side, and as they swam the spear handles protruding from their backs made a strange appearance as they stuck above the water, almost like gigantic porcupines with wooden quills.

As they came back, their reception was warmer than ever, but in spite of the cloud of spears thrown into them, the elephants forced their way to the edge of the water and tried to get up the steep bank. Two of them managed to break through and get out, but the other two were not so fortunate. The first got his front feet up on top of the bank, but the mud bank was too steep and slippery for him to throw himself out. There he stuck, half in and half out. This was just the chance the Shullas were looking for, and they stood above him and threw and jabbed their spears into his head and shoulders until there was nowhere left for a spear to stick. Still they stood just a spear's length away and repeatedly jabbed and thrust at the squealing and trumpeting elephant. The elephant was not going to give up, and neither were the blood-mad Shullas. When I arrived on the spot, the elephant's trunk had been cut off and both his eyes put out. I could stand it no longer, so I told the people to stand back while I finished him off. The first shot dislodged him from the bank, but he began to swim away, so I shot again and that seemed to have no effect on him, though I hit him right on top of the head. Then I remembered that I had used the last of my steel-jacket bullets. However, before I tried again, the elephant sank and did not come up, so we knew he had drowned.

The fourth elephant, after trying to get out again on this side, went back again to the opposite side and met with fiercer opposition. Again he came back and, swimming just at the edge of the river, he went downstream and, finding no place to climb out, he turned and made his way up against the swift current, occasionally trying the bank with his trunk and front feet. All the time he was being literally hacked to pieces with spears. But he was so dazed and crazed with pain that a few more made no difference, and he scarcely noticed that the Shullas were within six to eight feet of him.

Again I took matters in my own hands and determined to finish it all. I shot him in the ear without effect and again through the head and again through the open mouth as he started up the bank. But even though I was within ten feet of him, the .405 made no more impression than had it been a .22.

Of course, I was using soft-nosed bullets and they did not penetrate. It was effective proof to me that only steel-jacket bullets will kill an elephant, no matter how big the gun. Finally, as the elephant found a place to get out and came up over the bank, I shot him through the front leg at the shoulder. He turned and plunged down the bank again into the river and made straight for the opposite shore. I shot my last shell as he swam away, and he paid no more attention to it than he would have to another spear.

As he swam, he seemed to gather strength, and when he reached the opposite shore, with a tremendous heave he threw himself up over the steep bank and through a cloud of spears right at the Shullas. Then it was our turn to laugh. All morning those chaps on the opposite side had been laughing at us as we ran from the elephants and shouting as that half-dead elephant chased men and women through the village. The elephant had landed right in the midst of a village and scared all the women nearly out of their lives. Finally the weakened animal took his stand at the edge of the village and simply stood feebly waving his trunk as the Shullas got bolder and bolder in their spearing. He never made any attempt to charge and did not even seem to notice the spearing. Then the Shullas grew so bold as to run up and pull out their spears and jab at him with both hands, driving the spears in so far that they could not pull them out. After a few minutes of this, the great brute gave a lunge forward and fell dead. It was a marvelous exhibition of animal strength and how pitiful human efforts seemed to be in comparison.

With four elephants down, the Shullas had had enough for one day. They were satiated with blood, bone-tired, and cut and bleeding from their own spear wounds. Moreover, the spears were nearly all gone. What they had not lost in the river, the elephants had broken and smashed to bits, so that some men lost all they had and nearly everyone had lost at least one.

There never has been such excitement in Shulla country. In two days the word had traveled to all ends of the Shulla territory, and people came in great crowds to see the dead elephants. And whatever they may have thought of me before, they are all in general agreement now that there is no one quite like the "little red man with the big gun." I am greeted all over the countryside in every village like a long-lost brother. They, of course, want some more meat.[28]

The Shulla Church

Don McCLURE believed that he had been called to serve God in Africa as an evangelist. That is to say, his primary task was to proclaim the gospel of God's love to every person he could reach. It was true that the missionaries would need to be involved in many kinds of activities to reach their goal, but the focus was clear: as native people committed their lives to Christ they would establish a church with indigenous— rather than foreign—leadership.

During our vacation last summer I did some thinking about our lack of progress and decided that our problem is, we have been circling our wagons for defense rather than charging across our field as we ought to be doing. Thus we were holding one worship service on Sunday here at the mission that our schoolboys and workers are required to attend, but only six to ten villagers ever come except on a Communion Sunday. The Shullas look on a communion service as magical and not to be missed. It seems to me that if the villagers will not come to us, we ought to go to them. I proposed this plan to Mr. Heasty, but the other missionaries are afraid that if churches are established in the villages, we will lose control and evil practices will creep in. My answer to this objection is that we must trust the Lord to guard his own, that we cannot expect to be here forever, and that Shullas can lead Shulla worship better than we can anyway.

Late last fall one of our leaders, Aba Nyilek, who lives at Lyel across the river, asked permission to start a Sunday school in his village. From the beginning, this school had a remarkable growth. When it became generally known that there was a service each week in Lyel, the people began to pour in. The little girls almost always came carrying a tiny baby on their hip, and

90

when the babies joined the singing because they were thirsty they would be taken to their mothers for feeding and returned satisfied. The little boys, who had to care for the sheep, would chase the herds out to pasture at breakneck speed and come running back to learn the songs and Bible verses. Occasionally the boys would dash out to make sure the sheep were not in the crops. The older people also came, but only to listen to their children sing and recite memory verses (just like Children's Day in American churches). But it was not long before the adults were following the words with their mouths and then correcting the children when they made mistakes.

We pushed the cattle out of the cattle barn, which was the largest building in the village, but the group kept getting larger and larger. One Sunday morning we had more than a hundred people packed into stalls built to accommodate about fifteen cows, and the old women had to sit outside in the sun. Someone raised the question about what we should do, because there were no buildings any larger than the barn. The suggestion that we sit out under two small trees met with little enthusiasm from the older folks, who objected to the hot sun and strong winds. Then Aba finally spoke up—rather hesitantly, for at that time he was the only Christian in the whole village—and suggested that we build a church. At once there was a chorus of ayes, and every man agreed that that was the very thing to do. I was amazed at their response, for in that same village there is a temple to Nyikang, their pagan god, and the people were noted for their devotion to this god.

From the first I was hesitant because I thought they might consider the church as merely another altar, and the more altars, the greater their protection from the evil spirits that constantly lurk about. But soon I, too, was carried away by their enthusiasm. Immediately they began to plan for the building. The men and boys would do the mudding of the walls, the women and girls carrying the water. Then the women would cut and bring in the grass while the men cut and carried in the poles for the frame and roof. And finally they would all stand by and help when the roof experts started to do the actual roofing, because only experts do the difficult work of thatching the houses.

Then they came to the problem of doors and windows. At last one old man, who had been sitting back in the corner smoking his long-barreled pipe filled with charcoal (since the

Shullas have little tobacco), spoke up. *Ya ko kinia*—"Listen to what I have to say." Then he pulled on his pipe again as we all kept a respectful silence. Finally he took the pipe stem out of his mouth and, passing it on to his neighbor, said, "We are going to build a house." We all agreed that he had proclaimed a bit of rare wisdom. "Are we going to live in this house?" No one suggested that we were. "Who will live in this house?" No one ventured an answer to this difficult question. "Why, this is God's house we are building and God will live in it." Everyone eagerly agreed that was so. "Since this is God's house and we do not have any door and window frames, we should ask the man of God (me) to ask God to provide them." This suggestion was taken up with alacrity, and the group turned to me and asked me to put the proposition up to God, which I did.

It all happened so quickly that I was almost breathless. No meetings of the trustees, no congregational meetings, no bazaars or bake sales, no solicitation or pledge signing; yet all the plans for the church were complete, and it would be built without a mortgage or church debt. I am all for building that kind of church.

Work started on the new church about the first of April, and when the rains permitted, the villagers worked steadily. The women and girls carried the water while the men gradually built up the walls, layer on layer as fast as the sun would dry the mud. Then the roof was built up on bamboo, over which the grass was spread until it was absolutely waterproof and thick enough to make the room cool and pleasant. Finally, the Lord supplied the door and window frames, and in the incredibly short time of three months, the building was completed and ready for dedication. There are many churches at home much more ornate and impressive than this one. But this is the first unsubsidized native church in all the Sudan. I believe it is the longest step we have ever taken toward making Christianity indigenous to the Shulla people.

Already we have ten other Sunday schools started in different centers, and perhaps out of some of these will grow a need and a desire to have their own Shulla church. When the Shullas look to us and to our church here at Doleib Hill, they always refer to us as the foreigners and to our church as the "foreigners' church." Nor will it be otherwise until they have their own churches. Then Christ will begin to take his rightful place in their lives as the Savior of the Shullas and not just "one of the foreigners' gods."

Our dedication service was blessed by the presence of four district chiefs, who had to be recognized and who, in order of precedence, made four long and rambling speeches. All of them tried to outdo the other in praising us and extolling what we are trying to do for their country. A second interruption came when a woman appeared at the door and shouted at the top of her voice, "The sheep are in the grain." At that, there began a mad scramble to see which of the thirty or forty boys could climb over and around the sitting people the fastest and get out the door. They fell and scrambled out amidst the shouts of their lazy elders warning them what would happen if the grain was eaten. But all in all, we had a splendid service. More than 230 people were able to jam themselves inside the church, and a larger group, not able to get in, sat outside throughout the three hours the service lasted. Aba Nyilek spoke in a spirit that was indicative of the feeling of all the people and was a promise of greater things in the future: "If I could be sure that we would have a crowd like this every day, I would tear the church down tomorrow and start to build a bigger one." And that was said about a building on which he had spent three hard months of labor.

This church in Aba's village was only the beginning of a great movement among our surrounding villages that is still growing. About the first of the year, when this first school had proved itself and indicated that the interest was not just a passing phase, I called in all our leaders and proposed to them that we start other similar schools. They were very enthusiastic and at once took up the plan. So we laid out our territory and started a plan of rotation whereby each teacher would take a Sunday school in a certain village for a month and then pass on to the next village. We also planned our songs and memory work so that each knew what was being taught in the various centers and we would have a progression of religious education for all our people with no overlapping.

"Enthusiastic" is scarcely the term to apply to the attitude and action of these men as they started in this new work, and the results have been wonderful. Immediately the people seemed to sense that here was something different and what they were hearing was not something from the foreigner, but from their own. The response has been far beyond our highest hopes. In every one of the ten locations the welcome was cordial and the interest warm. We had about 150 in attendance the first Sunday, and the last Sunday there were 700. To get 700 Shullas to attend anything except a dance or a fight is nothing short of a miracle.

The most outstanding man among the Shullas at Doleib Hill was La Amoleker, whom the American Mission employed as a teacher. A few months earlier he had been planning a second marriage according to tribal custom, but forbidden by the rules of the little Christian church that was in the process of being formed. Don was desperate not to lose this natural leader and was overjoyed when La decided against the second marriage and consented to be baptized into the Christian faith and ordained as an evangelist. However, the governor of the province of Malakal, a Mr. Armstrong, absolutely refused permission for the ordination, insisting that such a practice involved government administration of native peoples that violated all precedents of government policy for the south Sudan.

Don would not accept this decision, because he believed that it was none of the government's business whether or not a Shulla was ordained. Thus Don applied to the civil secretary in Khartoum for a reversal of the provincial governor's ruling. When the civil secretary sent word that the government did not presume to interfere with the ecclesiastical affairs of the American Mission in Sudan, La Amoleker became the first native Sudanese to be ordained by any church body.

In the following month the Evangelical Church of Doleib Hill was organized under the general jurisdiction of Don's church in America. There were seventy-nine charter members, with more soon to be added, and Don felt that

We have attained a goal toward which the mission has been working for the past forty years. Some of the older missionaries might not think that we had been working toward that goal, and more of them might feel that we have not reached it. But I have a way of celebrating victories before the battle is completely over, so perhaps I rushed things a bit.

As soon as the church was organized, the Shullas elected four officers from among themselves who were then ordained as elders by a commission composed of Don, Lowrie Anderson, and others of the

American Mission. Don thought this was an historic event, since the new officers were the first black men of Sudan to be ordained as elders in the Church of Jesus Christ in nineteen hundred years.

It does not seem possible that it took so long, but it is a splendid stride forward after only forty years of Christianity among the Shullas. For ten days I met with the elders, all of them first-generation Christians, to explain to them something of church government and to impress upon them the seriousness of their responsibilities. They all took it very solemnly and made faithful vows that they would stand fast. I am sure that there are not five men in our American church to whom ordination means more than it does to these Shullas; largely because these men had to give up so much to make the vows and because they have come so far to be ready to make them. These leaders have been responsible for the building of native churches in their own villages and will now take charge of the services in them. Aba Nyilek has already taught and prepared forty-five people for baptism and is now teaching another communicants' class of more than twenty. What a joy these men would be to a pastor at home, and what a tremendous joy they are to us here at Doleib Hill! They have made our revival possible and kept it going.

A few months later, the church held a baptism and communion service for forty-one new Shulla Christians. Don and Glenn Reed participated in this service with La Amoleker, who, when he baptized his first convert, was so overcome by emotion that tears ran down his face and he could not be heard repeating the words of the baptismal formula. Then the new elders joined in serving communion to the largest group of Christians ever assembled at Doleib Hill.

Don thought it was wonderful how the elders had risen to the demands of their office, and he was not concerned about criticism from other missionaries that things were going too fast at Doleib Hill.

Suppose we do in fact baptize a few people who will later revert to paganism. That result is not unknown in America, and at least we are moving and not just standing still. We are just finishing five Shulla churches, and there will be nearly two hundred people ready for baptism when those churches are dedicated. That will make a total of more than four hundred baptized within the year. Yet the greatest joy to me is not so much the baptism of the people, but to see the way our Shulla leaders are taking an interest in evangelism. Six months ago I was preaching and teaching five and six times a day and as many as eight services on the Sabbath. But these men we have ordained, and especially the evangelist, La Amoleker, have taken over the burden of this preaching and are doing it far more effectively than I could ever do. A year ago I was going out almost alone; this week nearly forty Shulla men and women went out and taught their own people in as many different villages, and everywhere we have people asking for instruction.

Don spent his odd hours preparing a new baptismal service, because he thought that the one in use was disorganized. Moreover, in one place there was an entirely unintentional statement, in the Shulla tongue of course, which was so inadequate that it was heretical. Literally translated, the statement was, "I baptize you in the name of the Father, Lord of Heaven; of the Son, Lord of Earth; and of the Spirit, the soul of the Son and his Slave." Don was afraid that some internationally famous professor of theology who understood the Shulla language might hear that line and start a worldwide controversy on the relative positions and powers of the three persons of the Trinity.

Don was also planning to baptize two infants and their mother, which he thought might displease some of the older missionaries. The accepted pattern, although by no means uniformly observed, was that adult candidates for baptism were required to memorize the catechism, the Apostles' Creed, the Lord's Prayer, and certain passages of Scripture. In order to meet this requirement, a person had to attend a communicants' class that met once a week for two years. If at the end of that period the communicant could pass an examination, the person was considered ready for baptism. Don objected to this because the requirements made baptism possible only for the boys who had learned these things as part of their schooling.

We will never have a villager who is able to perform such mental gymnastics no matter how sincere he might be. For several years some of our most advanced Christians have asked that their wives be baptized, but have always been refused because the wives could not answer our questions. I want to set a new precedent. I believe that for the Shulla people, we should perform baptisms as soon as they show a desire to live a

Christian life and can assure us of their sincerity in giving up their pagan worship. I believe that such persons should be baptized as soon as they demonstrate their sincerity, but should not be received into the communing membership of the church until they have received sufficient knowledge to know what it is all about. I believe we should have a period of probation between baptism and confirmation. At any rate, on this coming Sunday I am going to baptize the two children and the wife of one of the elders. In our entire church membership we have only three women, and these were baptized a long time ago by our missionary George Sowash, who was no stickler for these standards. I am sure that after this baptism on Sunday, I will have requests from a dozen or so of our outstanding Christians to baptize their wives as well so that they can really set up a Christian home. I may comply if I think the applicants are ready, whether I get in trouble with my fellow missionaries or not.

Six months later, sixteen evangelistic teams started out after the church service and before evening had held sixty-five or seventy services and contacted close to three thousand people.

We started services in the outlying villages sometime ago, but only the teachers and those in the employ of the mission would participate. Gradually we got one or two others to go out and kept encouraging our people to share in this important part of their Christian duty. They were reluctant, since they knew so little to teach anyone else. Finally we got two women, then another two, and the group continued to increase until last Sunday there were thirty-five people who stayed after the service for prayer and instructions before starting to go out and proclaim the gospel that day. We usually send them out two by two, trying to include an experienced person with a new recruit, and in some cases we send out three together. It is proving to be a grand experience for them all, and the more they go, the more enthusiastic they become. As the group grows, I will plan to take a few of them out in the car and set them down at greater and greater distances from the mission, and then, as they make their way back, they will preach the gospel.

The Shullas take to this sort of thing very readily, because they love to visit distant villages and greet their friends. It is difficult for the younger men to call a crowd together to listen to them speak, but they gradually get over their fear and then they take a great pride in it. It has been marvelous to watch some of them develop and grow under the training. To me the greatest joy is the growth of Shulla leadership as more and more they become independent of the mission. I know that if we now had to leave Doleib Hill, the work would go on. I could not have said that six months ago, because the Shulla Christians had not at that time caught the vision of proclaiming the gospel to others.

Obviously God was blessing the local churches and the school.

I can only believe that the Holy Spirit is moving in the hearts of the Shulla people. Three months ago we were deep in the problem of polygamy among our leaders. It was not easy to go against a tribal custom in favor of the establishment of a Christian home, but our uncompromising stand has led to a blessing rather than the disaster we feared.

The first indication that something unusual was happening came when Kigokwic sent for me. He was very sick, and I had been to see him several times. But on Friday he sent and asked me not to delay. I went immediately, and he told me that he had believed in Jesus for many years but had refused to follow his way. "Now I am dying, and he will not let me die in peace. I want to be baptized." He surely was dying and I believed he just as surely had a great faith in Jesus. So the next day we gathered our leaders together and called the village together to baptize Kigokwic and his mother, who wanted to be baptized with him. Kigokwic died six hours later, and we had a Christian burial for him. Everywhere I went thereafter, people talked about Kigokwic and how happy they were that he had been baptized before he died. I was amazed at their interest in him and in baptism.

From that time on, people began to ask more and more about baptism, and I found myself going from village to village teaching people in preparation for baptism and church membership. Contrary to the former practice, I am baptizing them and then demanding that they come for further training before they can be taken into the church. I thought it would be difficult at first, but I find that the Shullas do understand that they need further training before they can grasp the meaning of the Lord's Supper and the duties of church membership. Following the dedication of the church at Lyel, the people of Appio, Pajur, and

Pathworo have all asked for permission to build a church in their villages. One church has been built in Palo and will be dedicated next week with more baptisms, and within the month there will be four other churches built in nearby villages. They are all vying with one another to see which will have a church first.

We now have a fine school here at Doleib Hill as the opening wedge to attack ignorance and superstition. We have over sixty boys coming daily for instruction. Forty-five of them are living here with us in the boarding school, where we can exercise very close supervision over them and exert a much stronger influence than if they lived in the village. The school is growing more and more popular every year. When the school started several years ago, we had to beg and plead with boys to come and had to pamper them to keep them here. That is no longer the case. We can now pick our boys and make demands of them in the way of school and outside work. We have tried to balance their curriculum in such a manner that classroom work is well integrated with practical work and agriculture. They learn all the native arts: weaving, pottery making, rope making, roofing houses, basketry, and the like. This will be exceedingly useful to them when they go back to their homes and settle down into village life. There they will begin to pass on what they have learned here, and after some years the entire tribe will have been elevated a bit in its standard of living. Our beginnings have been small, of course, and probably in the whole tribe there are not more than one hundred boys who can read and write. This is not a matter for discouragement, but rather a great challenge to us.

We are also endeavoring to open some out-schools. These mobile schools are established in villages that are at some distance from the mission. We train the teachers here and then send them out to gather together some boys who will consent to be taught. We cannot afford a school building. There will be no books, no pencils, no paper, no scissors, no blackboard, no chalk—none of the things that our American children take for granted almost as a birthright. But the teacher will sit together with some boys under a tree or perhaps go out to where they are herding sheep. Then he will use a large chart to teach them their letters, using stones to teach the children to count, and all the time he will be telling them stories of things he has learned—the history of their own people, some elementary geography, something of hygiene—but most of all he will be planting the seeds of God's love deep in those little boys' hearts. He will tell them stories from the Bible and of the life and power of God revealed in Jesus Christ our Lord.

In months past, the support of these teachers has fallen upon our local church here, for there was no money from our Foreign Mission Board to carry on this work. The native church has carried this burden nobly, and we are now urging them to add the support of two or three more teachers. They can do it if they will, in spite of the fact that the highest salaried man in the church receives only $7.50 a month—not a week, but a month. Of that he gives $1.00 a month to the church. The Shullas know how to give, and they would be insulted and hurt if they could not contribute something. They look on giving as a rare privilege and are richly blessed in it. But they need prayer as they undertake the support of a couple more teachers. It will mean only $2.50 per month for each teacher, but this is a big sum to our Shullas.

▼▲▼

Don later explained that it had become necessary to issue faithful Christians "communion tokens" so that only those properly prepared received the Eucharist.

On Sunday we celebrated the Lord's Supper in the small church here. Those who participated were required to present communion tokens. Tragically, eight of our former members are now practicing witchdoctors, ten have taken a second wife, and a large number are living in open adultery. Church discipline is always difficult to apply wisely, but it is important to try to separate the Christians from the pagans.

We had a big crowd of nearly 250. We have no pews, of course, so everyone sat on the floor. Many of the youngsters were completely naked. It was so hot that they would have taken off their birthday suits if they could find the button holes. One little girl was so interested in the service that she relieved herself where she sat. Her embarrassed older sister spread the moisture around on the dirt floor with her hand, and it dried quickly. That advantage, inherent in a dirt floor, is one that few

American churches can provide to its worshipers. According to Shulla social custom, it is disrespectful to exhibit the soles of the feet. Thus, in church they sit on the ground with their feet tucked under them and pointed away from the pulpit.

Don admitted that he had experienced great difficulty concentrating during this church service. Apparently one of the missionary women had thrown away an old corset, but a Shulla man had rescued it from the garbage and, with great dignity, came to church wearing the corset on his head and no garment whatsoever on his body.

The preacher was one of our Shulla evangelists whose pulpit robe was *really* too short. (Actually it was a pulpit loincloth.) Thus everytime he raised his arms, he gave us more of a "revelation" than he intended. I hope American preachers do not adopt this homiletical technique. Anyway, during the sermon an old dog wandered in, lay down behind him, and promptly fell asleep. A few minutes later, in the midst of some hell-fire and damnation exposition in a high and angry tone, the preacher stepped back and right on the dog's leg. Well, the dog yelped and, in a flash, had planted his teeth in the preacher's calf. Now it was the preacher's turn to yelp. They both nearly went over the pulpit. After a pause to kick the dog, the sermon was continued.

During all this I was watching a little girl about twelve or thirteen, just at the self-conscious age, trying to keep her knees covered as the white women do. Her mother, sitting placidly beside her, was almost naked and completely unconcerned about the fact. However, when the little girl got her knees covered, she was all bent over and uncomfortable. Every time she straightened up, her knees showed again. She must have covered and uncovered her knees at least fifty times. As she worked, however, a gust of wind blew her picture card out of her lap and across the floor. She started crawling after the card, and with the little black spanking place in full view, it was obvious that the whole back of her cloth was torn out. Having retrieved her card, she resumed her modest knee-covering stunt.

▼▲▼

In 1936 Don's brother-in-law and close friend, John Cummings, fell ill. Don wrote from Africa that he was praying for John's recovery and felt confident that he would be restored to health. John died on 23 October, two weeks short of his thirty-fourth birthday, leaving three small children. Don was heartbroken.

It is difficult to believe that John is gone and all the good times we had together are past and finished forever. In many ways, John was closer to me than my own brothers. I was able to confide in him, and he saved me from myself many times. What a strange world this is! So many things cause us to wonder "why?" We come to realize that we know so little about life and must live by faith in God alone. As I look out on the world and see all the pain and hunger and hatred and death, we seem to be fighting a losing battle; and the more we invest in the struggle for truth and justice, the more we seem to lose. If it were not for my faith in the ultimate triumph of the forces of goodness, I would give it all up and live for myself alone. But I believe that I have a task to perform on earth and when that task is ended, the Lord will call me to a new task in heaven. God must have decided that John was needed in heaven. He will not return to us, but we will join him someday when our work here is finished.[29]

▼▲▼

This is one of the most marvelous Sunday mornings I have seen in many a month. We had a heavy rain last night, and instead of the sun coming up hot and red, it is shrouded with fleecy white clouds. Without much stretch of the imagination I can feel myself in western Pennsylvania on a bright April morning with the air smelling deliciously of rain and the refreshed earth. I got up at five in the morning to have my quiet time, and the family is still sleeping now at six o'clock. However, it is time they were awake.

I love my Sabbath mornings, because everything is quiet and peaceful. There are no workmen about, no watercarriers, no people coming in to sell chickens and eggs, no one bringing sheep to gather tax money, no crowds gathering about the clinic door and chattering like magpies, no one coming to borrow boats or buy bamboo for their house roofs. I can look forward to an entire day in serving the Lord as I feel he ought to be served daily in teaching and preaching. The little things of everyday life so sap our energy and enthusiasm that I often feel the weekdays are almost lost to him. I know we can serve God in everything we do and honor him even in selling bamboo and buying chickens, or dickering about boat rental, but I find it very hard and very wearing, while a good worship service or a good chat with a friend about his spiritual welfare fills me with joy and enthusiasm. I go on from strength to strength and never seem to tire. I have held as many as fifteen services in a day in as many little hamlets, with but five-to-ten minutes between them, and come home from them refreshed and ready for more. But ten minutes of haggling over the price of a goat, or wasting half an hour explaining to a man why I will not loan him a dollar, simply drains me dry and I want to quit.

The church at Doleib Hill had recently increased from 95 souls to 209. In America a congregation that doubles its membership is a matter of pride and often self-congratulation. In Sudan, 200 Shulla Christians among a people numbering some 300,000 only reminded the missionaries how much remained to be done. According to Don,

The vast majority of Shullas still live in terrible superstition and therefore fear. Those Americans who have a romantic concept of the "noble savage" living a pure and simple existence close to nature should spend a month here. Last week lightning hit one of the houses in a nearby village, and because lightning is regarded as a punishment from the gods, no one even tried to rescue the woman and two children in the hut who burned to death. These, too, are children of God, and they need to know the truth that will set them free for abundant life. The Shullas have a concept of God and an inner craving that is not satisfied until it finds the truth revealed in Jesus Christ. Still, we have to be careful to preach Christ alone rather than to present a more advanced civilization in which he is just another technical trapping. I believe that those Americans who appreciate our efforts in agriculture, education, hygiene, etc., but reject our efforts in evangelism have lost their own faith. If you truly love a person, you will want to share the source of that love. Because Christ loves us, we believe he loves the Shullas, too, and we are out here to tell them about God's love and to live in a way that makes God's truth convincing. Of course, we often fail in what we say and do, but God will use our efforts in the upbuilding of his kingdom.

A brief stay in the hospital gave Don another opportunity to reflect on the Shullas' spiritual well-being.

I just got out of the hospital in Malakal, where I was laid up with a badly infected leg, which, after being ill-treated, turned septic and into erysipelas. I went in last Tuesday, and when the doctor examined the leg, he shook his head and said, "It is a bad one." And then he gave me the encouragement that I might be out within a month if they could confine the erysipelas to the present area on one leg. That prospect made me unhappy, since I could not afford the time or the money to stay in a hospital a month or more. So I decided to talk the matter over with the Lord. Not that the Lord did not already know all about it, but it is a good idea to take him into your confidence once in a while. This time it was an exceedingly good move, because it seemed that the Lord had other plans for me. I prayed and then left the whole affair up to him. The erysipelas was checked the next day, and within three days it had cleared up and I was ready to come home. The doctors held me a couple of days longer because they were not accustomed to such quick cures. I was afraid they would keep me a month just on general principles. When they realized that I was really well, the doctors began to take a lot of credit. I told them the credit belonged to God, but they were more than a little dubious.

While I was in the hospital, I had a chance to think about some things and one of them was, "What does Christmas mean to the people of the Sudan, and especially these pagan people among whom we work?" It is almost unthinkable that for more than nineteen hundred years the Christian world has been celebrating the birth of Christ and rejoicing in all the privileges and joys that he can mean to us, and yet there are millions here right within our reach who never heard of Christmas. What does Christmas mean to the pagan people of the Shulla tribe?

To about two hundred of them it means life and hope, light and joy, salvation and eternal life and everlasting companionship with their Master. To those who have been called out of death into life, out of the vile superstitions and customs of paganism into the glorious beauties of a new day, Christmas means far more than it does to most of us. There will be no presents here, no Christmas trees with all their bright ornaments, but the spirit of Christmas will be in two hundred hearts and there will be a song of joy on their lips, for "unto them was born in the City of David a Savior who is Christ the Lord." What need is there for presents and Christmas trees when the spirit of love is abroad and when the spirit of Christ is filling all hearts?

But what about the 299,800 Shullas who have not heard, or at least have not accepted? What will Christmas mean to them? What will their Christmas be like? It is terrible to think that as another Christmas passes we are so little nearer the realization of Christ's dream of the time when "every knee shall bow and every tongue confess that he is Lord." Have we Christian people failed our Lord? Have we turned a deaf ear to his pleadings? Have we become so engrossed in our little worlds and our little plans that we have lost sight of his great desire for us and for the world? I wonder how many of us would be celebrating Christmas with great joy and overflowing hearts if Christ had been as indifferent to our needs as we are for his and his kingdom.

Christmas morning in Shullaland will see 299,800 men, women, and children rise as on any other morning without a thought of what the day might mean. The men will go out to sit under the same trees, tell and listen to the same stories, plan the same kinds of dances they have known for centuries, indulge in the same superstitions, consult the same witchdoctors who will work the same incantations and charms that have been worshiped for centuries. They may go out to look at their ripening fields; they will plan the same evil, try to trade cattle, and perhaps buy a second, third, fourth, or fifth wife who will add to the strife in his village; all this will go on as if the day were not the birth of the Savior, because it will not have even a shadow of influence on their lives.

The children will run out to play in the same filth, play about the cattle barns, make fuel cakes from cow dung, collect cow urine for washing their hair. The same kinds of flies will crawl over their faces and into eyes and mouths that have been blinding and killing Shulla babies for years. Scarcely one in six of the children playing about this Christmas will live to be fifteen, and not more than half of them will see another Christmas. The simplest Christmas joys will mean nothing to them, for they never have seen a doll, a piece of candy, or a ball.

But the women will have the hardest lot, because Christmas will mean no rest for them, nor does any day until they die under the burden. They will have to grind the grain for food, go out and gather firewood to cook it, go to the river for water, although it may be a mile or more from their hut. If there is no grain in the hut, the women will have to hunt for herbs and roots to keep the family from starving. Then after the morning meal is prepared, she will go to the field and either hoe or gather the ripe grain. She will take the grain back home and start preparations for the evening meal. If there is any time left, she will mud the walls of the house or gather grass to repair the roof. And so Christmas Day will pass for man, child, and woman, never making a ripple on the surface of their lives. Will it always be so?

At the present time we are putting forth every effort to make Christmas mean something to all the people around. We will have special services in the little church this year, to which we will invite all the people within call. We will tell the old, old story that has been gripping hearts for all these years, and afterward we will have a feast for the Shullas. We will kill an ox and roast it whole. This will be our only Christmas present, for it would be impossible to give something to the hundreds who will come for the day. I hope next year we will have many more than two hundred Christians. We are preparing for a week of intensive evangelistic effort, culminating in Christmas, and we are to have the help of one of the pastors from the north Sudan, a man who is as black as any of these Shullas and whose history is an inspiration to everyone.

A month after this man, Toobia, by name, was born to a Dinka mother and father, the Arabs swept through the country, enslaving all they could capture. The boy's father escaped to the swamps, but the mother was captured and taken with her little baby to the boat that was to carry them far away to the north and slavery. The thought of their fate was too much for the father, and by night he returned and tried to effect their escape, but he too was captured and the whole family was carried to Omdurman. There they were sold as slaves and separated. Within a few months the father died, but the mother's stout heart clung desperately to life for the sake of her baby boy. After some years of the most cruel slavery, she too died when the lad was about five or six years old. He was then thrown on his own and had to shift for himself. As a man of thirty, he had never been to school, but longed to be educated, so he entered a mission school along with boys of eight or nine. In spite of all the taunts and jeers from his fellows, he persisted and soon graduated from the primary school. But he was not satisfied. Since there were no secondary schools in the Sudan, he decided to go to Egypt. Without money he had to walk most of the way from Khartoum to Assiut, Egypt, a distance of twelve hundred miles across burning sands. He traveled mostly by night to escape the bands of roving Arabs who might have taken his life simply for the clothing he wore, scant as it was.

After many torturous months filled with bitter experiences, Toobia reached Assiut and entered our American Mission preparatory school and later graduated from Assiut College. Still unsatisfied, he went on to the seminary in Cairo and graduated with honors. His life from this point has been one of glorious service for his own people. He might have remained in Egypt with great profit for himself and to the work there, but he wanted to return to Sudan. Since Arabic had become his mother tongue, he chose to remain in the north Sudan rather than come to the south, where he would have to learn a new language. So he has labored with ever-increasing success among the people who once enslaved and killed his parents and tried many times to take his life. There are many, many such faithful stewards laboring for the Master, giving love in return for hatred and giving life where before only death was known.

It is such a man who is coming to us next week. Toobia has never returned to the land of his birth since he was taken away as a baby, so he comes with his heart beating high and with a desire to tell his own people some of the glorious things Jesus has meant to him. It will be great for *us* to have him come, too. When we preach to and teach the Shullas, they say, "Oh yes, that is well enough for you foreigners and the white man, but such is not for us blacks." Now they will have a chance to hear one of their own people proclaim the saving power of the gospel.

▼ The Shulla King

TODAY I DO NOT REALLY have anything to write, but it helps to talk to loved ones. I always try to be cheerful and hopeful, but we have had no rain in two months, and the merciless and changeless sun beats us down. Poor little Marghi has an infected finger. She also has a temperature, which may indicate malaria or sunstroke and an eye infection. Her eyes are swollen and full of pus. I have to tie her down to put zinc oxide in her eyes, which burns like fire. As if that were not enough, she also has an infected foot. I had to wrap her in a towel and close my ears to her baby screams when I lanced her foot without anesthesia. So today I am tired and discouraged. I have never known a time when I did not profess Jesus Christ as my Lord and Master. My spiritual development has been a gradual growth in knowledge and appreciation of the faith. While there have been not a few mountain-top experiences, there has never been, to the best of my recollection, a "slough of despond." Each day my companionship with the Lord grows more precious. I expect that to be the rule of my life, but today, if not out, I am really down.

Last week all the Christian leaders got drunk on native beer, and there was a big fight. There has been bad blood between the two villages for a hundred years, and the men here like to fight. They do not have aggressive (but controlled) contact sports like our football, and when they pick up a stick it is not to hit a baseball. Our cook, Oman, had to jump into the fight on the side of his fellow villagers and was nearly killed. We were just finishing supper when friends brought Oman to our house for me to patch up. It made me sick just to look at him. His skull was laid open to the white bone in several places. Part of the fight was between our Christian cook and one of our Christian teachers. The teacher had bitten huge hunks out of Oman's cheeks. I suppose that in a world where Christian nations go

108

to war with each other, we cannot be too surprised that it happens here, too. Anyway, Oman was covered with blood. I am no physician, but I did what I could. Oman is tough and we expect him to live. Glenn Reed thinks we should warn them this time about drinking and fighting, but I think they should be punished. We are their brothers in Christ, but we are elder brothers and have a responsibility to foster their welfare in every way we can.

▼▲▼

Don always seemed unconcerned, if not oblivious, to social position and therefore was more than a little irritated by tributes paid to it, especially out in Africa. Thus he complained,

About ten o'clock Thursday morning a telegram came from Dr. Lewis of the hospital in Malakal to the effect that he was coming out to see us that afternoon and bringing with him Dr. Adeeb Abdullah, who was a graduate of our mission schools and a good friend of ours. We were glad to have them come and made preparations for tea and supper. A few minutes later a second telegram came from the senior doctor of the Malakal hospital staff, who had been up at Gambela, saying that he was coming down and would be in Doleib Hill early in the evening and would like to stop and see us. Well, since he had been looking after Lyda, we naturally expected him to stay for supper as well.

Both boats arrived at the same time, with Dr. Lewis from Malakal getting in just enough ahead to take the only docking place for boats here at the mission. Dr. Stephenson, the senior man, was forced to anchor in midstream and then make fast to the first steamer. I had a few minutes' talk with Lewis before Dr. Stephenson got ashore, and I could plainly see that Dr. Lewis was quite distressed. He had not known that the other doctor was to be on the scene, and being a new doctor and very junior to the other, it was presumptuous for him to be on the spot at all. The first meeting of the two doctors was decidedly cool, but as we sat on Dr. Stephenson's boat and they drank their sundowners of whiskey and soda to the accompaniment of my lemonade, the atmosphere was stiffly polite. I had asked them individually to come up to dinner at eight, and each accepted. With Dr. Stephenson was a second man, a Mr. Bell of the

Egyptian Irrigation Commission, also a senior official of high rank, so in his presence I repeated my invitation and again they all accepted. But then Dr. Stephenson turned to me and said, "I rather think Mr. Lewis will not be able to stay, as he ought to be getting back to Malakal." I looked at Lewis and saw him gulp a couple of times, but then, like a good government servant, he took his medicine and in a few minutes excused himself, and after good-byes to me, he sailed off for Malakal without his supper. Dr. Lewis would not eat that night at all, since he left at seven o'clock and it takes four hours to reach Malakal. Such is official British protocol reaching into the heart of Africa: a senior man cannot sit at table with a junior. What absolute nonsense!

Not long after that episode, Lady Symes, the Roman Catholic wife of the Sudan governor general (who was Anglican), came to visit Sudan and deigned to spend one of her afternoons at Doleib Hill. Don was not at all pleased with the honor—especially since they received only a few hours notice of her arrival, and it fell to Lyda to entertain the Lady and those attending her. Don insisted that Lyda could be Lady McClure if she would only change the order of the letters of her first name; nonetheless Lyda was rushing around trying to get ready to entertain a woman who was supposed, according to Don, to have a pedigree as long as the famous racehorse Man o' War.

Glenn and Don were assigned the task of meeting the boat, and Glenn was to make the speech of welcome, which he did in his best English accent. Lady Symes turned and said, "Why, you are not like the other Americans, you talk like the English." To which Glenn replied, "I believe when in Rome do as the Romans do," and then blushed furiously because the two Protestant missionaries had agreed not to mention anything that bordered on religion.

"Have you ever been to Rome?" she asked.

"No, I am sorry to say, I have not," confessed poor Glenn, who was then treated to a description of the beauties of Rome and more particularly of Vatican City.

The American women enjoyed the tea party, but if they had known then what they discovered the next day, they would have turned green and died on the spot. A few days before, Don had started to paint the porch furniture and had finished one chair. Since it was the nicest-looking chair, that was the one in which Lady Symes was placed. Unfortunately, the paint had not completely dried. Lyda later found a good deal of green paint on one napkin and was mortified. Don was not pleased either. "I will have to repaint that chair. I think I will send the governor general a bill for all the paint his wife took away with her."

A month ago I got blood poisoning through the infection of a cut and was ordered to bed. I told the doctor that my temperature stayed up because I was mad. If I could get in a fast game of tennis, I would be all right. The poison coursed around in my system and got localized in my leg, which is red and swollen. I am glad it settled in my leg rather than the end of my nose, which is large enough as it is. While I was recuperating, I was visited by a British official of the Sudan government. He told me that he had recently met a Roman Catholic priest who was asked if he believed the official would be damned to hell since he was not a Catholic. The priest answered, "Yes." The official was absolutely outraged; his eyes still flashed at the memory. "Here I am," he said, "from one of the finest families in England. I am an honors graduate of Oxford University, a high official in His Majesty's service, a believing Anglican Christian, and this miserable papist has the effrontery to tell me that I am damned!" I managed to be sympathetic while he was in the room, but as soon as he left, I rolled over in bed and roared with laughter. I have always assumed that God is interested in believing Christians, but this Britisher's confidence in family, education, and position is beyond me.

Protocol problems were not restricted to the British. So when someone murdered the much-hated, much-feared, but very necessary Arab storekeeper in the nearby village of Palo, the authorities made many arrests without any assurance that the murderer was among them. Don thought that the ramifications of this case were not only baffling, but impenetrable to Westerners. Thus it would take Sherlock Holmes "five pipes" rather than his usual "three pipes" to solve it.

In any event, in desperation the civil authorities sent for the Shulla king, Ayokar, and asked him to come to the scene and try his hand at ferreting out the murderer.[30]

He came, he saw, and we are overcome! Now, the world knows all kinds of kings, but a Shulla king possesses the romance of a Solomon with his multitude of wives, the chivalry of an Arthur with his round table of knights, the fierceness of a William the

Conqueror with his warlike bodyguard, and the pagan bigotry coupled with sympathy for other religions of a Cyrus the Great. In days gone by, the Shulla king was lord of all he surveyed, for according to royal theory everything belonged to the king, and he could call for whatever he wanted from his subjects. In his hand lay the power of life and death, and he is the personification of deity and rules by divine right. The king can do no wrong. We had no difficulty with our African monarch-of-all-he-surveyed as long as he remained some distance from us among his plurality of wives and held court for those who groveled before him and addressed him as *Nya Jwok* (Child of God).

But now the king has been forced upon us here in the narrow confines of our missionary compound at Doleib Hill, and we are expected to provide whatever hospitality he requires. We are overwhelmed with the honor of his presence. Immediately upon the king's appearance in our midst, a house of suitable appointments and size had to be provided. Unfortunately for him, we need our house for ourselves, so the headmaster of the school, La Amoleker, and his family were asked to abide elsewhere, for the king had desire for our headmaster's nicely decorated and newly roofed house. However, since the king cannot eat food cooked by female hands, our headmaster was pressed into service as his cook. The fact that school was in session and La was badly needed at his post only made his selection the more honorable for the king. Being the most important member of the compound, La was just the man to feed the king. I am grateful that I was traveling when the king first put in an appearance, or I might be writing this from the king's kitchen with one hand and grinding his grain with the other. Mr. Heasty looks so uncooklike that he was comparatively safe from kitchen service.

Next came an order for a bed. Regal bones do not rest well on the ground even though a tiang skin makes an excellent couch. So a bed was procured from the Heasty storeroom but, sad to say, Mr. Heasty came near to losing his head because he let the king down. The cot, being of canvas and having endured several hot and debilitating years in the Sudan, split from end to end from the weighty pressure of the royal rear end. Deeply humiliated, the Reverend Dr. Heasty produced another, though he was not so deeply chagrined as to comply with the kingly request that a mattress accompany the cot. Mr. Heasty fears his wife even more than he fears the king, for a bed louse is no respecter of kings. The cot now being supplied for the royal sleeping hours, we were expected to provide a steamer chair of proper proportions in which the king could occupy the time between meals. With the house finally and finely furnished, Heasty felt a measure of relief, because a king is very particular, and the mission station at Doleib Hill was not designed to accommodate monarchs who demand the niceties of life.

That was only the beginning! The king's Saturday night came along, and everyone enthusiastically agreed that he should have a bath. However, the king cannot expose royal limbs to the common people by bathing in the river, and no one in the court had ever heard of bathing any place in the house but in the bathroom. Unfortunately, poor La had never possessed a bathroom, because the river was always fine for him and his family. Thus a bathroom had to be built by our workmen, using our materials, under Heasty's direction. Perhaps Heasty looked to the king more like a plumber than a cook. Obviously, if there is a bathroom, there must be a tub, so an old washtub was found. It was neither wide enough nor new enough to suit the royal taste, but to our eternal shame, it was all we possessed. I have not discovered whether the bath water was wastefully thrown away or is being treasured as holy water by some devoted follower. The royal bath complete, there came request for tea, sugar, salt, and all those amenities that make a king's life bearable. The Arab storekeeper being gone, we could not excuse ourselves by sending the king's messengers to the store. We regretted that it was impossible for us to supply tobacco for the royal pipe.

All was going nicely and everybody happy, so I am at last coming to the point of my story. One morning, his majesty came to call in person. Mr. Heasty and I were alone, since Mrs. Heasty had just started for Khartoum and Mrs. McClure had not yet arrived. After the usual pleasantries, he eased the regal frame into a comfortable chair and we sat down opposite. We drank lemonades together, and then he and Heasty discussed the latest news of the murder, which was news to no one. Finally, after a long silence, the king blurted out that he had come for a new cloth. Heasty looked at me and I looked at him. What did we know about king's clothes? Now, we could easily make clothes for the schoolboys, since all you need is a yardstick and a pair of scissors. You look at the boy, and if he has a cloth, you estimate its length; if he is naked, as they usually are, you guess how much he will need to hang from his left shoulder to his knees, and after measuring, you cut a piece of unbleached muslin. The boy then ties a knot in two corners, throws it over his shoulder, and he is dressed. Two minutes will suffice to make a full outfit, whether it be for morning wear or formal evening clothes. But for a king! Heasty looked at the cloth he was wearing, a rather fine bit of broadcloth, not at all white, although it had once been. The king apologized for his present garment and said it was all of the royal wardrobe he had with him. Monarchy is not what it once was, since the king's traveling wardrobe consisted of one cloth that could be bought for a dollar.

After looking at the goods, Heasty said that we had nothing equivalent on hand. Under the circumstances the king agreed to be satisfied with less. I thought of Mrs. Heasty's silk dresses, but then realized that she would have taken them both with her. Heasty rose to the occasion, as he does to every occasion, and brought out a bolt of the same cloth we used for the schoolboys and asked if it would do. Grudgingly, the king opined that it would. So, yardstick in hand, Heasty measured off five yards, thinking he would be generous, since one and a half to two yards is usually plenty for the boys. But the king wanted more. An added two yards was counted off, then eight, nine, and finally ten yards before the royal desires were met. We thought perhaps he intended to clothe all his wives as well. But we soon had another thought, for as the cloth was handed to him all nicely folded, he filled our hearts with panic as he waved us back and told us to make the cloth. We were being gently ordered to tailor a king. Two missionaries who could not tailor a sock or sew on a button without endangering their lives with the needle and nearly choking themselves in the thread—we were to sew and seam and hem the royal garment. We did considerable hemming and hawing, and then I remembered Mrs. McClure's sewing machine that I had always wanted to play with but was only allowed to turn the handle of while she did the sewing. The reason I never learned anything in watching her was that she went too fast in the first place, and in the second I usually was reading aloud to her as I turned.

In our dilemma I saw that sewing machine as the way out. Far better to be beheaded after having tried than never to have tried at all. I marched out the machine and offered up a prayer of thanksgiving as I saw that it had white thread on and was ready for action. We were then instructed to look carefully at the present garment and make another like it. I wanted to ask the king to let me use his garment as a pattern, but it was all he had between him and nakedness. And I realized that I dare not get too familiar with the king even though we were to be his valets and tailors thrown into one. Heasty had the advantage of me, for he had already been the royal plumber. I was to be the official tailor, and he would turn the handle.

We learned that the ten yards of goods was to be made into one garment. Now, I defy a woman to make anything she will wear using ten yards of goods. Perhaps they will appreciate our problem if they try. We were to make the cloth double thickness and double width. Well, that looked easy, so we started bravely. We folded all the pieces together, four thicknesses, and started to run a seam as one would sew up a sack. We were getting along fine, although I did get it an inch wide in places and ran off the edge in others, and had about three-fourths of the cloth done, priding ourselves on our speed, when the king appeared to see what was going on. He looked and scowled. Was that like his present cloth? We saw that it was not, for he had a nice flat seam, twice sewn and neatly done. I wanted to say that at least his new cloth was clean, but I refrained. Nothing to be done but rip out the seam and start over, and somehow I knew that a new kind of seam would be harder. It was. We started with a nice quarter-inch seam and before long added another quarter-inch to that and then cut off about two-thirds of the whole until there was hardly enough cloth to catch the thread. What with my weaving back and forth, running too deep, and then suddenly tearing clear off the edge so that we had to reverse to catch the seam, it was a fancy bit of seam-*stressing!* The second running of the seam was a little better, though we did cross the former stitching a few times, but it will be stronger for all that.

Next came the hemming of all the edges, and we began to realize that the seaming was mere child's play. Instead of maintaining the proper decorum that tailors to a king should have, we began to go crazy with laughter, which showed how little we valued our necks. The king failed to see anything funny in our situation. After all, he had to wear the cloth whether we hanged for the deed or not. Finally he arose in all his dignity and announced that he was going. He could not be trifled with by a couple of missionary valets (or varlets) setting themselves up to be tailors. Nevertheless, he gave orders for his cloth to follow him. We sewed on (though not always on the cloth). Finally, after hours of torturous labor when we had done everything but break the needle, the end was in sight. Just six more inches to go as I raised my back for a rest. Heasty, already dizzy from turning, started again, and the bobbin ran out.

Now what were two grass widowers to do? We thought we knew, so we jerked the bobbin out and wound it full of new thread and got it back in the machine. The threading of the machine puzzled us a bit, but we got the thread through some holes and gadgets and started. It looked fine from above, but on the underside of the cloth, yards and yards of thread had all bunched up in a hopeless mess. We ripped it out and started afresh. Same story. Heasty then took the seat of honor at the machine and rethreaded the entire business. Now it was worse. We tried again with no better result. I tried my hand, but it had lost its cunning, so we both took time out to laugh ourselves silly. I trust the king did not hear us. Here we were—two normally intelligent, although by this time quite unbalanced, Christian gentlemen happily married to expert seamstresses, unhappily separated from them due to the exigencies of missionary life, in the very heart of darkest Africa trying to make clothes for a pagan king whom we hoped to convert to Christianity—and we could not even thread a sewing machine.

After a prolonged spell of laughter that brought tears to our eyes and left us weak, Heasty said he would try again. He started from the beginning and rethreaded the machine for the hundredth time. I then bravely, and not a little doubtfully, started to turn the handle. God threw a miracle our way, and it purred smoothly on; and while the hem looked like that of a circus tent, we finished with many a stitch but without a hitch.

Not a whimper have we heard from the king, neither have we been paid as befits royal tailors, but we are thankful that our heads are still reasonably intact. Perhaps the king is so pleased that he is thinking what he will do for us, and then again perhaps he is contemplating what our punishment shall be. At all odds it is a game of "heads I win, tails you lose" in being tailors to the king. I sincerely trust that Heasty and I will not have to rip what we have sewed!

▼▲▼

Glenn Reed and Don McClure loved to sharpen their wits on each other. Sitting in the gathering dusk of the African night after a hard day's work, Don would start on a seemingly innocuous subject until he found out what Glenn thought, adopt the opposite point of view, and the debate was off and going. The trick was to find a subject in which Glenn was interested and to rouse his pedagogical instinct without taking a position so outrageous as to disgust him. One legendary argument concerned the momentous topic of whether Jesus Christ, working in Joseph's carpentry shop, would or could have ever hit his thumb instead of the nail. Both men, of course, accepted the orthodox Christological doctrine that Jesus Christ was God and man in one person; but Don, starting from the position of Christ's divine (and perfect) nature, insisted that Jesus would never miss the nail. Glenn, starting from the human nature of Jesus, insisted that he could hit his thumb by mistake. Doubtless Glenn knew (and it was never safe to assume that Don did not know something) that they were debating the old and unresolvable theological chestnut technically called the *communicatio idiomatum,* or the relation between the human and divine attributes in Jesus Christ. But the point was not historical precision or theological tradition. The point was that two great friends were having a fine argument about a matter so obscure as to allow and engage the full range of their minds.

For months now, Glenn has been talking about taking his teachers down the Nile and returning the king's visit. Glenn could not go by car, since the rains are threatening and the road would be endless mud traps; and he would not go by launch unless I went along to take care of the boat and engine. I am glad I went, because we had a wonderful time together and with the teachers. We took six boys with us. One did the cooking (when I was not the cook) and the others washed dishes, so the work was easy.

We stopped at Malakal to load up with gas and oil, since it is the only "service station" south of Khartoum. We preached at four different villages that afternoon. The Shulla people are quite attentive and especially eager to learn songs and verses so they will have something to do when we are gone. They are very respectful of everything concerning God, or Jwok, but they are full of fears and superstitions. They fear lightning as God's club and thunder as God's voice, but they recognize Jwok as creator of all; from that place we can lead them into greater light.

The second day downstream was crocodile day. Glenn used his shotgun on the smaller ones, and I used my rifle on the larger ones. Together we accounted for twenty-five or thirty in a couple of hours. Few of them were large enough to skin for a shield, but we did have some fun with one big fellow. There were six or eight crocs lying on a small sandbar; all were asleep, and we were on them before they realized it. One of them was twelve or fourteen feet, and I wanted to try for him. I took careful aim and pulled the trigger, but the shell failed to fire. Throwing it out, I pulled the trigger again, and once more my gun failed. Then Glenn shot, and the big croc flattened out on the sand. All the others hit the water with a great splash. Glenn kept on shooting, but I could see that the big one was going to get away. I fired again and this time took him behind the jaw, and he stopped.

We all piled out onto the sand and tried to drag the crocodile up and away from the water, but he was too big to move. We took some pictures, and then the boys began to cut off his tail. Mr. Croc objected and, thrashing his tail around, hit one of the boys, knocking him down and hurting his leg. They all ran, but Glenn and I laughed and told them it was only reflex action. I then took hold of one front leg and called the boys to help me roll him over. Gingerly they returned, and over he went. I saw that Glenn had hit him once in the back of the mouth, knocking out several teeth, but the bullet did not go into his head. He had only been stunned. However, my shot had gone right through the neck at the base of the head, and we were sure it had broken his neck.

So again, with Mr. Croc on his back, the boys started to cut open his stomach. As soon as the spear penetrated the skin, he started to thrash his tail and legs and finally rolled over and started for deep water. I ran for my gun, hoping it would fire, and just as he was going under, I put a steel-jacket in the back of his head. Such a thing had never before entered his mind, so he stopped to ponder the experience. We finally recovered him and cut him up. Inside his stomach we found a six-foot crocodile that must have been swallowed a short time earlier.

Later that day we reached the village of the king. He was absent, and we learned that he was holding court at Kodok, twenty miles away, but was returning to Fashoda,[31] his village and the holy city of the Shullas, the next day; we decided to postpone our visit until then. That evening we camped in the king's backyard. It was a beautiful plain with thousands of cattle and sheep, all belonging to the king. It is said that he has fifty wives with him at Fashoda and thirty elsewhere over Shulla country. His custom is to marry every girl who is brought to him. Some father who needs cattle badly and in a hurry will take his daughter to the king, who will marry her, paying the necessary ten head of cattle and twenty sheep. Then, to keep his household from multiplying beyond all bounds, the king will occasionally give a wife away to some man who has pleased him and who deserves a reward, or often to some poor old man who cannot buy a wife and who has no one to care for him.

One might think that this would grow into a vicious practice and soon disrupt the marriage customs, but not so, for there is a price to pay. If the king should happen to keep the wife and have children by her, none of his daughters is allowed to marry for the simple reason that there are no young bucks good enough to marry a king's daughter. If a wife has children by the king, she is never given away, so the father of a girl thinks twice before he takes her to the king. He knows there is a possibility that his granddaughters will never marry and all her bride wealth will be lost to the family.

About noon on Saturday we were called to be presented. We approached the village with all our boys, who would not talk above a whisper as soon as they came in sight of the sacred city. The king is the personification of their deity, Jwok. None of them had ever before been inside the village. Just at the riverside there was a double house with an ostrich shell and a spear on top, which we knew to be the shrine of Nyikang, one of Jwok's earthly spirits. The boys, though all of them are Christians, fairly trembled when they passed the shrine and thought I ought not to take pictures of it. I did anyway and later got the king's permission to take more, to everyone's surprise.

The king himself came out to meet us and invited Glenn and me into his house. It is just an ordinary native mud hut, but made better than I have ever seen any other native hut. We later learned that it was the house in which he always received visitors. There were about fifty houses in the village, and all of them were really the king's houses, so we could hardly say that we were in the palace. He was very nice to us and talked of his visit to Doleib Hill. He then had one of the favorite wives bring us some drinks. We were hoping that he had become a bit civilized and was handling lemonade or the like, but we were disappointed. She brought the inevitable beer pot and handed it to Glenn to taste. Unfortunately, Glenn had been a bit sick in the morning, and his stomach rebelled at the smell, so he passed it over to me. I tasted it gingerly and found it very bitter and distasteful, but Glenn whispered to me to keep at it. So I sipped and sipped until the woman, thinking that I was going to drink all of it, went out to get some more. Glenn then merely touched it to his lips so that he could say that he had taken all he wanted. Sure enough, she came in with another pot and, thinking that I was the "big man" of our party, handed it to me first; but I declined, and Glenn was able to do likewise.

The king had been absent during all this, and when he came back he said that he was sending two sheep to our boat for our supper. We thanked him, but did not say that we thought two sheep would be a rather large supper for nine men, especially since seven of them were already full of crocodile. We brought one of the sheep home and are still enjoying it.

The next day being Sunday, we asked if we might have a service in the village. The king said that would be fine, but there was another village with many more people, especially children, just a little way off and did we not think that our time would be more profitably spent there? Well, we certainly did think so, under the circumstances, and the next day we had a fine service in that village. The king was afraid that he might lose face if a Christian service were held in his village, though he is very sympathetic with our school and what we are doing for his people.

▼ Shulla
▼ Superstitions

LIFE AT DOLEIB HILL often changed from boring to interesting to challenging to exciting to dangerous to dull to amusing to pitiful to tragic—all within a week. Don McClure found Africa endlessly fascinating, yet helping the Shulla people achieve the more abundant life was a constant battle against almost overwhelming odds.

Doleib Hill is a glorious place in the summer, but there are drawbacks, and one of them is snakes. I guess a snake is not really a drawback, but a slitheralong. I see and kill one nearly every day. Most of them are harmless and much worse scared than I, but they are snakes. However, there is an occasional bad one, as Dr. Sowash can testify. He nearly died when he was bitten some years ago. A boy was brought in today (one reason I brought up the snake subject) who had been bitten by a large snake with a very bad reputation. If the bitten person lives through the excruciating ordeal, the hand or foot usually begins to rot and sluff off.

This poor lad of about twelve was crying with pain as his father and two other men came running in with him from a village about three miles away. They had started immediately, and surely it was not more than twenty minutes on the road, because Africans can run very fast; but already his leg had swelled up twice its normal size and was as hard as iron. We have a clinic boy here who has had only a superficial training in Malakal hospital, but he keeps his head in emergencies. Unfortunately, he was out fishing and no one was here but me. I know what to do with an immediate case, but not one so far

121

advanced, so we sent runners in all directions to hunt Bwoga, the clinic boy.

In the meantime, I slashed the wound open a bit and rubbed in potassium permanganate, knowing it was useless at that stage but needing to do something. Finally Bwoga came running in and took charge like an old hand. He immediately slashed the poor lad's leg open from knee to ankle with great cuts, not two or three, but fifteen or twenty, ten or twelve inches long. The lad was screaming at the top of his voice and his eyes popping, literally out of his head. I thought he would die as we held him. I know I sweat blood for him, and I was ready to collapse. Then to make the treatment effective, Bwoga washed the open wounds in scalding saltwater. I never saw such suffering in my life as that boy went through. The boy seemed to gain some strength that day, and as evening grew on I felt sure he would live, but might have trouble with his leg. However, we could take him to the hospital for proper treatment later when he could bear the long trip into Malakal. But sometime during the second night the witchdoctor sent a summons that they were to bring the boy back to the village and he would make further treatment to save the leg. Unknown to us here, the father and two uncles stole the boy out of our clinic building and took him back to the village. The witchdoctor's treatment involved cutting rings around the leg from foot to thigh about every two inches and then burning the open sores and rubbing into them some horrible concoction.

The result was inevitable. The poor lad had nearly died as we worked with his leg, fainting away twice with pain, and we had been as gentle as possible. His leg hurt so much that he could not even bear to have anyone touch it to dress it. What terrible pain he must have suffered from the witchdoctor before God called him away! The little lad died while they were treating him. I am sure his heart broke under the strain of pain that we can scarcely imagine.

We had another tragedy here on Friday afternoon. About a month ago, two young brothers were brought in with gunshot wounds. They had been sitting around a fire in their village when someone slipped up through the cornfields to the edge of the village and fired into the village circle. The bullet was a slug of lead, and it hit one lad in the back of his hand and went through the other hand. Then the slug hit the second boy in the leg just below the knee and stopped in his ankle. They brought both lads in here, and I took the bullet out of the ankle. The wounds healed surprisingly well, and the boys were feeling fine. However, the first boy contracted pneumonia and nearly died, but he was recovering probably because I had pumped so much medicine into both of them. They could not have paid for the medicine with a year's work. Nor did I expect them to pay; I was just happy that they were getting better.

Last Thursday the boys pointed out to me a small swelling on the one lad's leg just below the wound, which was almost healed. I examined the swelling and decided that it was not ready to open, and I told the father we should wait a day or so until the pus gathered. But yesterday afternoon the father thought he ought to open the swelling. So he got out an old knife and made a hole in the leg. In doing so, he cut an artery and then could not get the bleeding stopped. He did everything he knew how to do except to call me, and he was afraid to send for me because he knew I would be angry with him since I had told him to wait. He tied cloth, vine, and grass around the boy's leg, but it continued to bleed from three o'clock in the afternoon until evening. Then as I went on my rounds of the sick, I heard this boy groaning and calling for help. I rushed into the hut and found the father holding the leg and the mother nestling the boy's head on her lap, and he was saying, *"Ana athow, ana athow"* (I am dying, I am dying). One look at him convinced me that he was. He was bled white, and the hut was full of blood. I ran for our house to get some plasma and saline solution, feeling that these things were more essential than trying to stop the wound at that moment. I was back in three minutes and found the old man holding his thumb on the wound, as I had instructed him, but the boy was sinking fast. I put a tourniquet on the leg and started to hunt for the vein in his arms, but the vessels had collapsed and I could not get the needle in. While I tried to get some blood plasma into him, he gasped once or twice and died.

My first reaction was one of great anger at the father for his stupidity, but with tears running down his face, he said, "Would a father kill his own son?" My mouth was closed, for I realized that he was trying to help his son and had killed him through ignorance. That has happened before and happens over and over again in this country. For the burial I took the family back to their village in the Jeep. I believe the boy had learned the way of the Lord in the weeks he was here, but he never made a profession of his faith.

So today when I was holding the clinic service, I had the opportunity to talk to the people about the things they do in their ignorance and what the results may be. It was a marvelous opportunity to teach them something both about their bodies as well as about the Lord. I had a very attentive audience. I would like to think that this poor young lad had come to know something of the love of his heavenly Father in the weeks that he lived here. In any case, his life is now in the hands of that Father.

▼▲▼

When a group of little American girls from the Junior Missionary League sent some money to Don, he explained in a personal way how it was used.

I think it is wonderful that you are concerned about the little black girls of the Sudan and want to help them. I know each of you has given up something that you wanted for their sake, perhaps some candy or a new pencil or a movie. Whatever it was, I bet you have received more joy from giving than from getting. Let me tell you what I saw in a nearby village yesterday afternoon, and I am sure you will agree that it is very good to help others.

Three weeks ago one of my Shulla friends came in to tell me that his wife had presented him with a new baby, and he wanted me to go out and see it. I almost forgot about the baby until yesterday, when something inside me said, "This after-noon you should go out and see that baby of Tipa's." I did not really want to see the baby, because little black babies are not very pretty for the first two or three months. Instead of being black, they are a reddish brown and have the biggest mouths you have ever seen; they look more like baby hippos than human babies. But I did want to please my friend, so I went.

Tipa lives in a small village of about ten houses. All of them are made of mud and grass. Tipa evidently had a good wife, because his house was as neat and clean as a house with mud walls and a mud floor can possibly be. All her cooking pots were nicely piled up at one side, and the skins on which they sleep were hanging from the poles of the grass roof—just where they ought to be. In many houses I have visited, the cooking pots have to be moved before I can sit down, and the skins would be all dirty and spread all over the place. But not in Tipa's home, and my respect for his wife went up a hundred percent.

When I arrived, the mother was nursing the new baby, but she was not in the least embarrassed. In this country, babies are fed during their waking hours every fifteen or twenty minutes, or just whenever they get hungry. That might be anytime and anywhere. If a mother is making a journey, she will often feed the baby as she walks and does not even bother to sit down. A baby is never allowed to cry, but as soon as it begins to fuss is fed at once—if not by the mother, then by any other mother who happens to be nearest to it. Mothers here seem to delight in helping to feed each other's babies. A baby is nursed until it is two years old, so for all that time it is scarcely out of the mother's reach except when sleeping.

Well, as soon as I saw this little reddish-brown baby, I thought it very ugly and skinny, and that is exactly what I told the parents—and they were quite pleased! I did not dare to say I thought the baby was pretty and strong, or they would have been afraid of the Evil Eye. No one ever tells the parents that their babies are pretty, because they are afraid that if the Evil Eye hears *that*, he will want to live in the baby. But if people say the baby is ugly and skinny, the Evil Eye will leave it alone. So I said that the baby was ugly and skinny.

Tipa's little daughter, Nyilwak, is about your age (ten years old) and was running around the village naked. She has never had a dress in her whole life, not even a secondhand one or a hand-me-down. But this little girl did not seem to mind, and she was just as happy as if she were dressed in the finest silk. Her name is funny. "Nyilwak" means "the little cattle barn." Many, many boys and girls are given just such funny names; they are named after whatever important event takes place in the village the day they are born. Some of them are called "the little dead thing," because a man died the day they were born. "Nyimac" means "the little fire," because there was a fire in the village. Or if the men of the village happened to kill an animal or catch a big fish, the children born on that day would be called "Nyirej" (Little Fish) or "Nyingu" (Little Lion).

But I must get back to Nyilwak and tell you about her. I said she does not have a single dress, nor a single doll, nor a toy, bead, or real plaything of any kind. While I was there, she came into the house and picked up an old bottle her father had used for oil. She wrapped a bit of grass around the bottle's neck and called it her baby. Then she sat down and started to "feed" her "baby" from her breasts, just as her mother was doing, and finally she sang it to sleep.

I felt so bad for Nyilwak that I wanted to come back home here and get one of the dozen or so dolls that Marghi has and take it out to her. (Marghi's favorite doll is named "Beany," because it is filled with beans.) However, I would not be able to give dolls to all the girls in the village. So it is better not to give any and make the girls jealous of one another and thus unhappy. They were happy without real dolls, because they do not know what they are missing. If they once had a nice doll as you do, they would never be satisfied without a doll.

I think it is very sad for any little girl in all the world not to have a baby doll that she can love and care for. But it is even sadder for a little girl not to know that Jesus Christ loves and cares for her. I want you to pray for little girls like Nyilwak that they will accept the love of God, and then they will be rich, no matter how poor they seem.

In the south Sudan, the birth of twins meant more than an extra mouth to feed. The Shullas believed that when twins were born, someone else would surely die. If one of the babies did not soon die, then the death of a parent or grandparent was necessary to appease the god Jwok. For all to escape was deemed impossible. In all of Shullaland there was only one set of twins living, and both the mother and grandmother died almost immediately following their birth. Considering the crude and primitive methods of birth, the death of the mother was no surprise, but the death of the grandmother at that time was a mystery. Thus it was the Shulla custom to let one of the twins die shortly after birth by the simple method of starvation. The mother would only acknowledge one of the babies to be hers; the other belonged to Jwok, and Jwok could take care of it. So the birth of twins was called "born of Jwok."

Just as we were finishing morning prayers, our older gardener came rushing in like a wild bull with his eyes bloodshot and almost popping out of his head. I looked around for the lion that I thought must be required to drive him to such speed, and I was ready to grab my big gun, when he burst out, *"Nyiola Jwok, nyiola Jwok, nyiola Jwok."* Literally translated, that means "My wife is born of God, born of God." My first impulse was to laugh and say, "I wish it were you," but with the rolling of his eyes, his foaming mouth, and his terrified look, I realized that there was more to it than would appear from a mere translation of the words.

When I inquired further, I discovered that just a few minutes before, his wife had given birth to twins. Then I did laugh and tried to congratulate old Ajak on his good fortune. However, I soon found out that I was treading on very dangerous ground and making congratulations on an event that is the direst calamity to a Shulla.

I was at my wit's end to know how to comfort old Ajak. Before he had come to see me, he had gone a long way along the road of comfort by filling himself with native beer, but it certainly did not calm his fears. Rather, it helped him to magnify the coming doom. He was certain that he had outrun death to our door by just a step, and if he dared to stick his head outside, he would be caught by Jwok and made to pay for the extra baby. This was a ticklish situation, because Ajak is supposed to be a Christian, and this was the first time twins have been born in the Christian community here. I surely did not want him to die of fright, and I thought he might do so any minute. I had a bright idea when I remembered that I had a picture of the Dionne quintuplets. I grabbed the picture and told Ajak about it. I think I came very close to manslaughter at that moment, for the poor distraught old fellow grabbed his head and said, "Suppose my wife had had five?" And he nearly died on the spot at the very thought.

Finally Ajak quieted down, and I gave him permission to leave his work and visit his parents, who live four miles upriver, to see if they were still alive and in good health. I remarked before he left that I thought their health would remain good if he did not tell them about the twins. But he insisted that they would already know, having been informed by Jwok the minute the babies were born. At any rate, he went off and the next day came back considerably sobered by his eight-mile paddle with the report that everything was all right. All are still living to date, though I am sure one or both of the twins would be dead if Lyda had not started to feed them about the fifth day. I never saw such emaciated little things in my life. They were quite evidently premature and the mother had no milk, so with a large, rusty tin spoon she was trying to feed them cold, half-sour cow's milk out of a rusty salmon tin in which several dead flies were floating. The twins were actually starving to death. Lyda now mixes up five bottles a day for them, and they are prospering.

By now the American Mission at Doleib Hill had become a relatively civilized outpost, although primitive Africa was not many steps away. The Shullas tended to be largely self-sufficient, but some of the missionaries expected immediate service.

Last week knocked a big hole in the work I had planned. One of the single American women is entirely helpless to do anything for herself and wants everything done for her immediately. I spent the whole week getting her stuff unpacked and fixed up. Her refrigerator came in late Saturday night, and I spent an hour at the river getting the thing unloaded, with mosquitoes flying in clouds two hundred to the square inch and breaking each other's wings to get at me. When I told her the appliance had arrived, she was peeved that she could not expect me to work on Sunday setting it up for her. She said, "Well, I guess I will have to wait until Monday to use it." I had a strong notion to tell her that she could jolly well wait until Tuesday, since I had other things to do on Monday. But not so; I spent Monday unpacking and getting the refrigerator operating for her. Some people seem to assume that others are designed for their convenience.

We had a series of tragedies this week. The boy who does our milking and takes care of our calves was dragged into the river by a crocodile and drowned. Heasty and I went to the river determined at least to kill the crocodile. In a short time the crocodile came up just opposite where Heasty was waiting and about sixty feet from the bank. It was holding the boy in its mouth. Heasty overshot, but about twenty minutes later the croc came up again about thirty feet from him. This time the boy was being held by the crocodile's front feet. I had to come home because of the unbearable pain of my infected eyes, but about half an hour later Heasty got the crocodile. Both the croc and the boy came to the surface yesterday.

The second tragedy occurred yesterday, too. We heard a cry from the upper village, and word soon came that one of our fine Shulla Christians had tried to commit suicide by cutting his throat. He was an old man who had worked at the mission for many years; his wife still works for us. For some months he had not been well, and his only brother had died, leaving a wife and child. His half-brothers insisted that he take the woman as his second wife, as is Shulla tribal custom. But while Agwet was willing to assume responsibility for her support, he refused to become her husband, because he was a Christian and already had a wife. In the last two years this woman has had children by the half-brothers, who refused to care for her and added to Agwet's burden. He protested to no avail. He could do no more, because he was afraid the half-brothers would curse his children. Thus he could see no way out except to end his life. I went to see Agwet, and he is still barely alive, but there is no hope that he will recover. The Christian faith brought Agwet the greatest happiness, and the church rule about monogamy brought such misery that he wanted to die.

There is more. My heart is very heavy, and I have little desire except to sit and grieve. I have just returned from the burial of La Amoleker's daughter, Nyiman Nya. She died this morning at five from something very much resembling typhoid fever, but on the other hand it might have been just severe diarrhea.

On Friday night, La came to me and told me his daughter was sick and constantly vomiting. I asked him about her bowels, but he said that he did not know anything. I gave him some milk of magnesia, but Saturday morning he came again and said she was worse. She had severe diarrhea and was still vomiting. So I gave him a dose of hot drops and told him to come back for more in three hours. I also sent some milk and bread, since she had not eaten anything for two days. La did not come back for medicine, so I assumed she was better. But about six last night he came and said she was worse. I again gave him some hot drops and told him that I would go and see her later. I did not get down until after supper and took more medicine with me.

As soon as I saw her, I was really alarmed, for I feared that she was dying. I asked La about the medicine I had given him, but he said she refused to take it. I was so provoked at La that I wanted to kick him. So I took his daughter in my arms and gave her the medicine, which she took from me without a word. She was already delirious. The girl was lying naked on the floor, and I told them to keep her covered, but when she kicked the covers off, they did not move to put them back again. Fearing what it might be, I waited until I could get a specimen of her stool to send to Malakal. This was easy to do, since she was constantly passing a bloody, watery stool that made me think the bowel was perforated. I sent the stool immediately to Malakal so it could be analyzed this morning. I feared that she was too far gone to move. Such proved to be the case, for at five o'clock this morning La came and woke me and said Nyiman was dying. I put on my bathrobe and went down, but before we got to the house she was gone. La took her death like the Christian man he is, though he was bowed down with grief; but Nyikak, his wife, who is not a Christian, simply went crazy and had to be restrained or she would have injured herself. After prayer with them she seemed to quiet a bit, so I came back and got dressed.

I never saw such a cloud over the mission as settled down over everyone this morning. Nyiman was a favorite of everyone and played in all our homes. Marghi played with her almost every day and will miss her little friend, though we have avoided saying anything yet about her death. It was decided to bury Nyiman in La's mother's village, and they started to dig the grave about seven o'clock. I had summoned all the elders and asked them to take part in the service, so about nine o'clock we went to the village. I had decided to let the family and people finish with their tribal rites before we had our service, because I did not quite know where to break in and begin a Christian service. As it was, I did finally break in, but the place opened up naturally.

When the officers of the church (Pakwan Deoker, Aba Nyilek, La Wad Wuol, Adwok Myom) arrived at the village, the grave was almost finished. It had been dug beside the house of La Amoleker's mother. It was such a pitifully shallow grave, but when you know that Ajak was doing most of the digging, one wonders that the grave was large enough to admit the body. It was not much more than enough. But when I chided him for his work, Ajak said, "She was just a baby, and a girl at that!" Why could not such a fine little girl have lived?

We found La Amoleker and Bwoga sitting off alone under a tree, so we joined them and had a prayer service as impressive as any I have ever known—La taking part with a splendid prayer of faith.

When the grave was finished, the mourning (there was a large crowd) rose in tempo as three women, preceded by another ringing a huge cow bell, took their water pots and went to the river, walking as to the tune of a dirge and with the incessant tolling of the doleful cow bell. I have never heard anything quite so funereal as that bell. The women brought back the water and with it the mud mixed for sealing the grave. Then a tiang skin (my donation) was cut up and half of it put in the bottom of a niche in the grave. Then as everything was ready, three or four women took whips and, with the one carrying the bell leading the way, they drove off the evil spirits, facing in all four directions as they shook their whips and rang the bell. Following this, four men charged the grave, brandishing their spears to further intimidate the spirits.

Finally the women, as many as could get hands on the tiny body, came carrying it, and they were shielded by a blanket held by two women so that the people could not see the body. The body was, of course, wrapped in white cloth (also my donation) and tied with string from head to foot. The legs were wrapped in the colored matting the Shullas use to cover pots. As the body was placed in the grave, all the people raised their voices in a general mourning and the body was covered with the skin. Then what remained of the tiang skin as well as a dead chicken, a gourd, some string, and a few beads were thrown into the grave, and the pitiful little grave was sealed with mud.

In the past it had been the custom of the missionaries at Doleib Hill to let the people bury their dead with their own pagan rites, because the missionaries had not been able to persuade the Shullas to abandon their tribal rituals. The older missionaries' attitude was that pagan and Christian customs should not be mixed and, if it was not possible to hold an entirely Christian service, then it was thought wise to avoid such ceremonies altogether. Don was not so sure that

American burial customs were entirely Christian either, but he was certainly uncomfortable about being absent from the Shullas in their time of sorrow, especially those who were trying to be Christians. Thus he had begun to attend the Shulla funerals of both pagans and Christians. The people came to expect his presence and were disappointed if he did not come to honor their dead. Don was even willing to conduct a Christian service and then let the Shulla people hold their traditional service afterward.

In one six-week period, Don took part in four funerals, although he refused to participate in one for a man who had no connection at all with the Christian faith. Sometimes the distinction was clear between Christian and pagan. However, Don felt that he was closer to the Shullas than ever before, because they are very anxious to have their dead honored and were grateful when he made some attempt to do so. When the plague took one elder's brother and another elder's little girl, the men came to Don and requested special prayer for their sick. Out of this meeting they began a fellowship of prayer in which all covenanted to pray daily for a real doctor to come to Doleib Hill.

The Shullas believe that the spirit of the dead cannot be ushered into the presence of Jwok until he has been mourned. Sometimes that spirit is at loose ends for several years until the family can gather enough grain and cattle to mourn him. If the dead man happened to be a "big man," he must have at least seven oxen killed for him and as many bushels of grain made into beer for the crowd to drink. Comparatively speaking, it is more expensive to mourn a man in Shullaland than with ourselves. We "burn and bury" money out of our opulence while they "drink and eat" it out of their poverty. A Shulla, if he worked every day for a year, might make fifty dollars, but out of that he would have to be feeding himself and family, so it would not be easy to gather enough for a big mourning. Often friends of the dead man help by giving an ox or some grain.

Then sometimes, and as is the case in a big mourning this afternoon in our lower village, several families will plan together to have their mourning at the same time and, though each must make separate preparations, yet the crowd can be more easily satisfied and a saving in both grain and oxen is effected. Of course, after the oxen are sacrificed, there is no further sacrifice, for the whole village feasts for several days. It is reported that eight or nine men (women are never mourned, for they are not admitted into the presence of God) are to be mourned today.

The butchering is an interesting process. Not everyone has sufficient rank to be a "killer." But like the Jews, the Shullas have their Levites, and from this group a young man or two is selected to do the spearing. These men station themselves someplace in the village, and one ox at a time is driven in their direction. With a special spear used only for that purpose, the *nyel a woup* lunges at the ox and tries to kill it with one stab. But these chaps are not trained as matadors and frequently miss their mark. Then the fun begins. Once the *nyel a woup* has drawn blood, the beast is anyone's game and there is a free-for-all to see who can kill it. After six or seven animals are killed, or perhaps only one if the family is poor, the dance starts. The dance will continue all day and on into the night. No one touches the animals in the meantime. The morning after, the now-bloated oxen will be skinned and meat distributed. I do not care to be within miles of that village during this process, at least on the windward side, for my sense of smell is somewhat depraved and cannot appreciate the odor of ripe meat, even at a great distance.

On another occasion Don wrote about chasing another kind of animal—hogs.

Some weeks ago a British official, one Captain Forbes, came out here to visit with us and stayed overnight. He wanted some of my eggs and chickens for setting, so I sent him three chickens and two dozen eggs. He had asked me if I should like to have some pigs, and I was delighted. In a few days I got a wire stating that the pigs were being sent to Doleib Hill by steamer. I pictured a couple or three small pigs that I could fatten and eat. A few days later, about nine o'clock in the evening, the steamer pulled in and the skipper announced that he had some pigs on board for me. I asked him to unload them and I would take care of them in the morning, thinking they would be in a crate; but he said that would be impossible, for the pigs were not crated in the first place and none of the Muslim sailors would touch them. I would have to unload them myself. So I called for a couple of the workmen, and we went down. To my consternation I was shown, not three nice little pigs, but nine full-grown hogs. The hogs were tied by their legs to various parts of the boat, and from their appearance they had not been fed for three days. This I later found to be true.

My problem lay in getting those nine huge hogs up to a pen I had built to contain the three little pigs I had expected. There was nothing for it but to grab the hogs by the hind legs and make wheelbarrows out of them. But the hogs vociferously objected to this treatment with such squealing and grunting as you never heard, and their state of starvation did not improve their tempers a bit. Instead of walking along nicely on their front feet while we held the hind legs high, with one accord they all went on a sit-down strike and had to be dragged. By the time we got the hogs in the pen, I was ready for a bath and bed. I got the bath and was about to write a letter before retiring, when word came in that the hogs were all loose and digging out my peanuts.

The hogs were so hungry that they had pushed the gate down and were out in the peanut patch having the time of their lives. Their long, hard snouts were just like plows, and in a few minutes they had dug long furrows along the peanut rows. I do not know who taught them how to dig peanuts. There was no help for it, even though I did not want the hogs and would have been glad if they all had run away, but I did want the peanuts. So I called out the schoolboys, and the game began. We chased hogs for two hours. The night was hot and sticky; in five minutes I was soaked with sweat, and at the end of a half-hour I was like a dishrag. The schoolboys were great on the chase but poor on the catch. They pretended great bravery, but as soon as they got close enough to a hog to grab it, they stepped aside and then made a lunge for it as it passed. As it turned out, I had to catch all but one of the hogs, and by that time I was really hog-tired. The next morning I shot two of the hogs, lean as they were, and for a week we enjoyed the first pork we have eaten since we left the States.

We have had some excellent fishing this month. Two weeks ago I put a night line out and caught two splendid perch. One of them weighed close to a hundred pounds, and the other about seventy. What brought fishing to my mind was that I was interrupted in my writing a few minutes ago by a Shulla standing outside and calling to me. It is about 10:00 P.M., and I wondered what he wanted. When I went out, I found that he had a big fish to sell and was afraid to wait until morning, knowing that I would not buy a fish that had not been freshly caught. His fish, also a Nile perch, weighed about thirty pounds, and I bought it for twenty-five cents. Last month the schoolboys, using my night line, caught a perch that I could not lift, and I am sure it was over two hundred pounds. It seems that during July and August the perch come up from the Nile to spawn in the swift waters of the Sobat and then hundreds are caught. We rarely see them at other times, though in every month of the year we have some kind of fish. Usually a different kind about every two months.

▼▲▼

Pagan superstitions also invaded the Christian church. Don was dismayed to report:

We now have our own "Christian witchdoctor." It came about this way: Years ago, as a young man, Obelgi became interested in Christianity and, after attending the communicants' class for some weeks, asked for baptism. After a reasonable measure of time, his request was granted and he became a member of the church. During the succeeding years, his life and faithfulness were such that he was honored by being named as one of the elders of the church. However, after several years as an elder he suddenly became rich upon the death of a brother whose cattle he was entitled to inherit. In addition, Obelgi secretly married a second wife and kept her in a distant village. But such carryings on can no more be concealed out here than in America, and the missionaries as well as the other elders soon heard of his activities. He was relieved of his eldership and suspended from the church. In a very short time this second wife died, and Obelgi became very penitent and was received back into the church as a member.

All that was years ago, and Obelgi has been a faithful Christian ever since, until just a few weeks ago. Two years ago he began to fail in health, but for some months he thought little of it since he was not in great pain. However, in these latter months he has been suffering greatly and dangerously close to death. He has tried everything available to a Shulla, which includes weird incantations by witchdoctors, bitter doses of strange medicines (which if a man survives ought to cure anything), and the most favored of all, burnings and bloodletting. A few weeks past, Obelgi came back from one of his treatments with his back and legs all burned and gashed in the most horrible fashion. Dirty and infected, he came to me for help. Great quantities of carbolic soap and iodine brought him healing from the superficial sores, but the pain in his back and legs persisted. He was almost skin and bones from his suffering and sickness and pleaded with me to do something for him. I was puzzled to know what more I might do, but decided to use a little of the "foreigner's fire," in the form of Sloan's liniment, to relieve the backache.

I got a large bottle of the fiery stuff, which I would not have recognized except for the bushy-bearded man on the outside. The label was written with strange Arabic figures and letters, which proves its universal use. However, I decided to try a little of it both inwardly and outwardly, not on myself, but on leather-stomached Obelgi. Since he had lived through all the doses of the witchdoctors, I was sure a little Sloan's would not faze him, and it would most certainly warm him up. So mixing the liniment with water and sugar, I persuaded him to drink a teaspoonful of it. The effect was immediate, for his eyes popped, his tongue came out, and he called for water. I was afraid that he would drown himself with the great quantities he drank, but I felt reassured that with so much water there would be little disastrous effect from the dose. Then I began on his back.

After a half-hour's rubbing, my eyes were weeping from the fumes and my hands were burning like fire. I wondered if he was feeling the warmth, but on my asking, he urged me to go on and rub some more of it. I did and left. All went well for about an hour, and then he began to call for help. He sent his wife for me, and she said his back was burning off and he could not lie still. I laughed, but told her to put damp cloths over his back and legs. I heard no more that night, and the next day I went down to see him. There he was, lying in the middle of his hut, naked in a pool of water, and his wife still fanning him with the wing of a goose. They both were haggard and sleepy and said they had not closed their eyes all night—he because of his pain, she in trying to keep him from burning up. He said that it felt as if I had built a fire on his back and no one could put it out. He did not want any more medicine.

To make a long story short, Obelgi got well after some weeks. To all his people it seemed to be a miracle, and secretly they planned to make him a witchdoctor. They reasoned that this man was possessed with evil spirits that would have surely killed an ordinary man, but he had overcome them. Therefore, he must have powers the rest of us do not have. Obelgi fell in with their plans because it is quite an honor to be ordained a witchdoctor. It is like being a bishop at home. So in a secret ceremony (for they all knew he was a Christian and could not do such things openly) he was initiated. He came home and went back to his work. However, such things are not easily hid, and we heard the news. Now what are we to do?

It is one of those affairs that brings sadness to a missionary's heart and makes him pray for more strength and wisdom to deal with the insidious attractions of established tribal patterns. We must come to some decision on Obelgi within the next few days, and what is to be done? Absolute expulsion will lose a good but weak man. To force him to burn publicly the insignia of the witchdoctor's office will generate hostility from otherwise friendly people, but these practices inimical to Christianity cannot be tolerated.

▼▲▼

As his years at Doleib Hill came to an end, so too Don completed his apprenticeship. He had worked at and learned about agriculture, animal husbandry, rudimentary medical aid, mechanics, building construction, the languages and cultures of black Africa, and most especially evangelism. In short, he was well equipped to be a pioneer missionary among primitive people, and he was eager to strike out on his own. While Don and his family lived in a relatively civilized situation at Doleib Hill, the unreached frontier up the river continued to beckon to him. Part of its appeal was that the Anuak tribe was still untouched by missionaries. Since no Christian had ever lived and worked among the Anuaks, no programs were under way and, if nothing had been accomplished, at least no mistakes had been made.

Like the apostle Paul, Don considered himself an evangelist, not a pastor. He did not enjoy building on the foundations of others, nor even on foundations that he himself had laid. The Anuak people offered a first-rate challenge to a pioneer with energy and ideas for African evangelism. Here was a "congregation" of some fifty thousand souls spread out over rugged terrain, and Don could reach them. And unless he was able to enlist some help, he would have to be doctor, teacher, farmer, herdsman, publicist, banker, engineer, and everything else required in those primitive conditions. Not many ministers are offered the opportunity of a task this immense. Since Don and Lyda were scheduled for a furlough in 1939 for Don to study tropical medicine as an "amateur physician" at Cornell University, there was some question whether they should start the Anuak project immediately and work for only one year, or stay at Doleib Hill and then begin the Anuak mission when they returned to Africa. Don's customary direction was forward, and he was ready to go.

Thus the McClures prepared to move farther up the river to begin work with the Anuak people. Don was by nature a pioneer rather than a settler and was happiest venturing out and pushing frontiers. He had become dismayed about the costs in time, energy, money, and personnel of maintaining relatively elaborate and fixed stations. Ministering to people in this way, he thought, was poor mission strategy.

Our future as American Christians in Africa is too uncertain to justify building on a large and extensive scale. We need to go in, do what we can as quickly as possible, and get out. If we stay too long, the native people come to depend on our presence. They become mission parasites, and *their* Christian faith is no deeper than *our* pockets.

In many ways Lyda and I feel as if a new life is opening to us, for we are on our way to the Anuaks at Akobo. At least we are well packed, and I am writing amid a great stack of closed boxes and crates. We have worked hard at Doleib Hill, and for three years the Lord has richly blessed us. During our time here the church has received more than six hundred new members, and seven native churches have been built. I have gotten very close to the Shulla people. But in spite of all this I have a feeling that my work is over here at Doleib Hill and the Lord has planned for us to push on to the Anuaks. It seems that I am destined to get things moving and then someone else must carry on the harder task of training and welding the people into the church.

I have no hankering for the slow, tedious process of school work and educating the church people. I know it has to be done and is vastly important, but it is not in my line, especially if the system has already been set up by someone else and I am expected to fit within a plan long ago inaugurated. At Akobo I will have the task of starting from scratch and continuing along the routine lines, but it will be a structure built by myself and I can change it at will. In a place like Doleib Hill, where the work was started forty years ago and the lines laid down, I find myself constantly hampered by precedents and custom, which to destroy would be an unkindness to those who sincerely laid them down, but the inertia of which today hampers the work, from my viewpoint. So I feel that I have done my part here and furnished some fire to the tinder; now it is up to someone with different skills to feed the flames while I go on to start new fires.

*Near Pokwo, an Anuak village
on the Baro River*

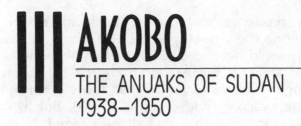

III AKOBO
THE ANUAKS OF SUDAN
1938–1950

▼ The Anuak People

WHEN LYDA McCLURE insisted to her astonished husband that she would be quite happy to spend the rest of her life—and raise their family—in a grass-roofed, mud hut with a hard, dirt floor, the central piece required for Don's pioneering missionary career fell into place. Missionary men and women had often lived in primitive situations for a while. But the major reason that the American Mission had never tried to reach out to the Anuak people along the Sudan-Ethiopian border was the never-questioned assumption that to properly establish a Christian mission it would need to invest in suitable missionary housing, which would cost about $20,000. Even in the McClures' denomination, which believed strongly in missions, that much money was not available to inaugurate work among the Anuak people. However, Don could build a mud hut for almost nothing, and while the house would not be grand, both McClures were willing to live under those conditions for years on end. The hut could be made livable with the single importation of screen wire for the windows.[32] Such a dwelling, using the same materials available to the Anuaks, would not only identify with their culture and instruct them in better building, but also avoid setting up an expensive and immovable mission compound that would take great energy to maintain.

Thus, in 1937 Don's small American denomination made a special appeal for funds to begin the Anuak project. Many people across the church knew Don and believed in his work, but the scale of this undertaking was something short of magnificent. That is to say, Don was expected to choose a site and build a house that would serve as the family residence and central headquarters for the Christian mission among the Anuak people, and for all of this the *maximum* expenditure could not exceed $1,000! There were not a few who were painfully aware that the American church had been talking about evangelizing the Anuaks for more than thirty years and only now had invested the ludicrously low sum of $1,000. But it was sufficient to give Don a start, and that was all he needed.

His first task was to explore the territory along the upper reaches of the Sobat, Baro, Gilo, Pibor, and Akobo rivers in order to learn more about the Anuaks and to choose a location from which it would be best to minister to them.

Here I sit at one end of a native canoe with a large Shulla sitting at the other end, as naked as the day he was born. Pakwan, my man Friday, is devoting his whole attention to guiding the canoe around the little eddies that might indicate the presence of a hippopotamus. We have already struck two hippos today, with almost disastrous results—but not to them. The river is shallow and narrow in March, with just enough water to cover a hippo. Since the swamps have dried up and they must have water, the hippos have come to the river to contest it with us.

A month ago I left Lyda and Marghi on the banks of the Sobat River at Doleib Hill. I did not know when I would see them again, because I had no idea how long this trip would take. Our canoe, propelled by a tiny outboard motor, is piled high with baggage, food, and gasoline. Since there are no restaurants or service stations along our way, we must carry with us everything that we will need. The first few days were an agony to me as the combination of a blazing sun, a strong wind that kept me wet with spray, and the reflection from the water turned me into a cinder. I could cover my arms and legs, but my hands were swollen and blistered; my hat covered the top of my head, but my face blistered from forehead to chin; my nose was like a hunk of raw meat. As for my lips, I would have murdered anyone who tried to make me laugh! My lips were so swollen and cracked that eating could only be managed with the utmost pain. All the salves and Vaseline in the world would have been useless. I simply had to get toughened to the sun.

Our progress was slower than I had expected, since the river was so low that we got stuck time after time and had to get out and push the canoe off sandbars. This was no pleasant task when we knew that we might step right into the waiting mouth of a crocodile. At first we tried traveling at night to avoid the sun, but getting stuck three or four times cured us of that idea. Even a blistering sun is preferable to a hungry crocodile, and they were in the river by the thousands. I have shot so many of the hideous beasts that my ears still ring from the noise of the gun; but my ammunition is running low, so all I can do now is watch them glide into the water as we approach. It will not be safe to swim until we get about fifty miles above Akobo on the Pibor River, and there the water is too shallow for crocodiles but also too shallow for us.

When we finally reached Nasir, our mission outpost among the Nuers,[33] we rested for two days until I had started to grow some new skin. Then we started out again up the Sobat to the Pibor. The Sobat (called Baro in Ethiopia) runs from Gambela to Nasir, while the Pibor and Akobo rivers turn south, the water flowing from the direction of Uganda. Most of the Anuaks I wanted to see were up that way. Leaving Nasir, we made good time until I shot an immense crocodile and Pakwan saw for himself the largest shield in all of Shullaland. He had to have it, so we stopped and cut his shield off the crocodile. In the crocodile's stomach we found eight anklets and four bracelets. I did not care to eat any of that crocodile, because it would have been too much like eating my fellowmen. After a day, we got to the mouth of the Pibor and started up its milk-like waters. The water is white because of the clay along the banks that looks like white sand and is not very fertile. Farther upstream the clay turns reddish, and the Nuers in that area cultivate splendid fields of corn, durra, and tobacco. In its lower reaches the Pibor is not pretty, since the banks are high and steep and this whole part of the country is a vast swampland during the rainy season.

Reaching Anuak territory, we stopped at scores of villages along the Pibor and Akobo rivers, looking them over and making some estimate of how many people were in that vicinity. Everywhere we went, the people gave us milk and eggs, and in one village we received four chickens. The Anuaks would not take money from us, but they were delighted to get a bit of salt, which they had not tasted in months. Some of the children did not even know what salt was. The river begins to take on more grace and is positively beautiful beyond the village of Akobo, which is the government post for the Anuaks of that district and is located where the Akobo and Pibor rivers meet. The Pibor here is more like an American river than any other I have seen in the Sudan. The long, sloping banks are covered with green grass, and their tops are lined with trees. I fell in love with the Pibor fifty miles above Akobo, but unfortunately there is no favorable site for us that far upriver. The river is so crooked and the corners so sharp that we almost had to bend the canoe to get around them. The best location I have found is only five miles above Akobo Post. It is near a large village of 400 people built on a big knoll overlooking the river. I estimate there are approximately 5000 Anuaks near Akobo, and that is not a bad size for a congregation—at least for a start.

However, by far the largest concentration of the Anuak population is on the Gilo River and entirely in Ethiopia. The Gilo is a branch of the Pibor that comes in about seventy miles below Akobo. Not only are the Anuaks to be found in vastly greater numbers on the Gilo River, but those who live there are the finest people of their tribe, the royalty of the Anuaks. The king lives on the Gilo in a large village called Gok, which I plan to visit on our way back. Someday I would like to work from that village and use it as our central headquarters for the Christian mission to the Anuaks. Such a dream is years in the future, if ever, because presently that territory is held by Italy. The administration of the Anuaks is very difficult, because about 20,000 of them live in Sudan and approximately 40,000 live in Ethiopia. Thus when an Anuak gets in trouble with one government, he simply crosses the border to his friends on the other side and cannot be touched. If the Italians will not turn the administration of the Anuaks over to the Sudan or vice versa, we may never be able to reach the heart of the tribe. Obviously, the best way to evangelize the entire Anuak people is to start from the center rather than the edge, and whichever Christian group is able to start from the center should have the responsibility of all. However, I am ready to begin now, and I can only start from the edge. So that is what I will do.

As I said, everywhere we went, the Anuaks gave us a cordial welcome, offering us milk and eggs. We were glad to buy both, because it is impossible to buy good eggs from the Nuers, and all their milk is mixed with cow urine. The Nuer believes that milk is a beverage for women and children, but he likes it so well that he cannot bear to see it all go to the women, so he makes a cocktail with a bite by adding cow urine, which makes it a man's drink. I must admit that I am not man enough to drink it.

We visited ten or twelve villages along the Baro River, and at each the chief asked us to tell them about our God. We had an Anuak with us who had learned to speak sufficient Nuer to attend our Nasir school, so through him we held services in each village. It was a wonderful experience, since we knew it was the first time many of the Anuaks had ever heard the gospel story. It gives me a strange feeling and a special urgency to know that this is the first—and probably the last—time that old man or that old woman sitting in the dark heart of Africa will have a chance to accept Jesus Christ as the light of the world. When I am called upon to speak to such a crowd, I do not need to search through the Bible for a text that will attract the eye and publish some gaudy subject on the bulletin board. There is only one text and one subject: "Jesus Christ came to seek and to save. . . ."

Some of the local chiefs gave us presents when we left and pleaded with us to return. Here is a great tribe of people, and not one missionary and only one poor teacher in the whole territory. The young Anuak accompanying us has received a smattering of education and wants to return to his own tribe, but his village had been burned out while he was in Nasir. As soon as we found a suitable place, I promised to open a school. The chief of the village I chose was delighted and promised to build the boy a nice house and a school building. I must return sometime in the near future and see how he is getting along. He will be the lone candle of light in all that great land of pagan darkness.

The Anuak village is entirely different from any other of the tribes in the Sudan. The Dinka, Shulla, and Nuer spread out over a lot of territory, with each family's settlement of five or six houses set off alone. But the Anuak has always had to fight for his life, since he has enemies on every side. Within reach of the Abyssinians, the Anuak has borne the brunt of slave raids. He himself is a fighter and makes long foraging expeditions into the Nuer and Shulla land to replenish the cattle stolen from him by the Abyssinians. The Anuaks have adapted their village life accordingly. Their houses are strongly built and very close together, with curious narrow-winding passages between each. The chief's house is always in the center of the village with a large palisade around his several houses where all the warriors gather for their final stand. The village is surrounded by a high mud wall surmounted with stakes. And around the wall is a deep ditch or moat, twelve to fourteen feet deep and in the rainy season filled with water. Thus the Anuaks defend themselves. In each village there are usually five or six old muskets and four or five bullets for each. These guns were captured from the Abyssinians at one time or another and carefully treasured against an attack. The bullets are not used to shoot game; spears are still good enough for that.

Don found the Anuaks to be wonderfully friendly and likable.

Married women wear little leather aprons, sometimes larger skins hanging from the shoulders as the Shulla women do, but the men and youths of both sexes are entirely naked except for an assortment of beads and brass ornaments, bracelets, and anklets. In contrast to the Shullas and Nuers, the Anuaks of both sexes shave their heads. Sometimes they cut the hair in a design of circles and squares, shaving the lines that make up the design and leaving islands of close-cropped hair between. The Anuaks are not quite so tall as the other tribes of the region, but seem of somewhat sturdier build. They are better fed than the other tribes because they grow two crops a year—one during the rains, and then, as the river goes down, they plant corn along the banks on both sides right down to the water's edge.

The Anuaks are much more progressive than any of the other tribes. They have their own blacksmiths, boat builders, and ropemakers. They grow and sell tobacco and grain; they kill elephants for ivory and ostriches for feathers. They make and sell spear handles to all the other tribes. They are also more willing to work for pay, doubtless due to the fact that they are not a cattle people in the same way the other Nilotic tribes are. The Anuaks have some herds and flocks, but these do not constitute their sole wealth or engage their exclusive interest, as is the case with the Nuer and Shulla. The Anuak combines more agriculture with his herding and establishes a more permanent residence. His language, though a distinct dialect, is related to the Shulla; his religious traditions, together with the practices of the witchdoctors, have some similarity to the Shulla religion.

The Anuaks are animists, seeing living spirits in everything. It is a spirit that makes the wind blow, the dog run, the tree grow, the river flow. These spirits can sometimes be heard. For example, when two sticks are hit together, the spirits cry out. Some of these spirits are good, but most are evil. No Anuak would start a journey by land or water without first making a sacrifice. He would not build a house or plant a field until the spirit had been propitiated. A sick child is possessed by an evil spirit, and so is an aching tooth.

These beliefs have been deeply held for many generations among the Anuaks, and critics are quite correct in insisting that it takes two or three generations for primitive people to learn what Christianity means if you are trying to teach them about *our* form of Christianity. But that is not what I want to do. I do not wish to foist my type of Christianity on anyone, because even I am not satisfied with it. However, I do want people everywhere to know my Lord, because I believe finding that Way is the Truth that leads to Life. I have no doubt that the Holy Spirit of the One True God is already at work among the Anuaks, and I am willing to do whatever it takes to be of assistance.

Among the Anuaks at that time, marriage did not begin with a wedding ceremony. The normal pattern of forming a new family was for a teenage boy and girl to have sexual relations until the girl became pregnant. Although both families were aware of these encounters and approved of them, the couple sneaked off for their liaisons. When the girl became pregnant, her male relatives (mostly her brothers) would descend upon the young man, kidnap him, tie him up, and give him a terrible beating for violating their sister. Then they would notify the boy's relatives that he was in their custody and that if his family did not come at once to redeem him, they would beat him to death. It was customary for the boy's relatives to delay for a few days in order that when they did appear, the captive would be extremely grateful to see them. By this technique Anuak families taught their normally undisciplined sons to appreciate family loyalty.

When the boy's relatives arrived at the girl's village, a lengthy and often heated negotiation was conducted until a bride price was fixed and the first installment was paid to the girl's father. Then the boy was untied and released to his family. The father-to-be would return to his home village and continue to live there while the girl, now considered his wife, lived in her village and was cared for and instructed by her female relatives.

The young bride and groom would see each other occasionally, but did not live together. It was considered improper for the father to be present or even nearby when his baby was delivered, although he was notified immediately after the birth so that he could come and visit his child and bring gifts to the new mother and her family.

After the birth of the baby, the father and mother were still not permitted to live together, since Anuak custom forbade sexual relations between husband and wife during the entire nursing period—which normally lasted two to three years. Occasionally the young father visited his wife and baby and was honorably received, but he was also badgered by his wife's family concerning gifts and additional bride-price payments. Often the husband would leave these visits in disgust and therefore make them infrequently. From his mother the young child heard idealized stories about his absentee father mixed with complaints about him from her and from his grandmother and aunts.

Sometime after the child was weaned, the mother would slip off one night to her husband's village to live with him until she once again became pregnant. Her child would wake up the next day screaming with the realization that his mother had abandoned him to the care of his grandmother in favor of the absentee father.

When the wife became pregnant, she would renew the sexual-avoidance pattern and return to her village and her first child. After a few years, when the father had made sufficient bride payments, he was finally permitted to bring his wife and children to live in his village, but by this time the husband may have acquired an additional wife or wives and other children. Therefore he would often be away visiting them.

▼▲▼

Don's evangelistic strategy involved approaching the men first, because they were more open to change. As in most cultures, Anuak mothers were the primary nurturers of children and custodians of tradition. Thus they would be extremely reluctant to change their old ways for Christianity. Anuak women had very little legal status, but many of the most important social customs centered around marriage and the family. Women were expected to marry and to bear and raise children; thus they had complete control over the early development of both sexes. A deep affection and appreciation for the mother persisted throughout the child's life, especially observable in the relationship between a mother and her daughter. A girl in Anuak society was dependent on her mother for all her training and never ceased to give her primary emotional loyalty to her mother.

The lives of Anuak women were filled with work, including the tremendously demanding responsibility of food preparation. Therefore they had little freedom to travel. Few girls would be allowed to go to school, because they were needed at home, and it was feared that education in new and strange ways would result in a lower bride price.

Because the Anuak woman's status was greatly dependent on bringing her children to maturity, she was very likely to take them to the witchdoctors. This is what her own mother did and what other women expected her to do. Moreover, children in this society were not weaned until two or three years old, so in addition to milk they also absorbed religious attitudes from their mothers.

To Don, this cultural situation meant that the men would be evangelized first. Once they became Christians they could support their wives in developing a Christian home. As Christians, Anuak men would be expected to gain a deeper appreciation of their wives, and the women could learn to form bonds with other Christian women with the conviction that it is possible—and important—to learn things that their mothers did not teach them.

In one sense, the grassy plains and great forests of the Anuak territory were romantic to Don. After all, the land abounded in game of every kind, and the people seemed interested in what he had to say. The fact of the matter was that the Anuaks thought of the Ethiopians as Christians, and since Don represented that same faith, many Anuaks wanted no part of it.

▼The Anuak Plan

T HE McCLURES proposed to spend the next fifteen years of their lives working among the Anuaks. Curiously, if a young American physician or educator chooses to devote an entire lifetime to *healing* or *teaching* in a poor and primitive area of the world, most people regard that decision as brave, sacrificial, and perhaps heroic. Even when a person who is not trained in medicine or education goes to a place so isolated that he is obligated to do both, most consider that admirable. However, when *preaching* is added to the activities of healing and teaching, in some minds the whole endeavor comes under suspicion. A theologian once wrote,

When one is *not* similarly committed to what a missionary is devoted to spreading, then the role of the missionary seems arrogant, fanatical, imperialistic and futile; and the missionary himself hypocritical and foolish. These people protest that missionaries have no right *to force their religion* down another's throat. On the other hand, when someone is willing to dedicate his life to spreading ideas in whose worth one *does* believe— such as modern medicine, democracy, modern methods and views of education, technology and the like—one tends to approve the changes in another society that this work brings about. As a matter of fact, the Christian religion has not been nearly so destructive of the patterns of life in traditional cultures as has the introduction of industrialism, the natural and social sciences, universal and modern education, democratic and socialist concepts, and medicine. The purveyors of these latter commodities are as truly "missionaries" of the West as the Christian evangelists are. The fact that we neither scorn nor castigate them as arrogant imperialists only shows that we

150

consider these ideas necessary to a rich, full life in much the way that an earlier Christian culture considered Christianity a necessary foundation for human fulfillment.[34]

Don McClure believed in modern medicine, universal education, and economic sufficiency, but he also believed that the Christian faith is a cosmic truth deserving and demanding entire commitment. Proclaiming the gospel of Jesus Christ was not an option to be considered, but a cause to be served. Don's church had been aware of the Anuak tribe and had been talking about sending workers among them for a long time. The Sudanese government, recognizing the value of having a Western presence in a former slave-trade area, had asked the American Mission to locate a station at Gambela. The missionaries talked and wrote and prayed, but the Anuak mission remained only a dream until Don McClure had served his apprenticeship and was ready to launch out on his own.

Don had come to believe that the established church's most important, challenging, and urgent priority was evangelism among non-Christian people. Among primitive peoples this involved a concentrated presentation of the gospel in a context of genuine concern for improving the overall quality of human life and a respectful understanding of the indigenous culture.

This evangelism had three components. First, the gospel must be freely preached and freely heard. That is, the preacher and the hearer must recognize the extent of their bondage to their particular cultures and the freedom that the gospel provides to both. Second, evangelism is not concerned merely about correct beliefs and words, although that is involved, but includes the attempt to make life fully human and joyful. Third, evangelism seeks to avoid cultural imperialism.

The purpose of the Anuak project, as Don conceived it, was to evangelize this isolated and primitive Nilotic tribe of about 40,000 to 60,000 people who resided in southern Sudan and western Ethiopia. The Anuak project was founded with the conviction that God would raise up some Christians from the Anuak people who would respond to the proclamation of the gospel and band together for support. A church could consequently come into existence that would be meaningful to the Anuaks and culturally authentic.

The strategy was to concentrate a large staff of fifteen missionary units in three different areas of Anuak territory about ninety miles apart. In each there would be five missionaries with a combined expertise in evangelism, medicine, agriculture, and education. They would work on preaching and Bible translation, public health, food production, literacy training, building, and economic development. In addition, all the staff members were to have some training in Bible, anthropology, and linguistics, and all without exception were expected to become fluent in the Anuak language.

The plan included a specific time limit; this was designed to maximize outside helpfulness without fostering dependence on the missionaries. Thus the Anuak project was to be completed in fifteen years—the amount of time it would take to train native leaders to carry on. It required "fifteen missionaries for fifteen years," and after that period all the foreign missionaries would leave to begin work with another untouched people, and the Anuak church would proceed entirely on its own. This time frame accepted the Anuak need for outside aid, but did not lose sight of their equally urgent need for continuing independence. Moreover, the withdrawal forbade the missionaries from making sophisticated plans that would require their own indefinite presence. No program or building or equipment would be introduced that the Anuak people could not maintain on their own. Thus the Anuak project intended to provide sufficient personnel to serve the major areas of compelling needs among primitive people and to avoid the crippling effect of an inadequate staff. Such a strike force, Don believed, could do the same amount of work in a concentrated attack that was normally scattered over sixty to seventy-five years through slow infiltration tactics.

To accomplish all this, the Anuak project had one goal: to plant and nourish a Christian church among the Anuaks before the arrival of "Complete Independence Day" fifteen years hence. This involved translating as much of the Bible as possible into the Anuak language so that the people could read the Word of God for themselves. This, of course, required that the Anuaks become literate. Therefore Don insisted that one team member, Harvey Hoekstra, have *no* assignment other than linguistic analysis and translation. With all the other problems of life among a primitive society crying out to be addressed, it was not easy to spend hours on translation; but when the Anuak New Testament was finally published,[35] the Anuak project took a quantum leap forward. Within a decade of the beginning of the project it had become possible for the new Christians to learn to read and to begin to study the Bible in their own language. As a result, indigenous evangelists did virtually all the preaching in the Anuak area. Missionaries went into the project expecting the Anuak church to be self-propagating as well as self-governing.

This meant that the Anuak project team would attempt *not* to introduce, or institutionalize, customary Western rules for church membership. The missionaries were to recognize that they were working with people who were culturally very different from themselves, and under an entirely different set of social expectations. In particular, they were dealing with a polygamous society and were keenly aware that earlier missionaries in other parts of Africa had imposed foreign regulations that had socially deleterious effects and had adversely affected new converts and infant churches. Some Sudan missions even forbade dancing and the wearing of beads as sinful! Don McClure was not an advocate of African polygamy and fought it where he could, but he did *not* believe it was appropriate for foreigners to legislate the prerequisites for African church membership. Rather, he trusted the Anuak Christians, under the guidance of Scripture and the Holy Spirit, to derive their own appropriate, culture-specific rules for church membership. In later years the Anuak church would require that a pastor or an evangelist have no more than one wife, although the same rule was not imposed on all other members. Even at that there was some difficult wrestling with a number of situations in which an evangelist inherited the wife of his deceased brother, since according to Anuak social custom, he was expected to be her husband rather than merely to provide for her.

Moreover, the project staff was determined *not* to establish a formal ecclesiastical structure for the Anuak church, but rather to allow the Anuak Christians to develop a self-governing organization that they deemed appropriate for themselves, and one that would presumably follow the customary decision-making process in the tribe. In the traditional Anuak political system each village was autonomous, and even though two villages might be directly across the river from each other, they did not share decision-making or economic resources on an inter-village basis. The reason for this political autonomy is that each village was ruled by a specific clan, and thus kinship regulations restricted the villages from sharing, or sometimes even from cooperating, with each other. Often adjacent villages were in a perpetual state of warfare, fueled by generations of hostilities. Don expected such warfare to cease when the peace of God was known among them.

It was not Don's intention to establish a church among the Anuaks that had the four-tiered judicatory structure of his own denomination. He did not believe his American system provided an absolute and universal model, and it did not fit the Anuak traditions or the authentic and dynamic leadership patterns in the new church. Unfortunately, and in spite of great resistance from field missionaries, the executives of his denomination, based in New York City, overrode Don's culturally sensitive model. They insisted that the emerging church be organized on the American model, which the administrators understood; this gave them the power to make decisions for people whose language they could not speak and whose culture they only thought they understood. Eventually this fact of American control, especially of organization and money, would replace the natural Anuak leadership pattern. Those Anuaks who learned to speak English and thus could communicate their desires to the New York-based executives became church leaders.

The final objective toward self-governance was that there would be no attempt to impose or even encourage a certain style of worship for the Anuak church. This was not easy to implement, because the missionaries did introduce Western liturgical components such as prayer, Bible reading, and preaching to the new believers, and they were adopted into the Anuak worship services. Some Western Christian songs and hymns were translated into the Anuak language, and some of these are still being used by the Anuak church. However, the missionaries focused on their desire for the church to develop its own style of worship, and one result was the Drum Hymn.

The Anuaks are great dancers and fabulous drummers. In addition, one of the traditional musical forms was the singing of songs of praise to the great leaders and chiefs of their tribe. These praise-songs were accompanied by beautiful drumming and handclapping. After some years the Anuak Christian leaders approached the missionaries to inquire whether it would be appropriate to use drums in the worship service to accompany songs that they had composed. The question itself indicates some uncertainty and dependence, but it also indicates some confidence and independence. The Anuak leaders had grown to the place where they desired to use their own customs to praise God rather than replace their traditions with Western ones. Since none of the missionaries were outstanding dancers or drummers, it was a tribute to their cross-cultural sensitivity that they unhesitatingly and enthusiastically said yes. What evolved in the Anuak church was a beautiful and profound form of worship, where a traditional musical style was transformed so that indigenous drum songs of praise to Jesus the Redeemer could echo from the throats of Anuaks of all ages, whether literate or not. The Drum Hymn became the core of Anuak worship and the primary medium by which the gospel message was transmitted throughout this Nilotic society.[36]

Don assumed that he had found his marching orders in the Scripture that reads, "The Spirit of the Lord is upon me to preach good news to the poor [evangelize]; to deliver the captives [educate]; to recover sight to the blind [heal]; to set at liberty the oppressed [emancipate]; and to proclaim the acceptable year of the Lord [do it now!]" (Luke 4:18). This verse makes a neat (if somewhat forced) summary of the Anuak project. In any case, it offered homiletic hooks on which Don could explain to his American friends what he was doing in Africa.

Almost from the beginning, the Anuak project was funded by those who had heard Don speak about what the Lord was doing among the Anuaks and wanted to help. Don's small salary and that of others who worked with him at various times were always paid by the denomination in the regular way, but Don had permission to receive funds outside the church's budget. Of course, he was under his church's jurisdiction, and he was expected to provide a strict accounting of monies received, but this funding procedure meant that people who wanted to support the Anuak project could designate their gifts through the Board of Foreign Missions in Philadelphia or send a check to Don's brother Tom, who managed his American bank account.

Some of these contributions, usually small gifts of five or ten dollars, were designated for an Anuak schoolboy or for medicine, but how other gifts were spent was left entirely to Don's discretion. Don felt that this direct and continued financial support not only gave him the flexibility to meet needs as quickly as they arose on the field, but indicated continued divine approval. Don believed that God would not provide resources for work he did not intend to bless.

In the early years the denominational leaders, led by Stillman Foster and Glenn P. Reed, thought it was important and necessary for the church to have such contribution channels in addition to the normal world mission budget. However, in later years a new breed of ecclesiastical administrators, based now in New York City, would oppose this practice with increasing aggressiveness. Obviously those who control money—control. Those who administer a budget direct what can be done by providing or withholding the necessary funds. Since Don McClure had his own funding network—and often people who made contributions through these channels were alienated by denominational policy—some of the New York executives could not forgive Don for his entrepreneurial skills and passionately resented the independence that such support made possible.

Such was the grand design for a pioneer mission in a primitive area of Africa: a team investing a maximum effort for a minimum time. Don was disappointed that J. Alfred Heasty thought nothing as temporary as this plan could bring permanent good. A mission, according to Heasty, required permanent buildings and a fifty-year plan. This is the old debate between settlers and pioneers. The settler has a "brick" mentality, which establishes an outpost by choosing a site, getting the necessary governmental approvals, and building a permanent residence that says to all who see it, "We are here to stay." The pioneer has a "canvas" mindset, which says, "We are always ready to fold our tents and move on." Heasty believed Don's strategy was too visionary and a waste of time and money, especially since it was directed toward a tribe living astride the disputed Sudan-Ethiopian border. That situation in the late 1930s was precarious; everything might be wiped out in a few years. Even Glenn thought Don and his family should not go out alone. But Don was convinced that the plan was right, Lyda was ready to go, and Don was not willing to wait any longer.

Of course, such a missionary strike team as Don envisaged was not standing by in any staging area. In fact, a full complement was never assembled on the field. After ten years there were still only three missionary families. People came and went; the immensity of the task, the ferocity of the heat, the isolation, health problems, financial problems, and family problems took their toll of those who wanted to participate. But through all these vicissitudes the McClures worked on: sometimes alone, sometimes with inferior helpers, sometimes with superb support.

▼▲▼

While Don was preparing to go upriver from Doleib Hill to Akobo to begin the Anuak project, Lyda, accompanied by daughter Marghi, went downriver to the hospital in Khartoum to deliver their second child. Don spent an entire week repairing his truck and made several false starts, but as each day approached he did not have the heart to leave for Akobo until he had news of his wife and child. As the days passed, Don became more and more anxious and restless. He came to the conviction that he was doing a very wrong thing to leave Lyda and his family just when they needed him most and when he needed them.

I had lost all heart in the work I was planning to begin, and my whole life became centered upon what was happening in Khartoum. Those were trying days for me as I imagined a hundred terrible things that might have happened. Finally I set 12 March as the deadline and, if no word had come by that day, I would push out into the wilderness without word, because those houses at Akobo had to be built before the rains came. On the morning of 11 March, just after we had finished breakfast at the Reeds, the phone rang and sent an electric thrill through us all. Somehow intuitively I knew it was from Lyda. Sure enough, it was a wire from Khartoum and I only heard the words "Donnie arrived at 2:30 this morning—all well—" when my knees buckled and my eyes filled with tears. I just leaned against the wall and wept for joy and relief. Gail Reed had to get the rest of the message for me, which was "Don, Jr. arrived at 2:30 this morning; nine pounds; everybody well and happy; say Amen." And "Amen" I did say, together with the most grateful prayer of thanksgiving that ever passed my lips. Lyda, eight hundred long African miles away, had gone through the birth ordeal alone and had come through wonderfully and safely. Donnie, our son, our hope and dream for months, was a reality in flesh and blood and one who could be held and loved. My eyes and heart fill to overflowing every time I think of the goodness of God toward us.

Well, after that, nothing in the world could hold me back, and by four o'clock on the afternoon of 11 March, my cook Oman and I were on the road with a very heavily loaded truck. I feared to carry so much, but I was taking only what was necessary for immediate use. Most of the load was bamboo to be used in making the roofs of the houses. My first obstacle, and the one I most feared from past experiences, was the crossing of the Sobat River on the rickety ferry. As the truck eased onto the ferry, it sank dangerously near to water level. But with careful handling we managed to get across and moored on the other bank. I knew I never could get up the steep bank with my load, so I called in a dozen or so men to dig away part of the high bank and make a road for me to climb out. I then saw to it that the ferry was securely tied and would not push out from me.

Finally, when all seemed to be in readiness, the truck put forth its best and we started to climb the bank. All went well for two or three seconds, the cables stretched tight as the truck pushed up the bank, but it was too much to expect as, with a backward lurch, one cable broke and then the other. I had no choice. I was too far off to get back on again before the ferry reached deep water, so I gave the truck all it was worth. With a rush the ferry swept out from under me and out into the river. The truck had just made the bank with the front wheels over the top (which was all that saved me) when the back wheels dropped down into the soft mud at the edge of the water and sank in deep. There I perched almost afraid to breathe. Indeed, I am not sure I had taken a breath for several minutes, and now it became extremely painful to do so.

I shouted for the men to come and hold the truck, and when they saw that it had settled in place and there was no danger to them, they came and gave me their moral assistance. Then the fun began. The accident happened at just about five in the evening. We dug and tugged and strained for four hours, but had not moved a single inch. I finally, much against my will, decided that I must unload everything. But that was going to be extremely difficult and dangerous, because the men had to stand in water up to their waists to take the things out of the back of the truck. No one likes to stand in the Sobat at any time and least of all at night when the crocodiles are hungry and frequent. So the men said they would do it in the morning, but not after dark. And no amount of persuasion would make them change their minds. I was in a predicament, for I did not dare leave the truck as it was. I felt sure it would settle into the mud and perhaps topple over. The front wheels were just barely resting on the top of the bank.

So finally I made many rash promises of bringing them tobacco and meat (the two things dearest to a native's heart) when I came back, if they would get me out of that hole. Calling more men from across the river, and even waking up small boys, they finally rounded up nearly seventy pullers, large and small. I set the engine going and with fear and trembling crawled into the driver's seat. I knew that if the cable broke when the truck was half out, it would drop back again and both of us would get a very wet bath. I was ready for a bath by that time, but did not care to have one at the bottom of the Sobat

River inside a truck. So as I stepped on the gas and shouted for the men to pull, I also offered up a little prayer, however mingled with shouts, grunts, and the incense of burning gasoline. With a roar from the motor and men, the truck hung for a moment and then rushed up over the bank and on to level ground. As the men jumped and shouted in glee over their strength and prowess, the "Anuak Special" and I dashed up the road for a few miles to get out of the mosquito area before I made camp for the night. I had already been bitten a hundred times and feared a dose of malaria.

Bright and early next morning, I was on the road again and made good time until we reached the "Slough of Despond" created by the elephants. It was one thing to go over this in an empty truck, but quite another matter to haul two tons or so in and out of the craters. It took us five hours to go thirty miles, but go we did and arrived at a large Nuer village just at 2:00 P.M. Stopping there only long enough to eat and fill my water bottles, I pushed on hoping to get into Akobo about 9:00. What innocence! And how little did I know what was going to happen before I saw Akobo.

The first shock came as we were spinning across a great sandy plain with an excellent roadway when suddenly the left back side gave a lurch and crashed down with a ripping, grinding noise that made my heart sink and gave me all I could do to hold the truck straight. Then the next instant, behold, our back wheel came merrily rolling along and whizzed past us on its way to Akobo alone, bouncing and jumping in great leaps as if it were glad to be freed of its burden. When Oman, who was sitting beside me and holding my big rifle across his knees, saw this wheel flying past and no one to catch it, he made a frantic leap out of the truck onto the road. Now, what he had in mind was very commendable, namely, to stop that wheel before it got out of Africa; but there were several factors his African head forgot to take into consideration. The first and most serious, from my point of view, was that he held my precious rifle in his hand when he jumped. The second was that, while the wheel was moving very fast and it seemed that the truck was standing still, yet that was far from the truth. We were actually moving about twenty-five miles per hour when Oman jumped. And the third mistake he made was to jump sideways and with his legs crossed.

Out of the corner of my eye—for I was having a struggle with the steering wheel—I saw Oman's crossed feet hit the ground, and then in a surprisingly short time, indeed with the speed of light, his head and feet changed places and he spun like an inverted top. To my shame, I fear I had little thought of Oman, for as he flopped I saw the stock of my rifle (the Winchester .405, which the Shullas called "the Old Gun") hit the ground and shatter into splinters. My heart stopped beating, and I wanted to cry—not for Oman, whom I knew had at least a broken head; not for the broken truck; not even for that wheel that was still dizzily spinning across the country—but I wanted to cry for my broken gun, which I believed was lost beyond all repair. That gun had been my companion on many a long hunt. I had carried it like a baby across my arm; it had provided food for many hungry stomachs; it had saved many from the mouths of crocodiles; it had only within the month saved me from the mouths of two lions. (Of course, I did not *need* to be *near* those lions' mouths, but there I was, and that gun had dispatched them.) It was all over but to pick up the pieces and mourn its fate.

As soon as I got the truck stopped—I mean, when it stopped itself—I jumped out and ran back to Oman. He was sitting up with the wreckage of the rifle lying about him. I said, "*Oman, wiji bogan* [You have no head]; didn't you know the truck was moving?" He sat rubbing the thing I told him he had none of as if to make sure I was wrong and then said, "I saw that wheel going and thought we had stopped." Poor lad, he was pretty badly used up. I did not worry about his head, for it was a Shulla head and toughened up with clubs, but he had taken the skin off his right side from his shoulder to his knee. His elbow and fingers were especially bad. The bone was laid bare on one finger. Fortunately I had my medicine kit with me, and I soon had him patched up and resting under the shade of a tree. Then I turned to the wreckage.

The pieces of the gun I simply gathered up and tenderly laid away in the truck and then turned to the broken wheel. It was not nearly so bad as I feared, for the wheel bolts had worked loose and finally, with a great wrench, due to the weight of the truck, the wheel had torn off and run up the road alone. The ground was sandy where it occurred, and the brake drum was not damaged. I found the wheel lodged in the forks of a small tree almost a quarter of a mile away. It had bounced over a log and was caught fast about three feet off the ground. I had to cut off one branch to dislodge it. Then I made a great mistake, and that was to try to lift the truck with its heavy load on a jack made only for the truck. As a result, the foot broke off the jack, and there I sat in the middle of Africa, eight hundred miles from the nearest gas pump and service stations, and no Western Union boy to send for help.

There was nothing else for it but to unload and pry the wheel up. For two hours I struggled with boxes and crates that had taken three of us to load. With many moanings and groanings (almost as pathetic as those Oman was making as he rested under the tree), I finally took out the last box and stick of lumber. By nine o'clock I was ready to start to work on the wheel.

I discovered that the threads had ripped out of the nuts, only leaving the threads of the bolts almost undamaged, except that they were filled with metal. It was fortunate that I could borrow nuts from the other wheels and make repairs. So by lantern light I sat down with a small three-cornered file and started to clean the bolts. As I worked, my mind went back to Khartoum, where I could see my Lyda lying in the hospital bed and at her side our little baby boy, not yet forty-eight hours old. And the rejoicing of my heart made my present difficulties shrivel to nothingness. However, two hours later when I got the threads clean and the wheel back on, I did not think it was nothingness as I tried to reload the big boxes. Finally my body just quit, and I crawled into the truck in all my dirty, greasy clothes and fell fast asleep.

The next morning Oman was so sore, he groaned with each bat of an eye, so I built an inclined plane and rolled the heavy things into the truck, and off we started. We had not gone far until we came across a truck stranded without gasoline. What a place to run out of gas! Fortunately I had some extra (so I thought) and gave them a five-gallon tin.

Pushing on at a good pace, though with very frequent stops to look at all the wheel bolts (I fear I now have a "wheel bolt complex"), we were making very good time and with good luck would be in Akobo within two hours. Then suddenly, right across the road, appeared an animal trail, worn deep by herds of antelope walking in single file. I should have remembered it—I had crossed it before; but evidently I was dozing or thinking of

Lyda and Donnie, because I saw it too late to stop or even slacken speed. We hit it with a crash and bounced, and then with a sickening crack our axle broke and we caved in. The truck quickly ground to a stop with the back wheels in the animal trail and its nose in the dirt.

I looked at Oman and then started to laugh, for the tears were running down his cheeks and he had the longest face I have ever seen on a human being. I laughed until I was almost hysterical, and he must have thought me crazy—and perhaps I was a bit. He cried, "Odon, we have been cursed; we have been cursed! Someone in the Shullaland has cursed us before we started!" Again I laughed and told him his curse was to have started out with such a bone-headed companion and driver as I.

I scarcely needed to look at the damage. I knew only too well what had happened. The front axle had snapped right off and—worse luck—it had broken just under the left front spring. Had it broken in the middle, my task would have been simplified. But how was I to mend such a major break? I took stock of what materials I had and found I had a piece of two-inch pipe, some smaller pipe, lots of lumber and plenty of wire and rope. So I set to work.

Again I unloaded and blocked the front of the truck up on pieces of four-by-four timbers—which I had expected to hold up the roof of my house, but not my truck. By evening I had the wheels and the axle off and the axle almost hammered out straight. I did the best I could with it, but had neither forge for heating the iron nor a big hammer, so I could not get all the twist out of it. I stopped long enough for supper, which Oman was able to throw together in a sort of a way, then went back to my job. By ten o'clock I had the wheels back on, and the axle ends almost met in place. I was elated, but too tired to do much celebrating, so I went to sleep.

The next day I spent most of the time cutting my two-inch pipe in half with the small three-cornered file. It was all I had with me, for most of my tools had been sent ahead to Akobo. By 2:00 P.M. I had the axle all tied up until nothing could be seen but pipe and wire. Then to reload and drive in to Akobo. It was becoming important that we get some place, because our water was giving out. I had brought enough from the Nuer village for just one day, and the terrible road had made our radiator leak so we had used most of the water for the motor before we broke down. Oman's hurts made him excessively thirsty, and I did not have the heart to tell him to conserve the water; so I went thirsty.

But with cheered hearts we piled in and, pulling out of the hole, started down the road. Alas, our hopes were ill-founded, for we had not gone more than one hundred yards until the wire snapped and down we went again. This time I, too, wanted to cry. I was sick and tired and about ready to give it all up. Not only was I worried about the truck and all my supplies, but I knew Lyda would be very anxious to get a telegram from Akobo stating that I was safely in. And I did not want her to be worried about me. It was important that she have an easy mind during Donnie's first days of nursing.

I was just about to curl up on the seat and have a nap when we heard a truck coming up the road behind us. It proved to be a Sudan government engineer going to Akobo. He took one look at the truck and pronounced it hopeless to repair and said I would have to leave it until I got a new axle. I did not share his scientific opinion about the hopelessness of the situation. I knew I could repair the truck and get it into Akobo if I had the materials and tools. However, I picked up my bed and, waving good-bye to the Anuak Special, we left it standing in the middle of the road with something of a down-in-the-mouth look about its front end.

We got into Akobo just at dark on Tuesday evening. I was a sight to behold. I forgot to mention that when the truck crashed, I had attempted to take a bite out of the steering wheel. Thus, when we got to Akobo Post, my four days' beard was full of grease and blood and my four days' shirt was covered with the same. I would have tried to clean up before we got in, but we were out of water. When I appeared before Captain Lesslie, who is in charge at Akobo Post and had expected me three days earlier, he asked, in some surprise, "Who are you?" "Don McClure," I answered. He replied, "Surely not the Reverend Dr. McClure?" "Yes," I said, "why not?"

The next day Don came down with fever and was not able to move the five miles from Akobo Post to Akobo to start building his houses. While he was recuperating, Don worked on his rifle. Since the barrel was not damaged, he was able to put the stock back together with glue, fine wire, and small screws, although it would never again be the beautiful gun it once was. Later he took a hundred-mile river trip from Akobo to Pibor, where he met the Beir (Murle) people.

They are very different from the other Nilotics and are very impressive. The Beirs have some of the dignity and proud bearing of the Ethiopians. There are about 60,000 of them in the Sudan, and no white man can speak their language. Needless to say, they have never heard the gospel. When we get the work among the Anuaks completed, I would love to come and live among the Beirs.

The next week Don broke ground for his houses with fitting ceremonies and prayer.

The Anuak boys working for me thought we ought to sacrifice a sheep, which I agreed to do as soon as I get hungry. These Anuak boys work hard, and every day the villagers come to watch our progress and to make suggestions. Only one boy knows the difference between a saw and a hammer, and he cannot use either. Thus I must cut and plane the lumber for my window and door frames. My theological training does not help much in building a house in the middle of Africa except that it provides a somewhat enriched vocabulary when I hit my thumb with the hammer. I would be working with a lighter heart if I were not separated from my family by eight hundred miles and for six or seven months—a family that now includes a son I have never seen. At night I have been enjoying my radio immensely. It survived the trip, and I can pull in KDKA from Pittsburgh and a Boston station. The only problem with a radio is that the news broadcasts from London take me out of peaceful Africa, where there is nothing more dangerous than crocodiles and wounded lions, into the maelstrom of the European war.

▼ The First Year

THE McCLURES HAD one year in which to prepare for the establishment of Don's Rapid Evangelism Project for the Anuak people before they were scheduled to return to America for a much-needed furlough. During this year they would learn to speak the Anuak language and start to reduce it to a written form into which the Bible could be translated. The first priority, however, was to build mud houses for the McClures and for those who came to Akobo to help.

Yesterday finally saw all our houses finished. Actually our house is a series of four round mud huts connected by verandas that will serve as sleeping porches and a dining room. They are works of art in mud and grass. I must pay tribute to Lyda, who drew up the plans. I departed from them here and there where it was easier to build on paper than on site, but on the whole, the credit for this place will have to go to her. I wish my family were here to glory in our houses and so I could glory in them. This is the fourth month of our separation. I am now filled with relief and joy in knowing that a big rainstorm will not wash away all my work.

Tomorrow I will cut my staff in half and keep on only enough men and women to clean up this place. I wish you could watch these Anuak women work, or try to work. I have had six women packing the dirt into hard mud for the floors and walls of the houses. It seems that no women can be found who are childless, so all of them come to work with babies strapped to their backs. Each tribe of people in the south Sudan carries a baby differently. The Shulla women carry their babies on their hip with the babies straddling the mother's thigh and hanging onto the mother's arm. The Nuer women put their babies in a long, narrow basket, which they cover with a mat, tied on, and this they carry on their heads. The Dinka women make a basket that resembles a laundry basket, and they strap it to their backs and the baby stands upright with straps under his arms holding him up. But the Anuak women make a little hammock of skin, and the baby sits in this with his little legs straddling his mother's back and sticking out each side. The mother slips her arms through straps that fit over her shoulders. Thus she will walk for miles and miles, or work for hours, and never take the baby off except to nurse, which is a very frequent occurrence.

These mothers come to work with their babies, and from early morning until nightfall I have been listening to crying babies and putting up with mothers doing nothing else while they nurse their babies. As I said, they nurse them about every fifteen minutes, and with each whimper the baby is nursed. There is one youngster at least two years old (he must be, for the mother is again heavy with child and they never break their custom to have children oftener than two to three years), and I have never seen him more than two feet away from his mother. All the time he has one hand on her, and most of the time he is hanging onto a breast either with his hand or with his mouth. Yesterday afternoon I wanted to get a picture of the mother and child, but the room was too dark. She was down on all fours sanding the floor (that is, making the dirt into mud and patting it down) and of course naked except for her small loincloth. The youngster was down on his knees with his face turned up, pulling away at a breast as hard as he could pull. Then she changed her position, and the lad rolled over on his back, hanging onto this breast with both hands, holding himself up so that he would not lose his mouthful. The mother was completely oblivious to the child and worked away, chatting to the other women all the while.

I have seen youngsters butt and strike their mother's breast just as an animal would when there is no milk for them. The cows in this country are hard "to start," and the calves sometimes almost lift their mothers off their feet as they butt at the udders trying to get milk. These little human "calves" or "kids" are just like so many little goats. Since both Shulla and Anuak mothers nurse their babies until they are two years old, it is tribal custom to dig out several front teeth with the point of a fishing spear.

In the late 1930s a special offering taken among his American friends raised $249.61 so that Don could purchase color film for recording life among the Anuaks. The first three reels were brought back by returning missionaries and reviewed for public presentation by the Committee of Directors of Young People's Work. To the committee's dismay, Don's pictures made it quite obvious that most of the Anuaks were something less than fully clothed. The shocked committee deliberated about this unsuitable situation and instructed Don to use the money to take lots of pictures of African scenery, but not to include naked or half-naked people in them.

Today the laugh was on me. I have been washing in the river every evening. At this time of year, with no crocs around, I have been enjoying my bath very much. Usually when I go down to the river, a group of people line the bank at some distance to watch the show of a "red" man playing in the water. Bathing is a custom the Anuaks do not understand, but find very amusing. This evening it was most embarrassing. I was already splashing around in the water when a large delegation of Anuaks came up. I have begun to understand something of their language, and after my visitors had greeted me politely, they sat down quite near to observe the strange action of washing. Since my admirers were of both sexes, I was in something of a dilemma. I did not know whether to try to out-patience them, or to crawl out and "face the music" and laughter. Knowing the patience of a sitting African who has nothing else to do, I feared that I would be outlasted and eventually have to climb out anyway. So, to their great delight, I boldly walked out and started to dry myself. The Anuaks certainly thought me a queer animal, and I overheard several remarks to the effect that "his body is covered with red hair just like a lion." I hope their curiosity as been satisfied, but I am afraid there will be more public baths.

▼▲▼

Not long after Lyda and Marghi and baby Donnie had come to Akobo, Don claimed that he had found a herd of splendid buffalo that were as tame as a mother lion with a litter of kittens. Several times after getting his first lion, Don had said that he did not desire to shoot anything else except a buffalo and invited his dad to come back to

Africa and hunt with him. Don had heard that some buffalo were in the vicinity and thought he would send out a scout or two to pet them up a bit and make them tame.

Last Friday one of my chaps came in and said he had seen a large herd about five miles away and there were some good heads. So that afternoon I started out to look for myself. After a long walk we crossed a swamp and came upon fresh buffalo tracks and spoor. As soon as we struck the tracks and started after them, I began to wish I was hunting rabbits instead of buffalo; but there was no turning back. The country was very unfavorable for hunting, because the high grass had been burned when it was still a bit green and the blackened stalks were hard to push through and furnished excellent cover for the buffalo. It was miserable stuff to try to shoot in, and if it came to a foot race, the buffalo would have all the advantage.

I knew that buffalo often charge in a herd and will charge even the scent of man although they may not have seen their object through the tall grass; I began to think that I did not want a buffalo after all. However, as we walked, it began to look as if we would not get a chance, because the sun was setting and still no buffalo. So just before turning back home, I climbed a tree to have a look around, and there—just three hundred yards off—I saw a big herd of huge, black buffalo. We had passed them as we hunted upwind, and when we got past they picked up our scent. Every one of them was facing us with heads high and tails switching. When I saw them, I did not know whether to stay up the tree or climb down. I wanted to stay up, but I thought of the six boys I had left a few yards behind; they had my guns. So I scrambled down, and we made a beeline to get out of that neighborhood and get the buffalo upwind from us.

We made a big circle through a tall patch of unburned grass that would take us out behind the buffalo. All the time we could hear the buffalo stamping and snorting off to our left. Because we were not able to see anything, we could only hope that they had good manners! The buffalo were standing in the open, and I knew as soon as I got through the high grass they would be close enough to shoot at. I had my boys sit down and, taking one chap with me, I pushed on. Coming out of the high grass on my hands and knees, I could hear the buffalo but could not see them. So I crawled on ahead about twenty yards to a large anthill and looked over the top. The buffalo were standing with their backs to me, still sniffing in the direction from which we had come. As I began to look them over for a nice head, the boys I left behind started to talk in low tones. Instantly the whole herd whirled around and lifted their heads and tails, looking right in my direction. I was glad the sun had set and it was getting a bit dusky, because they were not so liable to see me. There was no time to wait, so I picked out a big bull and let him have it. The bullet hit him full in the chest, like the sound of striking a drum, and he went to his knees. Much to my relief, the rest of the herd turned tail and ran.

Before I could shoot again I heard a snort and a rush behind and to the right of me. Quickly looking around, I saw a great buffalo dash out to the edge of the very grass through which I had crawled only a moment before. Evidently he was driven off from the herd and had been standing in the high grass. He stood looking at us with head up and tail straight out. Turning a bit, I took a shot at him from a difficult position and missed completely. He shook his head from side to side and started slowly right toward us. I turned fully around to face him, hoping at the same time that the buffalo I had hit in the chest was dead behind me, but I did not dare look to see. My next shot hit the second animal right on the Adam's apple and he too went to his knees, but only for a second; then he was up again and coming faster than ever. I could have run for it and likely made a tree in time, but I never thought to do so. Taking careful aim, I shot again. The bullet hit solid and full in the chest. The buffalo hesitated only slightly and started to run, still about fifty yards away. Just at that moment my boy's fright was my greatest blessing, because he felt things getting a bit warm, and he jumped to his feet and made for a tree a few yards away. As soon as the boy moved, the buffalo changed course and made for the running object. That was my chance, for I had a good side shot. My last bullet hit him in the shoulder and down he went.

Not knowing what might happen next, I took time to shove only two bullets into my rifle and, seeing the second bull down on his knees (although he was still struggling to get to his feet), I turned to have a look at the first buffalo. I had staggered him, but he was still coming on, with blood spouting from both nostrils. I then shot at the shoulder and knocked him to his knees, but he threw himself on his feet again and came right at me, dragging one front foot. I could not hit the other shoulder, and there was not time even to aim, since he was only ten feet away when I fired my last shell. I did not wait to see where it hit, as I jumped to the left and turned to run, but I ran smack into a thornbush. I just had time to throw up my arms and the rifle in front of my face as I crashed into the tight branches. The bush stopped me cold, and I braced myself for the crashing blow of those huge horns in the middle of my back. Then I turned and saw that the beast was down. He had slid to a stop just eight feet from the bush on which I had been impaled. My last bullet had hit him under the left eye and bored back into the brain.

The boys came rushing back and embraced me, trying to kiss my hands and feet, and they said over and over again, "*Jwok dwong, Jwok dwong*" (God is great, God is great). I agreed, and we slid to our knees to thank him, because my knees would not hold me up any longer. After a few minutes I slowly approached the other buffalo, which was still trying to get to his feet, and I finished him off with a shot behind the ear. He is a beauty and has a fine head. I never dreamed the buffalo were so large. This was as big as the biggest bull I have ever seen. He would weigh close to a ton! By the time we had looked him over, it was dark, so we decided to leave him where he was until morning. I hoped that the lions would not get at him, but then I was pretty sure they would not touch his head, so I did not care too much.

The next morning we went back and found both animals intact. I had a notion to follow the herd, but was so busy with my packing and getting ready to leave for our furlough at home that I did not want to waste any more time. We really need some time at home. Lyda and I are both so tired that we are literally dizzy. Lyda is troubled with almost constant headaches, and I tend to fall over for no reason at all. However, the worst feature of living in Africa, as far as I am concerned, is my teeth. They are falling apart in my mouth. I have had them filled several times in Khartoum, but evidently the dentist does not do his job thoroughly, and the teeth are continuing to decay under the fillings and they are falling out. Fortunately all the nerves are dead, or I would be in great pain just now. I still have enough teeth for a good smile, but I do have to hunt around to find a place on which I can chew hard toast.

It took us all morning to get the buffalo skinned, cut up, and into the truck. I was able to drive my truck within two miles of where I shot them, so the men had to carry the meat only that far. We found the meat very good. I now have one head and head-skin all dry and ready to pack for home. When I get it home I may find out that it will cost a small fortune to have it mounted, in which case I will just mount the head skeleton on a board.

I have another pretty fine trophy to bring home, and she is getting larger every day—a baby lioness. We captured her about three weeks ago when the mother lioness was driven out by a grass fire. The lioness managed to carry one cub away in her mouth, but she could not get back for this one. The chaps who brought it in were very anxious to get rid of it. They said that the lioness would be sure to follow and find it, no matter how far away the baby had been taken. I have had it three weeks, and if the mother is going to come along, she had better do it before we start for America. It is quite an experience to act as nursemaid to a lion. The lion has been sick for several days, and I am not sure that I will be able to get it home.

We are in the last stages of packing, and none of us knows where to turn around. We plan to leave here the day after tomorrow and will go by truck the whole way. Our original plan to go by water is impossible because of the rapid fall of the river. The water is now too low for us to get to Nasir with a full boat, and I am afraid to try lest we get stuck somewhere and held up for several days. So we are leaving early and plan to take it easy for Lyda's sake. Since she is pregnant again, we will not try to do more than one hundred miles a day. And believe me, that will be plenty over these roads. I am a bit shaky about starting out with all my family in the old truck, because after we leave Akobo we strike straight out into the heart of Africa for three hundred miles and will not see another town until we get to Doleib Hill. We will have to carry enough water for all that time, both for ourselves and for the truck.

It is quite an undertaking to start out with a nurse (Isabel Blair), a wife and two children, and another on the way when you expect to spend at least three days in an absolute wilderness and waterless waste. But I do not have the slightest worry about it, because Lyda is very capable and we will also place ourselves in the hands of the Lord. I know that he will see us through. We have only been at Akobo for a little more than a year, but we need some time at home and, at least, the Anuak project has been started.

In another letter Don continued their travel story.

Our first day was uneventful and the second day started out well enough, though Lyda was sick from sunburn and wind. Miss Blair especially was so burned from the wind that her hands and feet began to swell. The truck ran well for a few hours, and then the old trouble got worse and I spent most of the day out and under. We also ran into rains and got soaked thoroughly. What was worse, the road got so soft that we had to go along in second gear. The second night we camped out on wet ground, with threatening rain clouds and lightning making us nervous. During the night our camp was visited by several giraffe who paid their respects and left without hurting anything. They did scare Lyda, because she was the only one awake and in the dark did not know what the huge things were. She thought they might be elephants, which could step on us at any time. We did not even have a tent to protect us and were at the mercy of anything that came along.

The third day was a day-long nightmare. We were all tired, the women sick, and our two little kids restless. The road was almost impassable at times, and although I had apparently fixed the truck and it ran well, yet the road was terrible. With huge yawning holes, elephant tracks, and mud we could not make any speed and ran only a few miles before having to stop for a rest. One bright stop of the day was for a herd of wild boars. I had never before seen wild boars, and I was almost wild with excitement. I managed to get three before the herd vanished. It was a good thing, too, since we ate boar meat for two days thereafter.

During the afternoon of the third day the worst disaster overtook us, or perhaps we overtook it. We were moving along at a little better than our accustomed five miles per hour when the left rear wheel (the one of the bygone days, too) dropped into a hole in the road and broke off at the axle. It was hopeless to try to fix it even though I labored for several hours to try to patch up something that would enable us to crawl on. The only thing left to do was to sit tight and hope for someone to come along and help us out. That was a small possibility, because the rain was coming down in sheets for miles behind us and would likely close the road for several days. We made ourselves as comfortable as possible and determined to stick it out. There was no use for me to try to walk out for help, because we were still seventy-five miles from Doleib Hill and the road was a sea of water and mud. Lyda was feeling better even though her sunburn was painful. Miss Blair, on the other hand, was still feeling very miserable. Donnie, Marghi, and I were ourselves and we made enough trouble to keep the rest of the party cheerful. We slept on muddy, wet ground, and Easter morning dawned with no help in sight.

Before leaving Akobo I had made arrangements with an Arab merchant there to travel together. The morning we left, he promised to follow us within an hour and would catch up with us that night. He never did appear, but we had some hopes that he might come along. I had also sent telegrams to Mr. Heasty at Doleib Hill, and we felt sure he would send help if we did not arrive within a reasonable time. God surely answers prayers, since about noon, when we were sweltering hot, a government truck appeared far down the road. I immediately commandeered the truck and told the driver he was going to Doleib Hill! He hesitated a bit, but I said I would fix it with his boss in Malakal, so he agreed to transport us. I never would have let him do anything else. After we got all our baggage piled into the smaller truck, it looked mountainous, and the driver shook his head dubiously. We started about two o'clock in the afternoon, and he drove like the wind. The road was wet and full of holes, but he was so afraid he would get stuck that he drove like a madman and nearly killed us all. I was worried about Lyda and feared the worst from the terrible bouncing, although she insisted that she was all right.

We finally got to Doleib Hill at seven o'clock, all of us dead tired. Lyda immediately went to bed and this morning is as chipper as ever. I guess our experience did not do us any harm, but the old truck may have to stay out along the road through all the rains. I do not care if I ever see it again.[37]

The War Years

DURING THE furlough year in America, Don was allowed to study tropical medicine at Cornell University as an amateur physician. He also renewed acquaintance with his wider family and with those who were supporting the Anuak project with their gifts. In addition, their third child and second daughter was born. She was named for her mother, but as a baby was called Polly. In 1940 the McClure family was rested, healthy, and eager to get back to the Anuaks as they boarded a ship for Africa and traveled through a world at war.

We are still at sea. I know there are those who never thought I was anywhere else. Nevertheless, we are past the danger zones now and pointing our prow into the blue waters of the Mediterranean Sea once more. There is something about the Mediterranean that is far more alluring and entrancing than the cold, green waters of the Atlantic. Somehow the Atlantic seems morose and forbidding with its never-ending rolling, choppy waves and yawning valleys between the swells, while the Mediterranean is very warm and inviting and a beautiful deep blue as if its depths were beyond measure.

During the whole ocean crossing we were anxious about what we might meet lurking in the dark fogs of the Atlantic. You can be sure we moved very cautiously during thick weather. The French and British steamers used neither lights nor foghorn at any time. Several times during the night we passed ghost ships as they made their way past in complete darkness. I could not help but think that the darkness of the steamers was as nothing compared to the darkness of men's minds that made such a situation necessary. What dread and fear millions of people are continually carrying in their hearts.

In 1935 Italy had invaded Ethiopia, but because the conflict had widened into a world war, the Sudan government refused to permit the McClures to return to the Anuaks since Akobo was only three miles from the border of Italian-occupied Ethiopia. Thus Don and Lyda rejoined the mission at Doleib Hill to work there until the authorities would allow them to return to Akobo.

Now it can be told! Don McClure, missionary and superspy, has slipped behind enemy lines and returned to tell the story. The story is that the governor wanted me to sneak into Akobo and retrieve the motorboat that I had left stored there. This motorboat would have been of great help to the Italians, but I could not get to Akobo because the Pibor River had been guarded by two garrisons of soldiers, one just three miles from Akobo. However, early in the month, Captain Alban took his troop of Sudanese soldiers out of Akobo and destroyed both Italian outposts.

The governor came out twice to talk to me about the trip and the importance of rescuing the motorboat and at the same time not allowing our Doleib Hill launch to fall into enemy hands. I made several feinting trips up the river for strategic purposes, and then the governor called one Sunday evening to say that a steamer would be at Doleib Hill within an hour to tow the launch to Nasir. I was then to make a dash from Nasir to Akobo as fast as possible, which was all very well except that I was sick in bed at the time with an infected leg and high fever. However, I felt it was essential that I make the trip when the river seemed to be open. So I got some things ready and piled on the boat when it came. We tied the launch alongside, and I hobbled aboard and went to bed. A British officer named Captain Tiner was in charge of sixty soldiers. We had an uneventful trip to Nasir, save for shooting numerous crocodiles. I was delighted to get my hand and eye in again on the ugly brutes. My leg gradually got well, and I was feeling better.

I arrived at Nasir to find our missionaries there all under the weather. I stayed with them only long enough to get word from Akobo that all was well, so I started up the river that afternoon. I had only three boys with me, because my instructions were to carry only a skeleton crew. My crew was badly frightened and wished they were anywhere else than on the Sobat River. The first Italian post on the Sobat is just seventy miles above Nasir, and our people in Nasir are living in daily dread of an attack. However, we had to sail another thirty miles closer to this post before we came to the mouth of the Pibor River and could turn up along the Sudan-Ethiopia boundary. We took this part of the run at night so we would have less chance of being stopped. I had not the slightest fear that any of my boys would go to sleep at his post as we chugged along.

Before I left Nasir I was supposed to raise a white flag. However, I had forgotten to get one at Doleib Hill, so I borrowed a tablecloth from Blanche Soule. I expect that was the first time in military history that an American ship ever ran through enemy country flying a white tablecloth! Not up to the dignified canons of warfare, but strange to say, it gave us a measure of assurance that we would not be fired upon. Surely no self-respecting military man would waste his ammunition on a boat whose ensign was a tablecloth. And if they tried, they would doubtless be laughing too hard to aim straight. I knew that if I were fired upon, I would not return the fire but would run for it and try to save the launch. I had no intention of taking any man's life even to save my own. We chugged on through the night without any trouble, and with the sunrise we arrived at the mouth of the Akobo River and the Ethiopian boundary. Another three miles and I saw the familiar roofs of our houses at Akobo.

It was a great thrill to see my Anuaks again. A large crowd of people soon gathered, and I spent much of my time relating the events of the past year since I left Akobo and listening to all the tales of woe and sadness that had befallen them in the year. Everywhere people were hungry. I found my houses to be in fairly good shape; no one had been inside the houses since we left even though no door was locked or barred. All the doors were too badly swollen to shut, and I had tied them closed with pieces of string. The string was still intact, and not a thing had been taken. I think that is marvelous in the midst of a people who are hungry and who knew that I had foodstuffs inside the storeroom. I called the people together for a short worship service, and I thanked them for their care of our things. They had even shared their grain with my chickens, and I found a flock of five remaining out of eighteen left behind. The others had died of disease or had been taken by the jackals. I distributed what food I had, and some of the people wept when

I started back for Nasir having spent but one night under my own roof. I hope this war soon ends and I can get back to my Anuaks.

From that part of Sudan that the war hadn't touched, Don wrote,

In the quiet of this evening hour I can scarcely believe that the outside world is so torn and battered as our radio daily proclaims to be the case. All is serene and peaceful here at Doleib Hill, and it taxes my imagination to think of anything else. Today we have had news of bombing in Khartoum. There were three casualties in Omdurman. However, the war does not disturb us in the least, because we all are of the firm opinion that the Lord did not send us to Africa to be killed in this war, and even the Italians can be dissuaded by him. So do not be concerned about us. We are fine. If worse comes to worst and the Sudanese troops are forced to evacuate from Nasir and Malakal, we expect to stay on at our work here as long as the invaders will permit us. What we will do after that is not our worry, since the Lord will again take care of us.[38]

Just now we have more to do here than ever before, and our daily tasks take all our time and attention. Our greatest task is the guidance and discipline of our Shulla Christian leaders. In the last letter I sent home, I included a carbon copy of a letter that I wrote to Mr. Heasty telling of the problem we are having with some of our leaders getting married again. We have been in almost constant prayer for them ever since, but those who were already married are taking no steps to break their relationships with their second wives, and those still making negotiations are continuing to pay sheep and cattle for a second wife. I have talked with them until I started going in circles, but they are determined in their courses. They all feel that they can marry a second time and still live as Christians. Heasty thinks that it is acceptable to employ a man who has two wives, but not to allow him to be an evangelist or a member of the church. As a matter of beginning strategy we will try to discourage second marriages by our new Anuak Christians; but among the older Shulla Christians, second marriages have long been forbidden. For the Anuaks the very thought of refusing a second marriage is a step forward. For the Shullas the thought of accepting a second marriage is a step backward. Obviously it is an act of supreme selfishness for a man to marry a second time when he cannot adequately support his first wife and children.[39]

Jwodha, Heasty's cook, is a perfect example of this very thing. He married again about a year ago and ever since has experienced nothing but dissension in his home and bitterness between himself and his first wife and children. But that is not the worst. A few days ago I was called to the village to see Jwodha's brother and his wives. After I arrived in the village, I was also called in to see Jwodha's sister-in-law and her baby. The mother had been sick for five or six months, ever since the baby was born. When I saw them, I realized they could not live unless they get medical care and better food. I asked them if they had been drinking milk, and the mother said that there was none in the village to drink. They had only two cows, and they were both dry. In that same village, Jwodha's old toothless mother was gradually dying of starvation because she could not eat the coarse food. Several small children were rickety and sickly for lack of milk. Yet only a few months before, Jwodha had sent away seven (!) milk cows to buy his second wife. When faced with these facts, he became very angry and insisted that the cows were his to do with as he pleased. And still he thinks he can live just as fine a Christian life with two wives as with one. It is all eye-wash, and my eyes have been opened to see better and know better.

In spite of this problem, Don was encouraged.

We are having an excellent response from the people these days in preaching to them. We have large crowds in church and also in the villages. Last Sunday I spoke to about 200 in our church here and then went out into the villages and preached to another 300 people. We know that there are some results of our preaching, because people talk about what has been said; frequently when I stop in the same village again, they will ask me about the message of the previous day. I only wish I had more time to get out into villages farther afield. At one service, 36 Shullas were baptized, all of whom had been in training for weeks at daily services. Following the baptismal service, we held communion, and more Christians communed than at any one service we have ever had at Doleib Hill. The following Sunday was equally thrilling when we dedicated another church in the village of Palo and 56 people were baptized. In all, there have been 160 people baptized in the last four communion services, and all of them have undergone a period of training and have publicly denounced the evil practices of their pagan life and declared that they would henceforth live in Christ. Another native church is nearing completion, and a fourth one was started yesterday.

I hold three regular meetings a day and try to preach in one or two others in outlying villages, and now I am also doing translation work in both Shulla and Anuak languages every afternoon. I am afraid that my regular mission work of looking after the property, gardens, and so on has become a sideline and claims my attention only when I seem to have a spare minute. Still, we have an excellent garden. We have beautiful beans, cabbages, beets, carrots, lettuce, and all the fruits and berries we need. Every week I send about 1,500 limes and over 200 pounds of garden stuff to the army officers in Malakal. This is the extent of my war effort, and it is as large a part as I care to have.

Two weeks from now we will hold another communion service and will have approximately 50 ready for baptism, the majority of them being women and girls. It is a joy to see African women assert the dignity to make decisions for themselves. We know they will not marry again. But what we are to do if our Christians become involved in a second marriage through no choice of their own, I have not yet been guided to know. In any case, I keep insisting that the white man's time in Africa is short. Therefore I believe we must crash ahead with our evangelistic task and get out while we still possess the gratitude of African people. If we overstay our welcome, they will kick us out with their curses ringing in our ears. However, most missionaries expect to be here a long time.

Don not only served the Shullas as a missionary, but was frequently called upon to act as a judge. One case involved a dispute about the ownership of a club used during dances. It seems two boys had been at a dance and, because they left after dark, one of them had picked up the wrong stick. A few days later the owner recognized his stick being carried by his friend and demanded its return. The friend admitted that the stick had not belonged to him originally. However, this dancing club had caused him to lose his own because, by picking up the wrong stick, he had left the correct one behind and someone else had walked off with it. Thus he insisted that it was his right to keep the stick that made him lose his own. The original owner saw the logic of this position, but was nevertheless reluctant to surrender his dancing club and asked Don to adjudicate the matter. Don ruled that the stick itself should decide the case of rightful ownership. The two boys recognized the fairness of this procedure and reached agreement on which end of the stick was the head and which the foot. The boys stood apart, facing each other, and Don threw the stick into the air with the understanding that when it fell to the ground, the head of the stick would point to the rightful owner. The head fell pointing to the boy who had taken it and now joyfully claimed it. The original owner ruefully admitted that the cause of justice had been served, and they went off together.

The Shullas still look upon me as being a doctor, and most of the sick in the village will come to me or ask me to go out and see them. I have been going out every day to see one boy who has had tetanus for the last three weeks. In the early stages I felt hopeless, but now it seems that he is getting stronger every day. I feel sure that the Lord will spare him. Two weeks ago Donnie and I went out before church to see the boy, and I found a witchdoctor already on the job. The witchdoctor had cut the boy in small gashes up both arms, across his shoulders, down both sides and legs to his ankles. When I arrived on the scene, he was waving a freshly killed chicken over the boy and allowing the blood to run down over the boy's head and shoulder. All the time the boy was torn with pain, his head drawn back and his back bent in an arch by the tetanus. He was in such pain that he screamed every time they touched him.

I was furious to see the witchdoctor, and I wanted to take his knife and do some cutting on him so he could see how it felt. At least I gave him a tongue-lashing, and he picked up his chicken and left. While I was working on the boy and trying to close my ears to his screams of pain, I saw Donnie's eyes widen in fright. I glanced around behind me and saw a Shulla with a spear poised to plunge into my back. This man is severely mentally retarded, and he thought the white man was torturing the black boy. How was I to explain to him? I stood up slowly, and looking into his eyes as steadily as I could, I said, "I am trying to help the boy." Then I turned back to the boy on the ground, trusting that the Lord would protect me from the spear. He did.

The retarded man muttered for a few minutes and then walked away.

Glenn's special responsibility in the work here is the Boys' School and the bush schools that are attached to it. The school buildings are just next to our house, and the din is terrific. But they are darlings in spite of that! We have been surprised and very much pleased to see the enrollment stay so strong during the year. Usually some of the boys go back to their homes when the grain is ready for eating. For many, school is a good place to be only when there is no grain in the village! Nevertheless, we have been grateful that they have stayed, since they present seventy opportunities to witness for Christ.

The boys board here, but their accommodations are not swank. Indeed, I was a little shocked at the dormitory when I first saw it. It consists of nine, well-built but unmistakably *native* huts! They differ from the average *tukl* in the villages only in their screen windows and real doors. There are no beds for the boys; they all sleep on the floors of the huts. With the school so crowded this year, we have had as many as twelve boys in one hut, but that is nothing unusual for them.

It is only human for us to want to improve their condition and pamper them with some of the comforts that we consider necessities, but there is no point in raising their standard of living far above the standard in the villages. There is nothing more pathetic than a de-tribalized native, and our school program discourages the boys from trying to be very different from their own people. Christianity inevitably makes changes in their lives, and their love of imitation is hard to combat in the matter of clothes and other things. But our purpose is to improve their life without changing them more than is absolutely necessary. We are always disgusted when we see the people changing their dignified Shulla clothes for the shabby shorts and shirts and cast-off helmets that they love. We are especially amused at one of our most lovable schoolboys. He is about six feet, four inches tall and rapidly developing a marvelous physique to match. He has been begging Glenn to give him some work so that he can earn money with which to buy a pair of khaki shorts such as the men—missionaries and government officials—wear as their regular uniform. At least we can sympathize with his desire for different clothes, since the skimpy little cloth provided by the school looks ridiculous on him.

We lost one of our boys recently, and we were sad for days. He was taken by a crocodile while he was bathing in the river, and he drowned. His body was recovered the following day, and we were glad that at least he was not mutilated. It was obvious that his death was caused by drowning. The thought of it horrified us, but it is not an uncommon occurrence here. Glenn had been on his way down to the river to try to get a shot at the croc, which the boys had seen out in the middle of the river, when Olang was taken. The boys say that he fought his way up to the surface twice, and if there had been anyone in the river strong enough to help him, he might have been saved. When it happened, the only boys with him were small, and they were almost scared to death. The crocodile did not appear again for about fifteen minutes, and Glenn got a shot at him then, but missed. Olang was not a Shulla, but an Anuak and a very promising boy.

Don informed his father that the elder McClure's shooting prowess was at last being forgotten by the Shullas. For several years, whenever Don missed an animal or did some poor shooting, the Shullas reminded him that his father never missed, and since the gun he was using belonged to his dad, he ought not to miss either. After Don shot a leopard, his reputation went up several points. Moreover, Don made several good shots on crocodiles. However, a week before, Don had heard hyenas howling across the river. Taking his good friend, Pakwan, his gun, and his flashlight, he started out. Don did not get across until midnight, but before he reached the village he heard dogs barking and knew a hyena was near.

We took a circuit of the villages, and just when we came to the far side, I picked up some eyes about three hundred yards away. I was about to try to get closer, when the eyes started toward us to investigate the light. At least, he came in our direction and the light did not seem to bother him. I was standing ready to shoot as the eyes came on and on, until finally we could make out the form of the animal and I saw that it was a fine, big hyena. It did not seem to know that we were watching it, and since the wind was toward us, it could not smell us. On it walked, and when it was about fifty yards away, Pakwan began to get nervous and whispered, "Shoot, shoot," but I wanted to see just what it would do, so I waited a bit longer. Then the first thing I knew, Pakwan, who was carrying my shotgun, stuck it out over my shoulder within six inches of my ear. I grabbed the gun and pushed it down, but Pakwan was so excited that he did not know what he was doing. Fortunately I had the safety on, which he did not know how to work, or the gun would have gone off in his hands.

All that fuss disturbed the hyena, and it stopped and was very nervously looking this way and sniffing the air. Lest it get away, I took careful aim and pulled the trigger. There was a thud as the bullet struck it, and the hyena hunched himself up like a fighting cat, but with his head almost touching the ground, and never moved. Knowing that he was hit hard, I took the shotgun and started for him. But our movement brought him to life again, and he started off at a run. Quickly I grabbed the rifle and ran after him. Pakwan was less handicapped with clothes than I, so he ran on ahead and soon came up on the hyena lying down. Pakwan tried the shotgun again, and this time in my haste I had not put it on safety, so he pulled both barrels, missing the animal by yards, but knocked some skin off his own chin because he held the gun too high. The hyena once more made a supreme effort and started to run. I stopped running long enough to get another crack at it, and this time shot it right through the body from the hip to its front shoulder. Then it was all over except the shouting. And the Shullas who poured out of the village close by did plenty of that. This hyena was not nearly so large as the first one I shot, but had a much more beautiful hide. It is light in color and spotted like a leopard. I will send both hyenas home and see which one Mother wants to use as her winter coat.

Breakfast was the meal Don enjoyed most, and he liked to linger over it. The edge of this pleasure was taken away, however, because every day he knew there would be twelve to twenty people sitting outside the back door waiting patiently for him to finish morning prayers with his family and those who worked in the house. When his sense of duty overcame his enjoyment of the world's finest coffee, Don went out to sit on the ground among the people and do what he could to help.

The first man I talked to is a poor halfwit who has no home and simply wanders about the country begging food wherever he can. People will give him a meal, but nothing else, and then they drive him away. He was naked and begging a cloth. Even though our cloth is almost worth its weight in gold these days, I gave him two yards.

The second seeker needed tax money. The police were in his village, and unless he could dig up twenty piasters (one dollar) before noon he would be arrested and taken away. He did not want to beg the money, but merely borrow it. As security he had brought his fine spear, which he promised to redeem as soon as he could find the money. I looked around at the other faces in the circle and saw four or five other men reach for their spears to make the same plea, and in one case a string of beads of no real value but precious to the owner. I asked how many there were and found that six needed tax money today. I gave them the money and took their collateral, knowing that at some time, perhaps a month or a year hence, they would come in to claim them. As a pawnbroker I always lose, because I charge no interest and invariably, within a short period, one of them will return to borrow his own spear to go to a wedding or a funeral or a dance, and if, in a moment of weakness, I let the chap have his spear, he promptly forgets to bring it back and considers the debt canceled.

After dealing with four or five others, I noticed a poor old woman sitting in the shade of our woodshed and quietly moaning to herself. After I greeted her, she dropped her cloth off her shoulder and showed me her back. It was raised up in huge welts, and the skin was broken in several places. Her daughter is one of our Christian girls, and the father had sent this girl off to marry a scoundrel who was three times her age, already had four wives, and a bad reputation for mistreating them. Previously I had discovered her chained in her husband's village, and when I cut the chains off her hands and feet, she ran away from him. After three months, her brother found her and forced her to go back to this despicable man. When her mother resisted sending her daughter back, the son took a cow rope and beat his own mother! Women have no rights and no respect in this society, and we are determined to change that situation. We have made a start.

Never before have we had a Christian wedding at Doleib Hill. We have talked of it for years, but it was such a big step in the lives of the Shulla people that it was not to be taken lightly. When one considers that heretofore a man has always bought his wife as he would buy a sheep or a cow and after the purchase price was paid she became his property, you can begin to imagine what a tremendous step it is for a woman to say, "I take thee to be my husband." Women have never taken anything before but a beating or curses and hard work.

I admit I was a bit dubious about how the men would take my proposals for a Christian wedding, so I chose the men very carefully and, calling them in, I explained what I thought a Christian wedding should mean to them and their families. To my great joy, all of them were enthusiastic and said they had wanted such a wedding for many years because they felt that it was the first step after conversion toward the establishment of a Christian home. I quite agreed with them. It is wonderful how God prepares the hearts of his people. Then we called in their wives and again talked it over. The wives were very hesitant at first until they saw the eagerness of their husbands. The men urged their wives to make this great step and promised to help all they possibly could toward establishing truly Christian homes.

The men I had chosen were our ordained elders. They naturally should take leadership in any such movement, and they proved their worth and justified our faith in them when they so quickly grasped the great significance of Christian marriages for them and their people and willingly accepted whatever scorn and laughter would come to them from their fellow tribesmen. It was not easy for these men because, although they had once cut themselves off from any thoughts of taking second wives when they were ordained, their friends had not given up the idea for them. They thought that when the opportunity offered itself, these elders would marry again. But now they were about to take a further step and build an additional barrier to a second marriage, and they did it joyously.

The ceremony was very simple. I copied it after our own marriage service with a few variations. For example, the Shullas do not exchange rings. Then I translated the service into their language. Had I been given more time, I might have worked out something more creative and more suited to the context of

Shulla life. That may come later as we feel our way along. They
all wore the same costumes, a simple white cloth tied across the
shoulder and draped down across the body, as all Shullas wear
them. These wedding garments would not cost much more than
a dollar each and, strangely enough, the pastor furnished the
festal attire. Later, as others request Christian weddings, I will
encourage them to make gifts to the church.

Don was pleased that the first Shulla Christian wedding coincided
with a visit to Doleib Hill by the Reverend Dr. Neal McClanahan of
the American Mission in Egypt. Don thought of McClanahan as an
ideal missionary and was delighted that he could take part in this
important event.

On the afternoon of the wedding service the church was filled
with curious people. The six men and their wives, some of
whom had been married with pagan rites twenty years before,
stood side by side in front of the people. After Dr. McClanahan
addressed them for a few minutes, myself translating, I asked
them one by one to take the Christian marriage vows. Earlier,
when I suggested that they hold each other's hands while they
exchanged vows, they laughed. No Shulla husband and wife
had ever held hands before. It was a thrill of my young life when
I heard a Shulla woman say, "I take thee, La [her husband
already], to be my Christian husband" and then promise to
remain true to him until death. I feel it was the greatest forward
step we have ever taken in our work among the Shulla people,
and I am confident these six couples will not fail us.

After the wedding service we all went to our house and had
a wedding feast of meat and rice served in a huge cauldron.
Everyone sat on the floor of the veranda, and each family had a
common bowl, and it was the first time some of the husbands
and wives had ever eaten a meal together! Usually the wife
prepares the food and then the husband eats and what is left the
wife eats alone. She does not dare to place her hand in the same
bowl with her husband; according to Shulla custom, that would
make her equal with him. But as the first step toward a Christian
marriage, I insisted that they eat together. The women were
very hesitant at first, but soon entered into the spirit of the
event, and we had a grand time. I nearly burst with joy as I ate
with each family in turn and had to take my share from each

bowl. It was a bit strange to have newly married couples eating with their children already on the scene. However, we saw nothing incongruous about that. Fifty years from now it may be strange for them to have their children before marriage, but it is the expected thing now among the Shullas.

▼▲▼

At this time, home life for the McClures included the care of two Shulla babies that Lyda had assumed. The older one was not eating, probably because she was getting teeth. The second baby was gaining weight, although the doctor in Malakal had said there was little hope that she would live. Lyda had been afraid that the baby would die on her hands, but was glad to show the doctor that she knew something that he did not when it came to caring for babies. The babies began to thrive as soon as they were over their sores and infections, and the Shullas marveled that the babies were alive at all; they came from far and near to look at them. It seemed to Lyda that the babies had brought the Shullas closer to the missionaries. Shulla life was so hard and short that none of them would attempt to care for someone else's baby. They would just let the baby die, especially if it was a girl.

Three weeks ago a grandmother brought us a six-day-old baby girl and told us that the mother had died in childbirth and the father had thrown the baby away. Well, Lyda could not possibly manage another baby in the house, for in addition to our three children, she already had two Shulla babies. Therefore we made plans for the grandmother to live in a house on the mission, and Lyda would show her how to care for the baby and would prepare its food. The grandmother refused to stay at first, because her village was so far away and she said there were other children for her to look after at home. Moreover, she insisted that she did not want the little baby anyway and had brought her in to give to us and we could raise her. That would have been fine for a few years until the child could do some work about the house and the grandfather decided to start negotiations for her marriage. Then they would come in and claim this girl and take her without a word of appreciation to us for our care. Thus we insisted that the grandmother stay and care for the baby. She did so very grudgingly and complained every day.

After two weeks, the baby took sick and could not take any food. She began to spit up and pass horrible-looking, black stuff. Lyda brought the baby into our house and gave her constant care, day and night, but to no avail. We cannot prove it, but we believe that the grandmother killed the baby by feeding it dirt or some poison weed. This is the first baby Lyda has lost in all the dozens she has helped pull through their early months. She is now feeding three other Shulla babies in addition to the pair we have living with us.

▼▲▼

One day the district commissioner and his wife dropped in unannounced for tea. It was soon after Don had gone out to shoot some crocodiles that had been taking sheep and cattle in the neighborhood. One of the crocodiles measured eighteen feet and two inches and weighed about half a ton. On the way back to the house, Don shot two gazelles and carried them across his bicycle until he ran over some thorns and got punctures in his tires. Leaving the bike in the forest, he carried one animal while Pakwan carried the other.

I got home just at dark, covered with blood from head to foot. As I came in, I heard strange voices on the veranda, and I tried to slip off to the bathroom to clean up. But I was told that the district commissioner was waiting to see me and wanted to get started back to Malakal right away. I walked in on them just as I was—covered with blood. They did not stay long.

That evening, just as the children were going to bed, Marghi stepped on a big scorpion that curled up its tail and stung her between two toes. Her scream sent chills up and down my spine, and although I was outside taking care of a sick Arab I had housed in my bookroom, I did not need to be told what had happened. I ran to the house and in a few seconds had given her an injection of novocaine. This gave her some relief for a while, but soon the pain came back with renewed vigor, and since I did not want to give her too much novocaine, there was nothing to do but let her suffer. We sat up with her until midnight, and then her weariness became greater than the pain and she dropped off to sleep. She woke up several times during the night, crying with pain. There was little we could do but comfort her and quiet her until she fell asleep again.

The pain of a scorpion is the most exquisite and excruciating experience one can have. It feels like a hot coal, together with a stabbing needle and a severe pinch, and the pain quickly races to the groin or armpit and then into the stomach and heart. Except with the largest scorpions, the heart pain ceases after half an hour, then gradually, hour by hour, the pain recedes from the stomach, the groin, upper leg, knee joints, calf, ankle, foot, and finally the local sting. But this takes twenty-four to thirty hours, and during all that time the local sting does not diminish one bit in severity. At times one's nerve breaks down and there is a crying spell that seems to relieve pain, but it quickly builds up again. The worst feature of these houses of ours is that the grass roofs harbor scorpions, and it is impossible to get rid of them without burning down the house. After Marghi was stung last night, I made an intensive search and found sixteen scorpions! This evening we have killed five on the floor. If we used great care we would never be stung, but the children will run about in their bare feet and step on them. All of us except Donnie have had our baptism by the fiery insects. He seems to lead a charmed life.

▼ The Witchdoctors

IN MANY AFRICAN societies the witchdoctor has been a central figure for generations, both admired and feared for his power. Believed able to affect a person's physical and spiritual welfare, the witchdoctors inevitably came to resent and oppose the teaching presented by Christian missionaries. The struggle between them for the minds of the Shulla people was intense and often bitter. Thus Don McClure wrote,

One morning a few weeks ago, I went out to the workshop behind the house to make some repairs to the windmill pump. I took my .22 rifle with me to shoot any stray dogs that might drift into the compound. In recent weeks I have seen three children die in terrible, terrible agony from hydrophobia. All of them had their ears cut by the witchdoctors to keep them from becoming dogs, and it was so awful I vowed I would shoot every dog I saw. Ours was the first to go, and I have already shot seventeen others. So I always carry my rifle.

As I worked at the bench, several schoolboys crowded around La Amoleker. We were memorizing some Bible verses just recently translated, and as we talked and joked together, Dak Nyding walked through the compound and came over to see what we were doing. I glanced up, greeted him, and then noticed that he was wearing all the charms and bangles of a witchdoctor. Witchdoctors' beads and little bags of charms and bones are always distinctive, and they wear them on leather thongs around their necks. When I saw these charms on Dak, I was amazed to realize that he had become a witchdoctor, because we had been hunting together a few days before and I knew he was not a witchdoctor then. "Are you a witchdoctor,

Dak?" I asked him. "Yes, last week I became a witchdoctor." Dak then told me about the fight they had in the village. I already knew about the fight because I had bandaged his head when they brought him in. In fact, he still had the bandages just over his ear. Dak claimed that he had been killed in that fight and when he became alive again he was no longer Dak, but his name had been changed to "Badeng."

The point is, the Shullas believe that when anyone is knocked out or is unconscious for a few minutes or longer, his spirit leaves his body because he appears lifeless. If he recovers from this experience, whether it is of sickness, drowning, or a club wound, then Jwok must have sent him a new spirit. According to Dak, he now had the power to cure sickness by driving out the evil spirits. Moreover, he could make the rains come and put a charm on warriors when they go out to fight so that the spears of the enemy could not kill them. He could also put a curse on the spears so they could not hit what they are thrown at.

It occurred to me that I could easily demonstrate that Dak had no power. Thus I handed him my .22 rifle and said, "Here is my spear. Put a curse on it and see if you can charm it so that I cannot hit a target." Dak pushed my rifle aside and refused to be enticed into a trial of strength. I kept urging him. The schoolboys joined in, and La Amoleker said, "If you refuse to charm the spear-that-spits-fire, it is proof that you have no power to curse or charm or cure." The two men were about the same age, but La was a little older and had some education, so he was recognized as having greater authority. Thus his challenge was almost a command to the witchdoctor.

As they faced each other, I seemed to see a gleam come into Dak's eyes, and I should have been forewarned. Suddenly he grabbed the gun and waved me away because he did not want me to see what he would do. I started to leave, but I warned him that he could not tamper with the "eye," i.e., the sights of the gun. Aside from that he was at liberty to do anything he wished. After a long twenty minutes I was called back. The charming was over and the real test was about to begin. I examined the sights to make sure they had not been tampered with, and throwing a shell into the chamber, I confidently turned to Dak and asked, "What do you want me to hit?"—assuming that he would point out one of the many trees within a hundred yards of us and I would easily and quickly disprove his power to enchant. To my consternation, he pointed to a small dove sitting on the topmost branch of a tall eucalyptus tree slowly swaying in the wind. I pointed out to Dak that it would prove nothing if I missed a target so small, since I could not hit it with any rifle, charmed or uncharmed. I told him to pick out a nice big tree nearby and that would be a real test. If I missed the tree, everyone who knew me would know it was not accidental.

Dak would not change the target and, in suggesting that he should, I had already lost some credit with the schoolboys. I realized that I had been outsmarted and threatened to shoot at a tree anyway to prove that the rifle was all right, but Dak said he had only charmed the rifle against the dove on top of the tree. I had a real problem. I was sure to miss, and I was certainly going to be laughed at. Just then one of the schoolboys said, ''You must be afraid of Badeng's power!'' Of course, I was not afraid of Dak's power; I was afraid of my weakness. I had been given an impossible shot well beyond the skill of a superb marksman. And I did not want to be embarrassed in the eyes of our schoolboys and our Christian teacher. But as soon as that little boy's words hit me, I recognized that fear for what it was and the whole picture of our work swept over me.

For years we missionaries had been afraid of witchdoctors. We were not personally afraid of their powers or any ability to put a curse upon us, but we were afraid to stand boldly and confidently in the power of the true God. We had tried to placate these powerful men and attempted to win their friendship. We had given and accepted gifts from them and in every way made the native people believe we were their friends. But all this time the witchdoctors were working behind our backs among the people, cutting the ground from beneath our feet. They were turning the people away from the teaching of the gospel, and we were making practically no progress. We had been trying to win them with affection, kidding ourselves that it was the Christian approach. Compromise is a dangerous game to play with the powers of darkness.

With those young black boys around me, these thoughts raced across my mind, and there surged into my shamed heart an overwhelming conviction of God's power. Did I not stand in the strength of his might? My heart was gripped with the confidence that I could do all things through Jesus Christ who strengthened me. For the first time in my life I believed those words with absolute conviction.

I picked up the rifle, rested it against the side of the workshop, took aim at that swaying dove, and pulled the trigger. God sped that bullet straight at the little bird, which immediately fluttered to the ground. As the schoolboys whooped in glee and ran triumphantly to pick it up, I realized what this meant to them. Their bonds of fearful loyalty to witchcraft had been broken. That God-guided bullet had cut clear through the whole hellish system of Shulla superstition. The boys did not realize fully what it meant, but they had an inkling, and their little hearts rejoiced with me in the downfall of Badeng. Without another word I grabbed the tinshears lying on the workbench. Reaching out, I caught hold of the dozen or more leather thongs around Dak's neck. He thought I was about to kill him, for he cringed in terror and begged for mercy. I merely cut off the charms and bags of bones and threw them to the ground. Then I ordered Dak off the mission, never to come back again as a witchdoctor. As he ran away, I called after him that he was also never to come near one of our Christians again.

As the witchdoctor ran away, La Amoleker grasped my hand and said, with tears running down his face, "Why didn't we do this years ago? It would have saved many, many of my people from pain, fear, and death. God has given us new life this day!" I was never so humbled in all my life as at that moment when I was brought to a full consciousness of the power of God. I was ashamed that it had to come to me through a little Shulla boy of eight or nine years and a young teacher who had known the Lord only a few years. I went to Africa to teach them about Jesus Christ, but I am the one who had to learn what it meant to walk with the Lord in complete trust and faith.

The dramatic narrative of the witchdoctor Dak Nyding was told often by Don as he preached in America, but the story that it serves to introduce is even more remarkable.

Don had been treating a boy in a nearby village for pneumonia. Several days before, the boy had been at death's door. His family called in a witchdoctor to make a sacrifice, but the witchdoctor refused to come, insisting that Don had cursed the boy and he would surely die. Nevertheless, when the boy began to get well, the witchdoctor did come. One evening he made a sacrifice, said his incantations, and sprinkled the boy's body with the blood of the sacrifice. To drive the evil spirits out of the lad's pain-racked body, the witchdoctor then took a red-hot coal from the fire and laid it on the boy's chest. While four men held the lad on his back, the witchdoctor pressed the coal into the flesh and bone until the hot coal was dead and cold. When the boy fainted from the unbearable pain, it was taken as a sign that the evil spirit had left his body and he would get well.

Word of this treatment came to Don immediately after the witchdoctor departed, and he called a council of war with La Amoleker and a couple of other Christian leaders.

I asked them what we should do, and they all suggested that we go and see for ourselves what had happened. When we got to the village, I had to enter the little mud and grass hut on my hands and knees because the door was only two feet high and I saw all around the signs of the sacrifice. Blood had been sprinkled on the mud above the doorway; bones and charms were hanging in a tree outside the hut; more bones were hanging from the roof of the hut. The fresh mound of earth just inside the doorway indicated where a sheep's head had been buried. As I took the lad's feverish hand in mine, I saw the dried blood caked all over his body and a huge, gaping hole in his chest where the skin and flesh had been burned away down to the bone. The poor boy moaned and tossed deliriously in his awful pain as he lay there on the bare, hard dirt floor.

I was livid and threatened the family with all sorts of dire punishments unless they told me who the witchdoctor was and where he lived. I was determined to find the man and whip him publicly, but everyone was afraid to mention his name out of fear that he would put a terrible curse on them. I walked out of the village in a holy ferocity and refused to help them or even to treat the sick boy until I had the witchdoctor's name. That evening the love and compassion of the Lord overcame my anger, so I went back and did what I could to make the lad comfortable and left some medicine for him. The next day word came to me that the witchdoctor had returned to the village, taken off the bandages, thrown away the pills I had left for the boy, and warned the people that I should not be allowed back in the hut or the boy would die.

I placed a lookout in the village to let me know when the witchdoctor came back. I almost prayed that he would not come back, for by that time my savage anger had cooled. I felt mostly the pity that another young African was dying because of his people's superstition. I did not know what we were going to do if we caught the witchdoctor. The next evening my spy came running in and said the witchdoctor was in the village. I sent for La, and together we started for the village. As we ran past another teacher's hut, La called to him to join us. I still did not know what we would do when we confronted the witchdoctor. Would we take his charms? Would we tie him up and publicly denounce him? Would we whip him, inflicting some of the pain he had given to the boy? Would we turn him over to the government authorities and lodge some charge against him? Since most British officials refuse to interfere in any native religious rites, I quickly cast aside this latter thought. But what were we going to do when we arrived?

Before entering the village, indeed before the villagers knew we were near, the three of us knelt together in the tall grass for prayer. As we rose to our feet I still did not know what was to be done. But the Lord had taken care of that decision in another way. La laid his hand on my arm and looked earnestly at me. "You leave this to us. It is better that we do what has to be done. It will have more effect on our people." I was astounded. No Shulla in all the history of the tribe had ever laid hands on a witchdoctor. I was afraid that they might just sit down with him and spend endless hours in palaver without getting anywhere. I felt the time for talk was over and now was the time for action. "Well, La," I asked, "what will you do?" His reply has been the guiding principle of my life in Africa ever since: "You have shown us the Way," he said. "Let us follow it on our own."

As we hurried into the village, the witchdoctor ran out the other side and the two young teachers tore out after him. They were without weapons (which in itself was very strange, for never before had I seen a Shulla leave his house without a club or a spear in his hand), and the witchdoctor had both a club and a spear. As the teachers drew near him, he turned and hurled his spear with all his strength full at La's chest. La sidestepped the spear, which struck the ground. La pounced on it and continued the chase. Being much younger than the witchdoctor, the men soon overtook him and a fierce, if uneven, fight took place, with the whole village as witness. The teachers quickly took his murderous club. They tore off his charms and beads, stripped him of his bit of cloth, and then at the point of his own spear drove him back through the village naked, to shame and discredit him in the eyes of the people.

As the witchdoctor stumbled toward the village with that spear prodding him from behind, his curses were such that all the people covered their heads and faces, running to their huts for fear that some of the curses should fall on them. His language was so hot that I almost expected to see the grass roofs of the houses burst into flames. The witchdoctor declared that within three months all of us would be dead, but the Christian teachers, oblivious to his curses, forced him to stand in the middle of the village and promise never to come back to touch one of my patients again. With a final prod of the spear they sent him on his way, still naked and stripped of all the badges of his witchcraft. The villagers gradually crept trembling out of their huts to gather around La, to touch him reverently as a being with powers greater than a witchdoctor.

La's family did not have the same fearless attitude. They were terrified for themselves and for him. They begged him to go to other witchdoctors to have these curses taken off and his body sprinkled with the blood of sacrifice. His uncle even offered to give a bull for the sacrifice, which is done only when there is the greatest urgency; usually they kill a chicken or a goat for a blood sacrifice. La refused, but his family kept pressing him to do something about the curses. "I will do something," he said, "I will show you that I am not afraid of a witchdoctor with all his curses and charms. I will go and live with him to prove that I am not afraid and that he has no power over me."

La's family and friends, even more frantic, begged him not to do anything so foolish or rash. They believed that he was throwing his life away, that he would never come out of the witchdoctor's village alive. But La went. That took a kind of spiritual and physical courage that few of us possess. I would not have wished to go into the home of a man whom I had beaten and stripped and shamed before all his own people and who had threatened me with death, who had placed a terrible curse upon my head, declaring that I would die within three months of a horrible disease. I would have been afraid to go, and my family would have been afraid for me to go. But La went. What happened today is the direct result of his Christian courage.

Today hundreds and hundreds of people came in from all the villages round about. The church was crowded to overflowing, and many had to stand outside. As I waited at the front of the church for the people to come in, suddenly there was a stir of excitement. A lane opened up from the back for La Amoleker and Kaimybek, who was the most renowned and feared witchdoctor in all this country. He has been an enemy of this mission for forty years and, living close by at one time or another, he had cursed every missionary who ever came to Doleib Hill. He took credit for all the sickness and death around this place and claimed to have driven one family after another back to America.

The people parted as if by magic. No one wanted to touch the old man as La led him up to where I stood, holding him affectionately by the arm. Three men followed, carrying baskets of the old chap's charms and signs of his witchcraft. These were laid in front of the pulpit. The silence was intense. The old witchdoctor leaned on a tall staff, shaking as he tried to control his voice, to speak to his own people. We waited for what seemed to be an age before he spoke.

"Friends," he said, "I have lied to you and cheated you and robbed you for many years. I have even caused the death of some of your friends and mine." The tears streamed down his face as he bowed his head. Then he looked up with a radiance on his face and a wonderful new joy shining from his eyes. "I cannot undo the past. But I want to do something for you that I wish someone had done for me many years ago; I want to tell you about the joy I have found in Jesus Christ and how he has given me a peace that I have never known."

There are hundreds of Shullas who want to become Christians, but they are too afraid of the curse of the witchdoctors, whose powers over these people is unbelievable to a foreigner. When Kaimybek publicly laid bare his whole life, confessed his sins, and exposed all witchcraft as a fraud, it may have been the beginning of the end of witchcraft among the Shullas. All this came about because of the incredible courage of La Amoleker, who has not been a Christian very long himself. Kaimybek had allowed La to enter his house, planning to kill him in revenge while he slept. However, since Kaimybek could not understand La's calm fearlessness, he became afraid to touch him, and gradually La led Kaimybek to a knowledge of the Lord Jesus Christ.

From birth Kaimybek had been badly crippled with a deformed foot and humped back. The people said he was not normal, and thus even as a small boy he had been forced to practice witchcraft in order to eat.[40] When to become a Christian Kaimybek gave up his only means of earning a livelihood, the little church felt obligated to help support him, since he was now one of them. Don bought all the baskets and rope that Kaimybek had learned to make, but this would not entirely support him, and occasionally Kaimybek came to Don to ask for an advance of grain to tide him over until he finished his next basket.

▼ Famine Relief

IN 1941 A PATRIOT ARMY of British, French, Kenyan, South African, Australian, and Ethiopian volunteers recaptured Addis Ababa from the Italians and restored Haile Selassie to the Ethiopian throne. This army was commanded by the fascinating and wildly eccentric Orde Wingate, who, according to his biographer, preferred to brush himself all over with a toothbrush rather than take a bath. He "was also apt to receive visitors to his room completely naked, except for the alarm clock strapped on his finger." Before the patriot army fought its last battle with the Italians in Ethiopia, Wingate was recalled to Cairo and went on to die in Burma. Haile Selassie expressed his gratitude to Wingate by becoming the godfather of Wingate's only son.[41]

During the time he spent in Sudan, Haile Selassie came to a full stop in Khartoum when some problem developed with his chauffeur-driven automobile. No one in his entourage could start the car, and just at that moment the Reverend Don McClure happened to drive by in a Model T Ford and solved the difficulty by driving His Imperial Majesty to his appointment. Don was always delighted to help anyone in trouble, and while he respected the imperial office, he was absolutely certain that he was in the service of a Lord who outranked this emperor and all other monarchs.

By this time the war, as it directly affected that part of Africa, was over and Don and his family were finally allowed to return to the Anuaks at Akobo.

We are well on our way toward getting packed for Akobo. This is not as easy as it sounds, for not only do we have all our personal and household effects to pack, but we also have an entire mission to pack again. Everything has to go back in one trip. In addition, we have a vegetable and flower garden to

199

move with us and a young fruit orchard all ready to plant. We have planted some vegetables and have hundreds of flowers and flower roots in boxes and tins. We have thirty-one young orange, grapefruit, and lime trees ready to go. We planted a lot of trees when we were at Akobo in 1938 but, coupled with neglect, the goats and cattle roamed at will over our place, so very little is left. It is heartbreaking to see so much work disappear so quickly, but in a year or two we will have things in shape once more. We are eager to get started and will enjoy the hard work that is always the price of beginning anew.

We had a big time this evening. About 4:30, we heard the shrill sound of mourning cries coming from the nearby village of Palo. For a moment I wondered who was dead; I had not heard of anyone being seriously ill. But as the sound grew nearer, I could hear the tooting of horns and the sound of dancing mingling with the mourning cries, and then I realized the women were coming here to bid us farewell. There were hundreds of women, and each of them was dressed up in a dancing costume usually worn by the men. Some carried spears, and some were shouting at the top of their voices and dancing wildly as they do at the death of some village chief. When they reached the mission, they all stopped their shouting and began to sing a song composed for the occasion.

They marched up to our house and called for me to come and greet them. I went out and sat on the ground in the middle while they milled around and sang their song and shrilled their mourning cry. After a bit of this I left to get my camera, and when I reappeared they shouted all the louder. They seemed to enjoy having their pictures taken and gave us a good show. It was all very nice and thoughtful of them except for one thing—and it was a considerable joker, too—I was expected to give them a bull as a parting gift; nor would they leave until they had the bull. I did not have a bull tied in any convenient place to turn over to them, so after an hour or so of their singing, during which they sang their song over and over again, I finally asked them to sit down. I made them a short speech, telling them how much I appreciated their "mourning" for me, but that I was still very much alive and, although we would be some distance from them, yet I would see them frequently. I had no bull to give them, but promised that if they returned another day, I would have one ready. That means I must go out and buy a bull somewhere.

The song they sang was anything but pretty, although if one could believe them, it was very flattering. It ran something like this:

Jaldwong Odon [meaning me] is going to faraway lands,
He is deserting his Shulla friends and we shall all die.
The Foreigner is taking him away, he who is our father;
The Foreigner is taking him away, he who is our
    mother;
There is no one who will save us now.
Jaldwong Odon has saved us in times of hunger;
Jaldwong Odon has saved us in times of danger;
Jaldwong Odon has saved us in times of sickness;
He has given us back our babies when they die.
There is no one now who will save us.
Jaldwong Odon has been like a god to us.
He is like the Great God himself—
He is our king and our Nyikang [the Shulla ancestor];
He is our teacher and our savior;
Now he is going far away to a far land,
And there is no one to help us.

The first verse makes my gender a bit doubtful, and the last verse borders on blasphemy, but it is all very heartening and comforting to know that my years at Doleib Hill have not been wasted and that there will be a few who will miss me, even if only when they are hungry. I have heard rumors that the chiefs of the district are going to hold a meeting to protest my going, and they will send a messenger to the Shulla king asking him to send in a petition to "the Foreigner" asking him to require me to stay. Their feelings toward us make it all the more difficult for us to leave, but leave we must and that right soon.

I have just learned that before the war Mr. Heasty granted permission to the Sudan Interior Mission to send two missionaries to Akobo to study the Anuak language. These missionaries went up, built a house about a mile from our place, and expected to settle in for a long stay. When our field representative from America heard about this situation, he vetoed that permission and ordered the Sudan Interior Mission people out of the Anuak field. I quite agree. There is too much work to do in Africa for one group to duplicate what another is doing. I will have to pay the Sudan Interior Mission for the house they erected, and that will be a pleasure. I was wondering how I could possibly get another house built before our linguist and his family arrive, and the Lord has already built one for us. It will be a great help to have this extra house and will save me a lot of time.

Traveling upriver on a steamer to Akobo, Lyda noticed that the Anuaks on the boat gathered the grain that spilled from a pigeon cage. These seeds were then cooked and eaten. This was the McClures' first indication that the Anuak people were starving and that their most immediate and urgent task upon resuming the Anuak project would be famine relief. Previously Don had sent a couple of workers on ahead to organize the making of bricks for the anticipated repairs to his houses; when he arrived he found only a few hundred bricks rather than the thousands he had expected. At once he sent out for workmen and a few turned up, but they were so thin and weak that they did not have the strength to work.

We have landed in the midst of a starving people who have nowhere to turn. They have no voice to reach the ear of the world and for centuries have lived and died in miserable poverty and isolation. Plagues of rats and locusts destroyed last year's crops, and for months the people in this area have been living on fish and herbs. Many of the older people have quite literally starved to death, and the others survived only because they were able to spear enough fish to keep alive. Now that the river is rising, there will be no more fish, and I do not know what they will do for food.

Many are dying all around us, and stories of desperate hunger have been coming in to us. I heard this one today. One afternoon a man from a nearby village left his fellow sufferers sitting in the shade of the empty cattle barn and, taking his dog, started out presumably to hunt for some wild animal. Later in the evening he came back to the village without his dog and with a curious bulge in his stomach region where once had been a hollow and aching void. He sat down among the men and, although all of them wanted to know what he had eaten, none of them dared to ask him, because eating a dog is thought to be worse than death since the Anuaks believe their ancestors reappear in their dogs. They will eat crocodile and lizards and rats happily, but no matter how hungry an Anuak gets, he will never, until now, eat a dog. Well, this chap had not been long in the village until he got sick from eating so much meat on an empty stomach, and soon he emptied the contents of his stomach on the ground. Those poor devils in the village did not stop to ask what kind of meat he had eaten. They grabbed at the unchewed chunks he had vomited, and the dog was eaten a second time.

It is not funny, because most of the Anuaks had bartered the last thing of any value that they possessed weeks before, eaten their last cow or sheep, hunted the wild animals out of the area, combed the river for fish, searched the woods for edible roots, and still they were starving. Many of them are too weak to make any further effort. There comes a time when it is easier to starve to death than to search for food in a barren country. Today I got up at five o'clock for a quiet hour of worship, but I could hear the subdued voices of hungry people sitting outside in the darkness hoping for some food. Some of them have been here since yesterday morning, when I gave them what grain I had. I suppose they will stay here until the famine is over, because I do not have the heart to send them away to their villages where there is no food. I have given out a hundred bushels of grain, and Lyda has been feeding babies; but there are scores of people sitting about, including old folks lying under the trees, too weak to move off home. My food sticks in my throat when I try to eat, and yet everything we brought with us would not feed these people for a single day. When I go outside, men and women throw themselves on the ground, clutching my hands and feet and begging for what I do not have.

But I was determined that no more Anuaks would starve to death while I had one dime to rub against another. Fortunately there was sufficient grain in the government storehouses, but there was no provision to take care of people who could not pay for it. The Anuaks had nothing left except the utensils and fittings of their miserable, poor houses, and neither the government nor the Arab merchants would accept such things as payment. Women came in and offered their cooking pots for grain and then asked to borrow them back so they could cook the grain. They brought their hoes and spears, their sleeping skins and beads, their rope, wire earrings, charcoal, and even their few clothes. One woman sat here for two days insisting that I buy her dying baby girl in exchange for grain.

The Anuaks need food now—not after I have found sufficient money to pay for it. Thus I pledged my whole year's salary to purchase grain for them; but because it would take some time for the grain to be delivered by steamer, I was forced to drive to Malakal myself, get a truckload of grain, and start back to Akobo. When I got back I faced a heartbreaking scene. Hearing that I had returned, dozens of people came crowding in and begging for food, many of them prostrate on their faces and groveling in the dirt. I had only forty bushels, and that would not go very far, so I selected some of the older people and gave them grain, reserving the rest for my workmen. But I gave each man and woman at least some grain and sent them home to prepare and eat it. The next day they were all back and willing to work for food, but it was pitiful to watch them. A man would take a few strokes with a pick or throw a shovelful of sand and then have to sit down and pant for breath. I let them work about an hour and sent them all home again. The next day they worked a little longer. By the end of the week they could work for almost three hours without complete exhaustion. I was perplexed how to pay them for the work without money, but they soon settled that problem by refusing all money and begging for more grain. My supply was running low, and there was nothing for it but to make another trip to Malakal. Again I started back at night and got home early next morning. The Lord must have been with me on all these trips, because I was traveling without a spare tire and over terrible roads, yet not once did I have any trouble.

Again I started back to Malakal on the same day as I arrived home, but this time I could not drive through, because my eyes would not stay open. Not only had I been working from five in the morning until dark, but I had been doing all my driving at night to save daylight and tires, and I was beginning to feel groggy. However, I got into Akobo by noon, and before evening almost all of my grain was gone again and I had not scratched the surface of the needs. Yet I stayed on another week, trying desperately to get our houses rebuilt with new walls and new grass roofs before the rains came. Finally, the hunger of the people forced me again to go for more grain, and I made a third trip.

When the Anuaks were able to pay for grain, I accepted whatever they offered. In exchange I took 375 animal skins, mats, and even a few cooking pots when I knew there were others in the village. I am sure there are places in Europe where the people are in more desperate straits than the Nuer and Anuak people here; but none are in more danger of starving to death. The other day a tall, naked Nuer walked through the village, and Donnie said, "Look, Daddy, that man has no tummy." Sure enough, his skin seemed to be sticking to his backbone, leaving a great hollow where his stomach should be.

My budget is small in the first place, and there is no provision for a massive famine-relief campaign. In addition to my salary I have been using, and expect to continue to use, all the money that has come to me directly as special gifts to buy food for the Anuaks. How can we eat when there are thousands starving all around us? On faith I had purchased 30,000 rotls of grain from the government. I need still more and more because there are two hundred to five hundred people gathering at our door every day. Some of them come at daylight and sit until darkness drives them indoors or until they get a handful of grain. Already several people have starved to death because we could not get nourishment to them in time. One baby died almost in my arms because the food came too late. I made a mighty vow that as long as I have a bite to put in my own mouth, no one else would starve to death in this district. People would go hungry, but we would somehow find enough food to keep them alive. As I say, my faith was too weak to go on and purchase more grain from the government (even if I could get it) when I did not have the money to pay for it.

Daily I had been giving out 1,500 to 3000 pounds of grain to starving people. I had measured it out to each one by the half-cup, just enough to hold the soul within a fellow's ribs, not enough to keep the ribs from showing almost transparent through the skin. It was all we had. Some day try handing out 50 bushels of anything by the half-cup and see what happens to your arm and back. With pushing, clamoring, hungry, and pleading people all about, something happens to one's heart, too, and not infrequently to one's temper. I insisted on giving out the grain personally so that I could tell each person that it came from the Lord God and I was merely his agent. Nevertheless, I had used up all my money and credit. The local government official had gently suggested that he had to have cash by the end of the month, because he had to send his accounts in and could not carry the amount I owed. What could I do? A single day of even short rations would mean suffering for hundreds.

Just when I had reached the depths of despair, the wires began to come in: "Your father sent $250"; "Elwood City Church sends $400 Anuak relief"; and so on. Often, on the same steamer that came upriver with the grain for which I had contracted on faith, there would be a letter from America containing a gift of money sufficient to pay for it. This has reaffirmed my faith in God's loving providence. "And it shall come to pass that before they call, I will answer; and while they are yet speaking, I will hear." The good Lord answers us not only in terms of our obvious needs, but "is able to do exceeding abundantly above all we ask or think."

Money poured in from sources entirely unknown to me, and many of those who were giving did not even know there was a famine among the Anuaks. They just had an urge to give and so sent something. I know where that urge came from, and it makes me tingle from head to toe to think of it. It also makes me bow my head in shame that we use so little of God's resources in his kingdom's work. We are his only channels for pouring out his blessings and power upon his people, and yet we let so little of his love get through. How impatient he must get with us at times! But the experience here this year has given me new faith.

My heart has begun to sing songs of praise again. God has rebuked my faithlessness, not by punishing me as I deserve, but by heaping coals of fire on my head. My head is red enough without the fire, but those coals have warmed my heart, and I will never again forget that his resources are infinite and he expects us to use them in the service of his people.

Soon after, Don wrote,

During these months I have been able to clear thirty acres of virgin land and plant corn, durra, lentils, beans, and peanuts; build four native houses, a chicken house, two huge barns, a storeroom, and a large schoolhouse. Thus I got some return for the grain given out, although the people did not have the strength to do real work. In addition to this, I have exchanged grain for 120 sheep and 28 head of cattle. The Anuaks brought in their few remaining sheep and cattle for exchange, because the grain would last them a week or so, but the animals would be eaten and gone in a day. Fortunately the famine is now tapering off, and the people are able to eat small heads of grain. It is far from ripe or even fully developed, but at least it is something.

In retrospect Don was able to write,

After the famine months were over, I had given out 54,000 pounds of grain all with my own hand at about one-half pound per person. What is more, it is paid for and I have money left over.

Our next task is to prepare for the famine of next spring, which is almost sure to follow due to the rapidity with which the people are eating this crop even before it ripens. With the money given for the famine I am going to start a communal garden in ten or twelve representative villages and try to demonstrate to the people that it is possible to grow food even though there is no rain. We will have to build some kind of lift to get the water out of the river and onto the ground, but that should not be a difficult feat. Here at the mission I have already built a lift like a well sweep. These Anuak people never heard of such a thing and have been content to sit in their villages and starve even though a splendid stream is flowing at their feet. If they cultivated year-round, growing peanuts, beans, and corn during the dry season, there need never be another famine in this land.[42]

I will, of course, have to furnish the seeds for the first couple of years until they learn to preserve them. I will also have to subsidize the gardens for a year or two until they begin to see their value and undertake to do something on their own. A while ago I worked out such a scheme for the government officials and asked them to finance it, but they all think it impractical and the Anuak too lazy to take any interest. I have yet to see the man who is too lazy to better himself if he sees his neighbor has a good thing and he can have the same for a little trouble.

My working staff has shrunk from two or three hundred per day to just three men. I cannot get enough workmen to keep the wheels moving, and all the acreage I planted in millet and beans needs working. In addition, I want to build twenty houses for boys' dormitories, with all the accessory outhouses and cooking houses and so on. However, every man and woman is now sitting in the village with his or her back against the cattle barn, enjoying the feeling of a well-filled belly for the first time in eighteen months and the assurance that the next meal is also on tap. They are trying to drink enough beer in a single month to make up for all of the last eighteen beerless months. From the sound of things, they bid fair to do it. Recently I have had heads to bandage, human bites to cauterize, club wounds to tie up, and a lot of minor scratches to paint with iodine. All because people are feeling too happy and living too much in their cups.

When the McClures returned to Akobo from Doleib Hill, they had to prepare for the school year. The schools opened early in May, and instead of the 80 boys estimated, some 150 appeared. The previous enrollment had been about 50, thus 100 of the boys were complete beginners. The McClures could not handle such a great number of students and so had to select from among them. Forty of the boys had walked more than a hundred miles to get to school, and it was impossible to send them home, because the rains were on and the roads back to their villages were already closed. Thus Don decided he had to provide for 120 boys. There was not sufficient dormitory room for all of them, so many of the boys had to sleep in the temporary schoolhouses with their wide-open doorways, accessible to all the beasts of prey that might wander through. During that time Don shot five leopards, five or six hyenas, and three lions, any one of which might have made a midnight snack of a small boy. The boys stuck it out bravely, however—a testimony to their great desire to improve themselves.

We are having trouble with hyenas, and I have already lost ten or twelve sheep and one small calf to them. Of course, they only come at night and must be hunted at night. Lyda and I traipse around carrying a car battery in a box between us, with Lyda holding the searchlight attached to the battery and playing it over the landscape while I carry two rifles under my other arm. One night we stepped outside the kitchen door and Lyda flashed on the light. Not more than thirty yards away stood a big, beautiful cheetah that had been eating our chickens. He blinked in the light and blinked again when I missed him with the first blast of the .405. Then as he started to make for the woods, the .405 knocked him flat, but he got up again; to preserve my dwindling and precious shells I grabbed a long-handled shovel, conveniently at hand, and went after the wounded cheetah with it! Lyda yelled at me to stop, but my blood was up. I finished the cheetah off with a sharp crack on top of his head.

One of our boys was named Orop. He took care of his mother's goats and sometimes made a goat out of mud to play with. Orop was an odd-looking little fellow, since his head was absolutely flat on top. He loved to come to school, but he was not able to learn anything at all. He tried to trace the letters of his name with his finger in the sand (we have lots of fingers and sand, but no paper and pencils), but he could never get them in the right order. After a year I had to tell Orop that he was occupying a place that should be filled by a boy or girl who could learn. He was very sad, but he still came to school and stood outside the windows listening to the Bible stories.

Then Orop would gather a group of boys and retell the Bible stories. The trouble was that he got them all mixed up, like the letters of his name. This confused the villagers, and I had to forbid Orop from telling the stories about Jesus.

Finally, I told Orop that when I went out to a village to preach, he could carry God's Book (my Bible) for me. I came to think of Orop as "God's whip." Every day he was waiting for me as the sun came up and would carry God's Book to the designated village and gather the people, who would be singing hymns when I arrived. Orop was serving the Lord in the only way he knew how. He was always faithful in his task and proud of his part in it.

Yesterday a group of small boys were playing in the river when a crocodile grabbed one of them. The other boys ran away screaming, but Orop jumped into the water to fight the crocodile. He succeeded in freeing the boy who had been taken, but the crocodile seized Orop instead. I got to the river just in time to see the crocodile come up for air—with Orop in its mouth. I could not shoot then, but I followed the crocodile downriver and shot it when it came up again. Orop was gone. Greater love has no boy than to lay down his life for a friend.

I went to comfort Orop's mother, and she said, "Orop told me that he was not afraid to die, because Jesus would come to take him by the hand and lead him home. Is this true?" When I told her that it was true, she asked, "Will you teach me about Jesus? I want to be with Orop and Jesus."

Of little Orop, Christian, we recovered for burial one arm and one leg. Orop never owned a pair of shoes, he never learned to write his name, and he never finished the first grade; but when the roll is called up yonder—he will be there.

Of life in Akobo, Don wrote,

Out of my study window I can see the sun just coming up in a most glorious burst of color, and the world is awakening to the miraculous fact that God has made a new day. I call this my study, but it also serves as the children's schoolroom, Lyda's sewing room, and when we have guests we all move out and it becomes the guest room. Whatever it is, it looks out onto the Pibor River, which is now running full to the very lip of its banks. The fast-moving current carries down huge chunks of vegetation called sudd. Often the clumps of grass will be thickly inhabited with beautiful white egrets and small, brown wading birds called lily hoppers.

We are enjoying a period of excellent health when our youngsters are growing like bad weeds. They are fearless, and I wonder every day that they do not break their necks. A few days ago Donnie came in holding a small but very poisonous snake at the back of the neck (unless a snake should be considered all neck). The snake was still alive, and Donnie wanted to show it to me. A week ago I heard Marghi, age six, and Donnie, age three, saying strange things to each other; looking out, I saw Marghi near the top of the windcharger tower (about thirty feet above the ground) and Donnie halfway up. I went out quietly because I was afraid I would frighten them as much as I was frightened for them. As calmly as I could, I asked, "What are you doing up there?" Donnie swung around on the frame with one hand and one foot and, holding his finger to his lips, said, "Quiet! Don't talk, this is heaven; Marghi is God and I am Jesus and we are praying." I left them without a quiver of fear in my heart, because I knew there was One better able to care for them than I, and he certainly would not desert them at such a time. I was right, for in a little while they were down playing in the mud and building a pyramid. When I asked them what it was, they said, "A Tower of Babel. We want to go to heaven, and the windcharger is not high enough."

▼▲▼

Upon his return to Akobo, Don had to begin again his efforts to build a herd to supply milk for the Anuaks. Never slow to experiment, Don purchased two water buffaloes in Egypt with the hope that they would thrive in the south Sudan.

I must have been crazy to buy those buffaloes, because ever since, they have nearly driven me out of what is left of my mind. The story of the last two weeks could almost be called "The Tale of the Two Buffaloes," or if you prefer, "The Tails of Two Buffaloes." I have been following the travails of those two animals more closely than the travels of my own family. I felt that all was well since I had conferred with the necessary Egyptian government officials and secured all the necessary papers. However, I forgot to take into consideration the obstinacy of Egyptian bureaucrats, and I evidently overlooked one or two minor officials in my great desire to hurry things along. I had secured permission from the senior officials, but failed to placate all the intermediaries, and they have been making all kinds of trouble.

As we left Assiut, they refused to ship the buffaloes until they had a paper from a certain veterinarian in Cairo. So I telephoned Cairo four times and sent four or five telegrams. Finally we received permission to ship them, and I sighed with relief, but my relief was ill-founded. When we reached Shellal we found that the buffaloes had been delayed and could not go on with us. This was a situation we had not counted on, but after more calling back to Cairo we made arrangements for them to be exported unaccompanied. And contentedly we went on.

On arrival of Wadi Halfa we learned that the buffaloes had arrived at Shellal, but the veterinarian there had been overlooked. I had talked to him about the buffaloes and their care, yet I apparently had forgotten to *ask him if I might export them!* I supposed that the accompanying papers of export and permission from his superiors would be sufficient—but not for him. So I again had to call four times from Wadi Halfa to Cairo and Shellal to satisfy this man, and then I decided to stay over until the buffaloes came through to Wadi Halfa. Lyda went on south, and I stayed behind for three days to look after my buffaloes. While there, I made arrangements with the Sudan doctor for their care and inoculations against cattle plague and how he would ship them to Khartoum for me. When I learned that they were finally on the boat for Wadi Halfa, I took the next train for Khartoum. But I was far too optimistic. After I had gone, the Sudan veterinarian decided that he must have a separate set of export papers for the buffaloes. I had given him the import papers from the Sudan government, but that was not enough. He wanted to see with his own eyes that I had not smuggled two buffaloes out of Egypt, and he had to have the papers before he would send them on. So again I sent wires and letters to Cairo and got duplicate papers, and my buffaloes were shipped on.

The water buffaloes arrived in Khartoum yesterday, and what fun we had! I had just finished afternoon tea and was changing to go out shopping when a telephone call came in from the office manager of the shipping company we use there. He wanted to know if I was expecting two water buffaloes. When I said I was, he asked me to come immediately and get them, since they had arrived. I began to dress rather leisurely, and in five minutes another call came. This time the manager was frantic and asked me to hurry. I started to hurry, but three minutes later another call came, and he begged me to run because the buffaloes were in the garden of the general manager of the company and the general manager was having a garden party that afternoon!

I ran for my bicycle and dashed for the office. Arriving there, I found a half-demented Englishman who pushed me off and said, "No, not here in the office—at the general manager's garden!" I did not have the faintest idea where the general manager lived, so he sent a man with me on the run with orders to get the buffaloes. The general manager lived a half-mile away, but it was not hard to find the place, since a crowd of native boys were hanging over the wall looking at these two huge wonders. They had never before seen a water buffalo. I rushed in and found the buffaloes tied to the corner of a grass tennis court and calmly eating the general manager's beautiful flowering shrubs. As we rushed the buffaloes out the back gate, the general manager's guests began to arrive at the front gate. The general manager himself was greeting his guests and would soon be escorting them to his half-eaten garden. I think I will avoid that shipping company for a while. I am no longer very popular around there, although I did not take a single bite of his garden myself.

The men sent with the buffaloes had not been given instructions to bring the buffaloes to me, so they naturally took them to the head of the company that was shipping them. I wonder that they did not take the buffaloes into his front parlor! As far as I know, the buffalo incident is closed. I drove them out to our farm at Gereif this morning, and they took to the place immediately. The cow is still giving excellent milk and will be a great asset to us if we can keep her well. This one cow gives more milk than our whole herd of cattle gave at any one time. If the animals die, I shall be called a fool for investing so much money (seven hundred dollars) in them; but if they live and thrive, I will be acclaimed as a great man of vision and resourcefulness. On so thin a thread hangs fame! Well, you can have your fame or scoffing. Just give me a little milk for the children of Africa. We have already had lots of fun with the buffaloes, and it looks as if we may have more before we are finished. Now we will drive our truck from Khartoum to Akobo—one thousand miles straight south over bad roads and no roads. I expect the truck will need a little touchup paint after the trip.

▼▲▼

After nearly two decades in Africa, Glenn Reed was asked to assume the administrative leadership of all his church's overseas mission work. Don admitted that the thought of Glenn's leaving the field made him heartsick. "Glenn is by all odds the most able man in Africa and his going will leave a huge hole in our work. However, it will be a joy to have Glenn as head of our mission, because he will understand our problems and sympathize with our needs. Glenn will always be a missionary working out of an American office; he will never become a bureaucrat." As a matter of fact, Glenn Reed would only agree to work at an American desk for ten years. After that time he returned to Africa as the administrator of his church's evangelistic efforts in Sudan, Ethiopia, and Pakistan, with his office located in Asmara, Ethiopia. Because Glenn flatly refused to accept financial compensation beyond the amount paid to field missionaries, he was an acute embarrassment to all the other administrators who happily accepted the larger salaries. They begged Glenn to take the additional money and turn it back, but Glenn thought that procedure was not honest. With four sons to educate, including one in medical school, this was no empty gesture on Glenn's part. It was his conviction that he was a missionary wherever he worked and should be paid accordingly.

Back in Akobo, Don wrote,

It is obvious that the Holy Spirit is working even in places a missionary has never been. Recently an Anuak boy, a slave in the Murle country, was startled by a strange glow in his hut and a compelling summons to find someone who could tell him about the true God. Lado had never seen a missionary, nor had he heard anything of the gospel story, but he felt impelled to travel a hundred miles through enemy country, guided to find the only white man who could speak his language.

At that time Richard Lyth,[43] a devout Christian district commissioner, was stationed on the Boma Plateau about two hundred miles south of Akobo. Lado asked Lyth to tell him about his God, and when he heard the gospel story Lado responded with great intensity, "I knew it! I knew it!" Lyth later told Don, "Lado had never heard the name of Jesus Christ, but he did not need to be converted, because before I talked to him he was already a believer."
Don wrote,

Lado is now here with us in Akobo. Daily and constantly his life testifies that he has been born again. I have been trying to teach the way of Christianity to Africans. Lado demonstrates the transforming power of Jesus Christ. We cannot combat pagan animism with arguments, ridicule, or example, but with the revelation of the love of God that is effected by the Holy Spirit, whose agents we are.

Lado's great desire is to read and write and learn something of the Bible, then go back to teach the people who had enslaved him. Since there is no translation of any part of the Bible in the Murle language,[44] Lado will have to memorize the Bible in the Anuak language (he speaks Anuak with difficulty, since he was a very small boy when he was stolen) and then make his own translation for his former masters.

▼▲▼

I wish you could see our place. It really looks wonderful! Our houses are set back about sixty yards from the river, and from the front door we have a sandpath six feet wide lined with bricks. On each side of the path Lyda has periwinkles running from the door to the steps on the riverbank, then behind the winkles a row of tulip-like native flowers that are always green. Behind those there is a row of Mexican fire plants, which are red and green. Then we have long beds of Kenya lilies and just beyond the bed a trellis of different varieties of bougainvillea, which just now are a mass of marvelous bloom! All this leads from the front door to the riverbank. At the river we have beds of flowering cactus, more bougainvillea, some gardenia bushes, and frangipani. Then in semi-circles close to the round walls of the houses we have several varieties of lantana and beds of gaillardia and African daisies. Across the front of the two plots divided by the path we have hedges of lantana. On the south side of the house we have our citrus orchard hedged by mulberry trees, and on the east side our banana plantation and vegetable garden. But to me the most satisfying sight of all is the beautiful green forest about half a mile across the river.

When I look at our place, I marvel that not long ago it was a wilderness with big trees and brush growing right down to the riverbank. When we arrived we had nothing but our houses, and they were in poor shape. Now we have all the accoutrements of a first-class station in full running trim, including two schools—one here and one five miles downstream—and more pupils than we can handle. We have everything except a church. Some missionaries think a church building should come first, but our large cattle barn has been serving us in excellent fashion. If a cattle barn was good enough for the birth of our Lord, it is good enough for an Anuak service. I will construct a church building someday, but first I want to build a spiritual church among the Anuaks, who will soon demand something better than a cattle barn for the worship of God.

If we can accomplish so much in so short a time, what would a complete staff do in fifteen years? The progress made here at Akobo has convinced me that with an adequate program and staff to carry out that program, we could evangelize the entire Anuak tribe in fifteen years and train native workers to carry on the work themselves. I hope our church at home has the vision and faith to give it a try. If it proves a success here among the Anuaks, it will revolutionize our missionary program in all fields. The theory heretofore is that we have to work with the nationals of any country for two or three generations before they can be independent of us. So we build costly houses and institutions and prepare to stay on, hoping that the gentle and civilizing influences of living among a primitive people will be sufficient to bring them to Christ. It has not done so in any land that I know. Rather, we must go forth in the spirit of the apostle Paul and push ahead as if we had but a year to finish the job. We need a realization of the magnitude of the job and a determination to finish the task quickly!

We have already spent forty-five years in the Sudan and have barely scratched the surface of things to be done. In the north Sudan we are further behind today than we were twenty-five years ago, while here in the south we are gradually pushing ahead but without any definite plan of when we will finish the task. I would like our mission to set a definite goal and a fixed time limit in which to attain that goal. Then we can start toward the goal and make every effort count toward that end. As it is, we are aimlessly wandering about, each of us doing as he pleases and without any continuity of work. As soon as I leave this place, someone else will come in and turn things upside down. Then the new missionary will spend five years starting off in another direction. Such effort is wasteful, and the expense is terrific!

About this time the McClures took a short vacation in Egypt, and Don wrote,

We are having a marvelous time in Assiut. Yesterday we took a picnic lunch out to the edge of the desert, and the children played in some large caves with connecting tunnels. These caves are supposed to be among those used by Joseph in the Bible to store grain in preparation for the approaching years of famine. Our visit has not produced the rest and leisure I had expected. I have been kept busy talking about our work at Doleib Hill and at Akobo because our missionaries in Egypt are so eager to learn about a mission that is moving forward as fast as ours is. In Egypt the work is so slow that they measure accomplishments by years spent in the field rather than by the growth of the church. When our Egyptian missionaries hear of hundreds coming into the church, as we had at Doleib Hill, or the eagerness of the Anuak to hear the Word of God, they are amazed; it is all rather pathetic. If there is a sign on the road to heaven that says, "Go slow," I will have trouble obeying it.

It seems to me the fault is not entirely in the difficulty of preaching the gospel to Muslims, but in that our missionaries are not fighters for the cause of the gospel. As soon as they experience the slightest antagonism to their work, they draw back. I know that is a terrible indictment of our Egyptian mission, but I think it is true, and until they change their attitude, the mission will continue to decline. They must, of course, comply with government regulations about teaching religion, but instead of fighting the issues our missionaries meekly comply. Nor is this their only fault; here in Assiut there are so many prominent Egyptians who are personally friendly to the mission that missionary life is one endless string of social engagements. Day after day there have been teas, sporting events, lunches, and dinners. Since we arrived here, there have been days in which we had three social events in as many different homes. Maybe I am being unfair because I do not understand the situation, but it seems to me that when missionaries are so frequently entertained in the homes of non-Christian people, they are not in position to offer criticism of their host's beliefs and behavior. In any case, I would not be a missionary in this city for all the gold in Egypt. I do not have the temperament for this slow work.

At Akobo the Lord led us into the desperate struggle of famine relief that made the days and weeks fly by uncounted. What we were able to do for the Anuak people gave us a standing with them that we would not otherwise have gained in twenty years of work. It is no exaggeration to say that our Anuak mission schedule is thirty years ahead of the experience of the first missionaries to the Shulla and Nuer peoples. In the span of six months we were able to help in such a way that we have come to know a great many Anuaks and have become known by all the Anuak people in our area. Having been able to give them assistance in their time of desperate need, we have already won a confidence among them that normally would not have been developed except by years and years of service. All barriers between us have been broken down; the Anuaks call me their "father" and "savior." Obviously, when people are starving, the way to their hearts is through their stomachs.

Clearly, all this would not have come about without the generous help of people at home who believe in what we are doing. I will never be able to thank them adequately. They made it possible for me to do things among the Anuaks that usually require years and years of missionary effort. In a comparatively short time I have come to occupy a place in their hearts that many missionaries have not been able to earn in half a lifetime. I can take no credit for this, but must pass it on to all those splendid folk who made it possible to go ahead at such great speed as opportunities came. The Anuak project is off to a marvelous start, and I know we will go on from strength to strength.

If the love of money is the root of all evil, the accounting for it can be the source of considerable trouble, especially for those like Don McClure who had a lot of things they would rather do than keep financial records. For Don, groups of people always came before columns of figures. This eventually became a major problem between the administrators in New York and Don at Gode. But even while the McClures were at Akobo, the mission board, whose secretary was Don's dearest friend, Glenn Reed, voted to suspend the Anuak project until Don's financial reports were received and approved.

Don realized he was remiss, but he was also hurt and furious. This hot letter went to Glenn:

I am writing to you as the friend I love above any other human being outside my own family, and I am going to let my mind run free and empty out my heart through my fingers just as the thoughts and emotions come to me. Already more than an hour has elapsed since I wrote the first phrase above, and I have again committed this letter and myself to the Lord. I am writing to you because I cannot think the things I have thought without sharing them with you. In a wonderful prayer meeting we had at Akobo three weeks ago, we all opened our hearts to each other in a new way, and we also vowed to each other that we would never let the sun go down on any misunderstanding or wounded feelings that any of us felt for another. And although I have let many days pass since my hurt, yet I cannot go back to Akobo with all this in my heart.

I am penitent, contrite, and humbled, and I will write a polite, apologetic letter to the Board of Foreign Missions acknowledging my failures and asking their pardon. I want to live within the law. But on the other hand, I am angered and indignant, and I have been sitting here for an hour wondering how you were able to bury your personal feelings and better judgment under a mask of officialdom. I can understand how the board, as a board, can have little regard for God or man, but it is not possible for me to imagine how you could lend yourself to such a nefarious scheme in order to punish one recalcitrant missionary.

Your cable came through just a couple days before I left Akobo for our downriver stations, and I at once saw the seriousness of my failures to get my accounts in to you. I went to my desk one evening at seven and worked until the bell rang for prayers the next morning. I held six services that day and went to my desk again at eight that night, after a strenuous day when I had counseled with some forty men and women between meetings; I worked until dawn ferreting out my accounts. I brought the accounts with me downriver to complete, feeling elated and happy that it was soon to be finished.

Then to my amazement, as I traveled from station to station, my fellow missionaries asked me, "What do we hear about the Anuak project being closed?" I had to profess ignorance, because your cable gave me no intimation of a board action to shut down the work, other than to suggest that the hospital building might be delayed. On arrival in Malakal I received your letter as secretary of the board to me as general secretary of the mission announcing the action of the board to freeze all funds until I got my accounts in. My first reaction was a sickening heartache that you should suspect me of dishonesty, and my first impulse was to take the next plane home and face the board and the church and answer their charges one by one. It was only the faith that my fellow workers have in me and my own burning love of the Lord and the Anuak people that saved me from being on my way home right this minute.

Glenn, how could you and the board have taken such action? To get at one erring missionary, you drive a knife into the heart of the Anuak work. To punish me, you thwart the working of the Spirit of God in the hearts of this people. You rob twelve missionaries in his service of their confidence in me and in you. You have placed a big question mark in the hearts of three new missionaries, now en route from Khartoum, whose minds were filled with malicious untruths and half-truths, and they are already asking what it is all about. I know you will immediately answer that I am misconstruing the purposes and intents of the board. I am not! I know your motives and intents were largely of the best, but because your methods were of the spirit of the devil and not the Lord, only the devil could use them, and did, and is.

I am blameworthy and guilty of gross negligence and procrastination in not reporting my financial accounts to the board. But *I am not* the Anuak Tribal Plan; I am not God's sole representative in this area. To punish me, you have reached out and blighted the spirit of ten other missionaries. The board has received its pound of flesh, but it has also drained some of the life blood out of our work and put a barrier between missionaries. For this the board will be held accountable. Not to me, but before the throne of grace.

Why did not you, or some member of the board, give us warning of this impending action to freeze all our funds? In your letter you said that the board had taken action last October to stop funds. But you did not inform anyone in this field. You did not write to our treasurer. You sent word of it only to an official in Khartoum, who kept absolutely silent until two weeks ago when he gleefully began to give out the news that we were bankrupt. Why this silence on the part of the board and our general treasurer? I had received some letters, but in none of these was it even hinted that you contemplated closing us down. This bombshell you launched at us was unwarranted, unfair, and of a spirit other than the Lord's; only Satan can use it.

Again I state I am not the Anuak project. The board should have reached me in some other way than through the Anuak work—you threaten to block our whole work for a full year. Suppose I had refused to turn in these accounts? What then? Would you have continued to shut down until we all came home? And all because of a few paltry accounts? Glenn, I cannot believe it! I cannot! Why did you not have the courage to reach out and take hold of the man at fault? There were a dozen ways you could have done it and been perfectly within your rights, and I would have deserved them all. You could have repudiated me before the church (you did it before the mission!); you could have suspended me, stopped my salary, recalled me to face the board. Oh, so many ways other than trying to kill me this way!

Glenn, of all people, you *know* why I do not have my accounts in. You know I have nothing to hide, and if you do not know *that*, then I no longer want to be a missionary under this board. Oh, I know you will say, "Well, Don, you have opened yourself to suspicion by withholding your accounts." But, Glenn, that is just as unfair as the action of the board. I do not have my accounts in for two reasons. First, I detest bookkeeping, and second, which is the more pertinent, there have not been enough hours in the day to do all I have planned, or enough strength of body to keep up the pace.

I am a missionary, not a bookkeeper, and I have been working sixteen and eighteen hours a day at tasks that I cannot and will not slight. On two occasions, I have worked without rest for forty hours, and to get out my accounts for the board for fifty-two hours without sleep. These last two weeks are typical, for I have not had five hours' sleep any night since I left home. Yesterday I held five services at Nasir, finishing a marvelous baptism and communion service when we felt wondrously blessed of the Lord. At seven in the evening, half an hour later, I was in my boat heading for Akobo. I have been on the move all night long so that I might get home in time to put in a good day's work for the Lord at Akobo. In the midst of a life like that, when practically every minute of the day I am touching human souls, why must I spend time with bookkeeping? I came to

Africa to preach the gospel, not keep books. But my very real failures do not excuse the board for using the whip on many of my fellow missionaries. In punishing me this way, by the same token, you could stop all the work in the Sudan if our general treasurer did not get her accounts in on time. You could cut us all off.

What does the board look for in a missionary? I could name one or two—and one especially whose name immediately comes to your mind—who, if he lives in the Sudan another hundred years, will never win a single soul to Christ. Indeed, at this very minute he and his wife are bringing misery and distress and unhappiness into the lives of many of their fellow missionaries and robbing them of much of the joy and power of serving the Lord. However, he does get his accounts in on time and in good shape! Glenn, Glenn, I should not write to you this way, but never has my soul been so heavy! I know the board has lost all confidence in me, but I am not serving the board! I am serving the Lord, and only that keeps me on the field!

This action of the board was not of the Lord on several counts. Its very timing was of the devil. Your cable came to me in the midst of a great spiritual awakening at Akobo. Had I realized its seriousness, I might have been robbed of my power to awaken yearning souls and point them to the Savior. Fortunately your letter was delayed, or I could not have gone on. That was of the Lord. But when I finally received your letter in Malakal and answered the questions of the rest of our missionaries, I was ready to quit. I felt that never had a board so deliberately repudiated a missionary, yet I could not feel myself so reprobate and yet be so signally used of the Holy Spirit as I have been during the past month. Someone was wrong, and I felt it was not I. Negligent, yes, but not to such an extent as to warrant your action. The only other thing I can imagine is that you and the board are suspicious of my handling of the Lord's money. If this is true, I shall not labor under the board another day upon confirmation of this to me.

To this end, I am asking my father to contact you immediately, and if necessary, to make a trip to Philadelphia to canvass the board and individual members. If he feels that the board has lost confidence in me and is suspicious of the use of monies entrusted to me by the people of the church, then the board shall have my immediate resignation, and I shall be home to face the board and the church as soon as I can make it.

In the meantime we cannot stop our work here, whether you approve or not. During the famine period I spent all my personal savings and cannot fall back on that. But I have a wonderful father who will help, and I have Lyda's and the children's savings, which we will use now to keep going. By borrowing from our insurance, we will keep on, and the Lord will supply the rest. I thank God that the Anuak project has not received one cent from the budget of the board in the ten years that we have been in this work, and when we have to use it, I shall feel the Lord has removed his blessing and we might as well quit. I am writing to my home congregation to ask them to pay our salary outside the budget, if they feel they can. If they cannot, we shall seek support from churches that I know will be glad to do so.

In the face of this angry blast, Glenn Reed, ever the patient and tactful Christian diplomat, succeeded in calming all sides—especially the irate Don. As a result, Lyda McClure henceforth kept the financial records of the Anuak mission. The dispute over money resolved, Don went back to the work he loved with a happy heart.

▼ Snakes and
▼ Crocodiles

As FAST AS HE could and with his customary fierce energy, Don was pushing ahead
with the evangelism of the Anuak tribe. He
was farming to improve the nutrition available to all the people, and he was focusing
on reducing the spoken language to a written form into which the
Bible could be translated and the Anuaks taught to read it. In addition
to evangelism, agriculture, and education, Don's medical work was
attracting Anuaks to the mission.

With the mail today came some bad news. The new medical
inspector in Malakal (and of all this province) has written that
we can no longer treat anyone unless we have a medical license.
He intimated that none would be granted to such as I, nor
would I dare to ask for one. We have been ordered to use the
Akobo dispensary, more than a mile away and operated by a
very inefficient Muslim medical dispenser. If we follow strictly
the letter of the law, we cannot even doctor ourselves without
first consulting the local medical authority, such as he is.[45] It is a
bitter blow to us, because my clinic has been a means of
reaching thousands of Anuaks and is almost mandatory in
caring for the 120 boys in our school, some of whom need daily
dressings and drugs. Moreover, it is obvious to the Muslims in
the north of Sudan that our Christian schools are a great
influence on the pagan, black people of the south. Since the
Islamic north is the dominant political power in this country, it is
clear that at some point the Islamic religion and the Arabic
language will move south in force. We are no longer allowed to
open a village school without a special permit, and we must now

register the names of all our schoolboys. I assume that the purpose is so the Muslims can identify the Christians and work on them. We have heard that mosques are to be built near all the Christian missions and a Muslim missionary is to be stationed there. The increasing opposition of the government to our work is just another sign that our time as Christian missionaries in Sudan is very short, and we must accomplish what we can before we are forced to leave. In any event, I will be happy to stop trying to offer medical assistance to the Anuaks just as soon as a real physician comes here to live.

We had a wonderful testimony this morning in our workers' meeting. We hold the first service of the day at six o'clock, before anyone starts on the day's work, and always at these meetings we give an opportunity for the people to testify to the working of the Holy Spirit in their hearts. This morning one of our much-loved Christian women stood in the midst of nearly one hundred men, a most unusual thing for an Anuak woman to do, and said, "Last night the Lord came to me and said to me that the words of the missionaries are true and we are to listen and believe." Then she sat down. There was a most impressive silence. The Anuaks believe very strongly in visions and would hesitate ever to go contrary to them. They really believe it is the Lord speaking to them. In this case, so do I. I had to speak to the people following her words, and never did anyone have a more attentive audience, nor did a missionary ever weigh his words more carefully than I did this morning.

One would think that I was a real linguist because I use five languages every day. Most of the people at Akobo Post speak Arabic, as does our carpenter. The young man working in our kitchen came with us from Doleib Hill, so Lyda and I speak Shulla with him. Half my workmen are Nuers, so I must give orders to them in my stumbling Nuer. Everyone else speaks Anuak, and when I get to talk to my family I use English. I speak all these languages equally poorly, including English, but hope to be more proficient soon.

Don continued to treat people and wrote of some of his patients.

I am treating a lovely little girl whose name is Ariet. She comes to the clinic every day that it does not rain. She must be nine or ten years old and is too big for her parents to carry. Since she cannot walk, she crawls on her hands and knees for nearly two miles just to get some medicine and some treatment. I think she must have had spinal meningitis when she was small, because both legs are afflicted and are too weak to enable her to stand.

I have tried to tell her to stay in the village and I will send the medicine out to her, but she refuses and says she wants to come in for the worship service and to have me rub her. I massage her legs every day she comes in and rub her all over with oil, and she loves the attention. At home she gets only abuse because she is not able to help out in any way and is not likely to be married—though she will probably have children when she is old enough. Ariet is the most cheerful and happy youngster I have known among these Anuaks and utters nary a cross word when the other youngsters push in ahead of her. I am giving her shots of B_{12} and plenty of other vitamins, and she is looking much better. I have not yet persuaded any of the men or boys of her village to carry her to the clinic. I would do it myself if I had the time. Last Sunday she crawled in to attend the service and I did carry her home on my back, and she thought that was the most wonderful thing in all the world. I expect she will come in every Sunday just to be carried home.

Last Sunday she asked me a question that I am sure has been in the minds of countless thousands of people like her. I had been preaching in the service about God's love for them, and she asked me, "If God loves me, why can't I walk?" I did not have a satisfactory answer to that question, and I told Ariet I did not know why God allowed Satan to hurt her; but I also said, "I know God loves you, and I do too." I am sure Ariet will make a wonderful Christian, because she thinks a lot and is always talking about her *Kwaya*, or "Big Chief." I made a pair of pads for her knees, which were getting calluses like a camel's. I also gave her a pair of cotton panties to wear, because she could not wear a shirt while she was crawling. So she comes in with her knee pads and panties and tells everyone that her *Kwaya thinh* (Little Chief, or "the one under God") gave them to her. She is a lovable child.

This is a trying time. The temperatures in the last three days were 110, 112, and 114 degrees, and the humidity is almost 100 percent. We cannot sleep well in such heat. I am building five native churches and have a hundred Anuaks in training for baptism. In addition—and above all—I have a boil in my nose.

This is the third boil I have had in my nose in the last six weeks, and I call it unfair.

Don also had some battles with snakes.

We almost had a human tragedy in a nearby village early this week. About ten o'clock at night a woman came running in, screaming for help. I rushed out to see what was the matter. She said that a huge snake had crawled into her house and driven her out before she could pick up her baby. According to her, the snake was so big that it filled the house, and the baby was still lying on the floor in a basket. I grabbed my flashlight, and because I had loaned my shotgun out, I had to take the .22 rifle, and we ran for her village.

I fully expected to see the baby encircled by the snake and perhaps partially swallowed. The people of the village were running about with grass torches, but were afraid to enter the house. So was I, but I went into it anyway on my hands and knees. The doorway of the house was not more than two feet high, so I had to slide through, pushing my gun ahead of me and trying to see the whole interior at one time with the flashlight. It did not help that my batteries were weak and scarcely more than lit up the circle of its own beam. I looked at the basket first, and although I could not see the baby, I felt sure that all was well with him. This relieved my mind, but did not stop the pounding of my heart as I searched for the snake. I did not know what I would do if the snake came for me as I crawled through the door, because I knew I could not get back out in time. If it was a python, I would have a chance, because the villagers would help me; but if it was a spitting cobra, I did not fancy having it spit in my eyes or bite me on the end of the nose, and I surely could not do much shooting from that position.

I slowly pushed my way in, trying to see all sides at once. The house was filled with pots, baskets, a grain bin, and animal skins thrown over the floor, so it was hard to see anything that might be near the wall. Slowly I started to stand erect, and just as my head reached the level of the top of the wall, something rustled in the grass six inches from my bald spot. I hit the floor fast and hard. Then, holding the gun ready, I turned the flashlight on the roof, only to see a little lizard crawling along a roof pole. I looked into the basket to see the baby quietly sleeping, then began another search for the snake. It was a small house, and I knew if the snake came for me there would be no chance to get away, and I also knew that if it was a spitting cobra it could spit clear across the house at me, but I had to find the snake!

Cautiously I moved with my foot (a bare foot at that!) one pot after another. Just as I was about to push a spear handle under the grain basket, I saw it—a huge red snake, starting to crawl along the wall. I could only see a part of it and could not see its head at all. Holding the flashlight in my mouth, I shot twice in rapid succession at the snake and fortunately hit it both times, but it crawled on until it came to a hole in the wall. I shot again and missed as the snake pulled itself through. Then just as it was about to disappear, I grabbed for its tail and got a grip on eight inches of snake. Then I did not know what to do. I did not want the snake in the house with me, but I also did not want to let it go. So I started to pull. By jerks I gradually pulled more and more of it back. I could only do so because its back was broken and it had lost most of its strength; otherwise I could not have held it at all. Each time I jerked, I got another foot or so of snake back into the house and put another bullet in it. I was holding the snake with one hand, the muzzle of the gun close to its back with the other, and still holding the butt of the flashlight in my mouth. When I realized how funny it must have looked, I almost laughed and dropped the light. Finally the snake let loose and all of him came in, hissing and striking but fortunately almost paralyzed. I soon finished it off. Then, grabbing the snake by the tail, I again crawled through the door.

Quite a crowd had gathered, but being afraid to look in the house, they had not known what I was shooting at or the outcome. As I dragged this huge snake out and threw it at their feet in the light of their blazing torches, most of them screamed and ran. Coming back again, they said that it was *ywal* snake, and in hushed tones they said, *Jwok, Jwok*—which means "God, God." The Anuaks believe this particular type of snake is a god. Some of the women started to run off for some oil to pour over the snake as a sacrifice, and still others went for salt to sprinkle so there would be no curse on them. I called them back and, kicking the snake with my bare foot, told them it was not a god and if they brought oil and salt to throw on it, I would drape it about their necks. This was met with more screams of horror, but it was an effective threat. I then used the occasion to tell them what God thought of worshiping beasts and, after a prayer, dragged the snake away with me and threw it into the long grass where they would not likely find it until it began to smell.

The other day Marghi got up from her afternoon nap and was frightened by meeting a snake in our living room. It was a yard-long spitting cobra! She yelled for me, and we got it killed without much trouble, but it gave her a bad fright. And just yesterday our gardener was nearly attacked by a huge, seven-foot cobra that had just eaten a chicken and her chicks and some eggs. I have had enough of snakes. Unlike our mother Eve, I do not discuss theology with a serpent; I just dispatch them.

By now the three McClure children—thirteen-year-old Marghi, ten-year-old Donnie, and nine-year-old Polly—were attending school with other missionary children in Egypt. Spending the summer vacation with their parents involved a month's travel to Akobo, a month in Akobo, and a month's travel back to Assiut. The first part of the return trip from Akobo to Malakal was a family adventure.

For sheer fun, nothing beats a small, sixteen-foot boat and outboard motor, a family of five, a dog, and all the paraphernalia and baggage necessary for a six-hundred-mile trip down an African river. When we had the boat loaded with the bare necessities—our tent and sleeping bags, food and cooking utensils, baggage for the children and for us—the good ship "Heloise" was already low in the water and the waves lapped at the gunwales. In addition, the six passengers had to find places for themselves as best they could on top of all the luggage, but the trip had to be made; what has to be done can be done.

There were only five days remaining before the children were to meet their boat in Malakal, and if they had missed that connection, the next boat would be six weeks distant. We would have been happy to keep them at home with us for another six weeks, since one month is a very short time to get reacquainted with three growing children, but early in the morning we gingerly climbed aboard what was to be our floating home for the next five days. When the last passenger–Laddie, the little terrier—was aboard, we had just two inches of freeboard above the water. Very carefully I started the outboard motor for a test run while all held their breath. As we gathered speed, the boat sank a little lower in the water at the stern while the prow was lifted by the thrust of the motor. The water boiled up behind us much higher than the level of the deck. Those first moments were anxious ones, but long before we reached Malakal we had grown accustomed to our shaky platform and were doing all sorts of crazy things while running at full speed.

The sky was overcast, and in a few minutes after our start the much-dreaded rain began to pelt down. Perhaps I alone recognized the danger as we added pound by pound to our load, since the luggage began to soak up the driving rain. I knew we could not take much rain, so I asked the Lord to give us clear skies. Almost immediately we ran out of the storm and soon left it far behind. With that, all my fears vanished for the rest of the trip. I knew we were traveling in the hollow of his hand. And so it proved, for day after day as we were alternately drenched by the driving rains and scorched by the blistering sun, we continued to make our way down the Pibor and Sobat rivers to the mighty Nile.

The days were filled with things of interest. The banks of the rivers were lined with myriads of birds whose number and variety beggar description. Truly the Sudan is "the land of whirring wings," as Isaiah 18 says. Thousands of heron, crane, pelican, storks, and many kinds of lesser birds made the sky a vast sea of feathered motion and delight. But all the life was not in the sky. The waters of the rivers teemed with great schools of fish making their way up the flooding waters to their feeding ground in the swamps. Now and again we would see the snout of a hungry crocodile bob up to take a look at us. If they stayed a second too long, Donnie and I would vie with each other to see who would be the first to sink a bullet into the armored heads and send them to the bottom of the river forever.

There was one crocodile that we did not shoot but that almost sent us to the bottom and scared ten years' growth out of us all. We were camping at night along the riverbank and usually began looking for a likely place to stop about four-thirty in the afternoon, since we had to erect the tent and cook supper before dark. Darkness brought with it millions of mosquitoes, and everyone had to be inside the tent or be eaten alive. The first night out, we camped along the shores of the Pibor River, the second night we shared the luxury of the Jordan house at our

Nasir mission, but on the third night the children wanted to sleep on what we call "Crocodile Island" because of the great number of crocodiles always found there. So we had to push along until nearly dark. As we approached the island we saw some of the ugly creatures slide off the high banks and splash into the muddy waters of the Sobat, but we did not have a chance to shoot at any. We quickly chose a spot for our camp, and while Lyda spread the supper things out on the canvas tablecloth laid on the ground, the rest of us got the tent up and things ready for the night. Then we all went into the river for our evening bath, after taking the usual precaution of shooting down into the water several times to warn the crocodiles that it was bathtime for us and not feeding time for them.

When we first stopped at this spot and Lyda stepped ashore to tie up the boat, we had heard a great rustling in the tall grass as something rushed away. Lyda had let out a squeal and quickly stepped back into the boat, but the rest of us laughed at her for being afraid of a land lizard. Then, after the bath Lyda again stepped ashore to see about the things cooking on the fire. Just as she reached the top of the bank there was a great rush from the tall grass. With her call, I jumped to my feet, standing in the boat, only to see a five-foot crocodile come slithering at express-train speed out of the grass and right at us. He was moving so fast there was no time to do a thing but yell, "Look out! A crocodile!" He dashed right across the spread-out supper things, scattering food and dishes in all directions, as he made for the river and safety—his, not ours.

As I raised my head above the bank, I looked right into his half-opened mouth and felt that if I could reach down his throat and catch his tail, I could have turned him inside out. However, on seeing me he quickly swerved and gave a great leap toward the river. His leap did not carry him quite far enough to clear us and the boat, and he landed right smack on top of Polly, who was standing behind me. As the croc slid down her back, he wrapped his tail around her chest and would have pulled her into the river except that I had turned to ward off the blow and was able to grab her. Nevertheless, his impact was heavy enough to break the skin and leave a huge welt across her body. From Polly's back the croc slid into the water and fell right on top of Donnie, who was just climbing up on the boat. Without doing him any harm, the croc splashed into the water and disappeared. Yet he almost sank us, because we all lost our balance and fell to one side of the boat, which immediately began to fill with water. Fortunately the boat quickly righted itself, and we were able to bail it out before it was too late. It was an exciting five minutes and an event that taught us to make our camp elsewhere than in the midst of crocodiles, however scared they seemed to be of us.

Two days later we reached Malakal without any more serious incidents than burned noses and blistered lips from the intense heat and water reflection. It was obvious that the Lord had protected us on the trip downriver, because the day after our arrival in Malakal I started back up the river again alone. I was carrying some supplies for Doleib Hill as well as the personal baggage of some missionaries just back from vacation, but the boat was not so heavily loaded as it had been when we left Akobo. Without taking much care, I headed the boat upstream and pushed the gas lever to full speed. The motor roared into action and the boat, like a thing alive, leaped ahead. Then suddenly and without warning, I tipped to one side and shipped water, and in trying to recover I overcontrolled and tipped deep to the other side and shipped more water. With a swoosh the boat went down. Somehow a rope attached to the stern got tangled around my foot and I was dragged to the bottom of the Nile with the boat. I thought it was my last moment, when suddenly the rope slipped off and I bobbed up to the surface. Obviously, the Lord has some things for me to do on earth before I join the saints in glory. I expect the saints will be surprised to see me.

All about me were floating suitcases and packages and tins of gasoline. I grabbed a suitcase and pushed it in front of me to the shore. By that time all our possessions had already started to float away downstream. The people along the bank, seeing the upset, quickly came to the rescue, and with their help we recovered most of the things. A few hours later we were able to get the boat and the motor out, but after two days of diving and fishing I gave up the typewriter and cameras as lost. I must admit that every time I dived down through the twelve feet of water to search around in the mud on the bottom of the Nile, I wondered if instead of touching the smooth leather of my camera case I might not rub my hand against the rough scales of a crocodile.

Once Don arrived home, he wrote again.

▌am now alone at Akobo. Lyda accompanied the children on their long journey to school, but I felt I must get back to work, and this morning I produced the finest achievement of all my missionary career—I baked a splendid loaf of bread. Our regular cook is not here, and I have a young boy who can cook most of the normal things, but he cannot make bread. I have not tasted bread in a month, and since it began to rain early this morning, the workmen were sticking tight to the cattle barns. Therefore I decided to try my hand at bread. Lyda usually makes a quick bread, so I looked up the recipe. By 8:30 the bread was in the pans, and I instructed the boy that he was to call me when it had risen because I wanted to punch it down a couple of times. About 10:00 I came in to see how my bread was doing and discovered it was already in a very hot oven. It had been in only a few minutes, but was already getting brown on top. I rescued it and, after cooling the oven, stuck it back in, and would you believe a beautiful and tasty loaf turned out? You can bet I am going to mail a slice of it to Lyda. I remember vividly the first loaf she baked, and if I do not send her a piece, she will never believe I cooked some bread that I could eat.

I never thought life would be a bed of roses, but I did not expect it to be a pile of what I have been working in. At the beginning of the rainy season I dug a latrine sixty feet deep and six feet in diameter. I could not line the well at the time because I had no bricks, but I did put a reinforced concrete floor over the top of the pit. This "bathroom" has been a great joy ever since, because it eliminated (pardon the pun) the need to go outside or carry a bucket out every day. However, the heavy rains of the last two weeks undermined the walls, and the well caved in. The bathroom walls are now in danger of falling. I was standing inside looking at it when I heard two Anuaks talking outside. One of them said, "He [meaning me] is cursed to have his little house fall down. He will have to abandon this house." The other said, "You are crazy. You do not know Odon. When something happens to us, we sit down and cry, but when something happens to him he laughs, and then he prays, and God starts to work for him."

Well, I now have brick and cement, and this week I will spend all my afternoons putting a lining in our more-than-slightly-used latrine. The nearest mason is some four hundred miles away, so I will have to do the job myself. I will be working in semi-darkness, and all the bricks and mortar will be lowered to me through the toilet hole. (This experience has suggested some wonderful sermon titles, but I would never dare to use one of them.) I have found that the only way to finish a disagreeable job is to take a deep breath and get started. However, for this particular job, maybe I should not take a deep breath.

Toward evening I received a telegram from La Amoleker at Doleib Hill. Pakwan, my dearest friend and first convert among the Shullas, has died of pneumonia. It was Pakwan who had accompanied me on all my river trips of exploration; during all my years at Doleib Hill I never went on a hunt without him. Pakwan could tell whether I had hit an animal even better than I could. He worked with me here at Akobo until the middle of June and was planning to return as soon as his own crops were harvested. We were inseparable and shared in everything. I loved Pakwan better than a brother. He was my buddy. If he had to die, at least I wish I could have been with him. Since his death, I have received a letter, written just three days before he got sick, in which he thanked me for helping him to live closer to Jesus. Well, Pakwan is closer to the Lord now than any of the rest of us, and I believe that my work in Africa would have been worthwhile if only because of him. I shall miss him greatly, but I expect to see him before long. I hope the Lord will let us go hunting together again in heaven.

▼▲▼

The McClures were able to return to their work at Akobo and build a solid foundation for a Christian witness among the Anuaks. After this initial task was completed at the edge of Anuak territory in Sudan, Don became increasingly restless to move closer to the heart of the Anuak people, which required that the McClures cross over the border into Ethiopia. The American Mission in Ethiopia had already established an office in Addis Ababa and a station among the Oromo at Dembi Dollo, but Don intended to begin a pioneering work among the Anuaks in that country.

Don had recognized many years before that his strength was not in conservation, even of what he himself had established. Thus he wrote,

> I am afraid that I have done at Akobo what I swore I would never allow to happen. That is, this place has gotten too big for me to handle by myself without being forced to neglect the evangelistic work that I came to Africa to do. And it is my fault. After one piece of work is finished, one field cleared and planted, one school building erected—I cannot resist the urge to plant another tree, to clear another field, to take on more cattle, to try one more experiment. I now feel tied down here, and it is time for me to move on. Leaving the Anuaks in Sudan is a heartbreaking experience. We are never likely to go back to live at Akobo among these dear people who came to depend on me and on whom I depend. I am trying to get the place in shape so that the missionary who comes to take over can concentrate on the school. Like the church, a spear has several different parts, and they are all essential to its proper function, but I am only really happy riding the point.

Thus Don and his family prepared to leave Akobo for Pokwo.

The Gilo River in flood and the nearly completed airstrip

IV POKWO
THE ANUAKS OF ETHIOPIA
1950–1962

▼ The Lion of Judah

AT POKWO IN ETHIOPIA Don McClure's life's work as a pioneer missionary came to its fullest expression. That is, the Anuak project that Don initiated at Akobo and completed at the Gilo River station matured at Pokwo. Don accomplished a great deal in the years beyond Pokwo, but it was here that the Anuak project put down its deepest roots. The strangest feature of this period was the firm and warm (if necessarily distant) working relation between the missionary from America and the monarch of Ethiopia. This relationship between Don McClure and His Imperial Majesty, Haile Selassie I, King of Kings, Conquering Lion of the Tribe of Judah, Elect of God, Emperor of Ethiopia, is finally inexplicable, but its existence removed barriers that would have been otherwise insurmountable.

At last we are on our way to Addis Ababa to see an emperor. For a long time I have thought I should move on from Akobo and continue the mission among the Anuaks by establishing a new station in Ethiopia. We explored every avenue open to us, but for one reason or another it never seemed possible to go ahead. Now the way seems clear, and we are en route.

Lyda and I are traveling the hard way and enjoying the trip immensely. We left Akobo early yesterday morning in our outboard motorboat and after a long hot day arrived in Nasir yesterday evening. Parts of the trip were beautiful and delightfully restful, but on the whole, it is not exactly a pleasure jaunt to sit in a small open boat under the blazing African sun. I have arranged a canvas canopy over a rack, and Lyda stands at the back of the boat and controls the motor and helm. She is not wearing any more clothes than the law requires—and the law in Africa is rather relaxed in the matter of wearing apparel—with the sun helmet perched on top of her scanty attire. Much to her consternation, I have just snapped her picture. She is trying to get some suntan before we reach Malakal. I hope she does not get it in the wrong places and finds herself painfully sore. It does not take much for an African sun to make bare shoulders so painful that it is almost impossible to wear clothes. She has taken warning and put her blouse back on, so now I can concentrate on my writing. Tomorrow is Lyda's birthday, and I do not have a thing to give her except a kiss. I remember that I kissed her on her last birthday, and I guess if she can stand it again so soon, I can too. It is too bad that birthdays do not come around more frequently.

The Pibor and Sobat Rivers are beautiful at this time of year, just short of flood stage, and the waters are dropping rapidly, leaving beautifully grassed banks. Everywhere the grass and trees abound with birds of every description: egrets wading in the shallow waters looking for leeches and water beetles; herons slowly wading knee-deep looking for small fish; ibis and storks fishing for snails and clams; the bitterns just sitting and apparently not looking for anything; the many kinds of kingfisher hanging in midair and suddenly diving like a stone into the river reeds. On the surface of the water the stately pelican swims slowly along, then suddenly darts for a fish, while overhead the whistling teal and the spurwing goose fly back and forth to their feeding grounds. We have been disappointed, however, in the lack of crocodiles. Not one has been seen since we left Akobo. The swamps are not yet drained, and the crocs are still living back among the grasses. They do not come out to the river until the swamps get very shallow. We expect to arrive in Malakal in two days from Nasir. Tonight we may sleep on the boat and let it drift with the current to save time. There are no steamers on the river, and we feel safe to drift. The only dangers would come from an overinquisitive hippo or a hungry crocodile, and I think we can cope with any such.

We are trying to complete our building program at Akobo as fast as we can get materials. Harvey Hoekstra is making excellent progress in the Anuak language and will soon find his place in handling the literature and translation work. I am hoping that by the end of the next year he can take over the school entirely. It is wonderful to have a skilled linguist on our team. He will be able to correct my clumsy translations of the Bible into Anuak.

On arrival in Addis Ababa Don conferred with the American Mission staff working in Ethiopia. Everyone felt that Don should try to go directly to the emperor rather than the heads of the various departments of state that might eventually have jurisdiction over the Anuak project in Ethiopia.

According to Ethiopian tradition, Haile Selassie was a lineal descendant of King Menelik I, the child of a somewhat irregular union between King Solomon and the Queen of Sheba (1 Kings 10:1–13). One Queen of Sheba legend is contained in a fourteenth-century composition called *Kebra Nagast,* or *Glory of the Kings.* According to the story, once upon a time there was a great king who ruled a large country called Ethiopia. He worshiped one God only and was distressed that his people paid tribute to a multitude of wicked gods. In particular there was a huge serpent who devoured countless animals and to whom even humans were offered in sacrifice. One day the king fed poison to a goat, which the horrible serpent ate and then died, demonstrating that he was no god.

Another version says that the serpent demanded the sacrifice of a virgin every seventh day. When the king's own daughter was the chosen victim, a man named Georgis slew the serpent and saved the damsel, whom he married. This couple founded a dynasty of kings and queens in Ethiopia that lasted seven generations and produced Makeda, the beautiful Queen of Sheba.[46]

In one version, King Solomon heard of her great beauty and desired to see *her.* According to another version, she had heard of Solomon's great wisdom and desired to hear *him.* In any case, the Queen of Sheba visited the King of Judah; she was much impressed by his wisdom, and he was fascinated by her beauty.

One version reports that King Solomon had heard that the queen had a deformed foot, which she always kept covered. According to this account, "So Solomon had a floor made of glass so that the queen would think it was water and lift her robe. And she did so and revealed her deformity, and Solomon set his wise men to cure it." There is a window in Kings College Chapel at Cambridge that shows the Queen of Sheba standing in pale blue glass marked with wavy lines like water, while in the cathedral glass at Chartres her deformity is revealed as a webbed foot. There are still restaurants in France called *La Reine pedauque* ("the Goosefoot Queen").

King Solomon desired to have Makeda as the mother of one of his children (to put the matter delicately), but she steadfastly refused to accede to his demands. On the last evening of her visit, Solomon invited the queen and her dark-skinned maid to spend the night in his palace. Makeda agreed on condition that Solomon would not molest them. Solomon gave his word, but exacted a promise in return that neither woman would steal any of his possessions.

The meal that was served contained extremely salty and spicy food, and during the night Makeda awoke with a great thirst and sent her maid to get some water. "But Solomon had arranged that the only water in the palace was in a jar by his bed. When the maid started to draw water from the jar, Solomon reached out and caught her hand and drew her into his bed and lay with her. He then told her to lie under the bed and be silent." Then the queen herself came in search of water. "And thinking Solomon was asleep she began to draw water from the jar. And Solomon caught her hand and said, 'You have broken your promise.' And the Queen of Sheba said, 'Water is not a possession: it belongs to everyone.' 'In your country perhaps,' King Solomon replied, 'where water is plentiful, but here it is scarce; it is a man's most precious possession. But drink first, take your fill. Then, as you have broken your promise, so shall I break mine.'"

The story does not indicate the degree of enthusiasm with which the Queen of Sheba paid the penalty required by King Solomon. Suffice it to say that the next morning Solomon gave the queen a ring and said, "If you have a son, give this ring to him and send him to me." Nine months after Makeda's return to Ethiopia, Menelik I was born.

When he was old enough, the queen sent Menelik to his father with the ring, but on seeing him Solomon said, "I do not need a ring to know that you are my son." After Solomon had taught his son many things, he bestowed on Menelik as a parting gift the true ark of the covenant. Thus, for centuries the Jews possessed only a replica of that sacred object. The original ark is believed by some Ethiopians to be buried in their country. Presumably, no impious termite would dare to attack the acacia wood of which the ark was made.[47]

When Menelik returned to Ethiopia he brought with him the eldest sons of a hundred of Solomon's elders. Thus the Amharic ruling class of Ethiopia are supposed to descend from King Solomon and the Queen of Sheba through their son Menelik. The dark-skinned Oromos descend from the son of Makeda's maid and King Solomon. Therefore the Oromos are considered black Africans, but the Amharas think of themselves as Semitic.

▼▲▼

A few days after his arrival Don called Tafara Worq, the emperor's secretary and "minister of the pen," and asked for an interview.

After two telephone calls, this request was granted, and I explained to him our proposal and requests concerning a Christian mission among the Anuaks at Pokwo. I also asked for an audience with His Imperial Majesty, Haile Selassie, whose throne name means "Power of the Trinity."[48] The secretary was gracious but noncommital. After waiting two weeks, I determined to go back to Akobo and push on with the building program. However, about noon today Tafara Worq called and said that His Majesty had requested that I attend him that afternoon.

When I arrived at the Imperial Palace, an aide-de-camp asked me, "Where is your car?" I replied that I had left it outside.

"Will your chauffeur bring it around?" I almost laughed in his face, but said, "I do not have a chauffeur. I drove myself. Besides, my car is only a little Volkswagen."

"But you must have a car here," he said. "I have been given strict orders that I am to open the gate for Dr. McClure *and* his car."

"Never mind," I replied, "the Volkswagen is old and dirty and it would be out of place." I could see the British ambassador's Rolls Royce and a fine new Mercedes that belonged to the French ambassador.

"But you must come in a car," the aide said. "Let me have your keys, and I will send a driver for it." So I turned over my keys for a man to bring the car because "I must have a car," even though I was just fifty feet from the palace door.

I met Tafara Worq at his office, but he was glum and would not give me any encouragement. I almost felt that the audience was going to be a trying one, and I think the secretary believed that to be the case, because it was obvious that he did not know how the emperor would respond to my proposal. He instructed me on the protocol, and we started for the palace. Scarcely a word was spoken as we took the long walk, and I could not get a thing out of him. I approached the royal audience chamber in fear and trembling and almost wished that I was back in the wilds of the Sudan facing a lion instead of in Ethiopia facing the Lion of Judah. We walked up the long flight of steps at a breathtaking pace, and both of us were winded as we neared the closed door. Fortunately Tafara Worq paused a second to catch his breath and I was able to catch two of them before we went in. As I stepped into the huge room, I saw Haile Selassie standing behind an immense desk at the far end of the room. I bowed, and on straightening up and looking at him, I immediately felt at ease, for he acknowledged my bow with a cordial nod and a warm, friendly smile. Halfway to his desk I again paused and bowed from the waist; he stretched out his hand, which I took, and bowed again, not merely because it was proper protocol, but because he had a kingly bearing and great personal charm.

Immediately on waving me to a chair he indicated to me by a smile and by an inquisitive look in his eye that I was to state my business. I thanked him for being so gracious in granting me an audience and assured him that my mission concerned thousands of his own subjects. I reminded him that we had met years before in Khartoum when he had trouble with his car, but that meeting had nothing of the importance that this one held. Then very carefully I laid before him our hopes and plans for the Anuak people, working up to the crux of the whole matter—his permission to work unhampered among the Anuaks in Ethiopia. Tafara Worq translated as I went along, but I could see that His Majesty understood perfectly as I spoke to him in English.

After I had spoken for fifteen minutes, he replied in Amharic, which was again translated by Tafara Worq, saying, "I want to thank you for coming, and I want to thank your mission and your board in America for undertaking this work among the Anuak. I am deeply interested in these people of the lowlands and want to learn more about them. I will grant you immediate permission to open this work among the Anuak people in Ethiopia. When can you start?" By that time my heart almost leaped out of my chest, and my eyes filled with tears. I bowed my head in grateful thanks to His Majesty, Haile Selassie, but also to HIS MAJESTY in the heavens. As I raised my head, the emperor was smiling at me with a twinkle in his eyes, and the way Tafara Worq warmed up and became enthusiastic was revealing. It was apparent that the secretary did not know whether the audience was to be a success or not, and he had been afraid that he might be reprimanded for allowing a little missionary from America to come into the presence of His Imperial Majesty of Ethiopia.

Then the emperor began to ask questions about the Anuaks. How many were there, and where they were located? Where did we want our stations? How would we get to them in the rainy season and during the dry weather? Could the Anuaks learn quickly, and was I sure our program would be a success among them? Had the Sudan government given their permission to work across the border? Was Pokwo the best site for the headquarters for such a work? How many missionaries did we now have on the field, and how many would be coming this year? I tried to give clear and precise answers to all his questions. Then he said a very significant thing. He asked, "Have you heard that the Aga Khan of India has contributed one hundred thousand pounds for the conversion of the pagans of south Sudan and Ethiopia to Islam?" And had I heard that in Egypt, a similar fund had been raised for the conversion of the south Sudan to Islam? I replied that I was aware of these funds and it was the very urgency of the times and situation that made me bold enough to seek his permission to work among the Anuak in Ethiopia.[49] Christianity, of course, was introduced to at least one Ethiopian in New Testament times (Acts 8:26–39), and Ethiopia is the oldest Christian empire in the world. However, she is an island surrounded by an Islamic sea.[50]

I then pointed out to His Majesty that we would have to approach the Anuaks from Sudan due to the lack of avenues of communication within Ethiopia. He said that he appreciated these difficulties and would be glad to place at our disposal his own private plane for explorations and the choosing of necessary sites, and as soon as landing fields could be established, an air service would be made available to us. He said again that he was much interested in these peoples of the lowlands, and significantly he did not use the word *shankalla* (slave people) for the Anuaks as everyone else does; he called them "my people." I became the more bold and pointed out to him the difficulties of teaching these people in any tongue other than their own and said that we would want permission to use the native languages in all our schools until such time as we could learn Amharic and begin to teach it to the Anuak people in Ethiopia. He said he understood these problems and that I need not be concerned about them. He then said, "If and when you desire Amharic teachers and books, I will be glad to supply them at my own expense." I thanked him and said we would be delighted to accept his kind offer when we felt the Anuak people were ready to begin to learn the official Ethiopian tongue.

I then explained to him our desire to use small aircraft in reaching some of these outposts, and unlike the Sudan government, he immediately said there would be no difficulties about permission to fly in Ethiopia. Then, as I saw our audience drawing to a close, I asked about the necessity of visas, etc., in crossing back and forth between the Sudan and Ethiopia as we visited the various parts of our work. He replied that he would immediately write personal letters to all those concerned and give us letters for Gambela[51] and the border police posts granting us easy access to his territory. As he rose to close the interview, he again thanked me for coming and asked me to convey his thanks to the mission boards (I had explained that more than one board was behind the Anuak project) for undertaking this work.

It had been breathtaking, and as I bowed myself out, his warm smile followed me, and I thought I was walking on air. The Anuak project was one long step nearer fulfillment. I felt as though the Lord had placed his final seal upon it. He had blessed us above all we could ask or think. On my taking leave, Tafara Worq was a different man, for now he was beaming with delight that the audience had been so successful. He asked me to return as soon as possible to finish arrangements and get the necessary papers. I asked him if I should remain and wait, but he thought nothing would be done within three weeks or a month. We felt we should get back to Akobo and begin to plan the next steps with our crowd there and have the month with them before we returned to Addis.

Even before the McClures left Sudan it was evident that Africa's largest nation would have serious problems to resolve when it became independent in 1956, because the country was sharply divided between north and south. The more advanced and politically aggressive peoples of the north were culturally Arab and religiously Muslim, while the less developed black tribes of the south were chiefly pagan or Christian. Unlike the British, an independent Sudanese government dominated by northerners was not likely to continue to encourage the work of Christian missionaries.

In the early 1950s one of Don's missionary friends went north to Khartoum for his vacation and was denied permission to return to his station in Malakal because of "political activities." He was then compelled to leave Sudan altogether. Other missionaries became afraid to return to America on furlough unless they could get a reentry permit before leaving Sudan. In 1948 Don had predicted that his church did not have more than ten years left to work in Sudan,

And everyone laughed at me, and nothing was done to speed up our work. The old diehards refuse to turn over responsibility and mission property to the native Christian church. Someday soon we will be driven out of Sudan and all our property confiscated by the state. If we would now give it all over to the native church, they could at least hold the properties after we are forced out. The cry "Africans only in Africa," or "Africa for Africans," is being heard increasingly from all quarters, and the days of the white man as a ruling class are numbered. This attitude will affect missionaries and teachers too. It may be that the indigenous Christians will ask us to come back to Africa later on, but we will not return with strong missionary organizations but as individuals with certain needed skills. It behooves us now to prepare our Sudanese Christians for independence while we have some time left.

Don McClure never liked working under restrictions of any kind except those that belonged to the nature of the evangelistic task. Thus as restrictions were being imposed on Christian missionary activity in south Sudan even before independence, Don was delighted to be able to continue his work among the Anuaks by moving into western Ethiopia.

Don named his new station in Ethiopia "Pokwo," which in the Anuak language means "village of life."

We are located on a knoll, a beautiful spot high above the west bank of the Sobat (or Baro) River surrounded by low-lying land that floods every year. This river is called Sobat because it is red with silt from the Ethiopian hills most of the year. However, just now the water is falling and the river is a lovely cream color. When we set up camp, I laid out a kind of grass fence to designate our kitchen, another for my workshop, another for a storeroom, and two grass-fenced sleeping quarters for my helpers. There are fifty men and boys who have gathered to help us build this *Khal ke Jwok*, or "Place of God." We now have a grass-and-stick fence around our little compound so that we can eat and drink without bumping some Anuak on the nose when we bend our elbows. The fence gives us some privacy. The people are so curious to see all the ways of the foreigners that they will come here early in the morning and sometimes sit all day, following the shade around the big tree under which we live and just watching what we are doing. I occasionally stop my work and sit down with a few score of them and teach them some Bible truths. But I fear it is just as incomprehensible to them as why we own so many things.

In one of her relatively few letters, Lyda described her new home.

For now, we are living in two tents under a huge sycamore fig tree. The main tent is our storehouse for food and clothing and is also meant to be a dressing room, but it is seldom used. We live mostly in the mosquito tent. The floor is canvas, the walls are mosquito netting six feet high, and the ceiling is made of plain white cloth. It makes a fly-proof place to eat and a mosquito-proof place at night. In our mosquito house we have two camp cots with our mattresses, a sewing table used for a radio stand, a card table, two folding chairs, and a metal cabinet for dishes and clothes. All of this is in a floor space of nine feet square, and there is no room to spare! We hang our pressure light on a bamboo tripod outside so that we are free from bugs. Our kitchen and washroom are also outside. The gasoline stove is working hard these days until I can get charcoal made for the small charcoal grates.

The first night in Pokwo a fierce storm hit us with one-hundred-mile winds at two in the morning. Our tent blew down, although the dishes on the card table in the mosquito house were only blown off and the metal kitchen cupboard was blown over. After the terrific wind, rain poured down, and we had only our woolen blankets for protection until we decided the rain was not going to stop. So we got out our canvas bedroll cover. Don got it over our beds, but by then he was soaked to the skin and his bed was a pool of water. He shed his wet pajamas and crawled into my fairly dry bed.

We finally went to sleep, but the next morning we found that the dirt which had been blown in by the wind had turned to mud. I hung everything out to dry, and Don had to hang our mosquito house up so that the canvas could dry too. I had to take the sheets down to the river and wash them. It is not easy to wash sheets and heavy things by hand. While I was washing in the river, something brushed against me, and I got out very quickly. I had seen a crocodile out in the middle of the river, but I discovered that I had only been bumped by a floating cornstalk! When I finished, I was so wet that I took off my clothes and washed them too and put them back on wet.

Our bathtub is the river, which has a nice sandy bottom. It is so shallow that I am sure crocodiles will not come in so close, but we are always on the alert for them. We still do not have a canvas covering for our mosquito house, but tomorrow Don will fix it. It is the dry season, and we are not supposed to have rain. The weather is hot, but in the shade of our tree and with a breeze we are quite comfortable. We brought a refrigerator on Wednesday, so food is easier to keep. The Anuaks think that an ice cube burns and that we are strange to use so many of them. We had sandwiches with a choice of liver paste, peanut butter, sandwich relish, cheese, and a powdered milk drink with a chocolate malt to flavor it. The powdered milk is really the best I have ever had, and we are enjoying it.

According to Don,

The more we see of Pokwo, the better we like it. The Sobat makes a great bend here, and we can see the full sweep of the river for more than a mile upstream and downstream. Directly across from us is a large sandbar on which the crocodiles used to sun themselves, but recently they have been considerably disturbed by my shotgun, so most of them have moved away. Thus Lyda and I now find pleasure in having our twice-daily bath in the river, much to the amusement of all the local population. Since our arrival we have been living in a sea of Anuak people who have come to greet us and have stayed to watch the queer ways of the foreigners. They talk to each other about us just as if we could not speak their language. Many of their remarks are amusing, and some of them sobering. Among the amusing ones: "Wouldn't it be terrible to be born with red skin like those people?" "They eat three times a day like animals." (The native people eat only once a day.) But some of their remarks are sobering: "Look at all the stuff they have. Already they have brought three boat [truck] loads from Gambela, and some say they have much more." Again, "Why have they come to live in this country?" "Some say there is a war in their country and they are running away from it." "They will soon die in this heat." Our radio is a source of constant amusement to the Anuaks. They, of course, do not understand that the music comes over the airwaves, but think that it all comes out of the little box. Nevertheless, it amuses them.

Our river is full of fish, of which we are very fond. We have also come to enjoy crocodile meat occasionally. Only this last week Donnie shot a sixteen-foot crocodile and with the help of some Anuak boys proudly dragged it home. They skinned it and have dried the skin for sale. We are always glad when we have an opportunity to shoot the crocodiles, because many people are taken by them while washing or swimming in the river. We shoot a crocodile almost every day and sometimes more than one a day, but they never seem to diminish.

Our days are very full. I start the day with a six-o'clock morning worship service for all the people on the place and the nearby villagers. We always have more than one hundred in this service and sometimes as many as two hundred. It is a great joy to teach them the story of the Bible and of God's great plan of salvation. Many Anuaks have accepted Jesus Christ as their Savior and are being prepared for baptism. We hope to baptize them at Christmas time.

I always take off an hour at one o'clock for my inquirers' class, and it is a pleasure to teach this bunch because they are eager to learn. We have been studying the Holy Spirit, and it is hard for the Anuaks to understand the doctrine of the Trinity without believing in three gods. They are quite willing to believe in as many gods as I say there are, because a multiplicity of gods is their normal view. Again, it is beyond me to make adequate theological explanations in the Anuak language, and I must leave such matters in God's hands. Donnie and Polly are studying their catechism, and they have trouble with the doctrine of the Trinity, too.

Today I had difficulty keeping one chap awake, but he had been out in the hot sun since six-thirty in the morning cutting roofing grass, and I could scarcely blame him. If there is any job in the world worse than cutting roofing grass, I have never found it. In the first place, the grass is about eight feet tall and very tough. As one kneels and grasps a handful of it and then chews it off with a small sickle, every grass seed on the waving top falls down on one's sweating back and begins to dig in with its sharp spikes. Down there in the midst of the grass, there is not a breath of air and no shade. So if this chap dozed off in the middle of a theological discussion, he is not much to be blamed. I have had the men out cutting grass for two weeks because we need enormous quantities of grass for our roofs.

Every day while I am having breakfast, one of our Anuak men who is trained as an evangelist holds a service for the sick who come for medicine After breakfast I go to my "clinic." I have no clinic building, so I set up a table under the huge sycamore tree and spread out my medicines and bandages around me, and the people gather in. Sometimes we have a big crowd, but this morning I had only 47 patients. Monday is always a slow day, not because these folk do the family wash on Monday, for they have few clothes to wash, nor do they know that it is Monday. But always on Sunday I have a very large clinic of people who come in for the service and to receive medicines. During the month of October I treated 1,408 patients, and there were seven days when I had no clinic because I was away from the station.

The patients come in and sit on the ground. First, they must listen to a short sermon and learn a verse from the Bible, as well as sing a song or two. We want to bring healing to their souls as well as their bodies. Always there are more women and children than men. Some of them are covered with terrible sores. Many of them have venereal diseases, which are very widespread in these tropical countries. The poor little babies are the worst off, and some of them are brought in already blinded by the diseases inherited from their parents. Their bodies are a mass of putrifying sores. There comes no greater joy to a missionary than to see these little children begin to heal and their flesh become clear and clean as we treat them with penicillin to cure their diseases. There are many spear and club wounds resulting from village fights or encounters with wild animals. But the most prevalent cases are those with tropical ulcers, sore eyes, and malaria. Many of these we are able to treat and bring about swift and blessed cures.

When an American couple sent some money to Don, he wrote to thank them and to explain how the gift was used.

Last month I was called out to a nearby village to see a woman. They did not tell me what the problem was except that she was dying. When I approached the house where she had been carried, there were so many people milling around that it was almost impossible to walk through. When I finally pushed into the little mud-and-grass hut, I saw this woman lying in a pool of blood and her right arm and shoulder a mass of bloody rags and leaves. Bit by bit I pulled the rags and leaves off, and what I saw almost turned my stomach—and I am accustomed to seeing such things. Her whole upper arm had been shot away. Her husband had been sitting on the ground in front of her with his rifle, and it went off in his hand. The bullet hit her just below the shoulder and went up into the shoulder. These guns are old Italian army rifles, and they shoot a very heavy lead bullet. The bullet had shattered all the arm and shoulder bones. There just was not any shoulder left, and the arm bone was a jagged thing sticking out through the flesh.

As soon as I saw the woman, I thought she would die very soon because the arm was bleeding profusely. There was no possibility of getting her to a doctor, because the woman could not have stood the journey. So I went to work and tied off what blood vessels I could find and bound up her wound. I knew she would need penicillin if she were to be kept free of a killing infection. I had only a little penicillin, but she would need lots more and it costs money out here. One bottle of five injections costs $7.50. So Lyda and I prayed for penicillin, and I started to use what we had and sent off a runner to Gambela to telegraph for more. Before the penicillin arrived, word came to us of your gift, and I knew immediately why the Lord had prompted your hearts to send us the money. You will be glad to know that the woman is living today.

The mission's medical needs were always immense. Thus Don was pleased when he could report,

At last we are getting a nurse, and she will soon be starting out from America to us. When she arrives, it will relieve me of hours of clinic work, but even a nurse is not the answer for many of these cases. We have some terrible cases that would tax even the finest doctor. When I returned from a preaching tour, a man was waiting for me who has cancer of the lower bowel and rectum, and almost half of his large bowel is hanging outside his body and has been like that for three days. He was very sick, and when he heard we were coming back to Pokwo he tried to get up and walk into the clinic, and his bowels burst out. This was the most terrible thing that I have ever had to treat and dress. The pain was awful, and I could do nothing to relieve it. If he had been a horse or a dog, I would have shot him to put him out of his misery. It will be a blessing when he goes, but I hate to see him die and will not give him up until all hope is lost. My heart yearns to have the power of healing in such cases. I find such situations very hard on my nervous system and have wished many times that I was a physician. The medical needs here are so obvious and urgent.

For a few days Lyda took over the clinic work for me, excepting the injections and amputations, and was happy doing it for a while. However, one morning a woman came in with a horribly infected hand. It was all wrapped up with leaves, grass, and bits of filthy rags and string. As Lyda removed the pus-soaked wrappings and pulled them free, the first joint of the woman's hand came off with it. Lyda abruptly resigned from the medical profession and hastily made for the washroom. Thus I have taken over again. After a couple of shots of penicillin the woman began to get well, and her thumb has almost scaled over.

Don described his position among the Anuaks:

For several days the Anuaks have been urging me to attend a dance in a village about ten miles downstream. I have been very busy here and refused to go, but one after another of the old men came to see me and told me that they were postponing the dance until *I* could be present. Finally I told them yesterday that I would go this afternoon. Very soon after I gave my word to go, we heard drums all over the countryside calling the people to gather for the dance. Thus, when our boat arrived at the village of Patok we found hundreds and hundreds of people gathered. Our party consisted of Donnie and Polly and an escort of five Anuak friends who asked to accompany us.

When we arrived at the village, the people all ran to meet us and cheered and cheered as we walked up the path from the river. Many of the old men and women fell down on the ground and attempted to kiss my feet, and others tried to kiss my hands. It was not until they led us inside the enclosure of the chief's house and compound and asked me to sit on the stool always reserved for the head chief that I realized something distinctly odd was going on. I refused the proffered seat, but everyone insisted so vigorously that I could not gracefully refuse. Still, I moved the stool to the outer circle instead of the center of all the shouting people. Then I inquired about the purpose of the dance and learned to my dismay that it was called to acclaim me as the big chief of all the district. I tried to laugh it off and pointed out that I was a foreigner and Anuaks should have one of their own for their chief. They insisted that I was one of them and must be the head chief of the district; they were quite earnest, so I began to take the matter seriously.

After a great deal of conversation with the five or six lesser chiefs present, I stood up in the midst of all the people and spoke to them. I told them I was no chief, nor did I have any desire to be one. My purpose in coming to their land was not to take part in their government, but to tell them about God. I then proceeded to deliver them a sermon, and no preacher ever had a more attentive audience than those people, many of whom had never seen a white man or had ever heard a white man speak their language. Every eye watched my face, and they drank in every word as I spoke to them of the Lord Jesus Christ, their Big Chief, who had died for them. I said I had come to be their servant rather than their chief. This brought a storm of protest, because among the Anuaks a servant is scorned.

I insisted that as a Christian I was the servant of a servant master and was overwhelmed by the response. They all cried

out, "We will be Christians like you if you will be our chief!"
Again I pointed out that I had come to live among them only to
be their friend and helper. Finally they agreed to choose a chief
from among themselves, and I gave up my chance to be an
African chief. I hope I won't regret it.

After this episode we watched a most unusual ceremony of
the passing of a generation of young men into full manhood and
eldership in the tribe. About two hundred young men, ranging
in age from twenty-five to thirty, came crawling into the village
square. In complete silence they crawled on their hands and
knees and made a huge circle just outside the local chief's house.
The chief met them and spoke to them of the importance of the
occasion. They were taking the places of those who were too old
to carry on the business of the people, and the whole responsibility of the Anuak people was now on their shoulders. Then the
men were invited into a large compound prepared for the
occasion; they crawled in and formed themselves in small
circles. In each circle was placed a large gourd of cooked meat
and another of corn meal. The queer part of it all was the
absolute silence. The men serving them only whispered, and all
the others kept absolutely quiet.

Then the old men stepped into the circles and began stuffing
the meat into the mouths of the men. They would stuff a huge
handful into each man's mouth, which he is required to chew,
swallow a part, and spit out a portion as a sacrifice. At a given
word they were all told to eat. With both hands they grabbed for
the food and crammed it into their mouths until it was almost
impossible to chew. This went on for about two minutes. Then
the chief struck the ground with his stick, and like a pack of wild
animals the men dashed for the exits, fighting and pushing to be
the first out. Almost immediately they were recalled to sit again
in the circles, and the chiefs present all came in with large cow-
tail switches in their hands with an attendant carrying a gourd of
hot beef broth. The cow tails were dipped into the broth, and
the chiefs began to anoint everyone by violently switching the
broth in all directions. Everyone in the compound, including
ourselves, was covered with the spray, which, as it cooled,
became a thick, white grease. Following this, pots of beer were
brought in, and each man gulped a large mouthful, half of
which he swallowed and the balance spit out as a sacrifice.
Again the ground was struck, and like so many wild men, they

leaped to their feet once more and dashed for the exits shouting and yelling. They gathered in a large group for a few minutes, talking among themselves, and I learned that they were taking a new name for their generation. Soon they came out of their huddle with a new name, drums were beaten, a shout went up, and a new generation had been born.

Don, the agriculturalist, sent word home about his crops.

I am somewhat disappointed in my first corn crop at Pokwo, because the river flooded the fields before the corn was ripe. For weeks I had twenty to fifty men building levees by carrying dirt from the huge anthills that dot the landscape. Some of these anthills are fifteen feet high. The anthills are packed hard and the work is slow, since the dirt must be carried in five-gallon tins. On Wednesday the river began to rise. Usually it gets to fourteen meters (forty feet) and then begins to fall. This time it went higher, and our levee began to crumble. In a matter of seconds, millions of tons of water were pouring over our fields and gardens. All our corn, beans, and about an acre of peanuts are underwater. The corn was nearly ready to harvest, and we will get it out by boat. We got out most of the beets and carrots, all the onions, and a lot of eggplant, some of them as big as a football. Our kids are down in the garden picking tomatoes while standing in three feet of water.

However, this soil is so marvelous and the weather so perfect for growing that we will get a second crop, and if we try, we will get a third and perhaps a fourth crop of grain on the same land. Where else in all the world could this be done? Yet, in spite of it all, these poor people are on a starvation diet because they do not know how to plant new crops. Many families live entirely on corn year-round, supplemented by fish when they can get them; but this unbalanced diet makes them liable to every germ that puts in an appearance. Their poor physical condition robs them of all ambition and desire to grow more than just barely enough to get by.

We hope to change all that. Our peanut crop will be excellent, and already our first soybeans have yielded more than a hundredfold. During the last month I have traded seventy sacks of peanuts for seventy sacks of corn. Commercially I got the worst of the deal, but the people got the peanuts, and the way they eat them, without roasting, proves a great craving for any change of diet. I hope before we are through that we will be exporting tons of peanuts to other parts of the south Sudan. The possibilities of this place staggers me at times. I need a Christian farmer who will use his agricultural knowledge for the glory of God and the welfare of this people. Until then, it is up to Farmer Don.

▼ The Oromo
▼ Church

DON AND LYDA had just started establishing the station at Pokwo when the family returned home for a furlough year. Don spent most of his time criss-crossing America, renewing acquaintances with supporters and speaking to groups all over the country who wanted to hear about the Anuak work. Indeed, Don was in such great demand as a speaker that he often joked that he had to go back to Africa in order to get some rest! However, when the McClures returned to Africa, they found that it was impossible to return to Pokwo until their permission to live there was clarified. Don was not only exasperated, but furious at this delay. He had assumed that all the necessary documents from the Ethiopian government were in hand. During his absence, however, Don discovered that early permission from the top did not preclude later trouble at the bottom. Local officials had lost or destroyed many of his papers. He had to start all over again, and officials who had granted permission the previous year did not want to issue duplicate forms.

It cannot be that we are wrong in moving among the Anuaks in Ethiopia. Our methods may be wrong and our approach may well be from the wrong direction, but if this work now closes to us, then my faith in the guidance of the Lord and his blessing will receive a severe shock, and I will not know henceforth when to trust myself in interpreting God's will. I am confident that it was his will for us to enter upon this work at Pokwo eighteen months ago and that it is still his will. We must find how that will is to be carried out. The Lord must make his way plain before us.

Because of this delay, we are now missionaries without a station. We have been dismissed from Akobo in Sudan, and our former house has been assigned to another missionary family. They are living in our place with all our things stored, and we are not very happy about it because we were moved out without ever having been consulted! On three occasions the new missionaries have asked us to move *our* things out of *their* house. They seem to forget that *I* built that house and we lived there for ten years. Anyway, Lyda and the children and I will all be at Dembi Dollo until the missionary-in-residence comes back from his vacation.

I have already taken over the work, and together with the study of the Oromo language, we have been having a wonderful time in the hospital, church, and school. My day starts with a short worship service with the workmen at 6:30, then I take the clinic services at 7:30 and have the final service of the day at 10:30 in the school. In between times I try to keep the workmen on the job and squeeze in a few hours of language study. At this point I must still preach through an interpreter, and that irks me beyond measure. I cannot understand how any missionary could go on year after year using an interpreter to get his message across to the people! With each of my former visits here I have studied the language and now am able to direct the workmen and make most of my desires known in the native language; but I cannot yet teach and preach in Oromo.

It is a great joy to be here, for the Oromos are much more advanced than our Anuak people, and I feel free to really bite into a subject. At least I have the joy of preaching just about as profoundly as I wish,[52] and if the interpreter does not understand what I say (and I know many times he does not), then he can preach some other message and neither I nor the audience is any the wiser.

What we will do for a place to live when the missionary assigned to Dembi Dollo returns is still beyond us and is in the hands of the Lord. I feel that we are not wanted at Akobo; there is no house we can rent in Gambela, and I am unwilling to live in a tent with the children in the midst of the rains and mosquitoes. If the mission launch is ready for use, we may live on the launch and spend our time itinerating from one Anuak village to another, preaching and teaching as we go. I would greatly enjoy that for myself, but I am not sure it would be a very enjoyable vacation for the children. Still, it would be good for them to have a taste of real missionary work and certainly infinitely better than sitting cooped up in Gambela in the government rest house.

The country around Dembi Dollo is most beautiful. The high hills rise gently and then slide into wide, green valleys. The hillsides are dotted with settlements and farms. The Oromo farmer does not work very hard, because the seed and the warm summer rains do most of the work. Thus the Oromos grow marvelous crops with a minimum of effort. But withal they are miserably poor and improvident. I see a great need to teach both agriculture and house building. Our church and mission program is hopelessly inadequate, and everywhere in this country, as well as in Sudan, we are rushing into education on the higher academic levels when not a boy in our schools can build a decent house, plant a garden or a field of grain, or take care of a cow or chicken. And this is almost an entirely agricultural area. The only people who are not engaged in agriculture are those government parasites whom we are turning out in our schools and who can only work for the government or mission. We are doing our best to destroy an agrarian culture and civilization and create a parasite class of bureaucrats. Even the mission boys and teachers aspire to be paper-pushers. But I must keep off that subject!

Don found the work at the Dembi Dollo mission extremely challenging.

We had a baptismal service today, and it was a "howling" success. There were four babies to be baptized, and I did not know one from the other. They all were crying so loudly that I could not hear their names as the parents whispered them to me. It did not make any difference, because no one heard what was said; if the names were mixed up, no one is the wiser. There was one baby who was wet on both ends after the baptism. None of them wore diapers, and this baby was so scared that when the water was put on his head, he cut loose and soaked both himself and his mother; but no one seemed to mind, least of all the baby.

Word came in this evening that one of our pastors, who lives about four miles away, was arrested today for baptizing some people in his home. The church of which he is a pastor is closed, but these men have never been denied the right to hold services in their own homes. Now it seems that the persecution is going to reach even further. I think it is high time we brought this problem before the United Nations General Assembly. Ethiopia is a member of the United Nations and has pledged herself to religious liberty. Since she is denying freedom of worship to her own people, I feel some strong action on our part is called for in behalf of the downtrodden people of this area. The great and basic trouble is not religious, but tribal—that is, the rise of the Oromo people, or as they are usually and pejoratively called, the Gallas. The Amharas, who are the ruling class, are beginning to fear that the Oromos will become educated and demand a greater share in the government of the country. This is certainly true, since already some of the educated Oromos are pushing their way upward in government circles and the Amharas are beginning to see what may happen in the years to come. So some of the Amharas are determined to keep the Oromos down. It is not the case of the downtrodden minority, because the Oromos are far more numerous, yet most of them are still illiterate pagans. When the Oromos come to realize their strength and power, they may well make trouble for the Amharas.

Yesterday Lyda and I had an interesting time at a "mountain funeral." One of the Oromo pastors had been sick in the hospital for a long time, and last Friday night he died. I had not seen him, because we just returned from Addis Ababa at noon on Friday and were very tired after a long day of flying. We were preparing for bed when word came to us of the man's death. A few minutes later, some of the men of the church came in and asked us if we would be willing to take the man's body home for burial. His church was only forty miles away, but over a very difficult mountain pass with a very bad road, and I was not keen about the trip. On the other hand, unless we took his body back home, we would have to bury him here the first thing in the morning and before any of his family could arrive. So Lyda and I said that we would make the trip.

I drove down to the hospital for the body and could scarcely refrain from laughing when I saw the rough wooden coffin that had been hastily nailed together during the night. It was not the crude boards and rough appearance that struck me as funny, but the fact that it was fully nine feet long and the dead man was barely five and a half feet. I know that as we went up and down the steep mountain road, the body slid from one end of the box to the other so the men with us had to re-nail the lid on after we reached his village. Apparently the body had tried to pop out from time to time. We did not reach the village until 10:30 in the morning, and then the coffin had to be carried the last mile up to the little church on top of the mountain where only a donkey or a mountain goat could travel along the path with a heavy load. I remained with Lyda at the bottom of the mountain in the truck, and they were to call us when the grave was dug. We were grieved for the pastor's wife, who would have no intimation of her husband's death until we arrived there. A few minutes after our arrival, we heard the high, piercing keening echoing out over the mountains, and soon people began gathering from all directions, each of them moaning to themselves as they passed us. Then as they approached the village, their voices were raised to a shrill wail. This kept on for hours until there were hundreds of people gathered at the village and about the little church.

At 2:00 in the afternoon, two mules arrived to take us to the church for the service, and I realized that we were even then quite early because they were still digging the grave. With such a long box, the grave had to be correspondingly large, and the depth of the grave varies according to the importance of the deceased person. Since this was the pastor of the church, they wanted to dig the hole quite deep. After they reached about six feet, I thought they were finished, but then they had to dig a niche in which the body would fit and that took another hour. During all this time, I was congratulating myself that I would not have more than a prayer at the service, since there were three Oromo pastors present whom we had picked up along the way, and I felt it was their place to make any necessary remarks.

The head pastor Keis (or Reverend) Gidada Solon,[53] who is blind, opened the service with a prayer and song, then the other two ministers were called on for prayer, and finally Keis Gidada turned to me and said, in English, "You now make address and I will interpret." I gulped and started to protest, but he said, "The people expect it of you." So throwing myself on the power of the Holy Spirit, I rose and spoke to them on the verse "I am the resurrection and the life; if any man believe on me, though he be dead, yet shall he live." The words were truly put into my mouth, for I felt a freedom of speech and a wealth of material that simply overwhelmed me, and I spoke without knowing how long I had been on my feet. After the service we went quietly to the grave, and there Keis Gidada gave a short speech and the body was lowered into the deep grave.

After the coffin had been lowered into place, huge logs were placed over it to keep hyenas from digging down and trying to get at the body. This seems to be the custom even when the body has been placed in a wooden box. The wooden box is, of course, unusual and would only be used for an important man. After the earth was thrown into the grave, huge stones were placed on top of the grave and then completely covered over. The men and women of the village had been carrying the stones all day long from the creek bed at the bottom of the mountain. When the grave was closed, we again went to the house of the widow and had another short service with her and a few friends. Then we went to another house and were served a supper of fiery-hot Ethiopian food. The food is completely covered with red peppers, and my mouth and stomach burned for hours afterward.

We started home again at six in the evening, and while I drove as hard as possible over the mountain, it took us four hours to drive the forty miles back home. As I left Keis Gidada at his house at 10:00 P.M., he said, "I am very tired and have made no preparation for tomorrow. Will you preach for me?" After my extemporaneous sermon at the funeral, I could scarcely protest that I was not prepared either. So I had two services today, and tonight I feel the need for a bit of sleep.

Again Don wrote of the persecution of the Oromo church.

The Evangelical Church around Dembi Dollo has been under persecution for some time, and many of their people have been imprisoned for no other reason than that they held services in their churches. They have been held for weeks until they could dig up the money to pay their large fines. In many cases these fines amounted to three or four months' salary for the pastors, and the value of two or three head of cattle for the others. Every one of these men has been imprisoned because of his faith, and many of them are poor today because of the very high fines that they had to pay to various officials, often without receiving a receipt. What we would call extortion and bribery is considered by some government officials here a legitimate exercise of authority and the perquisites of office. One of the pastors was imprisoned three times, and each time he refused to pay his fine, but all this time he continued to teach the other prisoners and even his jailers. They took his Bible away from him, and he continued to teach from memory. They discharged him and he continued to preach, so they arrested him again, only to discharge him again. They did not know where he was a worse menace, in or out of jail.

The eighteen evangelical churches, one by one, have been closed by the local officials. In some cases the doors were officially sealed shut, in others just closed, and the people were threatened with imprisonment if they attempted to worship. A month ago I met with the Oromo Christian leaders for three days to discuss the problems arising from the closed churches and the needs of the people then in prison. The leaders were full of joy that they were being counted worthy to suffer for the Lord! Many of them had lost a half-year's salary and have not been able to plow or plant their fields. Most of them were wearing the only clothes they possess, and all were in their bare feet because they could not afford to buy shoes. Yet not a word was said about their own needs. They were only concerned for their people and the churches.

Blind Gidada spent seven months in Addis Ababa trying to reach the emperor with a petition for the imprisoned people, and finally one day he was with another pastor on the street when Haile Selassie drove past in his car. The pastor who could see immediately threw himself in front of the emperor's car and was very nearly run down. When the car finally stopped, merely brushing the pastor, Gidada thrust his petition through the window into His Majesty's face. The next day he was called to see His Majesty and learned that lesser officials had kept the emperor in ignorance of what was happening at Dembi Dollo, and he did not know that Gidada wanted to see him. After their conference Gidada was given two papers, one refunding all the fines his people had paid, and the other ordering that the churches should be opened and people allowed to worship freely.

The week Gidada returned to Dembi Dollo, everyone was full of optimism that the troubles would soon be over. But when he presented himself to the local officials with his papers for the refund of the fines and the verbal permission to open the churches, the local officials refused to recognize him and his papers (the order to open the churches had not yet come through from the governor general of the province), and they warned him that if he attempted to open his church they would arrest him. For three days Don met with the pastors and elders to seek guidance. Gidada wanted to defy the local officials and open his church in spite of them. Don agreed with him. These local officials were defying the church, the mission, and their emperor—to say nothing of their defiance of the Lord and his people's right to worship according to their conscience. But some of the others were more cautious and counseled that they should wait for a few weeks until all the papers had a chance to get through to Dembi Dollo.

I will never forget the words of Keis Gidada that evening as we parted at 10:30 P.M. after having met in prayer since 4:00 in the afternoon. He said, "I am not only ready to go to prison, but I am ready to die for the Lord and his cause here in Ethiopia." And he meant it. On Saturday I took Keis Gidada home after we had been in prayer with all the Oromo elders and American missionaries until late into the night, and as I left him at his humble, grass-roofed house, he said, "I do not know what I shall do tomorrow (the Lord's Day), whether I shall open the church or just hold the services in my home. I shall spend the night in prayer and shall do what the Lord guides me to do."

The next morning Keis Gidada rang the church bell for the first time in weeks. Instead of gathering in the church, however, he took the 158 people who had assembled into his own home. He said, "Perhaps some of them would be arrested for going to the church, and I do not want to make them suffer. I will suffer for all." They were allowed to conclude their services, but immediately afterward, as soon as the people had gone away, the police came and took Keis Gidada off to prison. They did not take him to the regular prison, but to a foul hole where they usually hold the worst drunkards and brawlers. It was a filthy place with no sanitary facilities whatsoever. When his friends and family tried to visit him, they all, including his wife, were denied the right to see him. Although a friend was permitted to take food to the blind pastor, he was not allowed to stay with him or to help him in any way.

His case was to have been heard yesterday, but the local governor went away on a picnic and refused to see Keis Gidada or hear his case. So Gidada remains in the foul prison where they first led him.

But the joy of it all is that both Keis Gidada and his people are rejoicing in the situation, for they feel that now the local officials have overreached themselves and that good will come out of it. The evangelical Christians have never been forbidden to meet in their homes and preach the gospel to their own people, but only denied the right of assembly in the churches. When the local governor heard the church bell, he assumed that Gidada was calling the people to church and sent his police to arrest him. The police did not realize that there was a difference between a church meeting and a home meeting, and they had not been given sufficient instructions to delay the arrest if the church had not been opened, so they went ahead and made the arrest. Everyone feels that the local governor will now get his fingers burned.

▼▼▼ Another Imperial Audience

IF THE MAJOR TROUBLES at Dembi Dollo were on the way to resolution, the problems at Pokwo remained. Since all government officials served at the pleasure of Haile Selassie, there was no effective constitutional system of checks and balances. Officials could enforce regulations as they chose as long as they did not offend the emperor. After the governor general of Illubabor province had canceled all his permissions, Don spent months trying to get new ones without success. Thus, in order to cut through the endless, official red tape Don determined to return to Addis Ababa in an attempt to see Haile Selassie again. He had been in Gambela for five days waiting for some kind of transport to start for Dembi Dollo so that he could catch the plane for Addis. Travel in this part of Ethiopia was never simple.

Each day I was assured that something would surely go to Dembi Dollo on the morrow. Of course, tomorrow never came, and if I had known on the first day what I knew on the fifth, I would have walked to Dembi Dollo. It is only forty-six miles up over the mountains, but by now I had only two days to get to the plane. So I decided to take my practically new truck out of storage. I had driven it down to Gambela from Addis Ababa sometime before to use in building our houses at Pokwo, and I was not keen to take it up over these mountain roads again; but I had no choice.

There was no trouble getting a load of freight and men to go with me. I contracted to haul a ton of salt to Dembi Dollo, and a dozen Ethiopians wanted to ride up. However, there was one very sick man, an official whom the district governor asked me

265

to transport, who needed medical attention as quickly as we could get him to the hospital. The man was so sick that I wondered if he would ever reach the hospital alive, and when I expressed this fear to the other officials, they shrugged their shoulders and said, "In any event, he wants to be buried at Dembi Dollo. Take his body there."

We left Gambela at noon on Thursday, and the plane was scheduled to leave Dembi Dollo at ten o'clock on Friday, but since we had only forty-six miles to travel that seemed like ample time. The first thirty miles up over the mountain were terrible, and I thought at times the truck would be twisted to pieces as we pushed up over boulders and fallen trees. Obviously an Ethiopian highway bears little resemblance to an American one. The rains had washed huge gullies into the road, and if we had slipped into one of them we could never get out, so we had to straddle deep ruts. Long before we reached the top of the mountain, my back was so sore from the twisting and bouncing about that I had to sit on the edge of the seat and hold myself erect with the steering wheel. There was never a still second, and at no time were any two wheels of the truck on the same level. Some of the driving and riding time was spent in holes, while other times it was spent climbing over stones and in the outcropping of rocks. Had the road been any worse, it would have been impossible to travel at all.

When we got to the top of the mountain, just about ten miles out of Dembi Dollo, the road did get worse. The rocks and stones disappeared, leaving the heavy red soil that the recent rains had made a quagmire. The huge diesel trucks that travel that road carrying salt and coffee had torn the road into ruts two feet deep and the width of three huge dual wheels. My small truck simply could not travel over the same ground. We tried it time after time, only to get stuck and have to dig out and build up the road with trees and sticks so that our wheels would touch bottom. We worked for hours to make a single mile and finally, at midnight, we were so badly stuck that I did not think we could get out without more help. I had left the road entirely and was driving through the high grass with an Ethiopian boy walking out in front. On one occasion, where he had walked was fine for him, but when I tried to follow in the truck, the back wheels slipped sideways and dropped down into what had been a trench, a relic of the Italian War in Ethiopia. The bed of the truck was resting on one side of the trench, with the back wheels hanging in midair.

Everyone was tired, and the sick man sounded as if he were dying. I wanted to leave the truck where it sat and walk the eight miles into Dembi Dollo and send someone back to get the truck the next day while I flew on to Addis. However, I could not leave the dying man or the ton of salt for which I was responsible. So I did my best to persuade one of the five healthy men to walk to Dembi Dollo for help, but not one of those men would move out into the grass and woods at night, nor would all five of them go together although I promised them a fine reward and threatened them with the death of the sick man. I was not afraid to go, but my back was so sore I could barely stand erect; I knew I could not carry my baggage, and there was no use going to Addis without it.

So we all slept except the sick man; he groaned all night. At 4:30 in the morning, just as the first light appeared in the sky, we were up again. This time I did get two men started off to Dembi Dollo while the rest of us began to cut trees to lift up the wheels. Within an hour I had built a sort of bridge under the wheels and then, with our digging away a part of the trench that held the back of the truck, our wheels finally rested on the bridge and in five minutes more we pulled out. We started for Dembi Dollo again and got stuck twelve times before we finally got there just at 8:30 A.M. The men I had sent ahead finally heard our truck roaring behind them, and they sat down beside the road to wait while we worked out of several bad places. I must have been a sight when I appeared, because all the folks at Dembi Dollo doubled up laughing at me. I had been under the truck a dozen times, much of it in the mud, and there was no opportunity to clean up. Even my hair was caked with mud.

As soon as I had a quick bath and a bit of breakfast, we raced for the airfield in the mission Jeep. The airport is another eight miles on the other side of town and the road almost equally bad, but the Jeep got us through, only for us to find that the plane was full and could not take a single additional passenger. Fortunately I knew one of the pilots, and he said, "If you are willing to stand in the cockpit to Addis, we will take you with us." I was dead tired and sore, but the chance to stand in the cockpit was too good to pass up, so I stood for the three hours to Addis.

Immediately on arrival in Addis Ababa, Don went to see His Excellency, Tafara Worq. Don did not want to telephone, since he knew he would be put off for a day or two. He went to the office, presented his card, and within five minutes was ushered in.

We spent forty-five delightful minutes together. Tafara Worq was most cordial and asked numerous questions about our work among the Anuak in the Sudan and about the Anuak people themselves. He wanted to know about their customs, numbers, political system, etc., taking copious notes all the while I was talking. Then, with a smile he came to the question both of us had uppermost in our minds by saying, "You have been having a few difficulties in getting this work started in Ethiopia among the Anuaks on the western border." I replied that the word "few" was something of an understatement—we have been having *many* difficulties and no little opposition. He nodded very sympathetically, sighed, and said, "Yes, I know and we do not like it." I then became bold and asked him, "Your Excellency, does His Imperial Majesty truly want us to carry out this project among the Anuaks in Ethiopia?" His eyes widened in surprise. "Of course, I have seldom seen His Imperial Majesty more interested than he is in this work." I became bolder and said, "Your Excellency, are you also in sympathy with our project?" Again he raised his eyebrows and said without any hesitation, "His Imperial Majesty's interests are my interests. We are very anxious that something be done for these people, and we will welcome anything that can be done and anyone who will do it."

For the next half-hour we talked of our problems. He wanted to know about every instance of opposition and about all the difficulties. I spared no one who had been responsible in making trouble for us. He said that after the first paper I received more than a year ago, everything else could have been taken care of by the governor general at Gore and we should not have needed to come back to Addis Ababa for any further permits. However, since those in authority at Gore had not proved helpful, he would see to it that we secured what we needed. As the interview was drawing to a close, I asked him if he thought I should see His Imperial Majesty to discuss the matter further. He was quiet for some time, and then said, "His Imperial Majesty is quite interested in what progress you are making among this people, and it might prove helpful to see him again. Hold yourself in readiness for an audience on Thursday. I do not say that we can secure such an audience, but I shall let you know Thursday morning." This practically means an audience, but I cannot be absolutely sure. It may not be deemed necessary.

Don continued later in the week,

On Thursday a telephone call came through to the mission office that I was to appear at the palace at 9:30. The last time I had appeared before His Imperial Majesty, I had been dressed in my best (and only) dark business suit and Tafara Worq was not pleased. Thus, to be more appropriately attired, I scurried around to locate formal clothes. In a closet at the mission I found a suit of tails and a tuxedo that Glenn Reed had left here. They fit quite well—that is, I could get into the trousers of the tux and the coat and vest of the morning suit. However, I could not button the coat across my lower chest; because of exercising so vigorously with a knife and fork, I have developed too much muscle. At nine o'clock the Honorable Reverend Don McClure, Ambassador Plenipotentiary of the Lord God of Heaven and Earth, was ready to go and feeling more than a little silly in such an outfit.

I was not only the ambassador, but also the ambassador's chauffeur, so I drove the mission's longest car (a Pontiac station wagon) up to the secretary's office, and five minutes before the appointed hour we started for the palace. As we entered the palace grounds, a guard stopped us, but the secretary impatiently waved him away and told me to drive on. Just as I started to turn into the magnificent gateway, who should appear coming out but Her Imperial Majesty with a three-car retinue, and we almost had a head-on collision. I quickly backed out onto the road while the secretary tumbled out and bowed himself to the ground. A near crash with the empress of Ethiopia was not a very auspicious start. However, we went on into the beautiful grounds and stopped at the palace steps.

After some last-minute instructions from Tafara Worq, we went in. The palace is beautifully decorated in cream and gold with deep red carpet on the floor. We walked through one large hall after another until we came to the emperor's parlor. The double doors were open, and we saw him standing awaiting us at the other end of the room. We bowed together as we entered the door, bowed again midway, and as I approached, he extended his hand and smiled. I assumed he was thinking that I looked as ridiculous as I felt. As we shook hands, he said in English, "Good morning. I am glad to see you again." From then on, he spoke Amharic with the secretary interpreting. He wanted to know everything about the Anuak work and what progress we had made. We talked for half an hour. Then he wanted to know of the inroads of Islam and communism in the west, the use of diglot (two-language) Testaments in all languages (which he approved), and the extension of our work among the Anuaks. Twice he expressed his appreciation for what we were doing, and twice he promised to help us in every way possible.

Then when I was about to leave, he picked up a small silver dish off the table and handed it to me, saying, "I want you to have this as a memento of our visit together." I thanked him and was about to slip it into my briefcase when he told Tafara Worq to take it and have my name engraved on it. So I relinquished it. I hope it is ready before we have to leave Addis Ababa.

Soon Don wrote exultantly,

We are now on our way to Pokwo. After conferring with His Imperial Majesty, I made an appointment to see His Excellency, Kenyasmach Asfau Abejie, the governor of Gambela. He is a fine-looking Christian man and has always been very friendly and helpful. I knew he would do what he could for us, but I was afraid that his hands were tied by the governor general's edict.

Dealing with officialdom is not easy anywhere, but it is especially difficult in Ethiopia. The confusion of some of these government offices is unbelievable. They have no real files. They put an assortment of papers into manila folders and then those folders are thrown haphazardly on the shelves in the "archives." Thus, when I go to a government office the clerk must first look up my files before the official will talk to me. I may have to wait for two or three hours before they locate my file, or it may be they cannot find it at all that day and will ask me to come back the next day. Hours and days when I could be teaching and preaching I have sat in offices all over Ethiopia. Even when an appointment is made well in advance, it never occurs to anyone to look up the file before I appear in person. That is not the way business is conducted here.

Before I left to see His Excellency, I called Iana, the interpreter who would go with me, and a friend or two, and we went to our knees to ask the Lord to prepare the way before us. On arriving at the governor's office I was surprised to see him come out and greet me in a very affable manner, since I assumed I must be out of favor. After the usual amenities I handed over to him the official papers we had received in Addis Ababa that gave us permission to start our work at Pokwo among the Anuaks within Ethiopia. He glanced at them and said that he had copies of all of them. Then I presented to him the letter we had received from the governor general of Illubabor Province revoking our permit and demanding that we start all over again. He read this document with great interest, then smiled, and finally laughed. I was puzzled, because I did not feel much like laughing, as this could have meant another delay of two years or more. The governor then pulled out his file and showed me a very official-looking document all covered with seals, which I recognized to be the royal seal of Ethiopia. With a smile he read, in Amharic, the contents of the letter. When it was translated to me, I was first stunned, then tears of shame welled up into my eyes, and my heart was stricken at my own weakness and doubt. The letter indicated that His Imperial Majesty had presented us as a freehold two *gashas* (square miles) of land that was to be ours, free of all rent or taxes, for as long as we wanted to use it. Then it would revert, with its improvements, to the crown of Ethiopia. We are the only mission in Ethiopia with such an arrangement. And His Majesty also asked that the work be started at once. I wanted to shout and dance with joy, but restrained myself to say, "Praise the Lord." To which His Excellency assented. According to the governor, we could just ignore the letter from the governor general, since we had a document granting direct approval from His Imperial Majesty.

This is not only a mandate from His Imperial Majesty; it is a mandate and a blessing from His Divine Majesty. During the course of my conversation with the governor he said, "His Imperial Majesty expects great things from you on this land he has given you." To which I replied, "Yes, and His Divine Majesty expects great things among the Anuak people. We will do our best to serve both His Divine Majesty, our Lord, and His Imperial Majesty, Haile Selassie.''

My first job is to get our permanent houses built. I have come to loathe this task, because it seems to me that I have spent most of my life in Africa building houses for ourselves or someone else. This past week I have worked on the cement foundation of our house every afternoon until dark. We have two of the stone and brick *tukls* ready for the roof, but we ran out of cement and were not able to get all the foundation in. I am sick of this building business and wish I could somehow contrive to spend all my time in evangelism. We must get more people into direct evangelism if we are to accomplish our purpose for being in Africa. Of all our missionaries in the south Sudan area, there is not a single one today who is able to give his full time to evangelism and only two who were appointed solely to do evangelistic work. I am one of those two, and I have to do everything else first and then devote what time is left to preaching the gospel.

▼ Close Encounters

LIFE IN AFRICA was so full of things to do that it was difficult to get bored. Building adequate shelter, producing sufficient food, fighting superstition, providing elementary education, and treating sick people—to say nothing of evangelism—were constant and time-consuming tasks. And there were curious things to see.

Orac, our Shulla houseboy and cook, is now learning to iron. He is wearing a fancy skullcap made of dried skin from the breast of a goose, with feathers stuck in it or feathers stuck out of it, depending on one's perspective. That is, whether the description begins with the feathers or with the skullcap. Never mind. Orac is actually a young man with three children named "Stove," "Tea kettle," and "Coffee pot"—all the things he has used so often during the fifteen years he has worked for us. Not many months ago Orac and his wife, Nyitwol, were expecting their fourth child. In jest, Orac said he might name this baby "Skillet," but he really intended to name a son after Donnie. From his birth something was wrong with the baby, and he died after two days. Orac and Nyitwol were disconsolate about the loss of their little boy, and so was I.

Of life in Pokwo, Don wrote,

Right now a native dance is going on, and the noise is deafening. I tried to listen to the Pittsburgh Pirates' baseball game on the radio, but I could not hear a thing. The dance is to celebrate the changing of the moon, because the Anuaks believe that the rains will soon come and they can start planting their crops. It is not exactly a rain dance such as the Shulla people

273

have and at which they offer a sacrifice to the goddess of rain. This dance of the Anuaks is just a social dance, somewhat like that of the Shullas but without the religious significance. The Shullas are very religious, but the Anuaks are quite the opposite and have very little of any religion or religious ceremonies. This is due in part to the fact that when they separated from the Shullas, the religious symbols were retained by the Shullas, whereas the political symbols were kept by the Anuaks. So the Anuaks have a more rigid political system than the Shullas, but practically no religion. In fact, I have never seen any of them make a prayer to their gods, although I have seen them make sacrifices. There will be no sacrifices tonight except of my peace and quiet.

Today, for the first time in many years, I spent an entire day in the garden. That is, if the hour I spent doctoring the sick is not counted. Heretofore I have only spent odd hours in the garden, and it had begun to look like it! Suddenly I realized that I would soon have a large family of four to feed again when Donnie and Polly get home for the summer vacation and I had better get busy. We will miss Marghi, who is now in the States finishing high school. Here at Pokwo I do not have the advantage of a trained gardener as I had at Akobo. There I spent ten years teaching an Anuak how to plant and irrigate, but when we came here, he had to be left behind. The same thing was true of my carpenter, bricklayer, and cattle herder. I spent long hours at Akobo training them to do things as I wanted. Then, when they were able to carry on without too much supervision, I had to leave them all behind and start over again. I have not yet found a man who I felt would make a gardener, so I am doing it myself for a while. Yesterday we ate string beans planted just fifty-nine days ago! We have been eating cucumbers planted at the same time, and of course lettuce, radishes, and green onions. Today I put in second plantings of everything, and the garden looks beautiful. All we need now is some rain to help it continue. Soon we will be getting rain by the barrels.

Our house is coming along slowly. All the stone and brick work will be finished tomorrow, and that leaves the roof timbers for me to set in place. Once I have the roof finished, the thatching will be only a matter of a few days and then we will move in. I was hoping to have it all finished by the time the children arrive, but that will not be possible. So until it is done, we will live in the nice grass house I have just finished. It is a big house with three rooms—a dining-living room, a bedroom, and a bath—and will give us some real comfort after having lived in this hot tent for so many months.

The weather is delightful at Pokwo. The early rains dispelled the heat, and now the days are dark and pleasant. I have never seen so many ducks and geese in all my life.[54] This seems to be their breeding ground, and all the ponds and lakes are covered with millions upon millions of them. The other day, with one rifle shot I killed three geese, all shot through the head and each several yards from the other. Crocodiles abound everywhere, and all day long people are calling to me to come and shoot this or that crocodile. If it is an unusually large one, I will drop my work and take a crack at it. The river is filling rapidly now and the sandbars are few, so every one left above water is covered with crocodiles. The big game hunting is also excellent. I have been able to get animals within a few minutes of the mission. The water buffalos are still about, but they are just a bit hard to get at, and the other game is so easy. When Donnie arrives, I shall take him out to see and have a shot at a buffalo. However, I will not let him follow a wounded beast.

This is a very beautiful country and just now, with all the green grass springing up, it is especially beautiful. This site is marvelous. We are on a high bank some thirty feet above the river and are almost surrounded by mountains, some of which are five thousand feet high but all covered with a blue carpet of grass and trees. This is by far the most beautiful mission site of all our stations, and by the time Lyda and I have finished with it, it will be the showplace of the mission. A few hours ago we had the most gorgeous sunset I have ever seen. The whole sky was a stupendous, mottled gold, blue, and many shades of red. From the west to the east, the sky was marked off in steps, and each step seemed to have a different color or hue. Across it all was a lovely spray of golden sunbeams like a pathway into heaven. If heaven is as marvelous as this preview we had today, then it will be a wonderful place to spend eternity with the Lord. I can imagine heaven will be a hundred times better.

I have a new playmate for the children when they arrive. Sheila, a baby leopard, has come to take up abode with us. Only Sheila is quite a big baby. Today Sheila spent the day following Lyda around all over the place, and whenever Lyda stopped, the leopard would throw both paws around her legs and lick her knee. The leopard spent most of the time in the kitchen, jumping up on tables and shelves, and it was all Orac could do to keep it out of the fire. When I got home at two in the afternoon, Lyda was in a fine dither and announced that either she or the leopard would have to go. So I got busy and made a cage for the leopard in which she can live. It is too much trouble to replace a wife.

The medical situation at Pokwo was always grave.

When we went home on furlough, I was treating twelve lepers at Pokwo. Some of them had been with us for a long time and others only a little while, but all of them were showing signs of improvement. Their old sores had healed and some of the cases were arrested, although none of them was completely cured except perhaps a small girl. However, when we went home to America and had to close the station, there was nothing to be done but send all those lepers back to their villages again. I did not dare leave large quantities of powerful medicine with them, because it was too dangerous. On a previous occasion when I gave a leper enough pills to last him a week, he gulped them all down in one swallow. He was unconscious for hours and very nearly died. So there was nothing to do but send the lepers back to their villages. It nearly broke my heart, because I knew that the disease would advance while I was gone, but there was no help for it.

When we returned to Pokwo, I found my lepers in deplorable shape. Their sores had returned, and some of them had lost additional joints from their fingers or toes. Two of the twelve had died, but in addition to the ten remaining and returning, there were another ten or twelve who had heard of our medicine and that we had arrived back on the field, and all of them came in for help.

It was a great joy to see them and to feel that we could begin again to do something for them. But we felt that we could do still more, so we prayed for the Lord's guidance. Out of this grew a dream of building a leprosarium in which these poor people could live, be treated, and perhaps be taught something they could do for a living, although many of them are without fingers or toes.

The medicine for leprosy is very expensive out here, but we estimated that $5,000 would build and get the leprosy center started. I did not try to raise any money or even write letters to people telling them of the need. On the first day of June I prayed for help and left it entirely with the Lord. Last week I received a check for $2,000 from a friend in Ellwood City mailed from Pennsylvania on 10 June. A few days later a gift of $770 arrived, and in the next mail two more checks of $165 and $75. All these gifts started from home in June. We see it as a direct answer to our prayer and the Lord's directive to build and operate a clinic for lepers at Pokwo.

About education, Don wrote,

Recently I located a very fine young Christian Anuak who was educated in our mission school at Nasir and the teachers' training school at Obel. He has consented to run a little village school near Pokwo, although he will have to make a great sacrifice in money and prestige. This young man had been offered a much better salary with the Sudan government as a clerk in one of their offices and a promise of quick advancement in salary and position. I had nothing half so attractive. The best I could offer him was ten dollars a month in the beginning and possibly a dollar a year raise.

The young man's native name is Ngany Gatwec, but when he was baptized he took the Christian name of James. Anyway, when I made my offer to James he said, "I have been offered a job with the government at twice the salary, but I would rather work for the Lord among my own people than to get rich working for the government." It will cost about fifteen dollars a month to cover the teacher's salary and expenses. I wish I had the money and teachers for a hundred more village schools.

Don's work was again challenged by superstition.

We have heard many rumors of the increased activity of witchdoctors in a village upriver from us. Indeed, we have hardly touched that village in all the time we have been here. Most of the people there have closed their hearts to us, but a group of ten boys had become Christians. Last Saturday the boys came to me and said the people were making a lot of fuss about a grove of sacred trees along the riverbank. One huge old tree, from which the others had started, was threatening to fall into the river, and the people were making sacrifices and placing charms to try to save it. The witchdoctors had been busy with their blood and gourds. These ten boys had gone to the chief and his elders and proposed that they cut the trees down because they knew God would not bless their village as long as the people worshiped these trees as Jwok. The chief and elders of the tribe laughed and jeered at the Christian boys and dared them to try to cut the trees down. They insisted that anyone who attacked a sacred tree would surely and quickly die. The boys told me that they felt the Lord wanted them to cut the trees down.

I promised to give the boys all the help I could. The next day, Sunday, a huge crowd from that village was in the worship service, and scores more could not get inside the church. The boys explained what they proposed to do and asked for our prayers. Then after worship, they took axes, saws, and mattocks. (I never encouraged men to work on the Lord's Day so heartily before in my life.) The boys asked me *not* to go with them. They said, "The village people expect you to be there to protect us against the evil spirits and against Jwok." So to my great disappointment, I stayed at home and about two hundred Anuaks crossed the river to watch the action.

It was not long before I learned that the boys were in serious trouble, but not from the chief and his elders, nor the witchdoctors, who had all fled away. Their problem did not even come from Jwok, but from some nasty little devils that almost carried the day. The big trees were full of bees, and these African bees are the most vicious in the world![55] The boys were stung all over and finally had to run for their lives. Soon some of them came back and got fires started at the foot of the trees they were cutting and then piled on green grass and leaves until the bees were stupified with the smoke. Then the boys went ahead with their cutting, but not without many hundreds of stings. They cut down eight or ten big and little trees, and only one was left standing when the bees drove them away again. But the objective had been accomplished, and never again will those trees be worshiped.

In the following services, twenty-one people from that village became Christians, and the next day another four came in. Since then, we have had an evangelist in the village every day, and he says many, many of them want to make a profession of their faith in the Lord Jesus. When their fear was lifted, they saw the light.

Don continued the story.

Soon after this episode, I went about five miles downriver in the outboard with James Jalaba, one of our evangelists, to hold services in three villages where we had not been for some weeks. We passed up the two smaller villages, calling to the people as we went by that we would be back in a short time for *Lum Jwok* (a worship service), and we pushed on to Enyeli for our first service.

I had my medical kit with me because I knew there would be plenty of sick people to look after, and I especially wanted to see a boy who had his eye knocked out a month ago. The lad had come home to this village only a few days ago after being discharged by the opthalmologist (me) with a big white patch still over his right eye socket. I was afraid that too much curiosity from the village folk might persuade him to take off the patch and let people finger the wound, which I knew would bring infection again. Sure enough, the first person to meet us was my patient with a large leaf tied over his eye by a filthy rag of bandage. The adhesive tape had lost its stickiness after having been removed a dozen times to show the empty eye socket. A dirty leaf had taken the place of the sterile gauze pad, and the eye was infected again.

Before we start the clinic work, we always hold a service and let the people know that every pill and bandage is given in the name of the Lord. This service is understandably short, and after the people have been treated we hold a second and longer service. Nothing unusual happened during our short prayer service, and then I was almost swamped as the sick and dying crowded in for medicine. During the next hour I treated more than one hundred patients. That is, I gave medicine to more than one hundred people. If the man with the chest cold got the medicine belonging to the woman with a stomach ache, that was his fault not mine. I gave out hundreds of pills, some of which I knew what they were good for (such as aspirin and cascara), and some I did not (such as Erythrocin-Neomycin).

On the other hand, I did not know what disease I was treating half the time either. So I assume everything balanced out. I had twenty injections to give and two abcesses to lance. All of this was done in the middle of a filthy, dusty village with hundreds of people milling around and kicking up the dust, and half a dozen holding down each child while I tried to pour the cough medicine into the forced-open mouth instead of all over the child's face and eyes. Usually the medicine comes spewing out again as soon as the child is released. Most of the time I enjoy my medical work because I know I am helping the people at least a little bit. I only get discouraged when I must try to treat dying men or women without the vaguest notion of what ails them or what to do for them. At such times I know that I am doing the work of someone whom the Lord intends to have on this field, but who has closed his ears to the Lord's call or her heart to the cries of human suffering. All I know is that some well-trained, committed American physician should be out here doing this medical work.

Today I had to operate on what I think was cancer of the mouth. The woman had a huge growth in her mouth growing out from her upper jaw. A few weeks ago some villager had attempted to cut it off with an old razor blade, but—as might be expected—she became infected. The infection disappeared eventually, but the growth became larger and larger and was hanging over her upper teeth is such a way that she could not chew. Against my better judgment I cut it off this morning and found the roots going deep into her jaw and face. I then had to remove two teeth and drain her ear, because the canal was still full of the former infection. Who am I to attempt such things, and why does the Lord allow me to work alone out here? I am the only "medical officer" for 25,000 Anuaks, and together with a nurse at Akobo we serve 40,000 people among the Anuaks alone, to say nothing of the hundreds of other tribespeople we treat who live on the borders of Anuakland.

All the above is an aside from the main story I am about to relate. After our clinic in the village of Enyeli (the record shows 108 patients treated and 223 treatments—which means all, or most of them, had more than one complaint), the evangelist, James Jalaba, held a second service. He gave a most moving message on the theme "My Sacrifice." It was not a chicken, nor a goat, nor a bull, but God himself who gave his life for us. I followed James with a few words on confession of sins. As soon as we finished, a strange thing happened. The first man who asked to become a Christian stood up and said, "I have a Jwok in my house, and I want you to come with me while I throw it out." The whole crowd trooped to his little grass house, and there in the courtyard was an old dried tree stuck in the ground; hanging from it were sheep bones tied in bundles and a number of metal bracelets. He broke off the tree and dug up more sheep bones from the ground. Then he went into his hut and dragged out an old gourd that contained bones and seeds. These he turned over to me and asked me to throw them into the river.

On the way down to the river, after prayer in the man's courtyard, the second convert dragged us to his house, and another gourd came to light. Then from all quarters people called us to come and destroy the gods they had in their houses and courtyards. Twelve trees were uprooted or broken off; scores of metal bracelets were taken off and turned over to me. The people said, "We do not want to see them again." And all were thrown into the river. Six large gourds were dragged into the open and smashed, and before we were through, the people were laughing and chanting, "*Gi anaka athow*" (the things of Satan are destroyed). In the beginning they had been—especially the old women—a bit apprehensive, but now they began to think it was a game, and they called to each other, "Bring out all the things of Satan."

I know we did not get all the things of Satan, especially those things in some stubborn and frightened hearts, but I also know they all want us back again to teach them more of the Word of God. This past week another fifteen have come to the Lord. The week before, there were twenty-five. Many of these have come because a few courageous boys dared to cut down some trees that their elders claimed were possessed of god.

▼▲▼

During the early years at Pokwo, Don made several quick trips to Akobo. During those times when the Anuaks learned that he had returned for a longer visit, they came in from miles around to greet him and to tell him their troubles. Don spent most of his time in their homes, visiting the sick, and calling on old friends.

On Sunday we had a baptismal service. It is a wonderful thing to see the second generation of Anuaks coming to be baptized. I was asked to baptize the baby of a girl whom I baptized years ago. When we begin to get the second generation, we know the Word of God is taking roots Even if we had to leave Africa today, the gospel will not be lost and the Anuak church will go on. However, witchdoctors have reappeared around Akobo. I assume the present missionaries are not as militant against witchdoctors as I was, and they do not get out into the villages to check on things as often as I did. People drift away and back into old patterns unless an intense personal interest and concern is demonstrated. Thus it seems the witchdoctors, once driven away, are slipping back and setting up practice again. One day while we were in Akobo, I ran two miles through the tall grass to the hut of a man who had taken a spear through the left side in a hunting accident. A witchdoctor had sacrificed a sheep and was pouring the sheep's blood into the wound. The man died before I could do anything. That evening I preached on the Lamb of God from John 1:29, saying that God's Son had made the *only* sacrifice necessary for us. Afterward I felt that I had never preached so eloquent a sermon.

It is a marvelous experience to be completely in the hands of the Holy Spirit while preaching. When that happens I find that there is no struggle for words or effect or even thought; everything just flows as naturally as water from a spring. Even when speaking in a foreign language, there is no groping for words and phrases. The Holy Spirit brings them to mind as naturally as if one were speaking one's native tongue, and not only this, but also grammatical mistakes and errors in pronunciation that I habitually make in Anuak disappear, and I find myself speaking perfect, idiomatic Anuak, much to my own delight and to the delight of those who listen to me.

In contrast to those who called in the witchdoctor, the son of one of our Anuak Christians was fishing when he was bitten by a very poisonous puff adder. The father calmly brought his son to me to treat and said, "If the medicine will not help him, then our prayers will. And if he dies, our lives are in God's hands." This boy is going to get well, and I teased his father by saying, "Why didn't you kill a sheep and pour the blood on your son as you would have done three years ago?" He raised his hands above his head in horror. "That was in other days. Now we believe only in the blood of Jesus."

Obudo, our former houseboy at Akobo, has just died of tuberculosis of the throat. Ever since we came back I knew he was very ill, and I went to see him nearly every day. On the days I could not go, I sent milk and medicine, but there was nothing else we could do for him. Obudo was six feet seven inches tall and always as thin as a toothpick. On my last visit he was able to whisper to me, "I know I am dying, but I am not afraid because the Lord Jesus will be there to meet me. Please tell my family that I am going to a better place." I did tell his family, but they are very much afraid, since someone told them that Obudo got sick because he worked for the foreigners. We loved Obudo and have lost a dear friend and a faithful servant. Our children will be deeply grieved to hear of his death, because he was very kind to them and they were very fond of him.

When I went to Obudo's village to hold a thanksgiving service for him and to visit his family, a young boy came to me and said, "I want to become a Christian. Will you baptize me?" I had never seen him before, so I asked him his name and whence he came. He said that he was a friend of Obudo's and had visited with him while he was sick. Obudo had told him about the Lord Jesus Christ and encouraged him to come to me and talk about becoming a Christian. The thrilling thing about it is that now we have our first-generation Christians going out and retelling the story of redemption and salvation, and soon there will not be an Anuak in all the country who has not heard the gospel.

Coming back to Akobo has been both a happy occasion and a sad experience. Obviously every person must do things his own way, and it was evident that when we left Akobo for Pokwo there would be changes in the mission. However, one of them breaks my heart. I put in ten years of back-breaking work at Akobo to clear the fields and get them in shape to grow crops that would benefit the Anuaks. Then, with high expectations I convinced an agriculturist to come out to teach and demonstrate how to farm in Africa. To my dismay, the new agriculturist has determined that the Anuaks are not suited to be farmers and that the soil is not suited for farming either.

In addition to this situation, each missionary will make his own friends among the local people and rightly so, but that does not make it easier on the special friends of the former missionary. It was sad to hear the plaintive stories of my old friends who are now out of favor. A score or so of these old-timers say they are going to move to Pokwo so we can be together again. I found that all the former employees of the mission who worked for me have been discharged on the grounds that they are too old, and the new friends of the new missionaries have taken their places. This is the way life goes, but it is hard on both the old workers and their old missionary friend.

From Pokwo, Don wrote,

We are now back in Pokwo, and I thought the rainy season was over for this year, but this afternoon we had a torrential downpour that all but washed us away. The grass in the yard came to life again and is a beautiful green. I run a meteorological station here on a small scale for the Ethiopian government. We have a rain gauge, maximum and minimum thermometers, a wind indicator, a relative humidity and present temperature thermometer. When I looked at the rain gauge after the big rain this afternoon, the vessel was running over. It was the biggest rain of the year and must have been more than four inches.

The mission station is crowded with sick people. The flu has struck with such intensity that there are hundreds of sick people all about us, and as many as are able come in here to sleep so that they can get treatment twice daily. Every house on the place is bulging with people. We have six Anuaks sleeping in my office; the clinic itself is full of sleeping people as well as all the outhouses. Even the cows have been driven out of the cattle barns to make room for sick people. It is pathetic and yet tremendously encouraging to see how people pile in here for help when they are sick. A few years ago that would not have been true. They would have gone to witchdoctors and burned great fires around their villages at night to drive away the evil spirits. Even though some of the people who come in are not Christians, they are beginning to think like Christians and adopt Christian habits. It is wonderfully encouraging and a matter of great joy to me. I can see some solid accomplishments here, and when I am inclined to get discouraged about the immensity of the task before us, I begin to count up the changes that have taken place.

We now have a real physician with us for one year, Dr. Paul Baumann. And we are having unexpected trouble with the sick. Over the years the Anuaks have grown accustomed to the diagnostic speed of my medical ignorance. I am able to treat fifty patients in a half-hour. But Paul cannot work as fast as I do. A lot of knowledge is a dangerous thing. Paul finds a place where the patient can lie down and get a thorough examination. Then he prescribes carefully. Thus he can only treat ten patients in an afternoon, whereas I can "treat" two hundred! I suppose there is some benefit in medicine as science rather than medicine as faith, but it slows things down a lot.

Dr. Paul has figured out that every patient averages two and a half treatments for each visit. No patient is just sick with one disease, so Paul has been treating them for two, three, four, and sometimes five different ailments. He describes one old woman who came in here a month ago. She was a leper, with advanced tuberculosis; she was running a fever from malaria, was anemic from chronic dysentery, possibly had syphilis, and was covered from head to foot with scabies. She came in complaining of a toothache and a headache. Apparently the other minor afflictions did not trouble her, but her teeth and head did. Paul said he gave her twelve different treatments that morning and would have to repeat those for months.

A few days ago one of our laborers left here and went to a village about twenty miles away and eloped with a girl. Of course, there was no marriage license; they just went away together. Soon they were caught, and the girl was beaten and sent home. The boy was tied up in preparation for his beating, but somehow escaped and came running back here for refuge. When the villagers came for him, I refused to protect him against them, but exacted a promise that he would not be beaten beyond endurance. I felt that the boy deserved punishment for stealing a wife, and I did not want to interfere with Anuak social custom, but I was not going to let them beat him unmercifully either. They promised not to be too severe and took him away.

When the group got back to their village, they tied the boy with his arms pulled back until his elbows touched the middle of his back. They left him that way for twelve hours. When I heard of it, I went out to the village and asked them to let up on him— which they did, much to his relief. But then somehow he worked himself free during the night and ran way again, this time to a village to which, being an enemy of the other village, they dared not go for him. Therefore the aggrieved village took a distant uncle of his and tied him as they had the boy and threatened to keep him that way until the boy returned. This uncle was so decrepit he was ready to die. He was at least fifty years, which is extremely old out here, and I knew the boy would never come back of his own volition. I heard about the old man about nine that night, and it made me so angry I was determined to free him. So I started out on foot to find him. We walked through the wet grass and corn for three miles, wading through water two feet deep in places. We finally found the poor old man tied to a stake driven in the ground. He was being eaten alive by mosquitoes, although his captors were sitting in the smoke of a fire just a few feet away from him, and their ears were closed to his piteous cries.

The men were clearly disturbed when I arrived on the scene, but they were polite to me and asked me to join them around the fire and in the smoke. I soon indicated the old man and asked why he was tied up. There was some mumbling, and then one chap said he had tried to kill a man and they tied him up for safety. The old chap yelled that this was a lie, and they tried to shut him up and convince me that he was crazy. I told the villagers that I knew the truth of the situation and wanted the old man released at once. They said that was impossible until the guilty lad had returned and taken his beating and made a promise to pay a fine of forty dollars. After an hour's futile discussion, I decided the time had come for action and whipped out my penknife and started to cut the bonds. They begged me not to cut the rawhide ropes, since they were valuable, and finally one of them untied the man. The blood was running from his arms where the ropes had cut him. Then I promised that I would find the boy, put him to work, and would pay over to them every cent of his wages until his debt was satisfied. This solution pleased them all and they happily agreed. I found the boy today, and he goes to work tomorrow. He might have been killed if I had not intervened for him.

Don later wrote of the Lord's work—and Satan's—at Pokwo.

Last week I thought we had the devil on the run at Pokwo. In one worship service there was a considerable period of silence except for the soft crying and sniffling of a young woman sitting near me. I did not speak to her, but I did pray for her, and in a few minutes she stood up trembling and frightened because it was the first time in her entire life she had ever stood in the presence of men at a public meeting. She professed her faith in the Lord and confessed her sins. Again we waited, and finally an old, old woman (possibly fifty-five years old) also shaking with fright asked to speak. She had in her hand an old gourd that rattled as she shook it, and she held it up, saying, "This has been my *Jwok*, and sometimes it has been my *Anaka* [Satan]. If I wanted something, it was my god, but if I wanted to curse someone, it was my devil. I want now to give it up and worship only Jesus." Again we sang and prayed, but this time with even more enthusiasm.

The woman broke her gourd in the presence of all the people, many of whom also have and use such charms. Later a man told me that he had some charms in his village that he wanted to destroy, but he was afraid of them and wanted me to take them away. I will not take them for him, but I will encourage him and will promise him the strength and protection of the Lord if he does so. These indications of change certainly point to the working of the Holy Spirit in the hearts of the Anuaks, and we are thrilled in their response. If this continues, there is no doubt that our program to evangelize all the Anuaks within the next few years will be successful. We expect that each person who becomes a Christian will go back to his village and lead others to the faith. In fact, we do not want to baptize anyone who has not been used by God to bring another person to the new life.

I was elated that so many people were coming to the Lord, and I thought that we were being wonderfully blessed. The very next day I learned something about pride going before a fall. Word came to me that one of the girls living on the mission compound was going to have a baby and had named one of our workers as its father. He vehemently denied that he was the father and even gave the girl a beating to discourage her claims. A day or two later, another girl had announced the pending birth of a child and named another teacher as the father. Then a third girl made a similar accusation, naming a former worker who had moved away.

All this happened a few weeks before we arrived back in Pokwo, and I worked for hours trying to get the truth, but the teachers insisted that the girls were trying to pin something on them of which they were innocent. I was almost but not quite convinced. I questioned everyone on the place, and the more I went into it, the more convinced I was that everyone except the missionaries knew the true stories and were hiding the truth from us. So one morning I announced that the mission was closed as of that hour and no one but the missionaries would do any work. We sent our cook and houseboy away and shut down everything at the station. I did open the clinic for the village people, but would not give medicine to anyone living on the compound. The first day all the workmen and others thought it was a big joke, and they had their laughs when they saw me doing things that they normally do. Lyda did all the cooking, and I washed the dishes and swept the floors. Our servants were horrified, but I kept them at a distance.

The second day it was not so much a joke, because some of them wanted grain and others wanted money, but everything was shut down. For the first time, we canceled our three daily services. The interdict was complete even to the cows. We turned them out and let the calves do all the milking, and we did without. The third day they heard that I was going to send all the staff away and get new people. And I intended to do just that unless they came across with the truth. So they had a meeting and brought in to us a half confession from one of the guilty parties. I would not accept it. They had a second meeting and came in with more, and I sent them away again. Then in the afternoon of the third day, they really had a rousing meeting. (We learned later that a group of Christians had held a three-hour prayer meeting about the situation.) After a stormy hour of discussion, they sent for us, and the truth emerged.

It was a wonderful meeting, and before it was over, many of us were in tears. We shared together as Christians should, and things came out of which we never dreamed, but obviously the Anuaks are tempted just as we are, and some of them commit adultery, steal, tell lies, slander each other, and so on. All these sins were confessed, and the three boys responsible for fathering the babies finally confessed under pressure of having the truth disclosed by others who knew it. Before the meeting was over, a wonderful spirit prevailed, and we all felt cleaner, although we had been listening to a terrible recital of evil.

After a fine time together in prayer, the hard task of disciplining the worst offenders fell on my shoulders, but also the joy of assuring the sincerely repentant of their restoration to Christian fellowship. I put the three fathers on probation and demanded that they make provision for the mothers and children, but the main instigator of the whole affair I dismissed from Pokwo.

This is a sad and tragic story. Ayey is a woman with four fine girls, and her husband, Okac, was our only elder at Pokwo until he died sometime ago. Ayey arranged for the young men and women to meet secretly in her house on the mission compound. Then she extorted grain from the couples. I was also giving her grain periodically, which she turned into beer and sold at night. For years Ayey refused baptism although her husband was our finest Christian. Now I know why. She has a home in Akobo, and I hope that in another environment she will be able to start a new life.

I was fearful that in determining to close the mission rather than to accept the betrayal of our workers we would lose all the men and women whom we have spent so much time in training. I was prepared for the risk that we might have to leave Pokwo, but I am glad the people finally trusted us with the truth. Still I realized more and more that it is a great mistake to hold around us the most capable of the people we have trained. They are the very ones who should be sent back to their villages. Yet somehow we keep them close to us, and more and more they become dependent on us and the mission for their livelihood. It is a serious mistake that I am going to try to rectify.

I am considering giving several of our men a bonus of about one hundred dollars (Ethiopian currency) and telling them to disappear into the Anuak villages for a year, not returning until they have established several groups of Christians. I want them to go to their own villages and create Christian homes for themselves and begin to live the things we have taught them. I am convinced that we would be further ahead to pay them to stay away from us rather than to pay them to do things for us.

▼ The Hot Hand
▼ of Satan

We have been favored recently with a visit from an anthropologist from Yale University. He was here a week studying the Anuaks, and his most profound judgment after that week's study is that we should *not* try to change the Anuaks. They are content as they are, and if we try to make Christians of them, we may make them very unhappy and give them complexes they will never be able to get over. After a week's study of the anthropologist, my most profound judgment is that he should go back to Connecticut and leave this work to us. If he thinks the Anuaks are happy in their fear, ignorance, sickness, and superstition, he should have his head examined.

Another visitor was an American army chaplain. To hear him tell it, the army would fall on its face if he ever left. In the week he spent with us he was able to solve many of our most difficult problems—some of which have plagued us for twenty years. It is really nice to have folks come out here for a few days who know all the answers and can tell us just what we should do. Most of the Anuaks now like to wear a piece of cloth, but the Nuers do not bother. The chaplain was a bit shocked to see a tall Nuer man, at least six and a half feet tall, walking hand in hand with a six-foot girl of about eighteen, both oblivious to the rest of the world and equally oblivious to the fact that they were stark naked. Young love is wonderful anywhere!

We are finishing our church building at Pokwo this week, and it will be great to have a place to worship after all those years of worshiping in cattle barns, under trees, and in makeshift structures. The local congregation is not large and is composed of the regular workmen and nearby villagers—all of whom contribute a tenth of their income to the church. I have always tried to give responsibility to our Anuak leaders just a little before they ask for it and a long time before they demand it.

It is a real thrill to see Anuak leaders taking their rightful place among their people. They cannot depend on us forever. And they often surprise us in what they do. For example, this little congregation of one hundred members proposes to send out ten evangelists! They figure it this way: If the evangelists are willing to accept the same wage as the church members earn, then every ten members should be able to support an evangelist. Obviously one hundred members can support ten evangelists. I suspect this is a record among Christian churches anywhere, and I am thrilled that the idea came from them. Christianity is *their* gospel, not the foreigners', and they want to share it with their people. We had eleven professions of faith today, and all of them were strangers to me. Each had been contacted and taught by Anuak evangelists. They may not be the most learned and articulate among the Christians of the world, but they are certainly among the most devout.

Once the building was completed, Don wrote of the Pokwo church.

We had a wonderful worship service today. It is true that our church building is not very inspiring. In fact, it is a nondescript grass-and-mud hut about sixty feet long by thirty feet wide, and the grass roof looks as if it were thrown on– which it was, since the Anuaks are very poor roofers. However, more than two hundred naked and semi-naked men, women, and children were packed into that little church in the heart of Africa singing songs of praise to the Savior as if they were going to raise the roof or burst their throats trying. The music sounded horrible to Western ears but the spirit of the singing was splendid.

I was preaching on the theme, "You Must Be Born Again," and truly, no audience on earth ever needed that message more than these people. The Anuaks are a savage, cruel and godless people. That is, they believe in a god, but one of terrible vengeance and despotic wrath who satisfies all his whims by bringing sickness and disease, famine and pestilence, trouble and sorrow. Indeed, their only name for sickness and disease is *Jwok*, or god. When they fall ill, they say, "I am taken by *Jwok*." Thus it was a joy this morning to tell them again of a God of mercy and peace who loves the Anuaks and wants to help them and do good things for them. I told them of a God who loved them so much that he gave himself for them. And his name is Jesus Christ. Of how he died for them and then became alive again that he might help them more. Afterward, one little naked boy came up to me and asked, "Did God's Son really die?" I assured him that he had, but also had come back to life because he wanted the little boys and girls to be happy and free from fear and trouble. The boy said, "How can God help me? I am an Anuak, and God does not help the Anuak."

That is the prevailing attitude. But I see more and more evidence that they are coming to know and love the Lord Jesus as their Savior. Not a little of this change of attitude is due to the medical care we have been able to give them. We now have twelve people living on the compound who literally have been pulled back from the grave, and they know it. It is nothing that I have done except fill them with penicillin, but the Lord is using it to bring new glories to his name, and these people are coming to love him.

I much prefer to evangelize by groups such as families, clans, or villages. Then we have a solid phalanx in that place against the witchdoctor and other evils and temptations of their old way of life. The single Christian man or woman has a hard time of it unless he or she is a very strong personality. We have a village of about four hundred persons just on the edge of our mission land, and I am encouraging them as a group to accept the Lord Jesus as their Savior. There are several individuals there who want baptism, but I would like to establish a complete Christian village and make it a model for all the other Anuaks to see. I know that in such a movement there would be many who would only be nominal Christians, but at least we would have a social hold on them with the expectation that they would live a Christian life. If we can encourage that kind of commitment, the Holy Spirit can do the rest.

We want to lead 25,000 Anuaks to the Christian faith in the next twelve years. To this end we are trying to establish a medical program, educational outreach, agricultural skills, and—most important—an evangelistic emphasis. We have been waiting for a long time to have an entirely Christian village in which we could carry out our complete program of the more abundant life in Christ Jesus. The Anuaks are naturally conservative people and at first seemed slow in accepting the gospel, but during this past year they have been coming in and making their professions of faith in ever-increasing numbers. A few weeks ago the whole population of this village sent for me and said they all wanted to accept Jesus Christ and to be baptized together. This is truly wonderful and almost unprecedented. I have been working very strenuously in that village ever since, trying to get them ready for baptism.

The next step is also very important. How are we going to do something about the miserable village in which they live? These people are desperately poor. In that village there are many people who have not had a coin of any kind in their hands for months. The older folks have not tasted meat or fish in months, and most of them live in rags (a good-sized pocket handkerchief would be larger than most of the clothes they wear). Their sole daily diet is a corn mush. But worse than that, this particular village is right on the river, and every year the water floods out over the bank and fills the village so that the people are living in the midst of water. The village is filled with sickness and death during the rains, because their grass houses will not keep out the water. I want to show these poor people what can be done with what they have and some effort. The people have nothing at all except a little grain to feed themselves. They do not have a single cow to give milk to their hungry children. For a long time I have been wanting to prove what could be done in such a village to clean it up, dam out the water, help them build better houses, improve and enlarge their fields, dig latrines and drains, and provide sufficient medical help to treat all their needs. Those things cost money, which we did not have until a gift of $2,000 arrived in the mail today.

Don wrote more information about the Anuak believers.

We had a fine baptismal service here last week. We are now planning these services almost monthly, and last week we had thirty-two ready for baptism. Since the river is so close and so much a part of the people's life, we baptize them in the river. (We also sprinkle the babies who are too young to be immersed.)

For this service, there were both men and women, and the first man was very old by Anuak standards. He came wearing a piece of cloth that he had just purchased the day before, and he had no intention of getting that cloth wet. So when his name was called, he took off his new garment and handed it to a friend to hold, and he walked down into the water completely naked. The next person to be baptized was a woman from a distant village, and she had never before seen a baptismal service. Observing the old man walk out of the water, she assumed nakedness was a baptismal requirement and started to untie her loincloth. Then she hesitated and called to me, "Do I have to take off my cloth, too?" I assured her it was not necessary.

I suppose that a skeptic might insist that the Christian Anuaks are motivated to exchange their traditional religion for Christianity only due to the foreigner's influence and with his encouragement. If I cannot refute the skeptic's argument, I do not have to accept it either. Undoubtedly, social, psychological, political, and economic factors are always involved in decisions, and out here there is a medical aspect; but I believe that primarily and fundamentally the conversion to the Christian faith is under God's direction and is therefore a theological matter. When Pontius Pilate asked Jesus, "What is truth?" I believe Jesus had already answered that question when he declared, "*I* am the Way, the Truth, and the Life." Anyway, if I sat down to sort out the human processes of decision making and their relative values in various social contexts, I would not get any work done—and there is a lot of work to be done out here.

▼▲▼

This day will long be remembered at Pokwo as "the Day of the Big Fire," and I am grateful to be around to tell about it. Today our fuel store went up in a great cloud of black smoke, and with it a year's supply of gasoline, kerosene, and diesel fuel as well as drums of lubricating oil, spare tires, some tools, two hundred new grain sacks, and a few odds and ends. With a gentle wind behind it, the fire also spread to our banana patch, chicken house (roasting some thirty chickens), and a small cookhouse belonging to our servant. Fortunately the wind was not strong, or we might have lost our workshop and other houses on the compound.

I have no one to blame but my stupid self. I had been working with a small electric generator, trying to get it running to take the place of our larger machine, which is temporarily out of order awaiting a spare part. One of our boys, Omot Okon, was working with me cleaning the machine with kerosene and a brush. I had just cleaned the sparkplugs and, testing them, found them to be in excellent working order. (They subsequently proved to be working too well!) Then I cleaned out the cylinders, using a little gasoline to cut the oil I had poured in. To facilitate this process, I took hold of the crank and turned the motor over slowly. This, of course, produced a spark from the plugs and ignited the gas fumes from the fuel. With a "whoof" the whole thing went up in my face, and the flames leaped six feet into the air, enveloping the motor, me, and the tin of gasoline I had been using. It happened so quickly that there was little to do except get out. I tried to drag the motor out of the door, but it was too heavy and much too hot. A pile of sand was nearby, and I tried to smother the fire with sand, but by that time the flames had reached the grass roof and in five seconds the whole roof was in flames. The fire quickly jumped over the brick wall that separated the generator room from the fuel store, and almost as quickly as we could get away from it, the whole area was burning.

What a fire it made! There were more than four hundred tins of fuel as well as seven or eight full barrels, and in a few seconds all of it was blazing merrily. The most we could do was to keep the fire from spreading, and everyone on the place was getting water or sand or dirt and putting out burning embers as soon as they fell. We got our water pump going very quickly, and its stream of water probably saved the other buildings. We could not do much except keep the roofs wet and watch the tremendous spectacle. It was everything one could ask for in a fire, and more than we cared to see, but it fascinated everyone. Great clouds of black smoke billowed hundreds of feet into the air, and the deep red flames occasionally broke through high in the sky. The brick walls of the building were so hot that they glowed red, and no one could get near the fire for hours. Finally, when the fire died down a bit, we were able to get close enough to the door to start pouring water in and gradually brought the flames under control.

As we cooled off the red hot tins and walls, the fire would break out again and again, indicating that some fuel was still in the tins. And sure enough, as we started to clear out the smoking debris later, we found a few tins buried under the pile still intact and full of fuel. The fuel was boiling in some of them, but had not ignited. So we salvaged a few of the four hundred tins. Fortunately the building was not a total loss and can be repaired. The walls withstood the heat very well and can be made usable again. I suspect this time when we come to put a roof on it, we will use metal instead of grass. The metal will help to contain a fire rather than spreading it. I am grieved about the financial loss, but I rejoice that no one was seriously hurt.

A few months later, his fuel supply replenished, Don had even greater cause to be grateful.

I am lying here in bed with arms and legs wrapped in bandages, and I can witness from personal experience that a gasoline fire is very hot. Last night about ten o'clock I went out to refill my fuel tanks in preparation for an early trip to Gambela. In order to see, I had taken a pressure light with me that I left outside the door, ten or twelve feet back from the fuel store. I had filled one can with gasoline, but in filling the second one I spilled about a quart of gas onto the floor. Just at that point, I looked out at my burning light and something told me to move it back even farther, but I decided that since it was out in the open air, it was far enough from the door not to be dangerous. However, a draft evidently blew the fumes directly out to the burning lamp, and suddenly there was a low boom and immediately I was standing in the middle of a fiery furnace and both my arms and legs were ablaze. The open can of gasoline from which I was filling the tanks was blazing like a blow torch, and though I could not see through the flames, I threw the can for what I thought was the door. The flames were so far confined to the doorway, although the tanks that I had been filling were burning. I knew I dare not stay there another second, for I feared the tanks would explode, and if they did, the whole fuel room with its hundreds of tins would go immediately and I would be on my way to heaven. The only thing to do was to make a rush for the door through the flames. I was in my bare feet and wearing a pair of shorts and a light shirt, which burned right off. Of course, I had gasoline on my feet and legs as well as on my hands, and everything was afire.

I had no sensation of pain, but I was conscious of keeping my mouth closed and trying to cover my face with my blazing arms as I made a dash for the door. Fortunately the curtain of flame was not very deep, and in two steps I was beyond it and into the cool night air. I remember brushing at my arms and legs to put out the fire and seeing the skin come off as I rubbed. Then I recognized that the only way to save the fuel store from a second disastrous fire was to get these blazing tanks outside. Since they were next to the door and I was still not feeling any pain, I reached in through the fire and grabbed one by the handle. The fire was roaring out of the spout like a blow torch, but I gave no thought to what might happen if it exploded. I knew that I would have to get it outside.

All this time I was yelling for help, and just as I was about to reach through the fire for the second time to get the other tank, one of the Anuaks arrived and, beating the flames off my burning arms, he held me so I could not return. Perhaps it is just as well. Fortunately we had a sand pile nearby, and soon three or four Anuaks were throwing sand onto the fire and, to the amazement of everyone, they quickly had it out. It was only then that I began to realize what had happened to me. The worst burns seemed to be on the soles of my feet, but I knew I had to walk to the house. I do not remember much until I was lying in bed in great agony. I must have been in a state of shock and could not possibly lie still, nor could I bear to have the touch of sheets against my arms and legs. Lyda soon had gotten ten or twelve aspirin tablets inside me and gave me a shot of morphine. It was only after the medicine took effect that I could bear to have my arms and legs bandaged.

As I lie here dictating this letter to Lyda, I am a grotesque-looking figure. I am swathed in bandages and look more like a mummy than a daddy, but I can praise the Lord that I am here to tell the story. It could easily have been otherwise. There is one thing of which I am very aware: the Lord knew my peril and tried to warn me of the dangerous nearness of the pressure light, and because I did not heed his warning he lifted his hand off me just long enough to teach me a lesson. I am grateful that he has given me another opportunity to practice obedience in the future. Obviously it is going to be some time before these arms and legs are normal again. I accept his discipline with praise and trust that I have learned a lesson. The Lord saved the fuel room from another tremendous loss such as we experienced last April. This time we lost only about ten gallons of fuel. The pain has already subsided, and I will soon be back at my normal tasks again. This time in bed will give me a chance to catch up on a little sleep and some reading I have wanted to do.

In the next few days, Lyda wrote,

I wanted to send this note along to let everyone know that Don is getting along fine. He is still in a lot of pain. He can use his hands a little, but he does not want to write for a while. The insides of his arms are raw, since he rubbed all the skin off trying to put out the fire. His legs are bad, swollen and purple; his ankles and insteps were very bad because he was standing in flames, but they are getting better. After the first day he has not needed painkillers, and he has a good appetite. Still, it is a miracle that he is here at all, because the funnel he was using to fill the tanks exploded right in his face. Yet only one eyelash was partly singed, and there is a small burn on the eyelid.

Two weeks later Don was again writing home.

This letter tonight will have two merits. First of all, it will be short, and its second merit will be that it is written by my own hand. This is the first time since the accident that I have been able to write with any comfort. My hands and arms are completely free of bandages, and they are almost normal. They look a bit queer because the new skin is a beautiful whitish pink and entirely free of freckles and hair. If I do not grow any new hair on the burned places, I will be an odd-looking creature indeed! Half of me will look like a woolly dog, and the rest of me will look like a lizard.

My legs are another matter. The last of the black and charred skin came off today, and they look like those of a newborn baby—a pinkish red. They are badly swollen and so tender I can barely stand a breath of air on them. The second day after I was burned, I walked to the bathroom, but today I simply do not know how I did it, because it would kill me to try to walk that far now. Yesterday Lyda helped me out to the veranda for afternoon tea. I made the ten necessary steps, but was exhausted, and when I got back in bed again, I had a fever. One of the strange things about it is that I have a fever every day despite the daily injections. There does not seem to be any infection, but every day I have a fever and feel ready to die. Then when the fever breaks, I feel fine and want to get going. There is some sign that the fever is lessening with each day, and perhaps it will soon pass.

It is obvious that I will not be up and out as soon as I had predicted. The first couple of days after the burn, I thought I would be out in a week, but it is now more than two weeks, and I know I cannot walk for another week at least, and then I will not be kicking a football! There has been one advantage to all this. I have been able to diet in a way I never would have done if working normally, and although my legs are about twice the normal size, the "muscle" around my middle has disappeared. The folks here at Pokwo have been wonderful through all this and have taken up my burdens and carried on. I have not yet attempted to open the school, but shall try to get it under way before the week is out. We already have more than thirty boarders eating their heads off, so I'd better get some classes started for them.

The time lying here in bed has not been lost. It has been an occasion for all my Anuak friends to gather in and, like Job's comforters, to commiserate with me. They have come from far and near, and even though the country is flooded with water, they have come by boat from considerable distances to ponder with me why God should let such a thing happen to one of his servants. One day a chief with thirteen of his followers filed into my bedroom and sat down for a palaver. After the usual greetings the chief got up and walked over to the bed and proceeded to bless me by spitting on the bandages of both legs. He would have spat on my hands and face if I had given him a chance. Then he said, "Nothing more will happen to you, and in a little while you will be better. I have blessed you, and you will be all right now!" Then, to Lyda's horror, each of the men solemnly got up, did his spitting, and made the same remarks. After they all sat down together, they agreed among themselves that I would soon be well. One of them earnestly asked, "How could this happen to one who is god?" I laughed and said, "This could not happen to God, and it proves that I am just a man like yourselves." And I said to him, "This was one time when Satan caught hold of me, and his hand was very hot and caused this burn." I said it as a joke, but they all agreed that must have been just the way it happened.

Sometimes the old women are the funniest, and they come in at times when my legs are unbandaged to give them opportunity to dry a bit. One old woman, when she saw how black my legs were, looked at her own skin and said, "When God made the Anuaks, he must have burned them too, and their skin never did change." I have one well-wisher, an old leper, who comes in occasionally. When he visits, it sends Lyda into a panic because the first time he came, he held out his fingerless palms as if to take my charred legs between them to give me a reassuring rub. It was a bad moment for Lyda, but he refrained and sat down with the others.

There have been times when I have deeply regretted the hours and days lost lying here on my bed. But recently I have come to see that the Lord has turned all this to his own advantage. More and more of the Anuak people, as they come in to see me, have said, "We thought you were going to die, and we were almost afraid to pray that you might be saved. But we did pray, and now we see that the Lord really does hear and answer our prayers. For you are soon going to be well and live among us again." I would be willing to go through the fire all over again if it would contribute to the increased faith and growth of the Anuaks. I do not think the Lord wants me to try the fire again, and I believe he can cause the Anuaks to grow in other ways. But if it were the only way for them to grow, I would not hesitate to face it all over again.

Later Don wrote,

This week I have gone back into circulation again, and I am on a half workday. That means I go to bed at eleven instead of twelve. I am feeling fine but do not seem to have much pep and am beginning to feel my age. I hate to admit it! We are expecting a lot of guests this week. Six women are coming from India to visit our station for a week to see how we do things here. At least I am certain that I can show them how to build a good fire!

▼ Education
▼ and Medicine

DURING THE TIME that the McClures were at Pokwo, the Ethiopian Ministry of Education determined to enforce the official proclamation of August 1944 concerning missionary activities. It mandated that the general language of instruction in Ethiopia shall be Amharic; all missionaries were expected to learn it and use it. In designated Open Areas, missionaries were allowed to use the local language orally in the early stages of missionary work, but only until such time as pupils and missionaries had a working knowledge of Amharic.[56] This law, of course, gave immense advantage to the Amharic tribe and meant that primitive people like the Anuaks would be required to learn an entirely new and extremely complicated language before they could be taught anything else. This would delay for decades the educational aspects of the Anuak project and make rapid evangelism with its Bible-reading component impossible. Therefore Don sent a petition to the Ministry of Education requesting permission to teach the Anuaks, especially the adults, to read in their vernacular language.

If the minister of education will give us permission to use the Anuak tongue, it may not be necessary to see the emperor, but everyone is pessimistic about the minister of education and feels that Kebede Michael is hostile to all mission work. He seems to be quite supportive of education for the Amharic ruling class, but not in helping the other peoples of Ethiopia. I believe this antagonism is based on fear because the Amharas are in the decided minority, and as soon as the various tribespeople become educated, the Amharas are afraid the downtrodden groups will revolt. That may be true, but if we are not allowed to

301

educate them in Anuak and the other tribal languages, we will lose two or perhaps three generations of people whom we cannot teach to read the Scripture. It is not the Anuaks alone that the Amharas are trying to suppress. There are more than one hundred different languages and dialects in Ethiopia, and all of them are forbidden as the medium of education.

None of the older people, and few above the age of sixteen, will ever learn to read Amharic. It is a very complex language for anyone, and to try to force it on primitive people even before they learn to read the language they speak is both foolish and impossible. The Amharic language has 256 different letters in the alphabet, and all of them must be memorized before the language can be read, to say nothing of the complicated grammar. I have great difficulty in reading the Amharic Bible myself; I could never teach it to those who know even less than I do. We all speak Anuak here. If we are to continue to go forward, we must be granted an exception to this demand. We have only recently reduced spoken Anuak to a written form, and if our people are required to learn to read a language they cannot speak, all our efforts will be educational rather than evangelistic. Doubtless, a common national language is a desirable thing, but I am a missionary, not a schoolmaster. I came to Africa not for the purpose of conducting Third World education, but to proclaim eternal world salvation. We are willing to use the Amharic script in teaching the Anuaks to read their spoken language, but unless we are allowed to use the native language, the Anuak project in Ethiopia is finished. The most we could do is evangelize an educational elite, whereas our goal is to reach the *entire* tribe for Christ.

With a heavy heart I had to close our little school and shut down the adult literacy classes and tell the Anuaks there was to be no Bible study for them. The immediate reaction of the Anuak people to this information was, as I fully expected it to be, that the government was trying to destroy their culture and customs. During the next month there was constant fighting between the Anuaks and government police. Three policemen and many Anuaks were killed. A dozen Anuak villages were burned to the ground, and the grain fields were destroyed by police.

Six months ago there was a fight between some Anuaks and the Ethiopian police at the village of Pokumo. When the Anuaks attacked, the twenty brave policemen threw down their rifles and fled, even leaving a machine gun behind. I was able to recover the machine gun and gave it back to the police, but the Anuaks are not willing to surrender the rifles until some compensation has been paid for the people killed by the police. I sympathize with the Anuaks, but now the government troops are going to attack the small village of about eighty-five men with a force of over four hundred unless the rifles are returned. It is not right, but there is nothing else for it. Unless the rifles are returned, the village will be wiped out.

Today I flew to Pokumo in the Missionary Aviation Fellowship plane, which can get there in about half an hour. It takes me four hours by boat. As we flew over Pokumo, we could see the people running for their lives in all directions. They thought they were going to be bombed. Finally we landed in the water and taxied up to the village. When the people saw me climb out, they shouted with joy and ran out to call the others back. Soon all had assembled, and we held a worship service. After the service I told them why I had come and that I had to have the guns. I left it at that, because I knew we had gained a lot of ground and the rifles would be forthcoming later. They also asked me not to fly in again because the airplane frightened the people too much.

On the way back, we flew over some more of the Anuak country to see some new villages. We were able to land on Lake Tatha, where hundreds of people came down to see us; we had a fine service with the people of Piny Bago. During the service, eighteen people accepted Christ. Then we treated more than two hundred when I opened my medicine bag. At the village of Piny Udo there were fifteen who accepted Christ, and over a hundred were treated for their diseases. It is wonderful to have a plane to get into these places.

Later I recovered the rifles and extracted a promise from the police that there would be no more reprisals. The police kept their promise for about three months, and then they sent out a large group of police to get revenge. But when they were marching down the river bank about fifteen miles below the mission, they walked into an ambush and an officer was killed and several men wounded. A few days later the police burned another Anuak village because they heard the villagers had harbored a renegade for a night or two. Then the police came to our nearest village, Akado, which is really on mission property. I met with the captain of the police, and he said the people of our village were feeding the criminals. I asked him for proof, and he could give only the scantiest hearsay. He then laid upon me the responsibility of finding out where the renegade chief was hiding. I spent a day questioning several hundred people, and finally two men said they knew where the bad chief had been hiding on an island in the river some miles away. I went to the island and found nothing but a little grass lean-to and a cold fire. I then went to various villages nearby, asking questions. Finally all the people agreed that the man had gone to a distant village back in the forest. It was a village I had always wanted to visit, but I did not want to walk the thirty miles necessary. It is on a small river, but the river empties into the Gilo River, which is much nearer Akobo than Pokwo. I did not have enough gasoline on hand to make the trip by boat, so I had to walk.

The next morning I started out with three boys as guides and carriers. I traveled light because I knew we had to walk fast before word of our coming preceded us. We went about eight miles downriver by boat and then plunged straight into the forest. It was just daybreak when we started, and a most beautiful day. The forest was hanging with millions of dew-drops from every leaf and spiderweb. As the sun came up and shone through them, it looked like a snow-draped forest at home. It was truly lovely, but we had little time to spend on the beauties of nature, for the tall Africans were making my short legs move along. One of Donnie's special friends was a guide because he lives in that area, and his legs are considerably longer than mine, so I almost had to run to keep up with him. We walked for six hours without stopping. Then we came to a splendid waterhole couched in the rocks and stopped for a drink of water and some meat sandwiches that Lyda had prepared for us.

After ten minutes' rest, we walked on and two hours later reached the village. It was a splendid village on the little river, Alwal, with almost one thousand people. It was strongly fortified with a high mud wall of trees, sticks, and mud. As we walked into the village, hundreds of children and dogs met us, and we had quite a reception. I thought it strange that none of the men came out to meet us, but we walked through the village, and everywhere the women and children stuck their heads around their houses and grass fences for a look at me. We walked straight through to the meeting place of the local chief, and there we found him sitting on his bull skin, smoking his pipe and surrounded by all his men. None of them looked hostile, but all of them had been expecting me, and I knew I would not find my man there. The chief greeted me very warmly and invited me to sit beside him while we talked to his people. We had a service first and then a long talk about spiritual things.

They had heard about us, and many of the men of the village had been into the mission; but this was the first time the gospel had been preached in their village, and they were very much interested. After a rest, I began to ask them about the renegade chief. They professed ignorance and said they knew he was still in the country but had not come into their territory. Indeed, as they warmed up to the subject, I realized that they were sworn enemies of the renegade, who had killed one of their men several months ago. I knew they were telling me the truth, but they would not tell me who had warned them of my coming. They just laughed at me when I tried to find out, and I knew that I would never be one of them, no matter how close they professed to be to me. I would always be a foreigner, and they would always keep secrets from me.

I spent a very pleasant night at the village, sleeping in the hut with the chief. Although I was disturbed by his snoring and his fleas, I managed to sleep. They could not offer me any food, since they were suffering from hunger. The ground is so sandy that they live almost entirely on peanuts, and it seems that their crop last year had failed. Now they were eating grass seeds and such things. The village was alive with sheep and cattle, but it never occurred to anyone to kill them for food. Sheep and cattle are set aside for marriage payments and could not be killed unless a sacrifice was in order. When I learned that wild animals were near, I went out late in the evening and shot two waterbuck for them, but the meat was not brought in until the next morning, long after I had gone. Some men slept in the forest beside the meat, but they did not want to carry it home in the dark.

The next day, before daylight, we started back for Pokwo. The second thirty miles I found to be very much longer than the first thirty miles. The renegade chief is still at large, and no one seems to know definitely where he is. Thus our Anuak people are very much upset and worried about the movements of the police. Tomorrow I am going to Gambela to get some assurance from the governor that no more villages will be burned without good evidence that they are supporting the rebels.

Don continued to try to secure permission to instruct in the Anuak language.

In August I came back to Addis Ababa to try again to gain permission to teach our Anuaks in their own language. No action had been taken on our petition during the intervening months, but on my appearance on the scene, the minister of education presented it to the Board of Education, where it was rejected on the ground that there is a law stating all teaching must be done in the Amharic language. When I tried to see him, the minister kept putting me off. Day after day I went to his office or called him on the phone, but some urgent business always called him away. We are not the only ones suffering under this law. Every mission group in Ethiopia is laboring under almost impossible conditions because of it.

After a month of vainly trying to see the minister, I sought an audience with His Imperial Majesty. I felt from the beginning that if I could gain his ear, our problems would be solved; but this time I had been counseled to try all the usual channels first and only go to His Majesty as a last resort. I had reached the place of last resort. Without difficulty, I saw His Majesty's private secretary and laid the case before him.

I pointed out that our work had been seriously curtailed by the directives from the Ministry of Education denying us the privilege of using the written Anuak vernacular as the medium of instruction. I also pointed out that the Anuaks had become resentful of the imperial government and of us for refusing to teach them in their own language. Moreover, the Anuak people can never be made good citizens of Ethiopia by force. If the Anuaks feel that they are despised and rejected, they will go back across the border into Sudan. The secretary gave me a patient hearing and seemed sympathetic, but did not commit himself. He asked me to put my case in writing and then give him some time to think it over. This I did, and after a few days I called him again. He asked me to come and see him, and we discussed whether it was necessary to see Haile Selassie. He said he would lay the case before His Imperial Majesty.

My situation was complicated by the fact that, years ago, some of our missionaries working in Ethiopia had accepted the Italian invaders and sold our hospital in Addis Ababa to them (although no money had been received). When the Italians were driven out, Haile Selassie assumed that the hospital complex belonged to him, and the Americans working there were ordered to leave. However, the Americans pleaded for more time and the use of two buildings. They are still there, and the American occupancy is embarrassing to the emperor; he is not eager to see representatives of the American Mission.

Nevertheless, a few days after I conferred with Tafara Worq, I was called to the Ministry of Education, but not to see the minister, who is ill. The acting minister met me with utmost cordiality and asked me to present my case. At the conclusion he thanked me and said, "We here in the Ministry agree with you in principle and have decided to make an exception of the Anuak project in this matter." Then he told me that he had received a letter from His Majesty's private secretary in which His Majesty had instructed them to satisfy my case. Apparently we will be able to use the Anuak language in teaching all the adults of the Anuak tribe, which is a great victory for us and may be the opening wedge for other missions to receive a similar permission. They have been trying to get permission to print the Bible in languages other than Amharic for fifteen years.

I am eager now to get back to Pokwo. I must build a clinic and a chapel and two houses for the new families coming out to help us. In addition, I must reorganize the school and start the adult literacy classes again. I have two communicants' classes of about forty each. Recently another entire village came in and asked for baptism, and I must begin their training. I have an evangelists' school with eight fine young men who must be trained for further work and prepared for going out to open evangelistic centers in nearby villages, in addition to the thousand and one things that crop up every day.

Don's celebration, however, turned out to be premature. He was called back to the Ministry of Education and informed that the Board of Education had denied the acting minister's recommendation. Thus it remained illegal to teach the Anuaks to read and write their spoken language. Don refused to accept that decision and so informed the acting minister. Though he was sympathetic, the minister stated plainly that the use of written Anuak, whether in Roman or Amharic script, was still forbidden. Don went back to Tafara Worq and requested an interview with Haile Selassie.

I am confident that full permission will be granted by the emperor, but I do not know how long we will have to wait. In this country no decision is final until made by the emperor himself, and over the years he has taken a personal interest in what we are doing. I need to return to Pokwo, because I left one of the single women in charge and she is not very tactful with the men who work on the station. They resent her authority, and when they do not jump to do her bidding—she discharges them. She has dismissed several of the men on whom I depend very heavily. I must get back and make peace.

The big mistake I made in the beginning was to take the advice of the folks here and apply to the Ministry of Education before trying to see His Majesty. Everyone felt I should go through the regular channels first and only then, if I did not get anywhere, go to His Majesty. I wasted a lot of time trying to get permission through the Ministry of Education before making any attempt to see the emperor. I will not do that again.

Tonight I am discouraged, and my tail is hanging low. My faith is faltering more than I care to admit. I have been in Addis Ababa for more than two months. I have written letters, telephoned several times, and had two conferences with Tafara Worq, but nothing has happened. If the Lord is testing me, I am buckling under the pressure. I believe that it is the Lord's will for the Anuak people to be taught his Word in their own language, but time is running away. I should be back in Pokwo preparing people for baptism, not negotiating with the Ethiopian government. It is a good thing that Lyda insists I be patient. Otherwise I would have quit long ago.

Finally Don was granted a special exception that enabled the Anuak project to continue its educational program in the Anuak language. Whereupon Don returned to Pokwo.

This seems to be a visiting day, and a group of Anuaks came in with their chief, who had heard about our box that could speak

Anuak and even sing Anuak songs. I have recorded a number of messages for the Anuaks on this tape recorder and find them most effective. The people will listen intently to a tape, whereas they might laugh and talk while a speaker is trying to get their attention. I have also recorded a number of songs and Anuak stories. So I brought out the tape recorder and entertained the chief and his followers. He then wanted to record a song of his own. I did not listen very closely, since I was thinking about the sermon I was going to give at the evening service; but the chief's singing brought loud laughs and cheers from the crowd of Anuaks gathered around.

Later in the afternoon we were visited by the Ethiopian district commissioner. He needed medicine for himself, and he brought a half-dozen soldiers with venereal disease for penicillin injections. The commissioner had heard about my tape recorder too and wanted to see if it would record in the Amharic language. I rewound the tape and played some of it for him. Then I began to play the song the Anuak chief had just sung. Immediately there was a great outcry from the Anuaks, and some of them jumped up and ran away. Others screamed at me, "Stop! Stop!" Without knowing why, I shut off the recorder and immediately asked the Ethiopian district commissioner to make a recording of his voice. He wanted to know what was wrong with the Anuaks, and I could truthfully shrug my shoulders and say, "They are always making noises like that. Now we will make our recording and pay no attention to them."

After the Ethiopian officer and his soldiers received their medicine, drank some coffee with us, and were loaded down with vegetables, they went back to their canoe and left. The Anuaks began to drift back, at first timidly, then with leaps and bounds, and they rolled on the ground with laughter and slapped each other on the back in high glee. Then the story came out. The song the chief had sung was about a pitched battle fought between the Anuaks and the Ethiopians a few months ago. The Anuaks had routed the Ethiopians and put them to ignoble flight even though the Ethiopians had superior numbers and were all armed with rifles. Then the song went on to tell about the Ethiopian officer who ran away so fast that he took sick and vomited up his food, which included a stomach full of red peppers. They described how during his flight his rifle got caught between his legs and tripped him, and he rolled down the riverbank into the river and cried like a baby to his soldiers not to leave him behind. I had recorded this song and unknowingly was starting to play the whole story back to the very Ethiopian officer the chief had been singing about. By the narrowest margin, we escaped a nasty situation that might have started another fight. I am determined that I will pay closer attention to what songs and stories I record hereafter.

▼▲▼

The attendance in our services is increasing. Our early morning services are attended by nearly two hundred people even though the services start at six o'clock. Today we had seventy-five at the clinic service, of whom sixty-one came for treatment. It is utter folly to send one man alone into a place like this and expect him to be builder, doctor, farmer, pastor, evangelist, judge, and father to so many, many people. The initial impact of the gospel on these people is the important one. Later, like Americans, they become immune to the message after hearing it so many times and not making a deep personal commitment to it. There are hundreds here right now who would become fast and sincere Christians with the proper encouragement and support. Today many Anuaks trust me as they would a loving father, and they will do whatever I tell them. I hesitate to storm their hearts, because I am not sure that I will be able to shepherd and train so many in the next years; but I could baptize hundreds right now because they accept my word that Jesus Christ is their Savior. I know many would learn to love the Lord if I had time to teach them. I pray that my reluctance to push them into Christianity with a quick decision will not mean that we will lose them.

Don wrote about several of the Pokwo believers.

On Sunday we had a fine service. I have been teaching a communicants' class of more than fifty, and I felt about thirty-five of them were ready for baptism. Before I had baptized one group of new Christians, another class started to form. It is wonderful to be moving ahead. The church was full this morning, and when I called for those to be baptized to come forward, many asked to become Christian who had not been coming to the training class. I had to explain to them why I felt they should not be baptized at this time. Then, as I looked over those to be baptized, my mind quickly ran over the story of several of them.

Akelo, a young girl, was standing with her blind father and sick mother. Akelo came to the mission nearly a year ago with her left ankle shattered by a rifle bullet. She had been tending the fire in her village one evening when an unknown enemy shot into the village and the bullet struck her in the ankle. All the ankle bones were shattered, and for weeks it looked as if she would lose her foot. Dr. Baumann was here then, and he took the pieces of bone out bit by bit until there was not much left. The leg bone was also fractured, and it has been a long time in healing. She still has to have it dressed, although she can now walk on it. Her mother came in with Akelo to take care of her, and we discovered that the mother had an advanced case of tuberculosis. Then a few weeks later, her blind father came in to stay. I had great difficulty in convincing the father to come to worship at all. He complained that since he was blind, he could not see what was going on. I persuaded him that all he needed was ears to hear and a heart to believe. First Akelo became a Christian, then the old father, and finally, a few months ago, her mother. Here they were, a complete Christian family but all three with terrible afflictions and little hope for real health in the days to come. Today they were radiant.

Also before me stood a leper with both hands and feet—or what remained of them—bandaged. Her face was badly affected, and the leprosy was so far advanced when she came in that it is questionable whether we can arrest the progress of the disease; but she, too, has come to love the Lord.

Another man standing before me had been a drunkard and a beggar. He was thrown out of several villages because he would not hoe enough grain to support himself, and the villagers refused to feed him. He had lost his wife because he could not complete the payment of the bride price. When he came in here with tuberculosis, he was a forlorn figure with no one to love him and everyone happy to see him die. This man became a Christian, conquered his drinking problem, and is now hoeing one of the largest fields in the community. He has begun to take steps to get his wife and small son back.

As the world counts power and prestige, we were a miserable, sick, dirt-poor, ragtag bunch of black Africans led by a crazy, white American missionary and the sober Anuak elders of the church of Jesus Christ at Pokwo as we walked in procession down to the river for the sacrament of Christian baptism. I waded out into the water, and after prayer, the elders led each new Christian down into the river. The obstacles these joyful people must continually overcome to remain faithful to their vows are tremendous, and there is no place on God's green earth that I had rather be than right here to try to help them.

Amid his efforts to evangelize the Anuaks, Don continued to practice medicine by faith.

Today I have not had any time for evangelism. I did manage to eat six pancakes for breakfast, and then I went out to work on the sick and dying. At least 120 were waiting for me. After I finished with them and was wondering what I should start on next, I heard cries out at the workshop. I rushed out and found two of our workmen fighting with garden hoes. One of the chaps was a Christian, so when I got the fight stopped I pointed out to him that Christians do not settle their differences in that way. "Yes," he said, "I know. But this man is a heathen, and he says that I am not a good Christian. If he says that again, I will split his stupid head open!" I call that a stout defense of the faith.

After dark I started for the house to clean up a bit for supper, but I was called back to the riverbank. Another canoe had come in through the rain, and this time a young girl was lying in bloody water. As two women lifted her out of the canoe, her big brown eyes looked piteously at me. Then I saw her trouble was caused by an umbilical cord that had not been removed and trailed behind her as they dragged her out of the boat and laid her on the wet ground naked, except for a loincloth. I was told that she had given birth to a stillborn baby yesterday and that the placenta would not detach itself. The poor little girl did not look to be more than thirteen, and she was frightened nearly to death and had lost so much blood that her eyes were glaring white and she was too weak to stand. I stooped over to pick her up in my arms and bring her into the house, where I could treat her. As I lifted her and straightened up, she suddenly clutched my neck and screamed in pain, and I heard one of the women cry, "It is out."

And so it was. In the dark the great Dr. McClure had stepped on the trailing cord when he stooped to pick her up, and in his lifting her with his foot still firmly planted on the umbilical cord, the whole placenta had pulled free. I daresay this is the only case on record where a placenta was removed in this manner. I think I will write it up for a medical journal. I may even become famous. After all, most surgical procedures are performed by skillful hands. I have done one with a clumsy foot. Maybe I will be asked to address a plenary session at the next convention of the American Medical Association. Doubtless, the doctors would like the opportunity to examine the foot that does surgery. I would certainly love the opportunity to tell those physicians that we desperately need a bunch of them out here in Africa. I do not know what I would have done if God in his grace had not taken care of that poor young girl. She is now sleeping quietly in my study and already feels much better.

▼▲▼

Our native evangelists are having marvelous success on the Gilo River, and we hear of great numbers of converts, but at Pokwo recently one of our lepers lost his mind under most distressing circumstances. This leper, Ocala, was a fine Christian and a hard worker. Although he had only his thumbs left on each hand, and no toes, yet he worked harder than any man around here. He hoed his fields and repaired his house as well as made cattle ropes for sale. One day he walked ten miles to a distant village to teach and preach God's Word to some relatives of his.

In that village was a sacred tree that the people feared and worshiped. Ocala told them that it was foolish to worship a tree and volunteered to cut it down. They warned him that a great curse would come upon him if he tried, but he accepted the challenge. It was a very large tree, and he could not possibly have cut it all down since he could hardly hold an axe with his fingerless hands. He did chop off a large limb, and the people ran from the village, but when he got the limb off and nothing happened to him, they came back and urged him to stay on and teach them more. The next day Ocala began to act strange, and two days later he lost his mind completely. He became so dangerous that they had to tie him up.

As soon as I heard about it, I went to see him. He talked naturally, but had moments when he waved his arms wildly and tried to hide himself from imaginary foes. I talked and prayed with him, and he seemed quieter. The next day they told me he was worse, and when I went down to the village I found that they had him tied down to the ground. Ocala begged me to cut him loose and bring him back to the mission. He promised to behave, so I gave him a trial and brought him back. He was quiet for a little while, but then went completely crazy again. We had no way of looking after him here except to tie him down, and I did not want to do that, so I took him back to his village. They made a set of stocks for him through which they put his feet and legs, and then tied the two logs to the ground. I have gone several times to see him, but he is raving mad. The people naturally attribute his madness to his act of cutting off the branch of the Jwok, and we cannot dissuade them. We can do nothing more than pray for him.

In my evangelists' school I start off with a service at six o'clock in the morning. Then the evangelists spend an hour in reading aloud from their Anuak Bible. Following this, they go out into the nearby villages for two hours of teaching and preaching. I teach Bible for two more hours. Later in the day, from five in the afternoon until seven at night, we study the Old Testament. I am glad to get this school started, because it is a shame that we have never made any serious attempt to train evangelists until now. We have spent years and thousands of dollars in training teachers and government clerks,[57] but never a cent in preparing the native people to take over the task of preaching the gospel. I just cannot understand what we have been doing all these years! So many of our missionaries feel that education is the answer for all of Africa's needs! Thus we pour our best people and the majority of our money into the schools while the development of the church is left to happenstance. We will pay for our neglect someday in watching the feeble church we have erected go down before nationalism and communism, and we will be helpless to stop it because we will have a few converts, but no deeply committed community with its own natural leaders.

▼ The Gilo River

B Y NOW THE McCLURES had spent ten years at Pokwo, and the mission was sufficiently established for others to complete. Therefore Don was ready to move on to the center of the Anuak tribe on the Gilo River and begin what he thought would be his final pioneering challenge. This was the place where Don had desired to start the Anuak project twenty years earlier. In the late 1930s he had been unable to initiate the Anuak project from within Ethiopia and thus had worked from Akobo in Sudan and then into Ethiopia at Pokwo. Now he was preparing to end where he had wanted to begin. One man can only accomplish so much in his lifetime, and the inexorable march of days had left Don with only ten years until retirement. He expected to finish his African adventure on the Gilo.

In recent months Pokwo has seemed to be more of a tourist resort than a mission station. Every plane brings in a new batch of visitors. Last week we had sixteen, and poor Lyda was feeding twenty-two at each meal. On Saturday they all said good-bye, and as they climbed into the truck to be taken to meet the plane, I could see the great relief in Lyda's eyes. However, when the plane landed, an Indian woman got off. She had come to see the Anuak project to get some ideas for her work in Pakistan. Also, there were two Americans—one a pilot for Ethiopian Air Lines and the other a doctor from Point Four. They had come down for a big game hunt—entirely unannounced and quite unwelcome—and expecting that I would drop my work to show them a good time. I knew Lyda would skin me, but there was nothing to do but take them to our house and make them feel welcome. Pokwo is entirely too civilized and accessible now to suit us, and we are ready to move on.

315

In 1960, as the McClures prepared to pioneer at the Gilo River, Don was able to report that the gospel had been preached in every Anuak village. In some villages there were as many as fifty Christians holding regular services, and in all the villages (except about forty) there was at least one baptized Christian. Don estimated that one-fifth of the Anuak tribe had become Christian and another fifth were being prepared for baptism. Further, starting from zero in Ethiopia, after ten years of work more than ten percent of the Anuaks were literate. Using English letters, the New Testament had been completely translated into the Anuak language, and seven books had been transliterated and printed in Amharic script. Primers and some form of literature were present in every village. More than half of the Anuaks had been treated in Don's medical clinics, and clinics for babies were established. Poultry and cattle were markedly improved, and fruit trees were multiplying.

We are now buying produce from Anuaks who ten years ago had never seen a fruit or vegetable. Moreover, we have twenty trained Anuak evangelists at work. Our central school has a complete Anuak staff, and we have students in advanced schools in Addis Ababa, Dembi Dollo, and Gore. Some of them are preparing for the ministry, some for medicine, and others for education. Nevertheless, we need help desperately in women's and children's work, agriculture, and medicine.

I still believe that the Anuak project provides a sound pattern for rapid evangelism in primitive areas. However, the complete team we originally envisioned has never been assembled on the field. We had hoped to have "fifteen missionaries for fifteen years," which would total 225 staff years. The personnel we have actually had and the years they have served equals only seventy. Obviously, if so much can be accomplished by so few in so short a time, a full team could work wonders.

I suspect that moving will be harder this time than when we left Doleib Hill for Akobo, or again when we left Akobo for Pokwo. We are older now, and somehow our roots are deeper. We have built a lot of our lives into this station at Pokwo and will be reluctant to leave it after all these years and the many friends we have here. Many Anuaks want to go with us to help start the new station, and it will be a joy to have them. It is always hard to train a new batch of workers.

We have had too many visitors at Pokwo. It seems that the reputation of Pokwo has spread from one end of Ethiopia to the other, and everyone, including tourists, wants to come out to see us, whether we want to see them or not. We do have a beautiful compound. It is beginning to look like a campus now, with all our buildings and the gardens and the trees; in another year or two it will be really spectacular. But beauty or not, Lyda and I are eager to push on to the Gilo River. We will keep things much simpler there than we have here at Pokwo. This place has gotten out of hand, and we have too much and too many buildings. We have nearly forty families living here on the compound, and at least fifty people not connected with families. They cause us constant trouble with their bickering and quarreling, to say nothing about worse things such as promiscuity between the men and women. It is nice to have the people here so that we can teach and train them, but the spiritual problems are great until they become Christians and are well founded in the faith.

A long time ago I wrote a letter to the Ethiopian minister of education asking permission to open the new station on the Gilo River. Then I went to see him. Neither letter nor interview moved him to any action. He was quite indifferent to my pleas and simply said the final permission was not in his hands. Nor would he explain what procedures were necessary to obtain the permit. He was just noncommittal. A few weeks later I went to see him again. This time he was very definite and said, "You must see His Imperial Majesty for this permission. He gave the first permission for your present station, and only he can grant you land for this second site." I asked the minister if he would assist me in seeing His Imperial Majesty, but he shrugged and said that audiences were in the hands of the private secretary. Thus started another series of attempts to break through barriers.

After my third visit to Tafara Worq's office, I was admitted and presented my case. He told me His Imperial Majesty was very busy, due to the Near East crisis, and was receiving only people of high priority. I tried to persuade him that my business was of the highest priority, but elicited only a wry smile. I kept going back as long as Haile Selassie was in Addis Ababa. Unfortunately it was just at the time of the Ethiopian fast before the feast of the Assumption of Mary, and His Imperial Majesty went down to Bishoftu with the Abuna to fast and pray for world peace. I decided to follow him, and Lyda and I spent four days at Bishoftu trying to see him, but he really was fasting and praying. His Majesty and His Holiness would go to the Ethiopian Orthodox Church at eight o'clock in the morning and would stay there until two in the afternoon. Ato Emanuel Gabriel Selassie was also in Bishoftu, and I enlisted his aid, but he brought back the report that His Imperial Majesty would see no one except in the gravest emergency. So we came back to Addis Ababa to wait.

After the feast on 23 and 24 August, I again went to see Tafara Worq. He admitted me immediately, but had no encouragement, because His Imperial Majesty had been out of town for two weeks and was very busy catching up on the affairs of state.

I do not have an empire to run, but I am responsible for a little bit of the kingdom of God, and I thought I ought to get back to it. Thus I wrote Tafara Worq that I would be leaving Addis Ababa on the 30th, and if we did not have this permission, it might delay our work at Gilo for a full year. Early in the afternoon the secretary called me and said that His Imperial Majesty wanted to see me, but had not set a definite date. However, I was not to leave town, because the appointment might be scheduled at any time. The next morning I telephoned at 8:30 as instructed, and Tafara Worq said, "Be at my office at 9:10 A.M., and we will go immediately to the palace." I had not finished my breakfast, but I quickly lost my appetite for scrambled eggs as I scrambled myself to get properly dressed. I walked into the secretary's office at 9:05 A.M. and was accompanied to the palace by a captain of the guard. There Tafara Worq met me and said, "His Imperial Majesty has many questions to ask you, so try to answer them briefly and to the point. Do not forget the usual three bows." Then he led me to His Imperial Majesty's study, and as we entered he was standing in front of a roaring fire.

I did not forget the three bows, and Haile Selassie advanced to shake my hand and said in English, "I have been expecting you and want to hear about the Anuak people and your work." Those were the only English words he used until he said goodbye. The emperor immediately began to ask questions about our work—what we had done; how many Anuaks had become Christian; were Muslims coming into Ethiopia in our areas; what success we had with chickens, pigs, cattle; how much grain we raised last year; how many boys and girls were in school; how much American money we were spending each year; if we had our full staff on the field; and many other questions that indicated he remembered our last conversation. Then after a half-hour, he asked, "And what can I do for you now?" I laid before him our plans to open a new station on the Gilo River and said, "I have not come to you impulsively, for I have been trying for eighteen months to get permission for this new work through the Ministry of Education, and they finally referred me to you."

Haile Selassie did not blink an eyelash when I made that remark, but subsequent events proved that he had taken full note of them. Officials in Ethiopia are appointed, not for their ability to do a job, but to balance and maintain the loyalty of powerful families to the emperor.

Haile Selassie asked me how much land we had at Pokwo and how much we wanted on the Gilo River. I replied that we did not want a large site there, since most of the agricultural work would be done at Pokwo and we felt that approximately one hundred acres would be ample. The emperor pondered for a moment and then turned to Tafara Worq and said, "See that Dr. McClure receives a paper granting him six hundred acres." I bowed gratefully. Then His Imperial Majesty turned to me and with a hearty laugh said, "Does this land belong to me to give to you?" I assured him that it was indeed his land, unclaimed wilderness that had never been occupied except by the Italians. He then indicated that the interview was over.

I would have been satisfied with what had been accomplished, but more was to come. The next day I was speaking to the Rotary Club at noon, to which belong several ambassadors, including our own, as well as several cabinet ministers. Following my address, among those who came up to speak to me was a young man whom I had not met. He said to me, "I am glad to inform you that the Anuak project has been transferred from the Ministry of Education to my ministry." My mouth dropped opened, and I exclaimed that I did not understand. He said, "Has Tafara Worq not seen you today?" When I replied in the negative, he said, "I am sure he has called, because he wants to see you." The young man then told me he was the head of the new Ministry of Community Development and was happy that we would be working together.

When I returned to our headquarters, I found that Tafara Worq had indeed been calling and wanted to see me immediately. When I got to his office he told me that His Imperial Majesty had ordered him to take the Anuak project out of the jurisdiction of the Ministry of Education and put it in the Ministry of Community Development. "I think you will not have so many delays in that ministry." And he said that since the Ministry of Community Development did not deal with foreign personnel, our new staff members would all be cleared through his own office. He then asked me for the names of all those who would be coming out to work at the Gilo River and said, "I will now give a blanket approval for their entry and registration." I was so amazed that I began to stutter. He smiled and said, "Do not thank me. This is not my idea. It is His Imperial Majesty's command."

This wonderful resolution was far more than we could have ever hoped for or dared to pray for. It is beyond our wildest dreams. Our work has the direct, personal interest and approval of Haile Selassie, and he is removing obstacles from our path. We see the hand of God in this, and Lyda and I will soon make a trip to the Gilo River and start work on the airstrip. We also must clear the forest for the building of our houses. I want to keep things simple at Gilo. We will build houses only for the missionaries and thus, instead of encouraging the Anuaks to come live near us, we will make all our contacts with them in their own villages. Even those who work for us will be expected to live in a nearby village. That will not only save a lot of money, but also prevent many a headache in problems of discipline.

One of Don's most creative ideas was to challenge young men and women in America to donate one year of their lives to serve without pay in Africa. These volunteers[58] had to arrange their travel expenses (usually with substantial help from their local congregations), and Don provided room, board, and plenty of work. These people were of tremendous value in what they accomplished in Africa, what they learned about Africa, and what they shared when they went home.

Since the Gilo River location was isolated and inaccessible, the station would have to receive supplies by air. Thus the first order of business was to hack an airstrip out of the rain forest. Don and Lyda and four American volunteers walked into Gilo, chose a likely spot in the direction of the prevailing winds, and started to work.

There were trees everywhere. During the next week we cut more than four hundred of them and cleared some three hundred yards of landing field. Eventually we will need six hundred yards for the larger planes of the Ethiopian Air Lines. Cutting trees is backbreaking work, and I was glad to have some help in making the landing strip. We also erected our first house on the Gilo River—a small grass hut to give us some shelter from the rain.

For a while the volunteers were left alone at Gilo to carry on other necessary work, but although they were supplied with plenty of food and an Anuak cook, they found they needed the guidance of someone with greater African experience. At that time Don was not able to return to Gilo, and no plane was available to fly in. In addition, the mouth of the Gilo River was completely blocked by sudd for three miles. Lyda tried to crash through the grass in their new jet-propelled boat, "The Dove,"[59] but discovered that even a jet-propelled boat requires some water, and the grass was so thick that it lifted the boat out of the water. Then she and her helpers tried to cut their way through, but the grass filled in as fast as it was cut out. Next they tried to pole the boat through, but after six hours they had advanced only thirty yards. Therefore Lyda decided to walk the sixty-five miles into Gilo, accompanied by twelve Anuak men carrying equipment.

Since she wanted to wear two pairs of socks, Lyda borrowed a pair of Don's tennis shoes and set off. For sixty-five miles she waded through crocodile-filled swamps with water up to her armpits, walked through fifteen-foot grass in which leopards were hunting for food, and at times crawled on hands and knees through the underbrush of rain forests. Before wading the swamps, her bearers always placed their shorts on their heads to keep them from getting wet.

After the first day, some of the carriers struck for higher wages, claiming that their loads were too heavy, although each had only forty pounds. They refused to go on unless they were paid more money than Don had promised them and to which they had agreed before they left Pokwo. Lyda simply fired them and hired new carriers at the next village. Everything and everyone arrived safely at Gilo after three and a half days. The entourage completed the final part of the walk after dark, to the bark of baboons, Colobus monkeys, and the calling of small geye monkeys.

According to Don, when the strikers returned to Pokwo, they claimed that he owed them for their walk back.

They may as well bay at the moon. In fact, they are lucky that I did not whip the whole bunch for deserting Lyda as they did. At present one of our missionaries has taken our old boat and a load of supplies downriver to start a new station among the Nuer people. As soon as he gets established, he will come back for his wife. That is not the pattern in our family. I am older and much wiser than he is, because I have been on the field longer and have learned all the tricks of the mission trade. I send Lyda out, and when she is well established, then I go and join her.

Don thought it would be hard for most Americans to realize how dependent the mission station was on what they could raise to eat, since there were no grocery stores nearby. Some months later he wrote of their crops.

Our first bunch of bananas are just ready to pick, and we will soon have papaya ready as well as pineapple. Lyda said today she had opened only one can during the whole month of November, and we have been living out of our garden exclusively for the first time since we arrived at Gilo. We now have melons, cucumber, cabbage, and cauliflower (which we never could raise at Pokwo), kohlrabi, eggplant, okra, beans, tomatoes, beets, lettuce, carrots coming, pumpkin, sweet potatoes, etc. Lyda and I put up forty-eight bottles of tomato juice and lime juice in the last ten days. We brought the lime trees over here four years ago.

The only thing not doing well is the cattle, and we have lost ten head of cattle in the past six months—I think to sleeping sickness. We had the cattle inoculated against sleeping sickness, but the injection is not one hundred percent proof against it, and we must have an especially virulent strain here. We will not try cattle again until we have the pastures ready and all the trees cut down within several hundred yards of the pastures. The tsetse fly must have shade and trees to live, and our cattle have been pasturing in the forest because there is nowhere else to go. In another year we will have cleared plenty of ground to give them open pasture. If we had grass growing on the airstrip, it would be ideal for the cattle, but we have scraped the strip clean. We will be planting clover and alfalfa eventually. Our turkeys are doing well, and we now have twenty-four eggs under hens and hope for a good brood of chicks.

Of course, Don's medical work continued on the Gilo River.

A month ago one of my patients, a young boy, was taken to a woman witchdoctor and soon died. Not long after that, we were sitting here in the evening when the drums in a nearby village began to beat and the people started to sing and clap their hands. It sounded interesting, so I suggested to our volunteers that we walk out and see what was going on. As we entered the village we could see hundreds of people sitting on the ground with a huge fire in the center of the circle; there in the light of the fire was this woman witchdoctor going through one of her dances. Several sick people were sitting near the fire waiting for her to touch them. She was in the middle of a dance that induces the spirit of Jwok to come and give her power to heal them. She was whirling around as the drums beat faster and faster and the people clapped their hands. As soon as she worked up to a frenzy, she would go into a trance and perhaps fall to the ground. Then she would have power to burn the patients and drive out the evil spirits that were making them sick.

This woman was almost to the point of falling into a trance when I turned my flashlight on her. The people had not seen us approach, and the witchdoctor fell to the ground in a faint. I walked over to her and opened her eyes and thought she was faking, so I picked her up and carried her over to the outside of the circle and put her on the ground. Then I started to speak to the assembled people. I talked to them about the evils of witchcraft, then told them of the Lord Jesus and how he healed the people when he was on earth and would continue to do so if we have faith and trust in him. All the time, I watched this woman out of the corner of my eye and saw her start to move and sit up. She became very attentive. So I spoke directly to her and asked her some questions about witchcraft, and especially about the small boy she had killed. Suddenly she broke into tears and begged me to stop. I asked her to come to see me at the mission in the morning, and she promised to do so. I never thought she would come, but while I continued our service in the village she sat through it all with great interest.

Sure enough, the next day she was at the mission at 6:00 A.M., and I talked to her about the Lord. She came back every day for two weeks, and I had a lesson with her daily and started to teach her to read. She was making amazing progress and had read two primers in the two weeks. Then suddenly she disappeared, and no one knew where she had gone. I was afraid she had run away and would never come back. But four days later she returned and told an amazing story of how Satan had taken her away into the forest deeper than she had ever been and where she was completely lost. He kept her there for four days without food, though she did find water. During all that time Satan was trying to make her follow him. But she refused and said she was going to become a Christian, which made Satan furious, and he threatened her and said she would never find her way out of the forest unless she worshiped him. But she refused, and finally Satan left her. She knew her general directions and continued south until she came to a village, where they took care of her. Then she came here and told her story and made her profession of faith.

Her account caused a sensation, and many others are following in her steps. I do not know how to interpret her experience except to understand it just as she told it. I believe that she was truly tempted by Satan, to whom she had once belonged, and he did not want to give her up.

Other Anuaks of the Gilo River believed as well.

Last Sunday we had a fine service and a wonderful baptism. Ojok looks ninety, but he is not more than forty-five. When I came through this country several years ago, he was supposed to be baptized, having become a Christian after hearing the gospel preached by an itinerant Anuak evangelist. However, he was too sick to come. Now he is sicker than ever. He knows that he is dying from tuberculosis and there is nothing we can do for him. He asked to be baptized before it is too late.

I have never seen a man so thin. He is nothing but skin and bones and unable to walk. Ojok had to crawl from the little hut where he is staying to the place where we held the service. When I called his name, he crawled forward and was baptized sitting on the ground. Ojok cannot stand up for Jesus, but he gave a splendid testimony. Ojok said that he had waited for more than three years for this day and had never wavered in his love for the Lord God. He said he was happy that he had made his profession of faith before the people and he was now ready to die and go to be with his Lord.

Although Don was often unable to help his patients, that did not prevent him from learning powerful lessons from those who died.

Today I had 148 patients in my clinic. The medical needs in the heart of Africa are so staggering as to become numbing, but these are God's children, too, and they desperately need help. Among those who came was a woman whose whole foot is rotting away. She crawled on her hands and knees several miles through the forest to get here. A man stumbled in, carrying two sick children who should never have been moved from their home. They were burning up with the fever of smallpox. Their little bodies were covered with sores and black with flies. They cried and squirmed in their efforts to escape from the flies. Where the father had held them in his arms the sores were bleeding and raw. To protect them from the flies he had covered the children with cow dung before he left his village. But the village is several miles away, and the dung had been rubbed off so that thousands of flies were eating away at the sores. I washed the children and then sprayed them with insecticide. For the first time in days they were free of the flies digging away at their bodies.

I had to treat the usual cases of yaws, dysentery, malaria, infected eyes, sores, and wounds. My lepers come in, because I do not have time to get out to see all the needy people who are dying all around us. The need for a real physician is tremendous, but I am here alone, and I must do what I can for the people I can reach.

Several days ago a man came in from a distant village and asked me to go to see his little girl. It was a twenty-mile walk, because the roads were closed by the heavy rains and I just did not see how I could go. I did not know what the child was suffering from, so I gave the man some aspirin and sent him back. The next evening he came again, pleading with me to go and see his daughter, for she was dying. Again I put him off, pointing out that many others nearby were dying and I could not see all of them. So I gave him some more medicine and sent him home. He must have walked all night, for the next day he was back again with the girl's mother. They threw themselves prostrate on the ground before me. Grasping my feet, they begged and begged for me to go to their village and see their sick daughter. Apparently the girl was too big to carry even if she had been well enough. Their pleas melted my heart, and I had to go. I gathered a bag of medicines, and we started on the long hike back through the woods and swamps. We arrived at the village after six hours in the hot sun, and I marveled how that father had walked over that same path six times in three days in his bare feet.

As I crawled into their little grass hut, I could hear the girl's strained breathing, and I feared the worst. As I knelt over her emaciated form and felt the burning face, I knew I was too late. I told her who I was and that I had come to help her. She opened her eyes and said to me, *"Kiperange yi keri oa cong?"* (Why didn't you come long ago?) My heart blazed within me. Why hadn't I gone immediately? I am a minister of the gospel, not a doctor of medicine, but I might have been able to help her.

Those words of that dying girl will never leave my ears and heart. I wish I could shout them in every church and into the ears of every American Christian. Over the last nineteen hundred years, God's children all over the world have been crying out, "Why have you waited so long?" I cannot rest or spare myself until I have used every last ounce of my energy and strength in sharing the gospel of Christ with these children of Africa.

A Somali woman and child in front of their home near Gode

V GODE

THE SOMALIS OF OGADEN
1960–1977

The Heart
of the Horn

WHEN DON BEGAN the Anuak project, he expected a team of fifteen missionaries to devote fifteen years to the evangelization of the Anuak people and then move on to a new frontier. However, since the full missionary team that he envisioned was never assembled on the field, a great deal of the Anuak project was carried on by the McClures alone or with a very few helpers. Nevertheless, the Anuak Christian Church had flourished with mission stations at Akobo, Pokwo, and Gilo. If there was always more to be done, at least Don's primary skills were as a pioneer, and the pioneering phase of the Anuak project was complete.

By dint of continuous years on the field, Don McClure had become his church's senior African missionary. During these years he had changed from a fiery redhead to a gray eminence. Don was quite well known, even famous, with a loyal following of people in America who had a very personal interest in his work and supported it with their gifts. In Ethiopia, due to his relationship with Haile Selassie, he was able to accomplish things that seemed impossible to others. Thus, after working only two years on the Gilo River, Don was asked to assume the office of general secretary of the American Mission, becoming the administrative head of the work in Ethiopia. With offices located in Addis Ababa, Don was ultimately subject to the mission administrators in New York City, but he was also to work as the field executive, representing and facilitating the missionaries.

Don was not keen to exchange his field for a desk, but this office was a new kind of challenge, and he agreed to accept the position on the condition that the Anuak project would continue on the Gilo River. Don moved to Addis Ababa, put on a necktie, and went to work. In addition to his full-time responsibilities as general secretary, Don tried to keep things moving forward at Gilo, but it became extremely difficult and problems arose continually.

Last week one of our men at Gilo, James Owar, got on the radio and began to call for help. Since he was not broadcasting during our designated time, we could have lost our broadcasting license, but someone in Jimma picked up his voice and called Addis Ababa by phone and passed on the message. Lyda and I flew down to Gilo as fast as we could and found that the police had taken over the mission. The police captain was living in one of our houses, and his men were running about as though they owned the place. Twelve of our people—our house servants, the schoolteachers, clinic workers, and gardeners—were all under arrest and had been held under a tree in the compound for ten days, not even permitted to go to their houses to sleep. They were not allowed to do their normal tasks about the station; no watering had been done and no cleaning, and the chickens had not been fed, although they were running loose and could forage for themselves. Everything was at a standstill.

I am afraid that I moved into the situation more like a cyclone than a meek Christian missionary. In a few minutes I had the men released and back at their work—but not before I paid fifteen dollars for each of them for five years' back taxes, which the police captain made his excuse for the takeover. Since he claimed that our people had not paid taxes for five years, he decreed that they would have to pay before they could be released. Some of the men had paid last year, but could not produce their receipts. Our head teacher said his receipt was in his village, but he was not allowed to go to get it. So I had to pay again for him. Others had not been in Ethiopia more than two years, having come from Sudan, but they, too, had to pay for the entire five years. I paid under protest and have written a letter to this captain's superior officer, which will build a fire under him, I am sure.

However, the captain and his men are still here and looking for more Anuaks to arrest. All the men of the nearby villages have fled to the forests, and only women and children are left. The captain says he has instructions to stay on the mission compound until all have paid their taxes. The real reason he is staying here is that he is afraid to go to any Anuak village, so he uses us as a shield. I do not relish the situation, but can do little about it now. I would not want to throw him out and have him run into serious trouble with the Anuaks. It might reflect back on us if anything happened to him. So we will sit it out. A charter flight came in yesterday and brought much-needed grain and supplies for the Anuaks, since they are facing a famine condition just now. The corn borers have been worse this year then ever before, and much of the crop is damaged. The people are up against it.

I am going to stay until we can get another charter flight in on Thursday, 11 February, and then I will have to go back to Addis Ababa. Lyda will remain on here for a few days more until I can arrange for someone to come in and relieve her. We love it here and wish we had no other job. We would be happy to finish our careers right here on the Gilo River and forget all about Addis Ababa and the work that has to be done up there.

Addis Ababa (New Flower), the capital of Ethiopia and the birthplace of the Organization of African Unity, was founded by Emperor Menelik II in the latter part of the nineteenth century. Due to Haile Selassie's international stature, Addis Ababa was both a traditional and modern metropolis. It might be called "the heart of the horn of Africa."

Life here in Addis Ababa is busier, if possible, than life on the Gilo. At least it is filled with more and different things that demand my time. Physically I am not working half as hard as I did on the Gilo, but I am on the go all the time. Yesterday, for example, I was doing business in five different government ministries, shopping for a half-dozen different people, and buying paints and building supplies for the mission. I made two trips to the airport to meet planes and had a speaking engagement last night for the Christian Teachers' Association. None of these things I would have to do on the Gilo River, and they are all important but time-consuming. I have been going back and forth to the Gilo station and at the same time trying to keep things moving here in Addis, but I find that I am not doing either job as I should and must concentrate on one or the other.

Right now I am sitting in my office high above most of Addis Ababa, looking out on a beautiful city that at this hour of the night looks like a Christmas tree with all its red, green, blue, and yellow lights. Our office is located on a hill overlooking most of the newer part of the city and on the top floor of the highest building in town. I can see right out to the airport and can work in my office until I see a plane coming in and be at the airport before visitors can clear through customs. This is a new Addis Ababa. Five or six years ago there were only a few multistoried buildings, but now the skyline is broken in all directions with new banks, hotels, insurance companies, and apartments. Just below us a new apartment building of fourteen stories is going up, which is very high for Ethiopia. It is true that in between all the new buildings there are tiny hovels and stores and occasionally a grass-roofed house. Twenty years ago when we first visited Addis Ababa, it was a city of 300,000 people, most living in *tukls* or tin-roofed shacks. Today there are 800,000 people, and many of them live in houses as fine as can be found anywhere. By day the city is still dirty and smelly and the streets are filled with lepers and cripples. Every day we see hundreds of beggars on the principal streets.

His Imperial Majesty has built homes for these unfortunate people on farms outside the city, and periodically the army trucks sweep through Addis and gather them up and cart them out to the farms. But they have to work out there, so gradually they drift back into the city by twos and threes to beg. It is the Orthodox Church that perpetuates the begging system, because it is one of the tenets of their faith that before entering a house of worship a person must give alms to the poor. Thus, in front of every Orthodox Church there are scores, and sometimes hundreds, of beggars waiting for their handout. The women usually bring bags of small rolls or cakes and pass these out, but the men give a small coin about the value of 1/4 of a cent.

I do not see how it can be raining anywhere else in all the world. Surely we are getting it all in Addis Ababa. Maybe the Lord is trying to wash this city off the top of the mountain. Addis Ababa could do with a little washing. In northeast Africa, only Cairo is dirtier than Addis, and that is only because Cairo is larger. Getting off the main streets is like going back a thousand years. There are still cows, donkeys, camels, and women carrying huge head and back loads of wood through the streets and blocking traffic. Menelik II planted the fast-growing Australian eucalyptus tree, and they are everywhere.

A few days ago I was hurrying over to the Sudan Interior Mission Chapel to preach. I took the back streets and got behind a herd of cattle. There must have been five hundred of them, and they filled the street from house to house. I was driving a little Volkswagen and did not dare try to push the cattle out of my way, or they in turn might have pushed me around a bit. The horn was completely ineffectual, and occasionally bumping the hindmost cattle did not affect the slow pace of the herd. The herders beat them wildly, but to no avail. I saw that I could not break through and had only ten minutes before church time, so I had to whirl around and go back the long way. The organ prelude had started as I dashed into the building. That is Addis Ababa. Not only do they drive huge herds through the streets and have horse-drawn carriages everywhere, but they fail to clean the streets afterward. There are no public restrooms anywhere in the city. I have seen two men shaking hands the way we do in America, but with one of them turned to the side relieving himself. I think I will try that the next time I am in Pittsburgh. In all this city there is not one sewer other than open drains. If you want a flush toilet in your home, you must build a septic tank, and where that drains is entirely your business. No one else cares at all unless you choose to drain it into a neighbor's front yard, as happens in many cases.

Though Addis Ababa is nearly 9000 feet above sea level, yet we are surrounded by mountains that tower over us, some of them reaching up to 14,000 feet. For all our height, we never get snow, because mountains in this part of Africa have to be over 17,000 feet to collect snow. Still, it can be quite cold here. We often wear winter clothes and sometimes wish for more. My heart goes out to the half-naked people who walk the streets looking for work and begging for money to buy clothing and food. All the poor walk around in their barefeet even when hail is inches thick on the ground and with their skimpy clothes soaking wet. We do what we can to help them, but it is an unending job. Also, we never know just how many of them are genuinely poor or just dress in rags and go barefoot for the begging hours of the day.

According to the *New York Herald Tribune,* there are 24 million poverty-stricken Americans living on $3,000 a year. The average Ethiopian lives on $53 a year and would be happy to have the garbage of the American poor. The average annual income of the Surma tribe is less than $10. All these people need food, clothing, medicine, and schooling in the most desperate way.

▼▲▼

The long history of Christianity in Ethiopia stretches back through the Kingdom of Axum into the mists of antiquity. According to legend, a young man named Frumentius was brought to Ethiopia after a shipwreck, converted the royal family, and was later consecrated bishop by Athanasius, the champion of the Nicene Creed. The main separation between the Ethiopian church and Western Christianity occurred at the Council of Chalcedon in A.D. 451. This famous ecumenical council attempted to work out a more precise way of understanding the relation between the divine and human natures of Christ, which had been declared though not adequately defined at the Council of Nicea more than a century earlier. This had been the subject of constant debate ever since. In company with large Christian groups in Egypt, Syria, and Armenia, the Ethiopian church rejected the Chalcedonian formula.

In the eyes of Western—and a good part of Eastern—Christianity, this rejection (the monophysite heresy)[60] of the continuing integrity of Christ's humanity led to an overemphasis on worship of God and an underemphasis on service to humanity. Thus, to Westerners the Ethiopian Orthodox Tewahido (Unity) Church stressed ritual observance to the neglect of service and ignored the rest of the world in its mountain isolation.[61] During the Middle Ages the legendary monarch, Prester (or Presbyter) John—most familiarly identified with Asia—was thought by some to be a king of Abyssinia.[62] After the depressing failure of the Crusades, Christendom was sustained by the hope of a powerful Christian ruler in a distant land who was sweeping away Islamic power.

Though isolated geographically, the Ethiopian church was administratively connected to the Coptic Church of Egypt. That connection began to weaken with the invasion of Ethiopia by Italy in 1935. After World War II, the church broke with the tradition that the Abuna, the patriarch of the church, should be a Copt sent from Egypt. In 1951 an Ethiopian patriarch was consecrated, and in 1959 the church became fully independent of Egypt.

The Ethiopians take their holy days very seriously. Someone calculated that there are over 1,000(!) holy days in Ethiopia, which, of course, is impossible for any one person to observe. However, fasting for 250 days a year is not uncommon.[63] People in some occupations, like those employed by Ethiopian Air Lines, must ask for exemptions in order not to be so weak from hunger that they cannot do their work. On 2 March we celebrate Adowa Day—the 1896 victory of Menelik II over the Italians who were trying to extend their influence over Ethiopia. On 23 July we celebrate the birth of His Imperial Majesty, Haile Selassie I, to His Highness Ras Makonnen Wolde Mikael and Woizero Yeshi Emebet Guemechu in 1892. In 1916 Ras Tafari Makonnen became regent and heir to the Ethiopian throne and, following the death of Empress Zewditu in 1930, was crowned Haile Selassie I, King of Kings (Negusa Nagast), the 225th descendant of the Solomonic dynasty. February 19 is Martyrs' Day, the anniversary of the 1937 massacre of some three thousand Ethiopians in retaliation for a bomb thrown into the car of Italian General Rodolfo Graziani.

On 15 May we celebrated the twenty-fifth anniversary of the liberation of Ethiopia from the Italians, and a huge demonstration was held in which Haile Selassie paraded before the eyes of the world every gun, tank, and military vehicle he possessed as well as miles of marching men and schoolchildren. I do not know whom he was trying to impress, but he wanted to show his might, and it was impressive for such a small country. However, during that time everyone talked about a possible coup or speculated that His Majesty would abdicate in favor of his son or that he would be assassinated; everyone seemed sure something would happen. It all turned out to be rumor, since His Majesty walked around through the crowds without a fear, rode in an open carriage, and stood for hours in full view and within a few yards of thousands of people, he being apparently unconcerned and without even a single guard.

Timkat (or John the Baptist Day) is one of Ethiopia's biggest religious festivals, much bigger than their Christmas. Everyone must take two days off. We would not dare to open our office, and no business house will be open except for bars and brothels, and they are busy. The whole city will congregate in their churches to be rebaptized. His Imperial Majesty will start the day at six o'clock with the patriarch, archbishops, and bishops, and thousands of people. Haile Selassie will baptize himself first, then the Abuna. The Abuna will then baptize the archbishops, they the bishops, and the bishops the priests, and finally the priests will start to baptize all the people. Everyone must be rebaptized. After the baptisms the people will feast for two days and attend some church service. There will be at least 250,000 people present in the sixty-four Orthodox churches in Addis Ababa.

Not long ago (25 September) we celebrated Maskal, or the finding of the cross of Calvary. The Ethiopians believe the true cross was found by an Ethiopian Christian and now every church has a piece of it. These bits of wood are extremely sacred and can only be seen and handled by priests. Once a year they are brought out of the churches and carried in procession. The wood is carefully concealed under many layers of cloth, so only the priest really knows what is being carried. With the opening of each new church, another piece is found and blessed for the purpose. Naturally these relics are of great spiritual value, and faithful Ethiopians believe they have power to cure sickness, to bring fertility, and to ward off any evil spirit. Even His Imperial Majesty takes part in the parade and celebration of Maskal Day, and I presume he believes the whole legend of the finding of the true cross.[64]

In addition to feast days, Don wrote home about religious traditions and customs.

Yesterday I ran across an odd custom. I met a large group of women on the street, each of them carrying a basket. They were gathering for a meeting called "the Women of the Bread." It seems that all married women within the Orthodox Church belong to these clubs. They meet once a month in someone's home, and each brings some bread. The meeting consists of each woman's confessing her sins as they break and eat this bread; if someone tells a lie, the bread is supposed to bring a curse upon her. After each woman has made her confession to the others, they all kneel down and ask the bread to forgive them their sins. This custom is all mixed up with the sacramental transubstantiation of the bread. The bread is first blessed by the priests, when it supposedly becomes the body of Christ and acquires the power to forgive sins, to heal sickness, and to make them fertile. The women then take the bread from the church and meet in private homes.

This practice must have arisen from the time many years ago when women were not allowed within the sacred precincts of the church. At these confessionals no wine is used, and all the bread must be eaten before the women leave. I am surprised that the priests let such power get out of their hands; I guess they get their share of money when they bless the bread. No priest of the Orthodox Church will perform the simplest service without a money payment in advance. They are paid for every house call. If the payment does not meet the priest's approval, then he will not bless the house as he leaves. For baptisms and burials, enormous sums are demanded and must always be paid in advance of the service.

Lyda and I want to attend a morning service in the Orthodox Church next Sunday. We will not understand what is going on, but neither will most of the others who are there. The entire service will be in Ge'ez, which was the language of the Ethiopian court until it was replaced by Amharic in 1270. Today only a few scholars can understand Ge'ez. Most of the priests just memorize the sounds by rote and mumble through them week after week. By tradition, Ge'ez is the language of the Garden of Eden and the only one God will listen to. Therefore the Ethiopian church continues to use it.

Because worship services are of long duration, the leaders lean on a praying stick called a *makutaria*. The worshiper does not even need to hear the service to get the benefit of it. Many people pray by touching the outside wall. The church is exceedingly wealthy, owning about one-third of the land of Ethiopia, while most of the people are miserably poor. In addition, every priest is a mendicant.

At least I should be able to get more done now, because I am working thirteen months a year. Ethiopia uses the Julian calendar, which has twelve months of thirty days and one month of five days. Leap year adds a sixth day to the thirteenth month. Each year is sacred to one of the four evangelists: Matthew, Mark, Luke, and John. The leap year belongs to Luke.

▼▲▼

After all these years I have finally been thrown in jail. It was only a temporary incarceration, but those who engineered it are now very sorry it happened. Four months ago, eighteen black South African refugees came to Ethiopia from Kenya, and the World Council of Churches asked me to take care of them. The Ethiopian government granted them political asylum, but apparently the governments of Kenya and Tanzania then asked Ethiopia to deport all of them. It seems that these men and women had refused to accept military training for the purpose of fighting against the present white South African government, and in the minds of most of the rest of Africa that constituted treason. The assumption that these eighteen are sympathizers with the present regime in South Africa is far from true, but in any case I was ordered to get them out of Ethiopia. When I began to try to find some place to which they could go, I discovered that for all their talk about freedom, no country in Africa would accept these refugees.

This search took months, and I was able to get scholarships for two of the men at Lincoln University in Pennsylvania. However, on Wednesday the director general of the Department of Immigration ordered me to get the rest out of Ethiopia within twenty-four hours. I protested that this was quite impossible, since no country would accept them and they would all be returned to Ethiopia, the point of departure. On Thursday I was called in again and threatened with arrest if I did not expel the South Africans. On Friday two policemen came to my office and said the director general wanted to see me immediately. Since I had some appointments, I let them cool their heels for an hour (which they later called "resisting arrest"). Then I went with them, and instead of being conducted to the director general, I was placed in a small room and informed that I was under arrest. I replied, "That is interesting. What is the charge?" They made it clear that I was being detained because of my failure to deport the black South Africans.

When I asked to use the telephone, the captain went out to see if this was allowed. In a few minutes he came back and told me to go ahead. For the next forty-five minutes I tried to get a call out. I first called Lyda, then the U.S. Embassy, then the executive secretary of the Organization of African Unity (whom

I know well), then the director general of the United Nations headquarters, then the minister of the interior, then His Imperial Majesty's private secretary, then the crown prince, and finally some friends I thought could help me. I was not denied the use of a phone, but the switchboard was jammed, so I could not get through to anyone.

About one o'clock the captain asked me what I was going to eat for lunch, and I told him I would eat whatever they brought me. He laughed and said no food was served there. I replied that I would go without, but I hoped he would not miss his lunch because he was guarding me. Then he suggested that I call my wife to bring some food. I asked if he had a phone that would work, and he went out for a minute. When he returned, I called Lyda, telling her where I was and to call the American Embassy immediately. Then, with a smile and a word of thanks I handed the phone back. The captain complained that I was supposed to ask only for food, and he went out again to report to someone.

Our ambassador stormed right over, and when he heard my story he cut loose with some marvelous American profanity and insisted someone would burn for this outrage. However, I assured him that I was only amused and did not want to antagonize these officials, because I had to deal with them almost daily on routine mission business. "Look," he said, "this would make a wonderful story for the newspapers of the world. A Christian missionary from big, bad, imperialistic America is thrown in jail in Ethiopia, the self-styled protector of all the downtrodden people of Africa, because the American defends some black South Africans who have fled for their lives."

After lunch I was taken to see the director general, who sweetly insisted that I had not really been arrested or detained, but only asked to come in for a chat. "After all," he said, "these South Africans cannot remain in Ethiopia." Another official seriously suggested I send them back to South Africa. When our ambassador heard that, he fairly blew his stack and said, "If I had not given my word to the prime minister to keep this out of the papers, I would call in the reporters right now."

That is not the end of the story. I have talked to representatives of the Organization of African Unity and the United Nations, the minister of the interior, and His Majesty's private secretary. On Monday I will talk to the crown prince, Merid Asfa

Wossen.[65] If he will not help me, I will talk to the crown princess, and finally I will ask to see Haile Selassie himself. Now that the iron is hot, I will keep striking until I get justice for these refugees. I suppose I do not sound much like a missionary who preached a sermon on peace a few hours ago, but at least I will bring peace to some harried South African refugees.

▼▲▼

When the moderator of Don's American church made a world tour that included Ethiopia, he asked Don to arrange an audience with the patriarch of the Ethiopian church. As the visitors arrived, they were placed in an absolutely bare anteroom to wait. A secretary came for them at the appointed hour and ushered them into the presence of His Holiness, who was seated on a splendid but rather dusty throne. The Abuna extended his cross and hand to the secretary to kiss, but not to the Americans.

After a few greetings, the patriarch demanded to know why Americans who had been invited into Ethiopia to work among Muslims and pagans were taking Christians out of the Ethiopian church and putting them in other churches. The moderator stumbled around trying to think of something to say, but Don got angry and could not remain silent.

I told the patriarch that I was one of those missionaries (which he had not known) and that I had been working among pagan people for many years—not one of whom had been a Christian before we came to Ethiopia. Moreover, I asserted that because of our efforts, there were now many thousands of them in the church of Jesus Christ. I pointed out that in fifteen centuries the Ethiopian Orthodox Church had made absolutely no effort to reach these people and was making none today. The moderator was aghast at my outburst, and I am sure he wished I was not there. In any case, he quickly changed the subject.

Don McClure was passionately committed to the evangelization of the world, and he had no high regard for Christian groups who did not share that missionary passion. Nevertheless, he was always eager to be helpful. Thus he was happy to comply when the dean of the Holy Trinity Orthodox Theological College in Addis Ababa asked him if he would find summer work for a small group of divinity students who were unable to return to their villages during the summer months. In this way was initiated the Summer Theological Institute as a joint venture between the Ethiopian Orthodox Church and Don McClure. The Ethiopian church provided the students, and Don provided everything else, funded by undesignated gifts that came to him from supporters in America.

Instead of finding the theological students some kind of manual labor so that they could make a little money during the summer, Don decided to attempt a joint study and service project. Don did not have the time or staff to provide a full course of study, but he organized the morning hours for the study of the Bible, church history, and Christian education and the afternoon hours for work.

The first summer program enrolled eight students, and they were charged with taking a religious census of Addis Ababa. At first the young men were afraid that they would be beaten by resentful citizens or arrested by the police. They wanted Don to get special permission from the Orthodox Church and city officials for them to make the survey, but Don felt that to ask permission was to invite denial. So he persuaded them to work unofficially. The young men were still afraid to go out alone, but finally agreed to go in two groups of four, carrying a Bible as their only credential. To their amazement the Bible opened the door to many persons, homes, and groups who were willing and even eager to discuss their religious beliefs and affiliations. Before the summer was over, the two teams had canvassed more than 20,000 people, a fair sampling of the 800,000 inhabitants of Addis Ababa. It had always been assumed by both Orthodox and Protestant leaders that the population of Addis Ababa was almost equally divided between Christians and Muslims. The census found, on the contrary, that 55 percent were Christian, 25 percent were Muslim, and 20 percent—about 160,000—had no religious affiliation at all. This was an astounding revelation to the young divinity students, and they immediately took it upon themselves to reach some of the untouched people of the capital city.

During the second year Don had fourteen students for ten weeks and added church music and singing to the study. To keep the students near the school, Don rented houses where they could room together and enhance the spirit of cooperation. A year later Don and his men conducted the first daily vacation Bible schools ever held in Ethiopia, with seven hundred students in three locations. The next year there were thirty-two theological students enrolled, then sixty, and then one hundred. By now, instead of living in rented houses and preparing their own meals, the men were living in a dormitory connected with the Girls' School of the American Mission and were provided three good meals a day.

As a result of Don's summer institute, he became a benefactor and friend of the Ethiopian Orthodox Church, which had always been suspicious of and often antagonistic toward Protestant missions. In fact, Don was invited to lecture weekly at the Orthodox seminary. He hoped his participation would lead in time to the appointment of a full professor to the theological faculty who would be from the Protestant tradition. In this way students could be sent to the Orthodox Theological College in Addis Ababa with the confidence that they could be prepared to serve in the evangelical churches of Africa.

The new patriarch, Abuna Theophilus, called me in yesterday and asked me to serve as his adviser concerning the various denominations and missions working in Ethiopia. I am not sure that I have the time or desire to do this, but the appointment indicates some gain. Previously the Orthodox Church has not even recognized that there were other Christian churches in Ethiopia. I accepted his offer with the understanding that if I cannot serve as I should, he will release me and appoint someone else.

In addition, the Ethiopian government and the International Leprosy Society asked me to serve as a trustee and the treasurer of a multimillion-dollar hospital and training center for all of Africa that is to be located here. We were incorporated as the All Africa Leprosy Rehabilitation and Training Center (ALERT) and have begun to collect funds from thirty different sponsors. Among the patrons are His Imperial Majesty, the minister of public health, the president of the university, and so on. It is our purpose to train doctors and nurses throughout Africa in leper care, but especially in plastic surgery and occupational therapy. I received the first gift yesterday from the Swedish government for one million kroner, or 500,000 Ethiopian dollars. I guess I was asked to undertake this job because I once amputated a leper's finger and thus am rated an expert in leprosy.

Last week was something of a "red letter" week for me. I had three meetings with the emperor. The first was at my request to report on our work in Ethiopia. The second was the official dedication of ALERT. As a director and the treasurer of the board, I had to accompany His Majesty to the rostrum and sat beside him through the ceremony. We then had a board meeting and the next afternoon were invited to the palace for a reception. Thus I have shaken the hand of Haile Selassie so often in the past few days that he probably thinks I am holding it.

Don wrote home with more of his observations on Addis Ababa.

I suppose college students are the same everywhere in the world. That is, they must let off steam somehow even if they are fortunate enough to get one of the extremely limited places in Haile Selassie University. Our student riots started two weeks ago as a protest against, of all things, a fashion show being put on at the University Creative Arts Center. The students piled out to demonstrate against *miniskirts(!)* on the grounds that this American fashion influence was destroying traditional Ethiopian customs. Of course, this was just a pretext to raise some cain.

Some months ago the government banned student organizations, especially one that called itself the Crocodiles, published a paper they entitled *The Struggle*, and went around referring to each other as "comrade." One cannot be anti-government in Ethiopia without getting into serious trouble, so students must protest something nonpolitical like miniskirts. Our riots have been quite serious by Addis Ababa standards. That is, we had some broken windows and heads, a few cars overturned, and rocks thrown. I got two stones in the side of my car, but our rioters are not very sophisticated. Just a minute ago I got a call from the president of Haile Selassie University asking me to serve on a board of mediation between the university and the striking students. I would rather not get involved in this mess, but I can scarcely refuse, since my name was suggested by His Imperial Majesty.

This has been a hectic week to be on the streets of Addis Ababa, because on Monday all cars, carriages, people, cattle, donkeys, sheep, camels, etc., were ordered to switch from walking or driving on the left to the right. Since the beginning of time, Ethiopians have driven—whatever they drove—on the left side as the English do. Now they have switched, and most people do not remember. No one is allowed to drive more than fifteen miles an hour for the first month, which by itself is enough to drive me wild. Many a time we have had to stop as cars came down what is now the wrong side and the driver wondered why we did not get out of the way. Then he would suddenly remember the change and swerve into the correct traffic lane.

▼ Islamic Attack

BECAUSE THE BLACK Christians of Sudan were naturally unwilling to order their lives according to Islamic law, there had been a long-standing tension between the dominant and politically powerful Arab and Muslim north and the primitive, pagan, and Christian south. This situation often broke into open rebellion and finally civil war.

During the riots in Khartoum, we lost all our mission property. Everything was completely destroyed. Two of our missionaries, Bob Meloy and Bill Philips, were beaten over the head as they tried to help boys from the south Sudan. More than a hundred southerners were killed in the riots.

At this time a British freelance reporter managed to slip into the south Sudan and travel for three months without the knowledge of the Sudan government. According to his report, a copy of which was sent to Don McClure,

About six to seven million Africans live in the three southern Sudan provinces of Equatoria, Bahr el-Ghazel, and Upper Nile. Only about 150,000 people, Arabs and Africans, live in the three provincial capitals and 15 small towns. Thus, about 98 percent of the population, entirely African, live in the bush. The Africans do not go into the towns, even when dying for lack of medicine, because they fear being killed by Arabs. There is no medicine at all in the bush, and no medicines sent to the Sudan government in Khartoum for distribution in the south will get there.

The only way to send relief to the African population in the southern Sudan is to transport it directly. The death rate is highest among children as a result of complications from measles, whooping cough, pneumonia, and diarrhea. Many of these deaths are easily preventable, and the world's relief agencies have the capacity and ingenuity to aid the south Sudan and the people have a right to this aid. Ignorance of the conditions or the political sensitivity of the situation is not a sufficient reason to do nothing. A precedent was established in Biafra when relief agencies were willing to aid both sides in a conflict even if only one side was recognized by most governments.

There is an immediate need for these things: First, seeds and agricultural tools to build up the supply of protein food. Malnutrition from lack of protein is the typical condition of the children, and more than half of the families I have met do not have such basic tools as hoes, spades, axes, scythes, or machetes. Second, in the region I surveyed, about one-ninth of the southern Sudan, there were some 180 primary schools still open with grades one and two. Twenty of them also have grades three and four. These schools have about 800 teachers and approximately 24,000 students. They need books (in English) and basic school supplies such as paper, pencils, blackboards, and chalk. Third, protein food supplements such as those sent to Biafra are available from food surpluses in America and would increase the working capacity of farmers. However, protein food supplements such as powdered milk, corn soya meal, and tinned meat have several disadvantages. They are bulky to distribute and will be seen by Africans as a luxury item to be sold in the market place, thus not reaching the people who need it. Protein food is better grown than flown.

In addition to these items, and even more crucial, is the immediate need for preventive medicine. The need is for several million doses of measles and whooping cough vaccine, the refrigeration to keep it, and spray injectors to dispense it. The people need tons of plastic sheets for rainwear and tons of cotton blankets, cloth, and thread for protection against pneumonia and bronchitis. For malaria, millions of chloroquine tablets, kerosene to pour on stagnant water, and tons of mosquito netting are required. For skin disease, millions of carbolic soap bars and tons of towels. For diarrhea and dysentery, millions of water purification tablets and rubber bags to hold water. For anemia, millions of multivitamin tablets are required.

This reporter concluded that the southern Sudan's immediate relief needs could be met quietly and nonpolitically and should be aimed at helping the people regardless of their political views. This relief could not be dependent on the agreement of the Sudan government, which presumably was willing to use death from starvation and disease as well as from force of arms to crush the rebellion in the south. Moreover, the reporter suggested that the relief effort should be regulated by Europeans to assure donors that it was being properly received and used.

The best relief representatives are missionaries who would be relatively secure in most areas of the countryside. The need is very real, and the means for meeting it is at hand. Whether it is appropriate to donate relief—not through the Sudan government, which is impossible, but directly to the victims of this conflict—is not so much a political question as a moral one.

Don McClure became deeply involved in refugee relief. From his years in Sudan, he knew many of the rebels. He felt that he and other Christian missionaries had to take some indirect responsibility for the conflict, because they had taught the people of south Sudan about not only Christian obedience, but also human freedom and dignity.

From the beginning it was unlikely that the scattered tribes of the south Sudan could capture the world's attention and conscience in their battle for independence, as Biafra was able to do earlier. Nor did the south Sudan have much in the way of the military personnel or modern weaponry required to wage a war. Even the rebels' superior knowledge of the terrain could not compensate for their lack of organization, leadership, and equipment.

Glenn Reed was with us for three days, having just come from Khartoum, Sudan, and told us terrible tales of what is happening in the south. The killings and massacres are continuing, and it is apparent that the Sudanese army is determined to exterminate all the intellectuals and Christians. They have announced that the only way to subjugate the south Sudan is to make everyone Muslim, and they seem set upon that policy. One of the first actions of the Sudan government was to expel articulate witnesses to the atrocities by closing all missionary stations in the south.

When his missionary colleagues were driven out of Sudan, Don sought permission for many of them to live and work in Ethiopia, but he had great difficulty, because the Sudan government officially asked neighboring nations *not* to receive them. Few countries were willing to risk the displeasure of Sudan for the sake of some missionaries who still wanted to serve in East Africa. When Don asked the American ambassador for help, the ambassador laughed and said, "You may not know it, but you have more influence with Haile Selassie than I do. I may be coming to you for help some day."

This has been a week of great furor in Addis Ababa, because the Ethiopian government has also capitulated to the Sudan by barring all missionaries expelled by Sudan from coming into Ethiopia to live or even to visit. This week three Sudan Interior Mission missionaries, who were just stopping over, were ordered to leave Ethiopia within twenty-four hours because they had come directly from Sudan. The Sudan has sent to Ethiopia a list of some three hundred former Sudan missionaries who have been expelled and has asked all the neighboring countries not to admit them into their territory. This is the most brazen piece of affrontery I have ever heard, and the point is that in the name of African unity all the neighboring countries, including Ethiopia, are going to respect this request.

It seems that the Ethiopian government officials are sharply divided on the question, and many of them think that Ethiopia has lost honor to accede to the Sudan in this matter. They argue that Ethiopia is a Christian nation and should open her doors to Christian missionaries who have been expelled from a Muslim country. Others, recognizing the strong political pressures, feel that the loss to African solidarity of refusing an official Sudanese request would be greater than the gains to be made by helping the missionaries.

Two of our Sudan missionaries, Lillian Huiskens and Dr. Mary Smith, were in Ethiopia a few weeks ago, and I got them out of the country before they were forced to leave. I will apply for permanent visas for them, and I do not want to have on their records that they were once expelled. The day when I picked up the visas for the Sikkemas and Dottie Rankin, one of the minor officials informed me that Dr. Smith's visa had been denied. I immediately asked to see the vice minister of foreign affairs. He put me off for four days, but I kept going to see him and sent in my card every morning and afternoon and indicated to his secretary that I would continue to come until I saw him. Finally the minister called me in. He was anything but cordial. He did not even ask me to sit down and was obviously on the defensive. I asked him about the status of Dr. Smith's visa, and he replied that his ministry had decided that she should not be admitted. I pointed out that she had been accepted by the ministries of education and public health, and I thought it only right for Foreign Affairs to grant the visa that other ministries had approved. He said, "Normally that would be true, but Dr. Smith's case is not normal."[66]

I asked for an explanation of why it was not normal, and he replied, "You know she is on the black list from Sudan, and we have to draw the line someplace and have decided to draw it with Dr. Smith." I replied that my name was also on that list and suggested they draw the line with me, since Dr. Smith would make a far greater contribution to Ethiopia than I ever could. He smiled at this and pointed out that I was already in Ethiopia and it would be more difficult to expel me than to deny visas to others. He went on to say that Ethiopia must keep her relations with Sudan on a friendly basis, and if they permitted all the ex-Sudanese missionaries into Ethiopia, it would be resented by Sudan. To which I replied, "You mean to say that you are allowing Sudan to dictate the foreign policy of Ethiopia?" He bristled at this remark, but insisted that Ethiopia had to cooperate with her neighbors.

We argued the case pro and con for nearly an hour. Finally he said, "Just how determined are you to have Dr. Smith in Ethiopia?" I answered, "Determined enough to explore every possible channel, and if I find them all blocked, I will apply to His Imperial Majesty in person." He looked at me rather quizzically, then said, "I believe you would," and I said, "You know I would." He shrugged, laughed, and said, "Okay, you win." He called in his secretary and ordered him to prepare the visa for Dr. Smith. While it was being prepared, we sat and talked amiably about conditions in south Sudan; we parted in the best of spirits. Sometimes it is nice to have a hard head, a thick skin, and the invincible stubbornness of the true Scot. I believe we shall have no further trouble with other ex-Sudan visas, though it is too early to know because I have been turning them in one at a time. Wilma Kats will be the next test, and if all goes well I should get her visa this week. If things do not go well, I will have to go through the laborious process of convincing the various ministries that I will not take no for an answer. Wilma's application has just been in for two weeks and is already processed through the Ministry of Education.

This was one of Don's most remarkable achievements. For compelling political reasons, Ethiopia had refused to accept Christian missionaries who were exiled by the civil war in south Sudan, but the government made an exception for Don's old colleagues. In this way Don was able to relocate experienced African missionaries expelled from the Upper Nile province of Sudan, thereby increasing his church's missionary personnel in Ethiopia from thirty persons to more than ninety.

The fighting in Sudan gets worse and worse, and many of our friends have been killed. Nearly every day we hear of another of our old boys who has been shot by Sudanese troops. From the reports we have received, they are being tortured, and even elementary schools are being machine-gunned to break the resistance. The Sudan army began to move after the rains, and one company of over a hundred soldiers was surrounded and ambushed by Nuer rebels. They fought for three days, and the soldiers were not able to break out. However, a couple of soldiers did manage to slip away during the night and get back to Akobo. They wired to Nasir for reinforcements, and another company of about one hundred men were sent out from Nasir. Before they reached Akobo they, too, had been ambushed and most of them killed by the Nuers. The government then sent out planes and dropped five-gallon tins of benzene on villages everywhere and sent word that they were going to annihilate all the Nuers in the Lau area. So now there are thousands of women and children fleeing to Ethiopia. We stand ready to help them wherever we can.

There is daily fighting between the Sudanese rebels and the government forces. The Sudan government has declared a state of emergency and closed all the schools in the south. Thirty-one Anuaks were massacred in a village near Akobo Post. Many of the women and children from that village have fled into Ethiopia, and we have some on the Gilo station. When the soldiers thought they had killed all the men, they set fire to the village and then stood guard and would not permit anyone to enter to get their things or to drag the dead bodies away from the fire. The people said they heard some of the men screaming who had been shot but not killed outright. The shock of this terrible thing has swept through Anuak country and, fearing a general revolt, the police arrested the king of the Anuaks, the same man who stayed with us more than twenty years ago at Akobo. He is being held as a hostage. The king has managed to get word out that the people are not to regard his life, but to rise against the government and fight back even though it means his death.

This is no time for me to be in Addis Ababa. I should be with my Anuaks, giving them what aid and counsel I can. Unfortunately that is not the way many of my fellow missionaries feel. They think it is a good thing that I am located in Addis lest I get involved in something political that would do harm to our total spiritual work. I would take my chances on that, because many, many Anuaks are in real need these days and we must do what we can to help them. Last week I chartered a plane and sent some grain in from Gambela. I will send another charter plane in this coming week, and then I hope to go down and see the situation for myself the first week in March.

Because of his work with the United Nations Committee of Refugee Relief, Don McClure had been classified as an enemy of the Sudanese nation. Thus it was extremely dangerous for him to go near the border, where he could be arrested. Nevertheless, he returned to the Gilo River, only a day's walk from the Sudan border, to help the refugees who crossed over into Ethiopia.

The situation in the south Sudan is still worsening, and we are being deluged with refugees, many of whom come with nothing but the few clothes they are wearing. Last week the police surrounded the village of Pakang, the first village just below our mission at Akobo and one where I have been many times and know almost all the people. The police were trying to locate some rebels they thought were hiding in the village. Not finding anyone, the Sudanese police took the village chief out, tied him to a tree, and shot him. The people raised such a clamor that it threatened the police, who seized another twenty people and tied them all to trees and shot everyone. Hundreds of people have fled the Sudan, and we are being swamped. I do what I can to help them, but my resources are limited and it is difficult to find grain here. It costs us five hundred dollars to bring a plane in with grain, but I am going to bring a plane load in next week so that we will have something for the refugees to eat. I received some unrestricted gifts this week that I shall use for that purpose.

Many of the refugees are Sudanese Anuaks who have been driven away from their homes and are seeking safety here in Ethiopia. The stories they tell of beatings, arrests, threats, and executions perpetrated by the northern Sudanese officials on the southerners are horrible. All our African teachers and hospital staff have run away from both Nasir and Akobo. This past week four of the boys I once taught at Akobo came through here looking for help. I have given them work, but they had to leave their wives and children behind. All these men were shot at by Sudanese police when they escaped. Everyone is watched, and there are spies everywhere.

Every day more and more refugees are flocking into Ethiopia. Yesterday Dr. John Apaye came to Addis Ababa and asked for help. He had been working in the hospital in Malakal, and the day Enoch and Bertran, two of our fine Christians, were arrested, a friend came by the hospital to tell Dr. Apaye (a Moro from Juba) of the arrest and that he was also under suspicion. He never went back to his house. He forged a letter on official stationery calling him to Khartoum immediately. He took this letter to the airfield that afternoon and managed to get on the plane for Khartoum. In Khartoum he got a friend in the Ministry of Public Health to certify that he must get to a cooler climate immediately and recommend two weeks in Asmara, Ethiopia, to recuperate from hepatitis.

Dr. Apaye bought a round-trip ticket from Khartoum to Asmara and was able to get on the next plane out before the authorities caught up with him. A friend accompanying him was taken off the plane as they left Khartoum. At Kassala, where they stopped for customs, the inspectors asked him why he had no baggage. John had left Malakal in the clothes he wore and did not even ask for his paycheck. While they were in Kassala, a telegraph operator showed him a telegram that arrived just a few minutes before the plane landed, instructing the police to detain Dr. Apaye and send him back to Khartoum.

The telegraph operator said he would deliver the telegram to the police after John's plane left for Asmara. John heard afterward that the army surrounded his house in Malakal and, when he was not to be found, killed his servant for letting him get away.

Just two weeks ago two cousins of John's were operating in the Juba hospital when soldiers appeared at the operating theater to arrest them. They leaped from a window and started to run. A helper in the operating room was shot and killed, but both doctors escaped and, still wearing their surgical gowns, jumped in a car and managed to get through to Uganda. And so it goes. A month ago there were nine south Sudanese physicians in Sudan, three from John's family. Three have been killed, and three have fled.

Harold Walker came in today with the news that Bishop Gwynne College[67] has been burned to the ground by the army and a number of staff killed, though he did not know who. Dr. Apaye brought a note from Bishop Allison of the Church of England, which was just a greeting and introduction for Dr. Apaye, but Bishop Allison did add that he had been denied a permit to go south and was told that he would never be allowed to visit the south again. The educated and Christian Sudanese are now running for their lives, and all are trying to get out of the south Sudan. Enoch and Bertran have completely disappeared, and no one knows where they are. We can only pray they have escaped. How can we bring the truth of the conditions in south Sudan to the attention of the world?

In recent weeks the Sudanese army invaded Ethiopia along the border and burned all the Anuak villages on both sides of the Pibor and Akobo rivers. When the Ethiopian government protested this invasion, the Sudan government handed them a list of grievances and listed more than three hundred incidents when rebels from Ethiopian territory had crossed the border and raided Sudan. The Sudan invited Ethiopia to discuss this matter at the same time that the Somaliland question was being negotiated in Khartoum. Some months ago, after nearly a year of border clashes, Ethiopia declared war on Somalia and wanted very badly to effect a solution to the problems of Ethiopia's eastern border—which is desert area, a waterless waste, not good for a thing except camel grazing.[68] Now Sudan has tied the Somalia issue to the conflict of Ethiopia's western border.

President Abboud of Sudan handed the minister of foreign affairs an agreement of extradition for Sudanese refugees, which is a threat that if Ethiopia gives aid to the refugees, then Sudan will not help on a peace treaty with Somalia. Ethiopia cannot afford hostilities with the secessionist province of Eritrea in the north, Somalia in the east, and Sudan in the west. Thus the Ethiopian delegation had to accept and sign the treaty of extradition and promise to repatriate more than five hundred Sudanese whose names were delivered to the Ethiopian government. This meant that most of them would be executed when they arrived back in Sudan. Last week one of our Christian boys, Timothy Odolo, was shot for no other reason than that he trespassed on the edge of a restricted zone in broad daylight. He was following a native path and was either ignorant of or had forgotten that it was a restricted area; when he walked through, he was arrested, taken to an officer, and shot immediately.

Last Monday I had an interview with the Ethiopian minister of the interior. He had sent for me on two previous occasions, but when I appeared at the appointed hour, I found that he had been called away for a meeting obviously more important than seeing me. However, on Monday he did call me in, and I met with him and two ministers. They were very grave, and the minister opened the interview with the words, "Did you know that the countries of Ethiopia and Sudan are on the verge of war over the border situation? A delegation from the Ministry of Foreign Affairs is now meeting in Khartoum trying to avert war, but we find the difficulties almost insurmountable as long as we permit Sudanese rebels to find sanctuary in Ethiopia and then abuse that sanctuary by crossing the border to attack Sudanese police and Sudanese villages. We have come to the conclusion that we must close the border and declare that all rebels shall be arrested and repatriated to Sudan."

While the minister of the interior personally disapproved of this extradition treaty, he was obligated to carry out the terms of the agreement. Thus he asked me to get as many of the rebels as possible out of Ethiopia before the deadline of 4 April took effect in six days! I was shown a list of the five hundred wanted men, but I was not allowed to keep it. They did give me a list of the eleven most wanted men, upon whose heads a price had been placed by the Sudanese government. They were all members of the Committee of Southern Sudan Freedom Group, and practically all of them were right here in Addis Ababa. I was told that I could get them out of Ethiopia in any way possible. The Ministry of the Interior could not help me, but neither would they hinder me for six days. However, at the end of that time they would have to pick up any men still in Ethiopia and send them back to Sudan. I knew that all eleven would be executed without question and without trial as soon as they arrived back in Sudan, so I was determined that none should be caught.

Two of the eleven had passports from Sudan, but none of the rest had any papers whatsoever. The two who possessed passports had surrendered them when they asked for asylum in Ethiopia, so I had to get permission from the Ministry of the Interior to have these passports released. The ministry did not dare to give me written permission; everything was done by telephone in a very roundabout way. After two days of contacting more than a dozen officials, I finally got to the Security Police; on being ushered in to see the assistant minister, he sent everyone away and tried to find out where the order to release these two passports had originated. He was reluctant to give them to me unless I would tell him who was responsible, but I could only tell him to start tracing the phone calls he had received and when he traced them to the end he would find his authority.

I got the passports. Then I had to see the British ambassador to get visas into Kenya for these refugees. At first he refused to help me, declaring that the whole thing was a "bloody awful mess," and he was not allowed by his government to touch it. So I called on the American ambassador and asked him to drop a word to the British ambassador and explain the circumstances to him. That afternoon I got my Kenya visas for the two men, and we sent them away on Friday to Nairobi.

Three of the other men wanted to go to Nairobi, too, but we could not get a visa for them because they had no papers. I hired a Jeep, and two of our missionaries, John Quick and Harvey Hoekstra, started off with them and two more Anuaks and two Nuers for the Kenya border. They left on Thursday, and the Jeep has not yet returned. It was quite a job to prepare an expedition for a week's travel over awful roads and then to outfit these men for a three-hundred-mile walk through the Kenya forests.

Some of the other refugees we sent out by truck to Dembi Dollo with instructions to slip off the truck before they reached the town, vanish into the forests, make their way back to the Nuer villages along the Baro river below Pokwo, and become primitive Nuers again until this war blows over. Still others we sent by bus to Jimma, and then the Missionary Aviation Fellowship plane took them to the Gilo River, where they will disappear into Anuak villages and live as though they had never been educated. Some of these refugees are university men, and others had training as medical officers and teachers. One had been to seminary in England. Now they must take off their clothes and go native again to save their lives. It was a heartbreaking business, sending these fine men away, but it was the only thing we could do to save them. I hope that when things get quieter they will be able to come back and live and work as civilized people. It has been a hard week for me, getting things ready and seeing them all off.

A few weeks later Pul, who was number two on the list of most wanted men in Sudan and was hiding on the Gilo River station, had to be moved because his whereabouts had become common knowledge. With spies for the Sudan government working along the border, it was not safe for him to remain any longer at Gilo. By now Don had his own airplane, which he flew mainly by sight and by faith.[69]

If Pul had been returned to Sudan, he would have been summarily executed, as has happened to two other Sudanese Christians who were caught. Moreover, he had to keep away from the Ethiopian police, who were now obligated to turn all declared rebels over to Sudan officials. Thus I had to keep Pul under cover until I could get him away. It took me four hours to fly from Gilo to Addis Ababa because the weather was so bad that I had to go miles and miles around the thunderheads. We finally arrived in Addis just after dark.

Fortunately Lyda was at the airfield to meet us, so we slipped our refugee into the back of the car and kept him out of sight of the airport police. Pul is a Nuer and so black as to be almost blue-black. He has such prominent scars across his forehead that even mixed among a thousand black people, it would be obvious that he was Sudanese.[70]

This past Sunday, Lyda and I drove our Kharman Ghia almost down to the Kenya border so Pul could walk across to freedom and safety. I had previously made arrangements with the vice minister of the interior to keep the police from stopping us on the trip, provided we drove straight through. Pul is the last of the most wanted men to leave Ethiopia. He hid in our house in Addis Ababa for a week, and none of the mission folk knew that he was there even though we had three dinner parties during that week. It would have been an unforgettable experience to conclude a dinner by having the host, hostess, and the unsuspecting guests arrested for harboring a fugitive.

It was with relief that in the midst of the refugee crisis Don and Lyda vacationed with their family.

Not long ago we had a wonderful camping trip. We traded in our old Volkswagen for a double-cabin pickup that can sleep six. Don, Jr. and his wife, Ginny, along with Polly and her husband, Drew, were coming out to Africa by boat. We drove to Asmara to visit Glenn and Gail Reed and then to the Red Sea port of Massawa, where it was 118 degrees. It was an exciting moment when we saw the ship and wonderful to have our family together, except for Charles and Margaret, who are in America. We decided to camp on the shore rather than stay in a hot hotel, but we did not tell the children that there was some danger in that two couples had been robbed not long before at the very place we chose for our campsite. I figured six people were a lot larger group than four. Besides, we trusted the Lord to take care of us, and I am sure the other party had not.

We swam three or four times a day and even at night. The sea was filled with phosphorescence, and swimming underwater made our bodies seem to glow with a million small light bulbs.

After three days we drove up the mountains to Asmara to spend a couple of days and on Monday started the six hundred miles back to Addis Ababa. We made our way leisurely over the mountains and through splendid mountain passes. Many times we could look down into valleys 4000 feet below and see the road looping like a twisted ribbon. In one place we could see thirty-four switchbacks as the road worked its tortuous way down into the valley. The road was very narrow and steep with no guard rails, but we negotiated it without mishap and stopped wherever nightfall caught us. We had to sleep under plenty of blankets, because we often camped at 10,000 feet and never below 6000. The road follows a high ridge, most of which is higher than Asmara, which is 7,500 feet above sea level; Addis Ababa is 9000.

▶▲▼

Don and Glenn Reed (no longer in New York, but permanently stationed in Asmara) recognized that the need for a permanent Anuak Resettlement Project in western Ethiopia had become imperative. They estimated that there were approximately five thousand genuine refugees, as distinct from rebels, who had fled Sudan because of the conflict. In most cases these refugees were old men, women, and children who were hiding in the forests, swamps, and grasslands of western Ethiopia. Doubtless, many of them hoped that someday they could return to Sudan, but their villages had been burned to the ground. In addition, the younger men who would be the leaders of tribal life had joined the rebels and almost certainly had cut themselves off from ever again living in Sudan. Already the general amnesty offered to the rebels had been rejected. The rebels still declared themselves for the independence of the south Sudan or at least some form of autonomy; this the Sudan government could not accept.

Perhaps many of these young men can be persuaded to build a life in their own villages in Ethiopia, but in the meantime the genuine refugees—mothers, young children, and the old—are suffering untold deprivations in the forests and swamps of western Ethiopia. If something is not done during the dry season, these people will spend another rainy season in the forests, where it is extremely difficult to get food and medicine to them. Their numbers are certain to be decimated. It is our desire to move these people back from the troubled border and get them settled as quickly as possible in new villages of their own. Once they are settled they can become self-sufficient within three or four months, which is the time required to plant and harvest a crop. Due to the wonderful soil of this area, there can be three harvests each year. However, when their government has driven them out and razed their villages, they are understandably suspicious; many may fear resettlement.

Thus we have decided on a pilot project to lead about 240 families away from the border area to a site on the Gilo River. Because the river is not navigable (except for canoes), all food stuffs, tools, etc., will have to be carried by porters. Then we will build an airstrip of sufficient length (1000 meters by 60 meters) to enable supplies to be flown in by Ethiopian Air Lines. The building of the airstrip will require a minimum of four months. We have people from four tribes living at the Gilo River station as well as Sudan rebels and refugees wandering around. Lyda feels that since I must be in Addis Ababa, she should remain at Gilo and do the work alone. I am proud of her, because there is not another woman in all our mission who will consent to being left alone on a mission station. They think it is too dangerous, but good old Lyda is not afraid of anything. The rest of the women just marvel at her fearlessness, yet it is not so much fearlessness as the simple trust that the Lord will take care of her.

About this time the Ethiopian government gave semi-official approval to Don's pilot project. The governor of Gambela province, in which all the refugees resided, had enthusiastically endorsed the plan. Don estimated that the 240 families could be supported for three months on approximately $20,000, which included the cost of food during the move, tools and equipment for building the airstrip, clothing and mosquito nets, medicines, farm tools, seeds, chickens, pigs, and other necessities. The American Mission and the Ethiopian government would work together to supervise and administer the Resettlement Pilot Project.

Because of the vast number of their people killed and their villages burned and razed by the Sudan army, some three thousand Nuers crossed over into Ethiopia. However, the Nuers could not move deeper into Ethiopia, because the Anuaks stoutly defended their tribal lands. The Nuers were unable to go forward or backward, yet they also could not stay where they were. Their presence was an open invitation for the Sudanese army to attack across the border, thereby infringing on Ethiopian territory and provoking an international incident. Worst of all, the Nuers were halted on the floodplain of the Baro River, and in a few months that would be completely underwater. Trapped in a no-man's-land, three thousand desperate people were without food or shelter or any protection from mosquitoes. They had no place to go. As soon as Don found out about the Nuers' plight, he used money sent to him personally to charter DC-3s from Ethiopian Air Lines. With them he began dropping food, blankets, and mosquito nets to the refugees. As can be expected, when the first of Don's planes flew over, the Nuers thought they were being strafed again.

When Don McClure, Jr., graduated from Pittsburgh Theological Seminary, he immediately returned to Ethiopia to help. The day Don, Jr. arrived, Don, Sr. finished work in the American Mission office in Addis Ababa, and the two Dons drove six hours by Jeep down to Jimma. There they removed a plane's cargo door, loaded sixty-six bags of corn, and flew three hours to the dropsite. They pushed the bags out to the hungry Nuers, all the while facing the obvious possibility that one or the other Don might slip through the open door and follow a bag hurtling to the ground. When they completed the low passes in the fierce heat, the plane climbed to 11,000 feet, and the sweating men spent the three-hour return flight in the forty-degree cabin with the wind whipping through the open door at 120 miles per hour. After the six-hour drive back to Addis Ababa, Don, Sr. had only two hours before he had to be at his desk again. He spent the time writing letters to his supporters.

Once Don received permission from the Ethiopian government to grant refugee status to these Nuers, he undertook to move them to a permanent site away from the border and Sudanese reprisal raids. However, the Nuers were afraid to take their families through the territory of the hostile Anuaks. They also wanted to make certain that the new location that Don had chosen for them contained unforested, grazing land, free of the tsetse fly so that their cattle could survive. By this time the rains in the Ethiopian highlands had made the river begin to rise; the pressure to get off the floodplain was intense.

Twenty-two clan heads agreed to survey the relocation site if someone would lead them to it. There were not enough canoes available for the whole group, so Don, Sr. could not guide them himself. His legs had never healed from their severe burns years earlier, and walking cross-country through saw grass would simply destroy them. In fact, since Don, Sr. had not arranged to have skin grafts done, his legs were not covered with skin at all, but with a thin, brittle fibrous sheath that often bled when he pulled on his socks.

Don, Jr. therefore agreed to walk the eighty miles with the Nuer leaders to their new home. One of the Christian Nuers had named the site "Kadesh" in memory of the Israelites who camped at Kadesh on their way to the Promised Land (Numbers 20).[71] The group set off with high expectations of a new life and expressed this with their traditional falsetto chanting. Earlier, two paddlers had started upriver in a borrowed, aluminum canoe with the group's food, mosquito nets, and Don's light bedding, tent, fresh clothes, and first-aid kit. The canoe expected to meet the larger group each night as they walked directly across the plain so as to cut off some of the long bends of the river. Don, Jr. knew he would get a very bad sunburn and was aware that his feet were still tender from his years in America, but he anticipated only a three- or four-day trek. He thought he would be able to keep up with the seven-foot Nuers, who are relentless walkers. These naked, graceful men of the plains with their long, smooth strides can walk barefooted for days on end over thorn and stubble. Don soon found himself taking two steps to their one, and after four hours and about ten miles he was feeling the jar of every step.

The parched, black African soil seemed to soak up the tropical sun, concentrate it, and send it burning right back through his jungle boots. Thus Don was glad when they reached an ankle-deep marsh. When the water became waist-deep, however, he wished for long trousers, because the saw grass began to slice away at his legs. The next hour Don had to take off his sodden boots and drape them across his neck along with his .22 Hornet rifle. During the third hour the group often found themselves swimming—Don with his boots and rifle held in one hand, and the Nuers holding their spears. Completely unexpectedly, the group lost sight of the high ground and found themselves in ten feet of grass and water on the rising floodplain.

As the sun began to set on the first day, and being in water over their heads, the group realized they could not reach the river to rendezvous with the canoe containing their food and mosquito nets. They knew they would get hopelessly lost if they tried to swim through the night. Following a calm, water-treading discussion among men accustomed to survival, they swam on until they saw in the distance a large anthill protruding from the surrounding water. At dusk the twenty-three men clambered onto the anthill to wait out the night. Their sitting space was already occupied by rats, snakes, and assorted vermin that had beaten them to what seemed to be the only dry spot in the world.

After getting out of the water and clearing the anthill, there was still sufficient light for Don to see that he was bleeding badly. At first he thought the blood was from saw-grass cuts, but soon realized that most of the bleeding came from under his shorts. Stripping them off, Don found hundreds of leeches attached to his body. Indeed, there were so many that he still appeared to be clothed. Don had no salt, no gasoline, and no hot coals to remove the leeches, so he had to slap his already bleeding flesh with such force that the leeches pulled their sucking heads out one by one. After he had removed all of them, Don bled for another hour until the leeches' anticoagulant wore off. As the leech trauma ended for Don, another one began for all the men. Searching for blood in the watery wasteland, millions of mosquitoes attacked the helpless men, and for twelve hours they had to endure the unbearable buzzing of swarm after swarm and bite upon bite.

As the second day dawned, Don determined to feed only one or two leeches at a time. Thus he tied both his boots and his shorts to his rifle and the men pushed back into the water. As they did so, they thought about where and when they would be able to eat—especially Don, who was not accustomed to going without food for days at a time. Expecting no difficulties, they had not made a contingency plan, and the canoe crew did not know where to meet them.

That second day, the group learned just how serious their situation was. Walking wasn't the problem; Don's feet did not burn as much this day, and he only suffered from the mud and grit that worked its way under what skin was left around the edges of his blisters. The water was the difficulty. Until the end of the previous day when they had sought refuge on the anthill, the men had only to swim fifty yards or so at a time before they could touch bottom and walk again through the water. However, on the second day the grass through which they were pushing was much more dense, and they often had to swim so long as to strain the limits of human endurance.

Don, Jr. (nationally ranked in America) was a better swimmer than the Nuers. However, while a person can normally move through water alone for many hours, having to swim and push high grass at the same time was like swimming with a heavy rope entangled around one's hands and feet. When the wading men lost contact with the ground, they quickly became exhausted, and no one knew how long they would be required to continue swimming in the tall grass. By now, with his rifle strapped on his back, Don had discarded his boots and shorts so that he could use both hands to swim and push the grass aside or under. Likewise, the Nuers had dropped their spears in their desperation not to drown and were swimming empty-handed. For a Nuer to travel anywhere without his spear is equivalent to an American abandoning his brand new car.

Had any of the men needed help, there would have been no one able to offer it. Every man needed all his strength just to swim alone. Don thought that some of them, and he with them, would surely drown. So desperate was their situation that these men, who had no food in their stomachs, were heaving the water that they had swallowed. This was the only time in his life that Don ever saw an African in such extreme distress that he became physically sick. That night, after a full day of wading in water waist or neck deep and often having to swim, Don and his men came across a dry-season cattle camp. Of course, only the grass roofs were above water, but the group split up and climbed onto the roofs. They were too steep to sleep on, but at least the group was out of the water for the second night. Scorpions hiding in the grass roofs stung two of the Nuers, and twice Don dozed off and fell into the water. These unplanned dips in the water were a momentary respite in another night of savage mosquito attacks.

On the third day Don managed to shoot a cormorant, and though he was very hungry he was not yet prepared to eat it raw. Later the men noticed some circling vultures and struggled over to the area to investigate, thinking they might find a dead fish that they could eat. What they discovered was a juicy treat for the Nuers. A lion had attacked a Cape buffalo that must have run into the water to escape. Apparently the lion had given up, but the buffalo had become entangled in the grass and drowned. It had been in the rising water long enough to be floating, and the vultures had torn the carcass open. The Nuers had no knives or spears to cut the meat off, but the flesh was sufficiently rotten to be very tender. Don had to move upwind from the banqueting Nuers, who had found a table set for them in the watery wilderness. Doubtless, Don would have died of food poisoning if he had joined the meal. Unfortunately for Don's nose, as they pushed on, some of the Nuers tried to carry pieces of the ripe meat in hope that they would not have to discard it to the fishes. They were soon swimming again, however, and lost their feast.

The third night found the group on another anthill. This one had a large tree in its center and some dead branches. Thanks to the Nuers' skill at starting a fire with two sticks, they soon had a blaze going with which to roast the cormorant. However, the bird was so tough that no amount of cooking made it possible to bite the meat off the bone. Still without food, Don slept in the tree at the top of the anthill. He did this not only because the smoke from the fire somewhat reduced the swarms of mosquitoes, but also as a way to escape the powerful flatulence generated by twenty-two men who had gorged themselves on extremely ripe buffalo flesh. They spent the next two days—also without food—in the water during the daylight hours and on anthills at night.

Emerging from five and a half days in swampland, the trekkers found the canoe waiting for them with food and medicine. They slept that night—the sixth—on dry land. Don's cuts and leech and mosquito bites were becoming very septic, so he was glad to clean them and let them dry. He was also able to begin taking prophylactic doses of malaria tablets. Since malaria incubates for ten days, if Don had spent three more days without medicine it is possible that he would have been in grave danger.

The next day was to be the last of their journey. As the men neared the relocation site, Don managed to shoot a waterbuck. The men carried it to their campsite, roasted it, and ate all they could. The rest they hung in a thornbush to protect it from animals.

During the night something tripping over the wires of Don's small pup tent woke him up. Peering out, Don was eye-to-eye with a huge male lion. Against a lion his .22 rifle was no better than a toy. In fact, a shot would have only served to enrage the lion. Lying on his stomach, Don could feel his heart pumping with sufficient force to lift him off the ground. The lion decided that he preferred already dead meat and sat within six feet of Don while he devoured the remains of the waterbuck and then disappeared into the night.

On the seventh day the Nuer clan leaders agreed that the land was suitable for their people and wanted to return to their families and bring them to their new home before the water got too high. However, to avoid having to travel through water again, they determined to find a better—even if longer—way through the forest. Don walked back to the river and settled into a locally borrowed dugout canoe, which the Nuers preferred to the wider aluminum canoe. His two refugee paddlers wanted to deposit Don in Gambela as soon as possible so they could join the big move to Kadesh. Without missing a stroke, except to dip their hand into the water for a drink, the two Nuers paddled upstream all day, all night, and until dusk of the second day. Almost the whole time the two paddlers sang to each other. The one in the back, singing in falsetto, would recount some episode of the just-completed first journey to Kadesh. The man in the front responded with a low-tone chorus chant, saying, "Really, and then what?" or "I can't believe it, tell me more!" or "Go on, that's interesting." When Don took over the front paddling position for a while, he was told that since he did not sing he was a boring paddler and made the man in the back go to sleep.

After thirty-six hours of unrelieved paddling, the two Nuers dropped Don off at Gambela. They faced a five-or-six-day return trip down the Baro River, but not once did either complain about their arduous task or even mention that he was tired.

▼▲▼

One of Don, Jr.'s later excursions proved to be more dire. He and another missionary, Peter Van Beyma, had tried a shortcut across a flooded plain in a sixteen-foot fiberglass boat. They soon discovered that the rising water had broken off large chunks of grass that the wind had jammed into the flood plain. Quickly surrounded by a seemingly endless and virtually impassable ocean of grass, Don and Peter lost sight of the forest and the high elephant grass that marked the river and a safe passage home. The sudd was so thick that they were able to walk on it, although if either stood in one place for a length of time he would slowly sink. Of course, the boat would not move through this grass.

In attempting to break free to the river the two men took direction by the sun. They carried the motor and fuel about thirty feet forward before returning to pull the boat. They had to keep moving or the heavy motor would sink through the matted grass. As night fell, the two men put everything back in the boat and climbed in to wait for dawn. During the night the mosquitoes became so unbearable that, using a hunting knife, each man cut a hole down through the thick grass and, covering his head with his shirt and shorts, crawled into the water to escape the mosquitoes.

The next morning when Don and Peter got back in the boat, they used gasoline to remove 113 leeches. Lost, hungry, exhausted, discouraged, and afraid they would die in the tall grass with heads hanging down, the two men continued to move slowly eastward foot by foot. Again they spent the night in the water to escape the mosquito torment.

On the third day they heard the rescue plane fly over, but the pilot could not see the desperate men or the white boat down in the grass. When he looked up at the plane, Don spotted a big tree that he thought must be on or near the river. They reached this tree after dark, and Don planned to climb it next morning in hope of discovering where they were. At dawn the tree began to hum, and the men saw that it contained a beehive large enough to fill eight bushel baskets. From earlier experiences Don knew that the African wild bee is both vicious and deadly. Don and Peter could not have survived an attack. Thus the two men moved as quietly as possible to get out of the vicinity before the day warmed up and the bees became more irate and active. By afternoon they found the river, and the search plane had them home by nightfall.

In spite of taking the normal preventive doses of chloroquine, ten days later Don and Peter came down with malaria. The cure required taking ten tablets in three days, but neither man could keep the medicine down. Unfortunately, they did not have injectable chloroquine. In addition, due to vomiting and diarrhea, both men became first dehydrated and then comatose. By now it was Sunday, and the two wives could not make radio contact with a missionary doctor until Monday morning; they feared by then it would be too late. In panicked desperation the women tried to rig up a garden hose to an intravenous needle, intending to restore body liquids with boiled river water. Fortunately for the comatose men, this procedure was not successful, for it would have proved lethal.

Don woke up on Monday to see a missionary doctor standing over him and injecting saline water and chloroquine. The Wright's stain diagnostic test showed that both men had contracted all three varieties of malaria at the same time. Primaquine had to be added to chloroquine to cure the falcipirum form of malaria. Although very weak, Don and Peter were up and about the next day.

▼▲▼

Later, after the Nuers arrived in Kadesh and were allocated an area, they promptly constructed homes, schools, and stores. They also hacked an airstrip out of the forest, but because of the approaching rainy season, the airstrip was expected to become unusable after a few days. Thus supplies would have to be airdropped. During this time, Don, Jr. and his wife, Ginny, lived with the refugees at Kadesh and, according to a United Nations observer, their mere presence did more to stabilize the situation than anything he could do or suggest.

The Nuer settlement at Kadesh quickly grew from three thousand to nine thousand refugees. Because of his leadership in this resettlement, Don, Jr. was accused of training guerrillas. Like his father, he was declared to be an enemy of Sudan, and a Sudanese army unit came across the Ethiopian border to murder him. By mistake the soldiers destroyed the wrong village and killed the wrong people.

Some months later, Ginny wrote,

> A few days ago a woman came in carrying a sick baby, with another child clinging to her animal-hide skirt. They had been walking for four days. The baby was bloated with a yellow fluid, and we had no idea about treatment. I knew it would cost us money that we did not have, but I persuaded the mother to let me charter a medical flight in here and out to a physician. She was terrified about letting her baby out of her sight and into a world she did not understand; but she was desperate with love. As the mercy plane landed, the baby died in his mother's arms.
>
> I wish those who think primitive people should be left alone because they are happy in their sickness, ignorance, and superstition had been with me when we buried that little boy and I tried to comfort that heartbroken mother whose grief came in soul-wrenching sobs for her dead baby. In the agonized face of that African mother, I see the suffering face of Jesus Christ.[72]

▼▲▼

Don, Jr. spoke fluent Anuak, of course, but very little Nuer. However, Kweych ("Leopard"), one of the two Nuers who had paddled the canoe to Gambela, spoke excellent Anuak because his mother was an Anuak girl who had been stolen in an intertribal raid. When Don returned to live at Kadesh and help the refugees, Kweych became his good friend and hunting companion. This was not only because they could communicate easily in Anuak, but also because Kweych was one of the bravest and toughest men Don ever knew.

Since the pilots of Ethiopian Air Lines consistently logged more flying hours per week than were allowable, no planes could be chartered to bring food into Kadesh. Therefore Don and Kweych had to hunt for animals sufficient to feed the nine thousand Nuers. Each morning at four, Kweych came to his tent and Don would pull on his shorts and a pair of Converse Allstars basketball shoes (at $7.50 the most expensive available then), grab his rifle, and slip off into the darkness with him. Passing through the pungent smoke of hundreds of smoldering cattle-dung fires, the two hunters would be seen at dawn leaving the forest and entering the African plains. Thirty or more women, with the help of a tracker, would follow their trail. In places where he thought it might be difficult for the tracker, Kweych bent a clump of grass. Each day Don would shoot six to nine large animals and cover them with grass to keep away the vultures. Beside the last animal Don and Kweych would build a fire to roast some of their favorite parts for breakfast. When the trackers came upon this fire, they knew the hunt was over for that day. The women carried the meat, often as much as a hundred pounds each, back to camp, where Don had to divide it. The various Nuer clans exhibited an enormous solidarity toward an outsider, but among themselves would fight to the death over a knucklebone. For six months Don's hunting provided the Nuers with their only food. In pulling his feet through the grass for six hours every day, Don wore out a pair of Converse Allstars every week.

Conditions at Kadesh were primitive, and amenities were in short supply. Surrounded by nine thousand Nuers, Don and Ginny lived in an eight-foot-square tent—and Ginny was expecting their first baby! The nearest water supply was a swamp three miles away. This stagnant water, trapped during the rains, lasted throughout the dry season and served the drinking and bathing needs of the wild animals, the domestic cattle, and the human population.

For Don and Ginny, bathing was a carefully timed affair. The three-mile walk had to be made in the late afternoon before the cattle got to the water. However, while the McClures needed to return to their tent before the mosquitoes came, they did not want to undo the effects of the bath by walking three more miles in the most intense heat of the day. Since in most of Africa men and women do not bathe together, Don and Ginny had to wash about fifty yards apart. Nudity created no problem, but proximity would have caused a scandal.

Because in tropical heat an infant can quickly become fatally dehydrated from a simple case of diarrhea, Ginny went to Addis Ababa to spend the last month of her pregnancy with the senior McClures. One night while she was gone, Don, Jr. heard a rat running around on the plastic floor of the tent. Don tried to find the rat because it might have rabies. Since he was unable to locate it, he went to sleep with the rat still in the tent. When he woke up, the rat was sitting on his bare chest. Not wanting to be bitten, Don knew he would have to kill the rat with one blow. Don smashed the rat on his chest with such force that there was rat blood, hair, and flesh all over his body as well as the inside of the tent. That night Don walked another six miles, round trip, to take a bath. Kadesh might be a city of refuge for Nuers, but it was obviously no place for a newborn baby.

▼▲▼

Kweych had been a member of the American Mission church at Nasir before fleeing the Sudan to save his life. As a fervent Christian he had no intention of living under Islamic law. He expected Don, Jr. to start and lead a Christian church at Kadesh, assuming that Don would preach in Anuak and he would translate the sermons into Nuer. However, Don insisted that the Nuer Christians form their own community with their own leadership.

Each day after returning from the morning hunts, Kweych cut timber and grass and had soon built a church. Since Kweych could not read, he came to Don on Saturday afternoon and asked him to read a story from the Anuak New Testament. The next day Kweych would hold the open Anuak Bible in one hand and preach in his church to an ever-increasing number of Nuers. One of Kweych's valuable items was the hoop of a fuel drum to use as a church bell. Kweych worked out that it took him exactly four and a half minutes to run from Don's tent to the church. So it became Don's responsibility to inform Kweych when 10:55 and thirty seconds arrived so that Kweych could run to the church and sound the bell at exactly 11:00 A.M.—the same time it sounded in Nasir.

Soon hundreds and then thousands of Nuers began to gather on the airfield (the church being too small) to testify to their faith and share their former experiences with pagan superstitions. These were gatherings of great humor and drama as the Nuer Christians acted out their encounters with witchdoctors. The Nuers spontaneously performed authentic African Christian music, and there was a great deal of dancing.

On one of their walks together Don and Kweych heard noises coming from a hut festooned by a witchdoctor with bones, amulets, gourds, and other talismans. Never shy, Kweych wanted to know what was happening, and on the pretext that "the white man" was a great healer they were allowed to peer into the bare hut. As their eyes became accustomed to the darkness and their noses to the stench, they saw a young woman spread-eagled and tied to stakes driven into the ground. This girl had refused to become one of the many wives of a powerful witchdoctor, and apparently her condition, extreme dementia, was her punishment. Her family had expended all its wealth in hiring other sorcerers to remove the curse, but all had failed and the family was resigned to her death, since she could no longer be fed or controlled.

Kweych announced to the family that Jesus could heal her and would do so if they would bring her to the church on Sunday at 11:00 A.M. That night Kweych asked Don to read him the story in Mark 5:1–13 in which Jesus casts demons out of a man and they enter a herd of pigs. Since the Nuers at Kadesh had no swine to cast the demons into, Kweych thought he might have to use goats instead.

Two days later the girl was brought to church bound with rawhide thongs. Don wanted no part of the service that Sunday, but he came out to watch. In the same falsetto voice that he had used on the canoe trip, Kweych began to sing of the joy and faith and power he had found in Jesus Christ. For two hours the Nuers responded with the chorus, "Tell us more."

Suddenly Kweych stopped and turned to the young woman in front of him, who by this time was covered with blood from the tight thongs, tears, saliva, and her own defecation. Addressing her demons, Kweych said, "I command you in the name of Yesu Kristo to come out of her!" And the exorcism was finished. In her right mind, the young woman, embarrassed by her filth, quietly said, "Mother, untie me." The only utterly astonished person present was the Reverend W. Donald McClure, Jr.

Kweych was not popular with the resident sorcerers, and when Don was absent from Kadesh, one of them waited for Kweych to emerge from his hut and crushed his skull with a club the size of a baseball bat. His congregation tenderly cared for him. After Kweych had been three days in a coma, one of the former witchdoctors whom Kweych had converted to the Christian faith performed a primitive trepan to lift some of the bone fragments pressing on his brain. Cow manure was applied to the wound as a plaster, and Kweych soon recovered consciousness. Since he suffered terrible headaches, Kweych eventually made his way to a missionary doctor. The doctor removed more bone fragments from Kweych's head, including one piece of three inches, and inserted a stainless steel plate to protect that stubborn Nuer Christian brain.

Kweych planted and nurtured four churches along the Baro River, and a few years later the Reverends Robb McLaughlin, Chuck Jordan, and Don McClure, Jr. of the American Mission baptized more new

Christians than they could count. Kweych could not baptize them himself, because he was not an officially "ordained" evangelist.

▼▲▼

On 18 June 1966 an observer reported that staple food was almost exhausted throughout the Gambela district of Ethiopia and about 15,000 people, a third of them refugees from Sudan, had entered a famine that would continue until January.

People are traveling throughout the region to see if friends or relatives in other areas have food. Women are going out at night to hunt for wild onions and to dig roots. The price of corn has quadrupled, and even those workers who receive wages cannot find corn to buy.

It is expected that 75% of the usual corn crop will be flooded in late July before it can be harvested. Thus at least 50% and perhaps 75% of the 75,000 people will be without food in July and August and again in October through December. No surrounding region in Ethiopia has a surplus. The U.S. AID minimum diet for famine relief is 300 grams of high-nutrition food per person per day, which provides 1600 calories. At 300 grams per person, one metric ton (or one million grams) would feed 3,333 people each day. Estimating 37,500 famine victims, 11.4 metric tons will be needed each day, or about 350 tons per month.

To meet this need, Don and Lyda and their friend Lem Tew—a pilot for Ethiopian Air Lines—flew down to Kadesh to airdrop six tons of grain.

A small plane can land on Donnie's airstrip, but not a big DC-3. It was a cold and noisy ride, because we had to fly with the cargo door off so we could get the sixty bags out. We tied ourselves in the plane so that we would not accidentally go out with one of the bags. We were elated that we managed to drop every bag on the airstrip and not one was lost. However, I had forgotten some things that Donnie needed, so I chartered a small plane and went in again a week later. Don, Jr. and his wife are doing a tremendous job, and the refugees simply idolize them. These poor people barely got out of the Sudan with their lives. Most of them were naked and had nothing more than they could carry in their hands, which was usually just a stick or a spear. I sat down and talked to the old man the refugees have chosen as chief, and he wept as he thanked us for what we had done.

The people at Kadesh were convinced that under the surface of his pale skin, Don, Jr. was in reality a Nuer! Accordingly, since all the men of the tribe are given an ox-name, the Nuers, following their custom of initiation, killed a *Kwe* (quay) bull. Don McClure, Jr. was thereafter known among the Nuers as *Kwe*—a creature for whom the face is white, but the rest is black.[73]

We have already taken care of more than 9000 people in the Kadesh camp and have settled 6000 of these on their own homesteads. We are now trying to get them cattle and sheep, since the Sudan army stripped them of nearly everything they had. A few hundred cattle got through, and these will serve as starters for the new herds; but it is essential that we find more funds for the purchase of cattle for these people. The Nuers are great lovers of their herds, and unless we find some cattle for these displaced Sudanese they will soon start to raid the neighboring Ethiopian tribes, the Anuak and Murle, and another war will begin.

Word has recently come through to us that we can expect another 3000 or 4000 refugees from the south Sudan within the next month or two as the Sudan army attempts to recapture some of the police posts wrested from them at the beginning of the last rains. If the army moves in, it will again burn villages and devastate the countryside. More people will then flee for safety to Ethiopia.

Our refugee troubles continue unabated and not only along the border. There are many Sudanese arriving in Addis Ababa every week, and it now looks as if we will soon have a hundred in secondary schools and the university. I have just rented a big house here in Addis Ababa to take care of some of the refugees. It is a five-room house, and we will pack about fifty boys in it, all sleeping on the floor. I have been trying to find places for them in schools around the city, but without much success. Most of the schools are filled to capacity already, and no one wants to accept boys of doubtful origins and who come without any certificates or papers from the Sudan. The boys have already missed the entrance examinations, which were given last May. If worse comes to worst, I will become an educator and open an elementary school, a high school, and a college all at the same time.

▼ Christian Retreat

IN THE LATE 1950s the small church to which the McClures belonged voted to unite with a much larger body of the same denominational family. Don considered this event to be a sell-out rather than a merger. He opposed the union mainly because his small denomination had always donated very generously to world missions, each year ranking ahead of most American churches in per-capita giving. The larger group contributed something like six dollars per family, which Don believed was not a sufficient amount for even an almighty God to bless. Because his denomination was small, it was relatively cohesive and had been able to ignore or resist certain kinds of changes of attitude or procedure; but this conservative attitude was difficult to maintain after the merger with the larger and more pluralistic sister denomination.

Don accepted that the new situation might have its advantages, but he thought that the mission fields had lost a great deal of independence and authority. It seemed that the new church was concentrating all the power in its administrative offices. Don felt that too many decisions that should be made on the field by missionaries were being made at the central offices of the new denomination. The decision-makers were mission executives who were more interested in the analysis of systems than the proclamation of the gospel.

Don believed that the New York office was increasingly unresponsive to the convictions of the church at large and the needs and opportunities of the various field bodies. For example, soon after this merger, the denominational executives decided that the idea of sending out missionaries to the world had outlived its usefulness and needed to be replaced with a more up-to-date theory. Thus those who served overseas and across cultures were no longer to be called "missionaries," but rather "fraternal workers." These workers were not to consider themselves as sent into the world to proclaim the gospel, but as sent to serve with a national church and under its auspices meet an identified need. The Board of World Missions was renamed the Commission on Ecumenical Mission and Relations.

Whatever merits this understanding might have in general, or even when applied to particular circumstances, it was not sufficiently dramatic or compelling for many Christians who were unwilling to support ecumenical relations with the same fervor and sacrificial giving that had characterized their previous commitment to world missions. Moreover, many perceived fraternal assistance as a shift of the church's focus from the proclamation of the gospel to the self-development of people. To many, improvements in political, economic, and social systems seemed to replace evangelism as the priority for overseas service.

In any case, Don McClure opposed the change. As far as he was concerned, he was a missionary, not a fraternal worker, and while no one worked harder at the self-development of people, it was—for him—always in the context of proclaiming the gospel with the direct purpose of establishing and equipping a Christian church.

I am not blind to the desperate needs of the human condition. I have lived on the continent of Africa for nearly half a century, and the social and physical needs of these 250 million people stagger the imagination. The amount of hunger, poverty, disease, ignorance, and superstition is unbelievable. Without doubt, making human life human is a worthy goal, but it is not the primary task of the missionary, which is to preach Jesus Christ![74]

Don objected furiously to what he perceived as a focus on the improvement of community life for its own sake rather than traditional evangelism that should carry these improvements with it.

According to Don, the social scientists had taken control of the administration of his church. They were more interested in engineering than evangelism. While they focused on improving the human condition, it seemed that to them, preaching the gospel was incidental or nonessential. Clearly, Don believed in social action, and most of the things he had done in Africa contributed directly to that end. However, for the church of Jesus Christ, social action without evangelism was neither proper nor sufficient. Thus Don could not understand how a low-cost housing project in Addis Ababa would be considered as a mission priority unless it served an evangelistic purpose. He could not understand why the total Ethiopian mission budget would be cut $25,000 while the church appropriated $50,000 for a well-digging project. Obviously, decent housing and good water were important, and Don spent countless hours working at both, but he did not think their production alone was a proper focus for a Christian mission.

Moreover, Don was grimly amused that the New York office was encouraging those who worked in Addis Ababa to join local service clubs such as the Rotary, Kiwanis, and Lions and was willing to pay their membership fee *from mission funds!* Missionary women in Addis were supposed to join women's clubs, including the Bridge Club. Don was more than a little dismayed that mission personnel were being encouraged to attend and to host cocktail parties instead of prayer meetings.

Frankly, I am dubious about the commission's commitment to world missions—at least as I understand it. They seem more interested in study conferences rather than direct evangelism; more interested in committee meetings all over the world than proclamation of the gospel anywhere in it. They are especially fond of organizing caravans of visitors from India to America and from America to Africa and so on. Recently the commission wanted to send a caravan to Ethiopia. The team was to be composed of youngsters sixteen to nineteen years old with their adult advisers. The board proposed to fly them to Ethiopia for a week at Pokwo, a week in Ghimeera, and two weeks in Addis Ababa, helping us with anything that needed to be done. I cannot imagine a bunch of kids like that doing anything worthwhile out here in one week. They would cause us more trouble in feeding and sleeping them than they could possibly contribute. I don't know what I would give them to do, unless it was hoeing corn, and I am sure the Anuaks can do it better.

I have a great burden on my heart for all the unreached people in western Ethiopia. In the area for which our church is responsible there are more than thirty different tribes who have never heard the name of Jesus spoken in their language. I think we should do something *now*, and I have proposed to the commission that they allow me to raise money outside the budget to support ten missionaries in a program we will call "the Forgotten Tribes Mission."

The plan involved several young missionary families who would make a commitment to devote their full careers to these untouched people. Don and Lyda were too old to take part in this project, but Don excitedly made plans for it. After a team of experienced Ethiopian missionaries made an aerial survey of Kaffe and Illubabor provinces, Don proposed in a letter to Haile Selassie that the American Mission was prepared to begin work with the Nuers in Ethiopia; the Masongos, estimated at between 20,000 and 30,000 people; the Shakkos, with between 15,000 and 20,000 people; the Mochas, with 40,000 to 50,000; the Teshenas, estimated at 100,000 people; the Tid-Termas, with approximately 20,000 and once thought to be two tribes; and the Gulebs, perhaps the least known and most inaccessible of all the tribes of western Ethiopia.

Many of these tribes are very difficult to reach, and the only possible way is to itinerate among them. For example, the Masongos live in the forests. Since they have no permanent villages, there is no place where a mission station could be located. The missionary who worked among them would have to establish several small centers and move from place to place following them. No foreigner can speak their language. Of the other tribes, some are as small as 1000, and others number 100,000, but they can all be reached. Recently I had a conference with Haile Selassie, and he gave me permission to start work in ten of these tribes. The emperor is virtually helpless, because there is no Ethiopian who can do what is needed among these peoples. No Ethiopian is trained and prepared to enter those tribes, to reduce their language to writing, or to open medical, educational, and evangelistic work. The whole burden rests with us.

As he surveyed the unreached areas and untouched tribes on the map, His Imperial Majesty looked almost pathetic. He cannot provide what he desires for his people without our help. The doors are wide open if the commission will only let us take up the opportunity. I do not know what kind of reception the new mission board will give my proposal, but the prospects are not very encouraging. Our field association asked the commission for four new evangelistic missionaries to start work with some of these tribes who live near our already existing mission stations. Since we would not be required to build new compounds, it was a modest request, but we were told that we should be thinking about curtailing some of our present work rather than planning new endeavors!

I fear that the missionary budget of the new church will never equal that of the two old churches. Far too much money is spent on setting up new agencies and administering them. Bureaucrats are the same everywhere. Already the forms and questionnaires have doubled, and the ecclesiastical paper-pushers are just getting warmed up! I am too busy preaching the gospel and teaching the Anuaks to read to fill out a questionnaire for some executive in New York City who wants to know what books we use in the schools and how many of our students come from broken homes. If they figure the kingdom of God will be advanced by this information on a sheet of paper in a file in New York, they can jolly well come out here and find out for themselves.

Last week we had a very fine meeting of our Ethiopian Executive Committee. The best thing we did was plan for a new advance in western Ethiopia among the untouched tribes of our area. I do not believe in retreating in the Lord's work, and I pleaded with our executive committee for two hours to persuade them to move forward rather than pull back, although New York sent us a directive that we should cut our budget 6 percent this year and 16 percent next year. Nevertheless, we dared to go ahead and increase our budget and ask for two new missionaries. It was a story about one of our Anuaks that turned the meeting around.

About seventeen years ago one of our district commissioners at Akobo found a lad living as a slave in the Murle tribe and took him to be an Anuak. We were glad to have the boy, and he is still with us—now a teacher in the school at Pokwo. Several months ago a woman came in and asked for Kony Jok. The woman was from the Masongo tribe and could not speak Anuak. She spoke through a second woman who knew both languages. When this Masongo woman found Kony Jok, she said to him, "You are my son. I have been looking for you for fourteen years, and at last have found you." Kony Jok would not accept her as his mother, because he thought she was only trying to get money from him. He said, "I am an Anuak and you are a Masongo; how can I be your son?" The woman said, "You have a twin sister who escaped with me after our capture by the Murle. I could not get you away, but I will bring your sister and you will recognize her." A few days later she returned, and with her was a girl who looked exactly like Kony Jok. If they had exchanged clothes, it would have been hard to tell which was which. When Kony Jok saw the girl, he immediately said, "Now I believe you. This is my sister, I know."

After a few days Kony Jok left with his mother and sister and only recently came back with some thrilling stories. His father is a chief in the tribe, indeed, the big chief. All the Masongos exist entirely on berries, nuts, bulbs, and edible roots as they move through the dense forests. They have no sheep or cattle and never plant fields. Their sole diet is what they can find in the forest. Kony Jok said he ate honey and grubs until he was sticky all over. When he returned, he tried to bring four boys who knew Anuak to our school, but after he got them out of the forests and started across the plains these boys became frightened and ran back to the protection of the big trees. So Kony had to come on alone. Sooner or later we will get some of those boys in the school at Pokwo or perhaps at the Gilo River station.

Kony is thrilled at being able to communicate with these boys a little and says he wants to devote his whole life to the Masongo tribe as an evangelist. This is the first of the Forgotten Tribes we have been able to break into. However, we are asking for a well-trained American to go into this tribe, learn the language, and reduce it to writing. We hope to prepare the Scriptures in nine or ten of these languages. One can argue endlessly about theory, but a story grips the heart. This one convinced the committee that it would be disobedient to retreat. We must go forward in the work of evangelism.

After a series of annual budget cuts, Don became more convinced that the commission in New York intended to dismantle the Ethiopian mission, and he came out fighting.

It appears to me that the Commission on Ecumenical Mission and Relations has lost its vision for the evangelization of our fields. We have been told by our executives in New York that at this point in history there should be no foreign mission bodies in Africa, and thirty missionaries—some of them our very finest—are being sent home. Why is that? Is the evangelization of Africa complete? Obviously not! In Ethiopia we have 108 tribes, and only 5 of them have the Bible in their own language. In the part of Ethiopia for which our church is solely responsible, there are two and a half million people in 30 tribes, 12 of which we have touched. Don, Jr. opened work among the Surma people just one year ago, and while he tries to build a house and learn the language, he and his family are still living in tents. As yet they have not even been able to talk to the Surmas, let alone do any real evangelism. Nevertheless, the bureaucrats in New York have decided that we are finished in Ethiopia and it is time to close all the various missions. I can only conclude that the zeal for the world-wide mission of the church has disappeared from the New York office, and when the church loses her vision for the outreach of the gospel, she is dead.

The commission has finally admitted that closing down our mission is not simply a problem of money, but a deliberate policy. We are being told the missionary task should be left to the national church, but those who say that do not know the condition of the national churches of Africa.[75] The shortage of money is just a good excuse for these executives to do what they intended anyway. At one time our church was the strongest missionary force in Egypt, Sudan, and Ethiopia. No more.

In the face of unparalleled opportunities with the naked, sick, forlorn people of Africa pleading for schools and clinics and churches, the commission in New York informs us that our staff and budget will be cut 30 percent this year (another year we were cut 35 percent), and by the end of the next year the mission office in Ethiopia will be closed forever and all field administration will cease.

According to Don, the commission had become autocratic and even dictatorial. There was always money for executive junkets around the world, but no money for a yearly field consultation among working missionaries. The commission's representative in Addis Ababa, who was not a missionary but an agent of the commission's staff, had $12,500 for his annual travel and entertainment budget, but there were no funds for a mission meeting. In addition, Don objected strenuously to the requirement that he fill out pages of secret and confidential information on fellow missionaries; he felt it broke down trust and love and led to dismissals. He objected to the recall of missionaries, the close of missions, the reallocation of mission funds to projects in America, the reassignment of missionaries within fields—all done from the New York office without field consultation.

As Don read the figures, the missionary budget in one year was cut by $476,755, but the administration of these cuts required an increase of $94,315 for the New York office.

I can understand the reluctance of our church people to send money to the commission when $300,000 of the funds entrusted to them for the world mission of the church is used for the crisis in American cities, and $250,000 to protest racism in America. The commission contributed $50,000 to build new bronze doors on the Egyptian Coptic Cathedral in Alexandria, and the New York executives fly all over the world on any kind of pretext. They sometimes come to Addis Ababa for one day and do not tell us anything that could not be contained in a letter.

A few radical nationalists yell, "Yankee, go home!" and our church leaders declare that the day of foreign missions in Africa is over. Where would we be today if the first-century Christians had stopped evangelizing when things got tough? It is true that funds are short, but withdrawal is a deliberate policy and strategy of the commission that started ten years ago when we had one hundred missionaries in Ethiopia alone. Now we have ninety missionaries in *all* of Africa. I believe we must continue to preach the gospel in every land and among every people until all have heard, especially here in Ethiopia, where the people are begging us to come among them and His Imperial Majesty and his government agencies implore us to continue our work. The cry "Yankee, go home!" may apply to diplomats, soldiers, and businessmen, but it does not apply to Christian missionaries who have been commanded to go into all the world, teaching, preaching, and healing in the name of Jesus Christ.

I believe that the Lord wants us to go forward as fast and as far as we can. Thus I cannot understand a recent letter from the commission insisting that we continue to retrench. I think that if we cut the budget in anticipation of reductions in giving, we will get just what we expect. I believe this procedure is utterly faithless and demonstrates a complete lack of vision. The Lord God is mighty and will provide for his work out of his infinite resources if we will trust him. However, the Lord will not bless the fearful timidity of our proposed withdrawals and deliberate cutbacks even when they are passed off as up-to-date mission strategy, as some of the administrators are insisting.

It seems to me that these reductions are a deliberate request of the Lord to withdraw his blessing from our overseas work. The gospel says, "Seek ye first the kingdom of God, . . . and all the rest will be added unto you." Our executives seem to be seeking "all the rest" first, with the assumption that then the kingdom of God will be added. We are building houses, starting businesses, defending legal cases, training professionals—all of which are good and useful, but not as the primary mission of the church of Jesus Christ. I think that our executives have lost faith and confidence in the Word of God revealed in Jesus Christ and his command to go into all the world and preach the gospel. The commission is doing such broad-minded, clever things as sending a homosexual, a kleptomaniac, and an atheist to serve with the Ethiopian mission and sending home highly trained and experienced missionaries due to lack of funds.

Needless to say, such remarks did not endear Don McClure to the executives in New York, but they could not fire him, because he had a great deal of financial support and could easily have continued his work independently.

When the commission refused to allocate funds for the Ethiopian missionaries to meet together, the missionaries agreed to finance the meeting out of their own pockets. They had planned to discuss mission policy, future aims, and their relationship to the commission. To their surprise, however, the top executive from New York flew out to join the field meeting and stayed to dominate it. According to one missionary, this man

> went to the Bethel church (membership about three hundred, leadership about six) and told them they could have all our available funds and take over the administration of all phases of the work in Ethiopia. Since no missionary was present at this conference, we believed him when he reported to us that, while he was "personally aghast" that the Bethel church made this "demand," he felt that the American Mission had no choice but to comply. Now we find that it was the big boss himself who initiated this demand and promised the Bethel church that they could have everything. The more realistic leaders of the Bethel church realize that they cannot handle so much responsibility, but others see this as an unprecedented opportunity to lay their hands on big money and enormous power. We missionaries are

angry and embarrassed about being so easily duped. We have been divided and conquered—outmaneuvered by New York—and it is the cause of Christ in Ethiopia that will suffer.

According to Don,

New York has ordered us to close our Dembi Dollo station and turn everything over to the Oromo church. We all realize that this is our ultimate goal, but no one in his right mind, or who knows the Oromo church, would think of asking them to administer a large hospital, elementary and secondary schools, teachers' training institutes, a dressers' school, and a very effective adult literacy program. We do not have a single pastor among the Oromo people who has more than an eighth-grade education; altogether there are not more than fifty Oromos with a college education, and most of them work for the government here in Addis Ababa. It is irresponsible to turn over large sums of money and schools and hospitals until the Oromo church is capable of managing them.

However, sitting in New York City, the commission has decided that the Bethel and Anuak churches are strong enough to carry on without the American Mission. New York is determined to turn over to the native church all our schools and hospitals and funds, together with the full authority to say which missionaries shall remain, and expects the native church to do the work that the mission has not been able to accomplish during the last fifty years. The Bethel Evangelical Church is a wonderful group of people, but it is composed almost ninety-eight percent of peasant farmers. I fear that these administrative responsibilities will be the death of this church, and I know that there is great danger in their handling more than a million dollars. But the real danger, to my mind, is that they will fail to reach the untouched tribes. We have been working in twelve tribes in western Ethiopia over the years, but there are still sixteen to eighteen untouched tribes, and our national church has no vision of preaching the gospel to them.

The Bethel church, being largely composed of Oromo people, is deeply concerned about the evangelization of their Oromo people, but the people of neighboring tribes are regarded as foreigners and are, in many cases, traditional enemies. It is simply not true that the African is a better missionary than the

American. The Oromos are undoubtedly better with other Oromos, but they will never minister to these other tribes. If New York really expects the Oromo and Anuak churches to evangelize other tribes, they are simply out of their minds. This decision to turn our work over to the native church will effectively halt the outreach of the gospel.

For Don, the whole issue came to a head when the commission in New York—at the same time it was withdrawing dedicated career missionaries from Ethiopia—decided to appoint seminary graduate Dick Blank to Ethiopia as a "frontier intern." When Blank's official papers arrived in Addis Ababa, the staff was amazed to learn that he did *not* wish to be classified as a professing Christian. Don McClure took him at his word: Dick Blank was not a Christian and should not be sent to Ethiopia as a Christian missionary. Moreover, the manual defined frontier interns as "college graduates who are deeply committed to the Christian faith" and willing "to involve themselves in the crucial issues of our time, in order to discover what it means to be present as a Christian in the structures of a rapidly changing world." As far as Don was concerned, Dick Blank had quite obviously disqualified himself. Don refused, as a matter of conscience and of judgment, to be involved in procuring a visa for him.

One of the New York executives felt similarly and urged that Blank's visa application not be pursued for three reasons: (1) obtaining a visa from the Ethiopian government was becoming increasingly delicate and, because it was delicate, the fact that other groups had decided against sponsoring him had a bearing on this situation; (2) since Blank did not regard himself as a Christian, he should not be appointed to Christian missionary work; and (3) if Blank entered Ethiopia sponsored by the American Mission and then became persona non grata, it would have harmful effects on the entire mission. On receiving this letter, Don thought the matter was closed. However, in the meantime, Dick Blank had flown to Geneva and then to Beirut and was waiting in Nairobi for a visa to enter Ethiopia.

At this point another New York executive, an old friend of Don's, wrote,

Dear Don:

The problem of Dick Blank is one where I agree with your position and do not agree with you about what should be done now. As a participant in the process by which Dick was given an assignment, I have shared in creating the problem.

How did this happen? Two ways. First, we tried to deal with a person and not a set of papers. Second, we want to challenge a part of the younger generation, whose commitment is real but whose vocabulary and thought patterns are not traditional.

We feel that Dick Blank, in spite of his theological uncertainties, has a contribution to make. You may think we are wrong in our decision, but we ask you to press for a visa for Dick Blank anyway.

I realize you have not had a good experience with the Frontier Intern program, but do not let that be the basis of judging the whole program. We have had some very creative experiences.

To this Don replied,

I do not know whether to thank you for your letter regarding Dick Blank or just weep. It sounds as if you are pleading to be rescued from a bad situation. If you agree with my position, then you believe that Dick Blank is not a Christian and that no non-Christian should be sent to Africa, or anywhere else, to represent the cause of Christ. If you agree with my position, then you believe that the church's money should not be used to send non-Christians to work in Ethiopia when you are requiring us to send Christian missionaries home because of lack of funds.

You may be dealing with a person and not a set of papers, but we have only a set of papers written by an articulate seminary graduate, and when he says, "I do not know what I believe, but I do not wish to be classified as a confessing Christian in any historic sense"—I think we should do just that.

You say he will make a contribution, but you do not say what it will be. I presume it will not be to Jesus Christ and his cause, because Blank does not believe in either. The last frontier intern who was sent here made a contribution all right; he contributed to the delinquency of several little Ethiopian boys.

Let me remind you that the staff in Addis Ababa (with the single exception of New York's representative), the entire mission field body, and the native Bethel church (as represented by the elders in Addis Ababa) oppose his coming. The Ethiopian

Orthodox Church in the person of the director of Inter-Church Aid refused to accept him or to work on his visa.

I am right now trying to help a couple get out of Ethiopia whom the commission has been supporting here for two years. Previously the woman was with one of the AID programs under the American government. When she started running around with Ethiopian men, her husband divorced her. Then she and this professor, who was sent out by the commission to teach in the university, got interested in each other, and they began to live together—as their children reported—"to try each other out." This woman had been divorced just a month before, and the man had been divorced for two years. He was sent to Ethiopia just a few months after his divorce was granted in New York—in fact, waiting for the final decree delayed his coming. The commission knew all this and yet undertook to sponsor this couple before they were married and while they were living together.

They were married only a few weeks ago, and last week they attempted to return to America. Just fifteen minutes before the plane took off, the police went aboard and arrested her because she was jumping bond since her former husband was suing for the custody of the children and she had been subpoenaed for a court hearing. So we now have a mess with two people supported by New York, and the woman is under arrest for trying to run out on a court case. We have become the laughingstock of all the other missions in Ethiopia, and we intend to continue to fight against such decisions and such persons representing our church.

▼ The Gode Project

IF DONALD McCLURE had a failing as a secretary-general, it was that he did not believe in retreat of any kind. As far as he was concerned, God's great engine had no neutral and no reverse. The only possible direction for the church's evangelistic task was straight ahead, and the only question was whether to travel in low-speed forward or high-speed forward; he much preferred overdrive. He thought that backing up or backing out was always disobedient and wrong. Therefore everything Don did was designed to advance this cause directly or indirectly. Since he was now located in Addis Ababa, it was easy for him to help many people in a way that advanced the cause of Christ.

A couple of weeks ago I was asked to set up an off-the-beaten-path Ethiopian itinerary for a group called the Young Presidents' Organization. The members were all presidents of some business that is capitalized at more than a million dollars. The reason I was asked is that the president of the Young Presidents had heard me speak in his church in America some years ago and thus felt he could call on me to provide this travel service.

The fifty men and their wives and forty-two teenage children arrived in Addis Ababa by chartered plane and took over the Hilton, our finest hotel. I chartered three planes for them. One was to take the children out east to Dire Dawa, Harrar, and some interesting geological formations. The other two planes were to visit three of our mission stations among three different tribes. I chose our Omo station, where the Bob Swarts are living among the Guleb people (Dasanech, they call themselves); the second stop was among the Surma people, where Don, Jr. is working; and the third at Godare, where the Hoekstras are working among the Masongo people. The Surma people are

387

strange and quite primitive. The women all make a long cut under their lower lip and insert a wooden lip plate, some of them eight inches in diameter. They also wear large earplugs. The men are completely naked, but the women—even little girls—wear animal skins softened with grease. When we tried to take pictures, the women covered their lips, not their breasts. Obviously modesty is culturally conditioned. We got back to Addis Ababa just at 6:00 P.M., and the group was delighted with their most unusual tour. They had seen three different tribes, visited their primitive villages, and taken hundreds of pictures of naked Africans. They saw things in Ethiopia that they had not seen in any of the fourteen countries they had visited.

The next day we had a reception at the U.S. Embassy, talked politics and commerce with a large group of Ethiopian business-men, and then to crown the whole visit we had a wonderful audience with His Imperial Majesty. There were eighty-four persons in the audience room, and Haile Selassie shook hands with everyone and had something nice to say to them. He was especially gracious to Lyda. Everyone had pictures taken shaking hands with His Majesty; then the group announced that they were going to make a gift to Ethiopia of sufficient money to build and support twelve schools in any villages I would choose. I am supposed to collect the money next time I am home in America. My being a travel agent has its compensations, and this seemed to please His Majesty. We finished up the day with a big party at the Hilton Hotel. About ten o'clock, just as the party was getting under way, a man walked into the dining room leading His Majesty's huge pet lion. There was a good bit of screaming and scrambling by the ladies as the lion walked past their tables.

I showed the Young Presidents a film that was made by a Harvard University team who visited Ethiopia last year and lived among the Nuer people along the Baro River for a few months.[76] I was so impressed with the film that I wanted His Majesty to see it. When this was arranged, the picture was shown to the whole royal family, and it was reported that His Majesty wept when he saw the Nuers living in such primitive conditions and asked, "Why has no one told me about these people living in Ethiopia? I will never rest until I have done something to improve their condition." Then Haile Selassie sent for me and asked me to prepare a program of education and medicine that would reach these 30,000 Nuer people in his lifetime (he is seventy-nine years old).

I worked for three solid days on the program, literally night and day, and then took it to him to study. The plan calls for sixteen schools and clinics as well as two technical schools and an adult literacy program. When I gave the program to His Majesty, he asked, "How many Nuers will this reach immediately?" I had to say that the schools would reach only about 640 students the first year and the clinics probably 1000 per day. He said, "The program is not large enough, increase it." I tried to point out that these numbers would increase year by year, and it would be very difficult to find teachers and medical people to operate the sixteen schools and clinics. So he was finally satisfied.

The emperor asked our American Mission to staff and administer this Nuer project, and he will finance it from his personal resources. The project will cost him almost one million dollars just to get started and then a quarter-million dollars a year thereafter. This is a tremendous opportunity for us, because with our limited support and resources the American Mission has been trying to reach these same Nuers for fifty years. We must pray that our church at home will accept the challenge and that the New York office will permit us to keep sufficient staff in Ethiopia to undertake this work immediately.

I had a very interesting audience with the crown prince, Asfa Wossen, and the crown princess this past week. I was called to the palace with only a couple of hours notice, and since the appointment was scheduled for 4:30 P.M., I knew it was for tea. Actually they had expected Lyda to accompany me, but the telephone call did not indicate this. Now, to make up for it, Lyda and I have been invited to lunch at the palace on Thursday of this week. The purpose of the audience was to give His Imperial Highness, the crown prince, some information about western Ethiopia and the southern Sudan. His Highness said he had been trying to get information and find some books about this area and that everyone he asked referred him to me. After I talked to them for an hour, the crown prince asked me if I would be willing to meet with him every ten days or two weeks to discuss the lives and customs of the tribes in the west. Obviously I will be delighted to do so.

Last week we closed our refugee program in Gambela. I thought I still had sixty head of cattle, thirty sheep, and two hundred chickens, but the animals disappeared into the Sudan with the two Nuers I had left in charge while my chickens went into local cooking pots. I hope the people enjoyed their chicken dinners at my expense. These people are only one generation from paganism, and yet the commission in New York thinks our missionary task in Africa is finished.

▼▲▼

The death of a baby is always a heartbreaking experience. It seemed especially so when the family was thousands of miles from home.

We had a terrible tragedy here in Addis Ababa last Wednesday. The whole mission had gathered for its regular prayer meeting at the mission headquarters. Harold and Polly Kurtz usually took turns staying with the children, but that night both parents decided to come to the meeting. They left the children, including four-month-old Kenny, with a nursemaid after tucking them all into bed. About ten o'clock they went home and got ready for bed before awakening the baby for his feeding. When they went to his crib, Kenny was gone. There was no sign of any suffering or struggling, and apparently he had just slept his little life away. Harold came running back to the mission for me, and I took the car and dashed back to see what I could do. When I arrived, the child was cold and lifeless. I tried hot water bottles and artificial respiration to no avail. We rushed to the hospital, but when the doctor arrived and examined the baby, he said he had been dead for two or three hours. It was a puzzling situation, and since he had not strangled in his bedclothes or suffocated in his pillow, we could not determine what could possibly have happened. Finally the Kurtzes decided to have a postmortem to try to discover the cause of death. They were very brave about Kenny's death, but wanted to know definitely that there was nothing they could have done to prevent it.

Lyda had gone to their house to take care of the three little girls, so I took Harold and Polly back home and then returned to the hospital. I arrived at the hospital after midnight and, much to my surprise, was not stopped by the police. There is a midnight curfew in Addis Ababa, and anyone out after that hour is taken to the police station for questioning. I got to the hospital safely and learned that the doctors had decided to wait until morning to do the autopsy. So I started home again. I had to drive clear across the city and was almost home when a policeman stopped me and demanded to see my permit to be out so late. I did not have such, of course, and explained the situation in three languages, but he was not to be placated and kept insisting that I pay him some money—which I refused to do. He held me in the middle of the street for more than half an hour, and when he saw that I would not bribe him to get away, in disgust he finally let me go.

The next morning at eight I went down to the hospital to be present at the autopsy. As soon as they had opened the chest cavity, they found the thymus gland in the chest had enlarged to twenty-five times the normal size and had completely surrounded the trachea and strangled the baby. This is called a thymic death. I had never heard of it before, and the doctors said it was quite rare. There was nothing that could have been done at that late stage. If it had been diagnosed weeks before, the child could have been saved. The thymus gland is very small at birth, and after the first year it normally disappears completely. But in this case it grew and grew until it was choking the heart and lungs. It was larger than either the heart or the lungs and almost filled the chest.

The Kurtzes had asked me to make all the arrangements and conduct the funeral service, so that morning I scurried around to find a casket. In the native market I found a little cedar box such as the Ethiopians use. Then I bought some nice white material to cover it. The burial service had been set for 2:00 P.M., and I did not get the little body back to the house until nearly 11:00 A.M. along with the casket and cloth. Lyda prepared the body for burial and then drapped the casket with the white cloth. When she was finished, it was beautiful, and Kenny looked as if he had just fallen asleep. It was a very difficult service for me because I had grown to love Kenny very much indeed. But the words of little Janie Kurtz, just three years old, to her mother helped greatly. Polly and Harold gathered the children together and explained to them that their little brother had gone to heaven. Of course, Polly shed some tears as she tried to explain to the three little girls, and Janie took her mother's face in her little hands and said, "Mummy, don't cry. Isn't it nice to go to be with Jesus? We all will go to be with him someday, won't we?" Out of the mouths of babes . . .

▼▲▼

Sometime earlier Don had secured the necessary land grants and visas for the Forgotten Tribes Mission. Five missionary families—the Swarts, the Jordans, the Hoekstras, the Muldrows, and the McClures, Jr.—had begun to work in it. In addition, His Imperial Majesty asked Don and the American Mission to assume responsibility for all the medical work in Illubabor province. This would involve operating a fifty-bed hospital at Gore with two doctors and two nurses in charge there and a third physician to be medical director of the entire province (all of these being members of the American Mission). As a pilot project, the Ethiopian Ministry of Public Health agreed to pay four salaries and all the expenses of the staff and equipment if the American Mission would fund one physician.

Don had heard that if his church turned down this request, the Ethiopian government intended to contact the Roman Catholics and if they too refused, turn to the Russians, who had already offered to undertake this work at their own expense. In fact, a communist Indian doctor was then in charge of the Gore hospital. Don saw this as an unprecedented opportunity and, as field secretary and without consulting anyone, immediately agreed to do it. Employing an old American football tactic, whenever Don saw an opening, he went through hard and fast. The emperor wanted medical help for his people, and Don wanted complete freedom to evangelize everywhere in the area. Don thought that this proposed medical cooperation between the Ethiopian government and the American Mission could be coupled with their established work among the Oromos and Anuaks and the developing evangelistic outreach of the Forgotten Tribes Mission. It was an initiative not to be missed.

Don immediately and excitedly began to draw up a contract that he believed would be "an historic document because no mission in Ethiopia has ever been asked to take such a major role. This new medical work will fit perfectly into our evangelistic program for that area, since we can locate our education and evangelistic work side by side with the medical service."

The executive staff in New York had already agreed to seek funds for one physician at Gore, but when Don sent word about this expanded medical project, many commission members were outraged. While Dr. Andrew Thakur Das, regional secretary for Africa, was personally in sympathy with what Don had done, he gently suggested that Don should have first consulted the commission's department of medicine before committing them to this large-scale project.

In any event, the commission as a whole was unwilling (or unable) to make the kind of commitment to Ethiopia that Don had envisioned. The medical program was never implemented, and this humanitarian and evangelistic opportunity was lost.

▼▲▼

Ethiopia had begun to take steps to resolve her border disputes. To handle the long-standing problem with the province of Eritrea[77] in the north, the emperor sought a military solution. Ethiopia resolved its refugee problem in the west through diplomacy with Sudan, and Haile Selassie hoped to avoid a greater problem with Somalia in the east through economic improvements. For generations the Somalis had drifted back and forth between Ethiopia and Somalia, chiefly seeking water and grass for their cattle and camels, but often marauding the smaller tribes on both sides of the border. At one point these raids had brought the two governments into open warfare, and a number of soldiers had been killed on both sides. To avoid renewed hostilities, both countries agreed to attempt to settle these nomadic tribes into a number of villages well back from the border. The governments would make houses, schools, medical care, and pastureland available.

The Ethiopian government started building a model city along the banks of the Webi Shebelle River in Harrar province, about 150 miles from the Somali border. This village, to be called Gode, was being laid out with a school, a hospital, and a community center for 5000 people, an Orthodox church, a mosque, and a residence for Haile Selassie (to demonstrate the emperor's commitment to the region). Additional plans made it possible to expand the settlement to accommodate 30,000 people. The government constructed a dam across the river and prepared one hundred thousand acres for irrigation to provide for crops and pastureland.

A few days ago I was at Pokwo attending an Anuak planning conference* when a plane flew over and dropped a note stating that I had been called to the palace for five o'clock that afternoon. It was then just after two o'clock, and I was hundreds of miles from Addis Ababa and dressed in shorts. However, I ran for my plane, gathering up two passengers as I went, and we took off a few minutes later. Fortunately we had good tail winds, for we arrived in Addis Ababa just two hours and ten minutes later. I expected to find Lyda at the airport with my "meeting-the-emperor" clothes, but she was not there, so I drove for home as fast as I could. I changed my clothes and dashed for the palace. It was five o'clock when I left the house, and ten minutes later I was at the palace five miles away and through the entire city traffic. I still had not seen Lyda.

I quickly learned that I had gone to the wrong palace (that is the trouble with having so many palaces). Fortunately the Jubilee Palace is very close to the Grand Palace, so I turned into the gate of the Jubilee Palace, called to a doorman to park my

---

*Although sharply reduced, due to ecclesiastical developments in America and political conditions in Ethiopia, the Anuak project continues. As of 1990, Marie Lusted, R.N., and the Rev. Niles Reimer are still serving the Anuak church. Their primary task is to complete the translation of the Old Testament into the Anuak language. In addition, Reimer trains Anuak evangelists who are permitted to come to Addis Ababa.

At the Gilo River Station on 28 March 1973, Beth Reimer was bitten by a small animal. That night she developed a high fever and chills. Thinking she might have malaria, Don McClure, Jr. flew in with chloroquine, but Beth did not respond to the medication. A few hours later Harold Kurtz flew into Gilo to take Beth and her mother, Ann, out to a missionary physician at Dembi Dollo. When the plane landed at Pokwo to refuel, the volunteer nurse observed generalized small hemorrhages over Beth's entire body, suggesting massive infection. When they reached Dembi Dollo, Beth's temperature was so high (more than 108 degrees) that it would not register on the thermometer; she was slipping away. Before Niles could get to Dembi Dollo, his daughter was gone. Any father who has loved his daughter can understand the desperation of Niles's prayer that Beth be raised from the dead.

On 29 March 1973 Beth Reimer (age eight) was buried behind the little Christian Church at Pokwo, the village of life.

An American statesman once said that what Christian missionaries have done in Africa is almost beyond belief. "They fought superstition, ignorance, suspicion, and a terrible host of diseases. They walked for years across a dark continent to bring light, and many of them fell before they could even reach their destination. But of all their great sacrifices, the most pitiable are of their own precious children. Dear God, I saw the gravestones of children all over Africa."

car, and ran in. I met one of the palace secretaries, and he asked me what I wanted. I told him I had an appointment with His Majesty at 5:00 P.M. and was sorry to be late. He said that His Majesty was with an Italian cultural group, and I would have to wait my turn. Just then Tafara Worq, His Majesty's private secretary, came out and looked at his watch. He smiled and said, "You are a bit late." I explained that I had received the message in Pokwo only three hours previously and had flown in as fast as I could. After I finished my long explanation, he smiled again and said, "So you did not know that the audience has been postponed until 9:30 A.M. tomorrow." I was about ready to collapse, but also greatly relieved.

The next morning Glenn Reed and I went to see His Majesty, and as usual it was a most delightful audience. He was as gracious and kindly as an emperor should be. He thanked us for what the American Mission had been doing in Ethiopia through the years and then almost apologetically said he was asking us to do more—and that was to supervise the medical and educational work in the city of Gode, which was just now being built. We tried to point out that we had received word from the commission in New York that our budget was being cut again and some of our present work would be closed. Therefore we were not confident that we would be able to start a new and formidable project on the other side of Ethiopia among Muslim people and requiring the use of a new language. When I asked His Imperial Majesty if he could not find one of the other missions in Ethiopia already working among the Muslims who would undertake this new work, he smiled gently and said, "I am not asking the other missions. I am asking the American Mission to conduct this work along the lines of your Anuak project on the Sudan border."

Apparently Haile Selassie thinks our protests are only the modest American way of talking. In any case, after half an hour of pleasant conversation the emperor asked me to propose the Gode project to our people in New York, and this I could not refuse to do. Haile Selassie usually gets his way without ever losing his temper or raising his voice, and I can understand why he would not need to do so. His voice and eyes are so persuasive that it would be difficult to deny him anything. It would be thrilling to start this new work, but Glenn retires next year at age seventy, and I do not have many years until I reach the retirement age now set by the commission at sixty-five.

The next day Don was called to the office of Tafara Worq to discuss the Gode project in more detail.

After a few preliminary remarks, Tafara Worq reiterated, "His Imperial Majesty wants the American Mission to open a station in the Ogaden region." I responded, "Your Excellency, the Ogaden is clear across the country from the area in which we are working and among a different type of people. Furthermore, according to the comity agreement of 1935, this area is assigned to the Sudan Interior Mission." He asked, "What is a comity agreement?" And I explained that a committee designated the areas in which the different missions would work so that they would not duplicate services or encroach on each other.

Tafara Worq waved aside the comity agreement and repeated, "You evidently misunderstood me. His Imperial Majesty wishes the American Mission to start a station in the Ogaden." Then he went on to explain the situation. Gode is being built as a model city in an area where no town has previously existed with the hope that thousands of nomads will settle there. The Ministry of Education is building the school, the Ministry of Public Health is building the hospital, and the Ministry of Community Development is building a community center. The American Mission would supervise these services and be responsible for the medical and educational work.

Since time was short, we did not go into more detail, but I understood that budget and buildings would be provided by the Ethiopian government and we would provide the staff. This would mean someone to direct the school and community center and a doctor or nurse to supervise the health center. I did not discuss salary or housing for these Americans, but I assume that would be our responsibility.

I think that the Gode project would be a tremendous opportunity for the American Mission. First, the mission and government would be working together rather than at cross-purposes. Ethiopia needs help with its Muslim people, and we could provide it. Second, we would add a Muslim witness to our Ethiopian field. The Sudan Interior Mission has a site on the border at a place named Callafo, but there are hundreds of square miles and hundreds of thousands of people yet un-touched. Third, if we undertake this work, I think it should be in cooperation with the Ethiopian Orthodox Church, which should share in station personnel and administration; any converts would become members of the Orthodox Church rather than a foreign-sponsored body. Our staff in Addis Ababa is concerned that this project might cut into our present work and needs, but I think it should be seen as an expansion of our service in Ethiopia.

People often came to see things as Don saw them. More than once at the beginning of a meeting in which the Ethiopian Mission was to pray about an issue, Don McClure was a minority of one. The meeting ended when everyone recognized that the Lord's will was exactly what Don had, from the beginning, thought it was.

To the New York office Don explained that this was

Simply a preliminary report of my conversations, but I am sure the Ethiopian Mission would be prepared to work at Gode if the commission approves. Tafara Worq indicated we should begin as soon as possible. I scarcely need say that I think this is a wonderful opportunity for us, especially if it comes as a joint effort with the Orthodox Church. Abuna Theophilus has expressed deep gratitude for our summer program with theolog-ical students, and the possibilities of cooperation are increasing greatly.

In all previous missionary endeavors in Ethiopia, Don had received special permission from Haile Selassie, but for the Gode project he received the emperor's direct request. Don did not see how he or his American church could refuse to comply—whatever the difficulties might be.

Having flown out to Gode as a guest of the district governor, Don informed his friends and supporters,

Colonel Desta Gabre Mariam had me up at 6:00 A.M. to go to church with him. When Colonel Desta learned that there was not going to be a sermon, without speaking to me he interrupted one of the four priests participating in the service and told him that I would give a sermon. Then he came back to me and said that in about ten minutes I would be called upon for a message and he would translate. I spoke for only ten minutes, but the interpretation required fifteen minutes, so I guess his sermon was better than mine. The whole service was two hours and fifteen minutes long, and having no chairs or benches, we stood the entire time.

Yesterday the governor drove me out to a town that he had built for the Somalis six years before when the first trouble with these nomadic tribesmen brought him down as the commander of the Sixth Battalion of the Ethiopian army. At that time he forced these Somalis to settle there just six miles from Gode. More than one thousand people have given up their nomadic way of life and built a permanent village of mud huts. There are a dozen small stores where goats and cattle are bought in exchange for salt, cloth, knives, and beads; the largest-selling item is plastic shoes. The Somalis find that the plastic shoes protect their feet from the heat and thorns, and everyone wants a pair. I saw scores of women carrying their shoes on top of their heads wherever the path was smooth, but they put on these shoes when they get out into the bush, where there are sharp stones and thorns.

We found the people happy and apparently very content. Most of the men were out with their cattle and camels, but increasingly they are finding something to do in the town and becoming interested in the life of the community. It was the experience in this village that led His Imperial Majesty to invest so much in Gode. I am encouraged with what I saw yesterday. Also, I found that most of the Somalis could either speak or understand Arabic. So instead of learning a new language, it may only be necessary for us to brush up on our Arabic, which we have not used very extensively for many years.

Don was reaching retirement age, and his office as field secretary for the American Mission's Ethiopian work was being phased out. With the deep cutbacks in mission personnel over the years, there was now no field to administer. Don had strenuously opposed these cutbacks, but he was helpless to prevent them. He had promised Haile Selassie that the American Mission would initiate a mission at Gode—yet nothing was being done.

A year ago I wrote to the commission about the Gode project and received a most enthusiastic response—then silence. I wrote several times about plans for recruiting staff—more silence. Finally I told the commission that when I retire I would become a "Volunteer in Mission" and undertake the Gode project myself. I will raise the necessary funds over and above the present budget. I will try to recruit a staff, but in any case, Lyda and I will work at Gode as long as we are able. To that the commission gave its approval (since I was going to do it anyway), and the Gode project has begun.

Some people feel it may be impossible to persuade the Somalis, who are fierce lovers of the desert, to give up their tents and the freedom of movement they have enjoyed for generations to live communally in a settled village. However, the success of the project does not depend entirely upon the Somalis, although they are our primary target. We have discovered hundreds of villages clustered along the Webi Shebelle River composed of approximately 90,000 people who call themselves "Suri" and are neither Somali nor nomads. According to the Suri people, the traditions of their tribe go back to a time when they lived in south Sudan. Many years ago they trekked across Ethiopia and settled along the Webi Shebelle. Through the years they have been greatly influenced by the Somalis, and most of them have adopted Islam but without knowing what it means. The Suris do not observe the Muslim prayers or fasts. They seem open and fairly easy to reach with the gospel. A year ago Colonel Desta started a first grade in the school with two teachers and no benches or books, and 176 pupils appeared the first day. Obviously we will have plenty of people to serve. No Christian has ever approached the Suris, the gospel has never been preached among them, no word of the Bible has ever been translated in their language, and their literacy rate is zero. The need is there, and the opportunity is ours to grasp.

I must now begin to think in terms of a budget. We are fortunate that the Ethiopian government will provide all the buildings—including the hospital, school, and staff residences—except for our house, which I will build. The Orthodox Church is looking for a doctor and a nurse, but we may be required to pay their salaries and expenses, which we estimate at $22,000. We need an educator (and family) and an evangelist (and family) at $15,000 each, and a house and Jeep station wagon for us at $20,000. We already have $55,000 in hand and the same amount in pledges from individuals and churches. Lyda and I are ready to move to Gode, put up our tents, and begin work on our house, which will be built with a raised cement floor because there are so many scorpions.

The primary goal of the Ethiopian government is the peaceful rehabilitation of the Somali nomads, but our primary purpose is the evangelization of that region. In any event, the Gode project is launched, and we will be living in Gode from now on. It turns out that I will have to build and equip the community center with a library, reading room, and bookstore. The land is set aside for this building in the center of town, and I will get started just as soon as funds are available. I estimate the library-bookstore at $20,000; tractor and farm equipment, $8,000; a movie projector and sound equipment, $2,500; a van to get out into the villages to preach and show movies, $12,000; a pump for our water and irrigation at $6,000. I have already received the gift of a motorboat for river transportation and several other large contributions for various aspects of the Gode project.

▼ The Great
▼ Deception

DON McCLURE thought his church had promised Ethiopia that a Christian mission would be established at Gode. On that basis Don had given his word to His Imperial Majesty, Haile Selassie, and when the administrators in New York made no move to implement the Gode project, Don felt honor bound to begin the work himself. Thus, although the McClures had reached retirement age, they reenlisted in the cause of world evangelism as Volunteers in Mission—a concept, now an official program of his denomination, that Don had initiated many years before as part of the Anuak project. Now Don was serving as a volunteer himself. Years before, on the conviction that the Lord would always provide, Don had refused to enter the American social security program. Thus it was only his small pension check that made its way to Ethiopia.

One more time, Lyda and Don McClure were starting out alone with the hope that in the near future they could enlist the help of at least one physician and one educator. A Kansan who had served with the U.S. government in Ethiopia suggested to a group of Kansas physicians and veterinarians who wanted to work in Africa that they ought to get in touch with Don McClure. This group of twenty-five doctors, under the leadership of J. Alfred Larson, M.D., and Martin Douglas, planned to devote part of their lives on a voluntary, rotation basis to a pilot project in some developing country of Africa.

Based on the conviction that there is a very close relation between animal health and the health of the human community that depends on these animals for food, the doctors planned to work together but in their special fields. The physicians proposed to improve human health by using the very newest and finest available medical procedures, drugs, and equipment. They would provide the staff of a hospital, build a research facility, operate mobile clinics to treat those who would not come to the hospital, and train public health teams. The veterinarians would also set up a research center, operate clinics, and immunize all the animals of the community. Moreover, they would improve cattle and poultry by selective breeding and then distribute these superior breeds to local people and train the nationals in animal husbandry and poultry raising on a commercially viable scale. Don was overjoyed by the prospect of two first-rate medical teams working at Gode. The addition of the Combined Medical Services would make the Gode project, not the small-scale operation that Don had originally planned, but a major service to Ethiopia and a model of inestimable value for all of Africa.

Don set about to assess the feasibility of a large medical program for Gode. First, he estimated that since approximately 90,000 people were within reach of the Gode area, there was obviously a sufficient population to treat. Second, the medical needs were overwhelming.

These include tuberculosis (75 percent); intestinal parasites (100 percent); malnutrition (80 percent); smallpox (10 percent); malaria (60 percent); measles and whooping cough (25 percent); venereal diseases (10 percent); trachoma and glaucoma (30 percent); conjunctivitis (100 percent at one time or another). The incidence of brucellosis and ungulate fever is unknown. The incidence of tropical ulcers is high, as is death at childbirth of both mother and baby. Third, the population of the area is widely scattered over many kilometers of territory, and there is only one hospital at the town of Gode. However, since the medical project proposes to travel to the places where the nomadic people are located, they are available to be helped. Fourth, in many areas of Africa the indigenous people resist all efforts by outsiders to meet their medical needs, but the Somalis around Gode are quite open to such help and will accept and welcome a major medical program. Fifth, our staff of physicians can expect to use the very finest available equipment; to administer the Gode hospital and all public health facilities and training; to establish a research center; and to have several mobile clinics in order to reach small settlements.

The animal health aspect of the project intends to start by building a clinic and research center in order to improve the health of the present animal population, including cattle, camels, and goats. All these animals are presently infested with some disease and need treatment by inoculations, dips, and the isolation of sick animals. In addition, the veterinarians intend to breed a strain of cattle, to be known as "the Ethiopian," that will be second to none in the world. Some of the very best cattle breeders and herd managers in the United States will plan and direct this program. The doctors expect a gift of high-bred animal semen valued at three million U.S. dollars, and by use of artificial insemination the Somali cattle will quickly be improved. To increase the number of cattle and improve the quality of the meat, they will irrigate fenced pastureland and cut thousands of tons of desert grasses, which are rich in proteins. Large quantities of oil cake will be produced by extracting oil from cotton, sunflower, groundnut, sesame, and other oil seeds.

Moreover, poultry will be raised in sufficient numbers to make cheaper and more abundant chickens and eggs available to all Ethiopians. At present, poultry is a luxury for the high middle class. We believe that the climate and soil at Gode is ideal for raising both chickens and turkeys that can be produced and priced so that even the poorest can afford them. Since there is a world-wide demand for chicken and turkey meat, it would be simple and practical to export large quantities to Middle Eastern and European markets. Chickens and turkeys are now being imported into Ethiopia and into most European countries from the United States, but we believe that Gode can compete with the finest American poultry in European markets in terms of quality of meat and cost of production and transportation.

During the recent droughts in Africa, millions of cattle have died, and the demand for meat will be high for many years to come. Moreover, the Middle East has never been able to supply its own beef needs and must import from the United States and Australia. We propose to raise sufficient cattle to supply all the market needs of Ethiopia and to export the surplus. An abattoir and freezing plant will be built at Gode that will meet any standard set by importing countries for high-quality meat and poultry. The beef will be killed, prepared, and frozen under the supervision of inspectors who will be acceptable in any area to which we ship. It is more feasible to ship processed meats by air rather than trying to drive large herds over great distances to market. At present, we do not anticipate canning meats or tanning hides. Later on, we may expand our facilities to include these processes.

Finally, we expect to train large numbers of Ethiopian nationals to manage herds and flocks, to prepare both beef and poultry, and to sell the product in local and world markets. According to Dr. Larson, major medical and agricultural development companies are considering additional investments of tremendous importance to Ethiopian and a major pharmaceutical company is considering locating in Addis Ababa for the manufacture of drugs for Africa—all of which is contingent on the speedy inauguration of the Gode project.

This program was extremely ambitious, and the cost over a five-year period was estimated at $10 million. According to Don,

The Kansas doctors are all Christian men who want to serve mankind through their various skills. They have joined the Gode project not simply to bring physical and economic health to the region, but also to support the spiritual health of a needy people. Most of the doctors involved are not wealthy men, but they are willing to give up their practices in America to serve for a time in Ethiopia; they must be furnished the necessary tools, equipment, and buildings. Providing a herd of one thousand head of cattle for breeding alone will cost many hundreds of thousands of dollars. Of this amount the Gode Combined Medical Services has a present balance in trust of $2.5 million; another $2.5 million is expected from medical foundations; $1 million from Christian churches; $1.5 million will be sought from private donors and governments (including a request for funds from Ketema Abebe of the Ethiopian Ministry of Public Health to Earl Butz, United States secretary of agriculture); and $2.5 million will be raised from the sale of commemorative Ethiopian coins.

To help defray the costs of this immense project, the doctors proposed to mint, at their own expense, 800,000 commemorative coins. They would be sold in sets of four with a face value of five Ethiopia dollars each, for a total of $4 million. These coins, produced according to the highest standards of international proof quality by Huquenin Medailleurs of Le Locle, Switzerland, were to be sold to collectors and would never circulate as currency, since each coin would be worth many times its face value. Originally the coins were to portray Haile Selassie, Dwight Eisenhower, Charles De Gaulle, and Winston Churchill, but the board of the Ethiopian National Bank absolutely refused to consider permission for minting a coin that pictured a non-Ethiopian. Thus the proposal was changed to bear the likenesses of Haile Selassie, King Solomon, the Queen of Sheba, and Menelik I. Don told his supporters,

> These men who want to help in the Gode project will give guarantees that every dollar raised in the sale of these coins will come back to Ethiopia and be used for the benefit of the Ethiopian people.

With this coin program Don went in over his head. From the beginning he was uneasy about funding a project with anticipated revenue from collectors who might be interested in a set of coins but not in the project that the purchase was designed to aid. Don had always raised money from individuals and groups, like the dear ladies of the Women's Missionary Society, who knew him and believed passionately in supporting what he was doing. Don had no experience with—and of course, no loyalty from—the world of collecting and high finance. However, his great desire to see the Gode project established on the splendid scale proposed by the Combined Medical Services plan overcame his scruples. He worked hard to get the necessary permissions from Haile Selassie, to overcome the suspicious inertia of the National Bank of Ethiopia, and to make the legal and financial arrangements with a trustee company represented by an attorney and counselor of law in Zurich. Don confessed,

> I am not very enthusiastic about this method of raising money and will not have any responsibility for the sale of the coins. But I have had to work out all the problems here in getting permission to mint the coins. At last I have the agreement almost in hand. It has been promised for tomorrow (as it has been promised a half-dozen times before), but this time I think I will get it. I will leave immediately for Geneva and Zurich to get started on buying the silver, finding the artists, signing the contract with the mint, and so on.

Despite all his efforts, Don was able to secure the permission to mint only the first coin. On the obverse side of this coin there was a profile of His Imperial Majesty, Haile Selassie I, in the central space. Along the top border the name "Haile Selassie I" appeared in Amharic lettering, with the same words in gothic Latin lettering along the lower border. To the left was pictured the emperor's crown and to the right, the imperial monogram. In the central space on the reverse side was the traditional design of the Lion of Judah. Along the upper border in Amharic lettering was "Empire of Ethiopia," and the same along the lower border in gothic Latin lettering with the year 1972 just above the border. The value of the coin (five Ethiopian dollars) was printed on the left in Amharic and on the right in gothic Latin and Arabic numerals. Two hundred thousand copies of this coin were produced with the hope that the other three could be minted at a later date.

I am writing on a marble-topped table of rich green and red with gold legs. My appointment to report to Haile Selassie on the first coin was scheduled for noon, but his secretary came in and apologized that His Imperial Majesty would be a little late. I graciously told the secretary that was perfectly all right. This anteroom of the imperial palace is gorgeous. The huge, crystal chandeliers are brilliantly lighted and dominate the room. The ceiling is in cream and gold with flying cupids (or fat babies) on each panel. Around the walls are gold pillars with three golden candlesticks on each and mirrors in between the pillars. The furniture is in cream, gold, and blue. The carpet is blue. It is all very grand. . . . I had a delightful audience, and His Majesty was very interested in every aspect of our program for Gode and kept me for forty-five minutes asking questions.

Anyone who is consumed by a great passion becomes vulnerable to the conviction that others are equally committed to that cause. Thus we may hold in abeyance the skeptical detachment that prevents us from being deceived by those who only *seem* to share our concerns. It is difficult to believe that from the beginning the Gode Combined Medical Services was designed as a scheme to make huge sums of money for its leaders—but that is apparently how it ended.

On 16 February 1977 a newspaper reported that former backers of an alleged charity used an Ethiopian missionary organization as a "front" to solicit nearly $1,000,000 in contributions. Dr. Leonard Volbeda, a veterinarian, claimed to have lost over $100,000 dollars. Ralph Brown, a businessman, had been swindled out of about

$250,000 by Ethiopian Call, which, the paper reported, was founded by Dr. J. Alfred Larson, Martin Douglas, and John Pritchard, president and chief stockholder in a Brinkley, Kansas, bank. A Marianna minister named Bruce Marshall was president of Ethiopia Call and, according to the newspaper account, 200,000 Ethiopian silver coins were used to solicit donations of $50 for each coin in units of $25,000.

The newspaper reported that Douglas was unavailable for comment on Ethiopian Call, and Pritchard declined comment although both Brown and Volbeda said they believed Pritchard contributed to Ethiopian Call and was himself a victim of the scheme. The newspaper account also reported that Larson denied any association with Ethiopian Call except for one contact with Marshall's former attorney. Marshall defended himself, saying that he had been fooled into becoming Ethiopian Call's figurehead leader; he did not know the organization engaged in questionable practices.

A suit brought by Joe Taylor, Brown, and Volbeda in Kansas Western District Federal Court named Larson, Douglas, Pritchard, Marshall, three Swiss corporations, and two Kansas banks as defendants. It was dismissed on 29 December 1976 at the request of the plaintiffs. According to the newspaper, Volbeda said that from the suit he received a cash settlement amounting to approximately twenty-two cents on the dollar. Attorneys said some of the defendants borrowed money from a Kansas City bank to pay the settlement costs and as collateral deposited a large number of Ethiopian silver medallions.

A year earlier (29 and 31 December 1976), another newspaper reported that Marshall, a well-known evangelical figure in the area, had been arrested by FBI agents and charged with interstate transportation of stolen funds. The federal complaint filed in the Central District of Florida alleges Marshall "willfully, knowingly, and unlawfully" devised a scheme to defraud Bank Peterson A.G. of Basel, Switzerland, through a $5 million issue of Gospel Outreach Inc. bonds. The newspaper said that Marshall admitted to FBI agents that in September of 1974 he had printed $5 million in worthless bonds to help raise money for Gospel Outreach; it also reported that Marshall became president of a missionary group known as Ethiopian Call, which had been organized by several Kansas doctors and veterinarians.

On Larson's recommendation and guarantee, Don McClure had loaned some of his own money to Marshall and others connected with the Gode Combined Medical Services. When a supporter sent these newspaper articles to Don, he wrote to his brother Tom, a banker,

I guess this is no time to try to recover my money. I know you think the Kansas bunch is running some kind of racket with me as the fall guy, but I still trust them and believe that the project will get started. However, I will hold on to my own money from now on until I see some of theirs.

On 6 February 1976 the pastor of a California church wrote to Marshall,

We are tremendously distressed to learn that Don McClure has not received anything of the financial contributions which we sent to him through Gospel Outreach. Our little church has always had an interest in Don's magnificent work and because of that interest and our love for him we made these contributions. We are not interested in Ethiopian Call, but in Don McClure. We specified that our gifts be sent directly to Don. We have not sent money for anything else, and such expenditures of our contributions would be a total misappropriation of funds. We are intensely distressed to know that Don is serving so faithfully, but without the financial help we promised him and to which we committed ourselves.

On 16 September 1978 a local newspaper reported that a U.S. District Court jury had found Bruce Marshall guilty of interstate transportation of fraudulently obtained securities. By that time Don McClure had been dead about six months.[78]

▼ The Last Labors

WHEN IT BECAME painfully evident that the Combined Medical Services was *not* coming to Gode, the McClures could have used the occasion to retire gracefully and return to America to rest and reflect on a lifetime of Christian evangelism in Africa. Instead Don scaled down his plan, and with the continuing support of his many loyal and generous friends, he and Lyda set out to accomplish what they could.[79]

From the beginning at Gode we have been praying for a Christian Somali who can teach us the language as well as conduct worship services. God has sent Abdi Nur Abdi to us. He is tremendously energetic and has a burning desire to share the gospel with his own people. Abdi has agreed to go down to Gode with us and be our evangelist. Since he is a convert from Islam himself, he knows how to approach Muslims.

At this time the accumulated effects of four years of drought brought thousands of starving, sick, and dying Somalis into Gode in search of water.

The lack of water is a perennial problem in the Ogaden desert region. All year long people gather around their waterholes, and as the dry season approaches they dig deeper to reach the lowering water table. For centuries, they have always been able to find enough water to keep themselves and their animals alive. This year was different, because for the previous three years rainfall was far below normal. Because there was no rain this year, the water table sank lower and lower until it was impossible for the people to dig down into the sand to reach it.

409

Nevertheless, they continued to sit around their dry water-holes expecting the rains to come. All that time the cattle and camels were dying, but the people were unwilling to go for help and leave their animals behind. When the people finally began to move off in search of water, they walked through the desert from one dry waterhole to the next. As soon as the Ethiopian government realized the gravity of the situation, aid was sent, but it was too late to save most of the people. When we went home on a short furlough, conditions were just getting serious, but rain was expected every day. Now it is estimated that 100,000 have already died from thirst. I have learned that many people moved to the Webi Shebelle River, where they could get water, but there is no forage for their cattle, so they are almost as bad off except that death by starvation comes more slowly than death by thirst.

When the McClures returned to Gode, the refugee camps were trying to cope with the needs of ten thousand persons. For a time deaths averaged twenty each day. Don and Lyda supervised the distribution of grain and the dispensing of medicine until the rains came and the drought abated.

Many of the refugees had settled down in the camps, and as long as they were being fed, they were content just to sit. However, the Lord had other plans for them, and he brought them about dramatically. Many of the people at home had been praying with us for years that this terrible drought would end. They should not have prayed quite so vigorously, because it rained harder than anyone could ever remember and the camp was flooded out. The rains swept away the refugee camps, but fortunately no more lives were lost, since the people had time to get to higher ground. In a few hours the flooding did what we had been attempting for months. It swept the camps away and got the people moving. They had nothing to return to, so they willingly moved to the land we had marked out for them and began to work at irrigating their own five-acre plots.

We intend to prevent a recurrence of this catastrophe. All those tens of thousands of people died of thirst with water only 150 feet away, but it was underground and they could not get to it. By hand I have dug one well down to 65 feet. I got lots of water, but it was brackish. It is drinkable for cattle and for people if they get thirsty enough, but it is too salty to use for irrigation. We hope to get out into the desert, drill wells, set up windmills, and teach the people how to irrigate their land. We must go ahead with our windmill project because a windmill needs minimum care and the Lord provides a constant wind across the desert. I have ordered twenty-two windmills and expect to buy sixty-four in all. None of them has yet arrived because the shipping backlog at Djibouti, our port of entry, is colossal. Relief items have priority, but the narrow-gauge, one-track railway is swamped, and it may be months before our windmills come through.

Our well-digging rig has not arrived either, but the people's needs for food and water must be met daily. I have discovered a drilling rig in Addis Ababa left behind by the Tenneco Oil Company when they moved out of Ethiopia some months ago. I have written to the chairman in Houston, Texas, asking Tenneco to donate the rig to us. If we have to pay the full value of the rig and equipment, it will be in the neighborhood of $80,000. We do not have that kind of money, but we have the faith to believe it will come if we must make the purchase.

Here at Gode we have bought diesel pumps to get water from the river onto the land. But diesel pumps are not the permanent answer, because they require expensive fuel and constant maintenance—neither of which is available in the desert. Still, these pumps are helping those who have moved onto their own homesteads. One of our greatest joys is to watch the peoples' pride and hope return as they work for themselves and anticipate the day when they will harvest their first crops in four years and become independent of relief handouts.

In the midst of this refugee crisis, Haile Selassie was deposed and a Marxist-socialist military junta seized power in Ethiopia. Haile Selassie had ruled Ethiopia since 1916 and was venerated by the peasantry. He had convinced most of the powerful territorial families and the Ethiopian Orthodox Church that their interests were best served by his reign. There was unrest, however, and it was focused among the military, the wealthy elite who desired even more privilege, and the educated, many of whom had studied abroad with the emperor's encouragement and blessing. This was not the first attempt to depose the emperor. A palace coup, attempted in 1960 while Haile Selassie was visiting Brazil, was thwarted by loyal elements in his government. These elements were not able to prevent the junta from seizing power this time.

As a Christian country surrounded by Islamic nations, Ethiopia had long been isolated in fact and in spirit. Therefore Haile Selassie believed that it was essential to maintain a strong army, which had been trained and equipped by the United States. Ethiopia was America's staunchest ally in Africa, and a symbolic contingent of Ethiopians even served in the United Nations forces fighting in the Korean War.

In his later years the emperor was unable to placate and control the powerful military. When they seized power, they moved to discredit His Imperial Majesty, picturing him as unconcerned about the terrible drought. According to Don, however, the emperor had not been informed of the drought by officials responsible for supplying such information because they did not want bad news about conditions in their areas to reflect on them.

Haile Selassie fell while Don was in America on a short visit. Don admired the emperor as an enlightened and benevolent ruler with a deep concern for the welfare of his country and all her people, a desire to bring Ethiopia, with all deliberate speed, into the twentieth century. When Don was asked to comment about the Ethiopian situation on Canadian television, he used the occasion to plead for humane treatment of the emperor. This upset many people who thought Don was jeopardizing the future work of the American Mission in Ethiopia by engaging in political activity.

On his return to Ethiopia, Don had an hour-long session with the Coordinating Military Committee about the Gode project.

They assured me that the agreements signed with the former government were still valid, and they hoped that we would do our best to carry them out. They guaranteed us full cooperation and whatever help they could give us. Early in October I had the privilege of a last interview with His Imperial Majesty. He was under arrest, a broken and failing man who has since died and been buried in an unmarked grave. The Conquering Lion of Judah and King of Kings did not have much to say except to give me his blessing on the work at Gode and to thank me for past years of service to Ethiopia. How quickly passes the glory of the world. Lo, how the mighty are fallen!

One of my last promises to Haile Selassie was to build the community center at Gode with a large auditorium that can be used for Christian worship services. Gode has now grown to 20,000 people, and the Christian congregation is too large to meet in our small house. Much of the money for the community center was given as a memorial, but building costs have more than doubled and we do not yet have sufficient funds to complete this part of the Gode project.

As I look out my window, I see a little ostrich running around the yard. This ostrich was born in my study about a week ago while our grandchildren were here. A man came in one morning with three eggs, and I bought them and put them in my bookcase. That afternoon we heard sounds from the bookcase, and sure enough, one egg was beginning to crack open. We placed it on the floor, and Don, Jr.'s three children lay there all afternoon watching an ostrich being born. Now Oscar the ostrich is ready to take over the place. Later on he will become a nuisance, and I will probably take him out on the plains and let him go. At this stage he is fun as he runs around trying to catch grasshoppers and crickets.

Now that I am a rancher, my herd has been growing until I have over one hundred head of cattle. I was gradually giving a few to the Somali people, but they could not feed them properly and the cattle died. I must wait until the people here have better pasturage. Don, Jr.'s cattle down at Surma have died, too, but from disease, not drought. So I decided to send some of my cattle to Donnie, who has lots of good grass for them. We chartered the Mercy Airlift DC-3 for the trip. Don, Jr. came into Gode, and we selected fifteen of our finest animals. The Mercy Airlift plane was designed for passengers, but converted to freight by taking out the seats. However, the carpeting was still on the floor, and it was glued down so that we could not lift it without destroying it. Well, our cattle were not accustomed to carpets in their barn, and we knew what would happen to this nice carpet. We bought a huge tarpaulin in Addis Ababa that would cover all the interior of the plane along the floor and up the walls.

Since we had not experimented with sedating the cattle before the plane arrived, we did not know whether to tranquillize them before we drove them to the airstrip (about one and a half miles from the mission) or wait until we started to load. If we tranquillized them at the mission, we might have to carry them onto the plane; but if we did not, we might have to wait a long time until the medication took effect. Anyway, we took the chance and waited until we got to the plane. Most of the cows we did not have to sedate at all; they walked quietly up the ramp and into the plane as if they were frequent flyers. Some of the young calves we had to tie and throw on, but when we came to the big bull, it was a different matter. He was going to be bull-headed and he was not going on the plane! Moreover, he objected to being injected. Finally about twenty of us manhandled (or bullhandled) him while Donnie got an injection into his neck. The medicine took effect immediately, and he became so sleepy we thought he would fall over—and he was much too big to carry onto the plane. Eventually we got him started up the ramp, three of us pulling him by the nose, three or four pushing behind; and then four men had to take his legs and lift each leg and move it forward to make him walk. If I had been a bystander I would have died laughing, but being a participant was just hard work. When the bull fell on the ramp we were not sure we would be able to get him up again. The plane had to fly seven hundred miles that day, and it was getting late, so that made us all the more anxious.

At last all were on board, and we shut the doors on Donnie and his youngest daughter and locked them in with all those cattle, not really knowing what might happen when the plane took off. All went well, except the bull soon woke up and stuck his head through a window, so Don had to give him another shot. The bull got four shots altogether during the flight. Don and Miriam had quite a trip; before they got home to Surma they knew they had been in a flying cattle car. Working with eight or ten Surmas, it took Don two hours to clean up the plane, even with the tarp covering most of the floor. Mercy Airlift says they will never again transport a herd of cattle, but Donnie is delighted to have them. The Surma people have never seen a bull as big as the one we sent, and hundreds have been coming in to look at him. When the bull was being led out of the plane, he jumped off the ramp and took off after Don's wife, Ginny. I got a letter the other day from eight-year-old Carrie. She wrote, "We luv the cows, but Mommy got butt by the bull. Mommy has a big black and purrpul and red brooz, but the brooz doesn't hurt much and it is in a place where only Daddy can see it."

Concerning his work among Muslim people, Don wrote,

Many years ago I complained about how slow and difficult it is to make a Christian witness among Muslims, but there are rewards, too. Before we went home for a short furlough I had three young men who were being trained for Christian baptism. I did not think they were ready for this huge step, but they were making good progress. Shortly before we left Gode, one of them, Hadj Omar, came to me and said that while we were in the States he wanted to go home and tell his family about the joy he had found in faith in Jesus Christ. I was reluctant to have him go, since his family is entirely Muslim and his older brother was studying for the Islamic priesthood, that is, to be a reader of the Koran. I thought it unwise for Hadj Omar to go home at this point and boast of his change of faith—especially since he had not been baptized and still had a lot to learn. I was afraid that when Hadj Omar was subjected to the ridicule of his hostile and angry family he would not be able to stand by his convictions. But he thought he was ready, so he and his two companions left to walk the hundred miles to his home on the Somali border.

When we got back to Gode we were told that Hadj Omar had proudly announced to his family that he had become a Christian, and his older brother in a rage, and in the presence of the family, had taken a knife, killed him, and fled into Somaliland. I was crushed that our first Christian convert at Gode had been murdered even before he was baptized. As a result I expected that the thirty men who had been studying the Bible with me would not return; but on the same day I heard about Hadj's death, twenty-seven of them came forward and asked that their studies continue so they could soon be baptized. According to them, "Now that Hadj is gone, we must take his place." The Holy Spirit is at work out here on the Somali border, and it is still true that the blood of the witnesses is the seed of the church.

Two weeks before Don McClure died, guerrillas operating in the Gode area stole eighty-six head of cattle. Since Don was breeding these cattle for the hungry Somali people, he wanted them back. The local governor sent eight policemen with Don, and they followed the rustlers for two days before they found them near the Somali border.

When the cattle were stolen from our feedlot, there were only six thieves, but when we caught up to them there were seventeen, all armed to the teeth. The police exchanged a few shots with the rustlers and then ran for their lives. My cattle are gone. It is hard to help people who steal from you the very things you want to share with them.

In one of his last letters, Don wrote,

It is truly wonderful to be serving the Lord in Africa. This desert country often reminds me of my first years in the Sudan. Last night when the electricity was turned off at 10 P.M., I went out to sit for a while under God's heaven. The air was so clear that every star seemed to shine with an extra brilliance. I am sure I could see twice as many stars as I have ever seen before in all my life. The sky was white with points of light, and the Milky Way (which one of the Ethiopians called the Milk Road) was so bright that it made shadows under the tree. This morning I woke up early and walked outside just as the first faint glimmer of light began to appear in the eastern sky. The quiet whispers of the new dawn were the same sounds I heard as a new missionary nearly half a century ago in the countryside around Khartoum. As the stars faded away, the first wisp of the morning breeze sprang up, and it was identical with the desert winds of the Sudan—and I felt young again.

The gravesite of W. Donald
McClure at Gode

▼ A VALEDICTION
▼ THE FINAL REFLECTION

WHEN DON, JR. returned to the mission, he found the covered body of his father still on the lawn.[80] He carried the body into the room in which his dad and he had talked only a few hours earlier and laid his body on the bed. Then Don, Jr. drove to the Gode hospital to see the other missionaries, who were amazed that he was alive. They assumed that he had been dragged away, wounded or killed. After a while, Don, Jr. returned to the mission to make funeral arrangements. He decided that his dad would desire his body to remain in the land he loved and among the people he served and that his wife and family be spared the additional trauma of a later funeral. So Don, Jr. prepared to bury his father. A wooden coffin was made. Don selected a gravesite at the highest part of the mission compound and under the largest tree, and digging began.

Don, Jr. went back to the house and sat down at his dad's desk and forced himself to accept the fact that his dad was dead. A bullet had gone through Don, Sr.'s heart and spine. He had died instantly and lay unattended all night on the ground. He was now lying in the next room, but he was not breathing and never would again. It was final, and not easy for Don, Jr. to grasp.

Just then the two Ethiopian nurses came in and asked timidly if they could dress the body for burial. Don said, "No, it doesn't matter. Dad is gone." And so the Reverend Dr. W. Donald McClure, Sr. was buried still clad in a worn pair of his son's cut-off jeans.

Don, Jr. had previously arranged to talk to his mother by radio at 9:15 on Sunday morning. The guerrillas had taken the large radio that Don had only recently installed, but they abandoned the small two-way radio. Don found this radio on the porch, brought it into the house, hooked up the antenna, and called his mother in Addis Ababa

419

while, unbeknownst to her, the little group of Christians at Gode was singing at her husband's funeral.

Lyda reported that she had managed to charter a small plane to fly into Gode. However, Don told her it was urgent that they all be evacuated and a plane large enough for the entire group be sent immediately. Since Don knew that his mother would be alone at the radio transmitter, he did not tell her that she was now a widow, but he did ask if there was anything special that she wanted him to bring out. She answered, "I don't care about anything except that you and your dad come back safely."

The government offices in Addis Ababa were closed on Sunday, and no one was available who could authorize an emergency flight. It seemed impossible to get a large plane to Gode until late Monday at the earliest. Lyda decided that the best plan was to try to contact the World Vision office, since most of the people needing evacuation belonged to that organization; but she knew that those offices were also closed. Yet she remembered that Lindsay Nicholls, who was in charge of the office, worshiped with the Sudan Interior Mission, and she called that number. Providentially Nicholls was walking by the telephone as it rang. He answered it and was apprised of the situation in Gode. Nicholls contacted Marvin Michaels of Mercy Airlift, who in turn reached Al Temple, a pilot connected with the American Embassy; Temple had tickets in his pocket to go to Europe that very day, but agreed to fly to Gode if permission could be arranged. In the space of four hours—miraculously short for Ethiopia—clearance was granted from the highest level of the government and the plane was in the air for Gode.

Putting down the radio transmitter from his morning talk with his mother, Don saw his dad's gold watch on the desk, still ticking from its last winding, and slipped it on his arm. He washed his face and went out to join the mourners at the graveside. He read 2 Timothy 4:1–2:

> In the presence of God and of Christ Jesus, who will judge
> the living and the dead, and in view of his appearing and his
> kingdom, I give you this charge: Preach the Word; be
> prepared in season and out of season; correct, rebuke and
> encourage—with great patience and careful instruction.

Then he spoke through fresh tears and could not afterward remember what he had said except that his dad would always remain in Africa and his family and friends hoped and trusted that his death might be the occasion to bring many more to an understanding of God's love for them.

As the knowledge of Don McClure's death spread, a considerable correspondence was addressed to various members of the family expressing heartfelt sympathy. Some of these notes were dutiful, but many were warm and eloquent tributes of gratitude for Don's life and influence. One letter came from Otho Odier, an Anuak who had been speared through the stomach many years before and nursed back to health by Don, and who had become a Christian in the process. Later, after Otho had lost his wife in the forest, Don had comforted him. At the end of his letter Otho copied these verses from his Anuak Bible and sent them to comfort Don's family:

> I have other sheep that are not of this sheep pen. I must bring them also. They too will listen to my voice, and there shall be one flock and one shepherd. The reason my Father loves me is that I lay down my life— (John 10:16–17a).

> Do not let your hearts be troubled. Trust in God; trust also in me. In my Father's house are many rooms; if it were not so, I would have told you. I am going there to prepare a place for you. And if I go and prepare a place for you, I will come back and take you to be with me that you also may be where I am (John 14:1–3).

> We do not want you to be ignorant about those who fall asleep, or to grieve like the rest of men, who have no hope. We believe that Jesus died and rose again and so we believe that God will bring with Jesus those who have fallen asleep in him (1 Thessalonians 4:13–14).

The circle had come around. Don had devoted his life to evangelism in Africa and now the gospel was being proclaimed by these Africans in turn.

▼▲▼

The original title of this book was *Life Unto Life*, a phrase from 2 Corinthians 2:16 (KJV). It is embedded in a section that begins with thanks to God who in Christ always leads us triumphantly and through us spreads the knowledge of God everywhere. It is descriptive of, and therefore appropriate to, Don McClure and many like him, who live in constant thanksgiving to the God revealed in Jesus

Christ and in the absolute confidence that victory belongs to him and therefore to those whom he has called to the task of spreading his gospel. The passage goes on to say that we are the fragrant offering of Christ to God among those who are being saved and among those who are perishing—to one a fragrance from death to death, to the other a fragrance from life to life. Don McClure did not doubt the importance of the Christian mission in God's plan for his kingdom or the urgency of obedience to it. He accepted that there were those who went from death to death and were lost, but he believed even more firmly that there are those who—with faith in Jesus Christ—go from life to life.

Such a book title would not have been inaccurate. Don McClure did indeed believe that the good news of Jesus Christ would bring abundant life to all who believed. However, without expecting to, I became convinced that Don saw his life—and all Christian life—as an adventure . . . a venture out. More than that, it was a life filled with joy. No matter how tired or discouraged or sick or frustrated or lonely or unsuccessful he might be, Don believed that God was in control.

The ancient Greek philosophers argued long and learnedly and somberly that "happiness" or "pleasure" is the goal of human life. Christians, by contrast, insist that the goal of life is service to God and this service brings with it the deepest happiness. In other words, if God takes each of us absolutely seriously, we do not have to take our lives so seriously—we can relax and enjoy our opportunities.

Don McClure made a pilgrimage of service. He started in the desert region around Khartoum along the Nile, traveled across the lush forests of the Upper Nile plain from Doleib Hill in the Sudan on the Sobat River among the Shulla people, to Akobo on the Pibor River among the Anuaks, to Pokwo on the Baro River, to the Gilo River, to Addis Ababa, and finally across Ethiopia to Gode among the Somali people along the Webi Shebelle at the southern edge of the vast Ogaden desert.

I think if someone had asked Don to describe his life, he would have answered, with a merry twinkle in his eye, "It was fun. It was a lot of fun! I had a real adventure in Africa. Thanks be to God, who always leads us in triumph."

ACKNOWLEDGMENTS

I would like to express my appreciation—

To my editors: Michael G. Smith, Martha Manikas-Foster, James E. Ruark;

To my friends: Russell E. Grable, Jr., Carl H. Templin, Opal G. Smith, Raymond F. Luber, Gail N. Jones, and John Lowrie Anderson;

To my wife: Margaret McClure Partee—as always;

To my brother-in-law: W. Don McClure, Jr., for invaluable assistance, and

To my mother-in-law: Lyda Boyd McClure, who was there when it all happened.

A special and immense debt of gratitude is owed to
GWENDOLYN KERR

▼ NOTES

1. This book is designed primarily to tell a story rather than to recount a history. Nevertheless, the following dates in the life of Don McClure may be helpful in setting the general frame of reference:

1906	Birth
1924–28	Westminster College (Pa.)
1928–31	Khartoum, Sudan
1931–34	Pittsburgh Theological Seminary
1934–38	Doleib Hill, Sudan
1938–50	Akobo, Sudan
1950–60	Pokwo, Ethiopia
1960–62	Gilo, Ethiopia
1962–70	Addis Ababa, Ethiopia
1970–77	Gode, Ethiopia

2. My first contact with the Reverend Dr. W. Donald McClure was through an airmail letter to distant Ethiopia in which I asked, in what I took to be proper form, for his eldest daughter Margaret's hand in marriage. His return letter indicated that I could have her *hand* and inquired what I proposed to do about the rest of her? Over the following twenty years I came to respect and admire Don McClure. He was many things to many people and, happily, far from faultless. Still, what remains my dominant impression of him is that his enthusiasm was boundless, his energy relentless, his cheerfulness unnerving, and primarily, his dedication to his missionary task unlimited. He is the only man I have ever known whom I believed to be perfectly content in every situation in which he found himself: whether dining with the filthy rich or eating with the filthy poor; whether preaching the gospel to people covered with animal skins or to the entirely naked; whether flying across Europe or walking across Africa; whether conferring with an emperor or bandaging a peasant. I think it was because wherever he found himself at work, in a task large or small, he also found his God at work.

3. The vast beauty of Africa has more than once been the subject or backdrop for great movies. For the motion picture enthusiast I would mention the spectacular scenery of *Out of Africa* (with Meryl Streep and Robert Redford); the classic *African Queen* (Humphrey Bogart and Katherine Hepburn, with Robert Morley in a truly wonderful cameo role as a missionary); the delightful *Gods Must Be Crazy*. *King Solomon's Mines* (1950, Stewart Granger and Deborah Kerr) was one of the first

425

American movies to be filmed entirely on location in Africa. There is a more recent post—*Raiders of the Lost Ark* remake with Richard Chamberlain and Sharon Stone.

King Solomon's Mines is based on the adventure novel by H. Rider Haggard, which does *not* contain a leading female role (see Alan Moorehead's comment, note 24). In the book, Quatermain, patterned on Haggard himself, is a much older man. The 1937 movie version starred Paul Robeson as the native, Umbopa. The story of Major-General Charles George Gordon (note 5) is pictured in *Khartoum*, with Charlton Heston as Gordon and Laurence Olivier as an unconvincingly civilized Mahdi. Beau Bridges starred in a 1978 remake of the romantic and adventurous *Four Feathers*. I was intrigued to be told that Don McClure had helped in the splendid 1939 version of *Four Feathers*, which featured Ralph Richardson, but alas, Lyda McClure said that was not true.

The gripping story of Burton and Speke, summarized in Moorehead's *White Nile* (see note 24), appeared in a 1990 motion picture version entitled *Mountains of the Moon*.

4. The immensity and mystery of Africa's dark interior seemed to fascinate the Scots, a major component of Don's denomination. Of course, the challenge of Africa had long been known. Around the time of King David (1000 B.C.) the seafaring Phoenicians, sailing from Tyre and Sidon, established trading posts on the coast and about 820 B.C. founded the city of Carthage in northern Africa. In the poet Vergil's classic version of the legend, Carthage was founded by Dido, who fell in love with Aeneas and was abandoned by him. Centuries later, the great Christian theologian, Tertullian (A.D. 150–220), who contributed significantly to the development of the doctrine of the Trinity, was born there. About two hundred years after that, the Greeks founded the city of Cyrene, whence came Simon who carried the cross of Jesus (Matthew 27:32). Apollos (Acts 18:24) was from Alexandria—the cosmopolitan African city of the famous catechetical school of Clement (150–220) and Origen (185–245). And the greatest theologian of the first five hundred years of Christian history, St. Augustine, was bishop of Hippo in Africa. A good deal of Catholic energy that might have been used in evangelism was devoted to combatting the Donatist heresy. The Donatists, sometimes considered an African nationalist party, had some success in evangelizing the indigenous population. Still, the Greek and Roman influence was confined to the coast.

The vast interior remained essentially uncharted until James Bruce's eighteenth-century journeys in Ethiopia and Mungo Park's (1771–1806) travels along the Niger River. The nineteenth century included such daring explorers as Richard Francis Burton, John Hanning Speke, Samuel and Florence Baker, James Grant, and H. M. Stanley. Among the pioneer missionaries were Robert and Mary Moffat (who lived seven hundred miles inland at Kuruman for forty-six years); Alexander Mackay, an engineer in Uganda; and Johann Ludwig Krapf. As an explorer, Krapf and his colleague Johann Rebmann (the European discoverer of Mount Kilimanjaro) had seen snow-capped mountains in East Africa, but European geographers ridiculed them.

Perhaps the most famous explorer of them all was David Livingstone, who spent over thirty years in Africa. The now legendary Livingstone combined both the vocation of explorer *and* missionary, a fact symbolized in the title of one of his books, *Missionary Travels*. Nurtured in a strict Scottish Calvinism, Livingstone was studying medicine when he met Robert Moffat and was enthralled by the possibilities of service in Africa. Accepting Moffat's suggestion, Livingstone determined to push north of Kuruman where no missionary had ever been and where Moffat had seen the smoke of a thousand villages in the morning sun.

Arriving in Kuruman (1841), Livingstone made several forays to the north. In 1843 he was mangled by a lion and suffered a broken arm that never healed properly. While recuperating at Kuruman, Livingstone fell in love with Mary, the eldest daughter of the Moffats, and they were married in 1845.

Livingstone was convinced that Christian mission stations across the heart of Africa would help to stop the slave trade, and in 1852 he began his first great exploratory journey. Although he was now forty years old and had been in Africa eleven years, Livingstone had never suffered from malaria. While making this trip riding on an ox that he named "Sinbad," Livingstone contracted malaria and had so severe an attack of dysentery that he was unable to stay on Sinbad for more than ten minutes at a time.

In 1856, after sixteen years in Africa, Livingstone returned to England to find he was acclaimed as a hero for his geographical discoveries. Two years later he returned to Africa with the hope of blazing pathways across the continent that would promote the spread of Christianity and encourage civilized commerce. Livingstone was no longer sponsored by the London Missionary Society because they were unwilling to finance an expedition that seemed to them only indirectly connected with spreading the gospel. However, the British government was willing to support a geographical investigation of the possibility of using the Zambezi River as a trade route to the interior. In the following years, most of those who tried to follow Livingstone into the interior died of fever, including Livingstone's wife and Bishop Charles Mackenzie, whose death seemed "so useless, so foolish, so extravagant, a magnificent venture of devotion and self-sacrifice that had ended in nothing but dust and soil vanishing among the bindweed." See Owen Chadwick's splendid *Mackenzie's Grave* (London, 1959), p. 212. Chadwick's descriptions of the characters and assessments of the personalities involved are especially memorable, including David, Mary, and Charles Livingstone. In 1863 the ill-fated Zambezi expedition was recalled and Mackenzie's Africans abandoned, except that Daoma, an African girl whom Mackenzie had once carried on his shoulders, lived on to become a serene and Christian adult, dying as recently as 1937 (p. 237).

In 1866 Livingstone began his final African trek, sponsored by the Royal Geographic Society, which was interested in resolving the questions of the watersheds of central Africa, especially the Nile and the Congo. His wife had been dead four years. Their eldest son, Robert, forced to join the Northern forces in the American Civil War, had been captured and died in a prison camp at age eighteen. Beset with difficulties, Livingstone's porters deserted, leaving him with only eight men. One of the deserters returned to the coast of Zanzibar and reported that Livingstone was dead. In 1871 H. M. Stanley found Livingstone alive. After some months with him, Stanley, unable to persuade Livingstone to leave Africa, left food and medicine. Livingstone was determined to make a last attempt to find the origin of the Nile in order to obtain evidence to verify the legend that Moses had followed the river to its source.

One of Livingstone's remaining porters had dropped his astrolabe, and his calculations were off by ten to thirty miles; the party often found themselves chest-deep in swamps. On his sixtieth birthday, weak and ill, Livingstone was carried to

Chitambo's villege, where, on his knees as if in prayer, Dr. Livingstone was found dead on the morning of 13 May 1873. Livingstone's five faithful companions (including Chuma, one of Mackenzie's boys, p. 240) began a nine-month journey to the coast with his body, which was identified by the improperly set left arm that had been mauled by the lion some thirty years previously.

Before they began this journey, the heart of David Livingstone, missionary-explorer-physician, was buried in central Africa. When David Livingstone died, he had, as far as he knew, failed in *everything* he set out to accomplish. He had *not* evangelized the native people; he had *not* established Christian missions in central Africa; he had *not* ended the slave trade; he had *not* found the source of the Nile.

C. P. Groves, in *The Planting of Christianity in Africa*, 4 vols. (London, 1948–58) says that Christianity has had three opportunities in Africa. In the early Christian centuries, strong Christian churches existed in Egypt, North Africa, Abyssinia, and Nubia. The advance of Islam in the seventh century finally destroyed the Christianity of Nubia and left the Coptic Church of Egypt "much diminished in numbers and influence." The Christian church in Abyssinia has lived on, but "in enfeebling isolation." Christianity's second opportunity came seven centuries later as the Portuguese, led by Prince Henry the Navigator, found sea routes to the southern parts of Africa not reached by Islam. This church-planting opportunity faded with the decline of Portuguese power two centuries later. The third opportunity began in the closing decade of the eighteenth century (pp. vii–viii). Groves is especially relevant in 2:79–117; 3:162–74; 4:137–47. Also, J. du Plessis's *Evangelisation of Pagan Africa* (Cape Town, 1929) helpfully tells the missionary story by country.

In the nineteenth century the great African scourges, especially in the interior, were malaria, yellow fever, and dysentery. The causes and cures were unknown. Still, the missionaries (and others) came—often dying within a few days of landing. Week after week, in letters, reports, and diaries, the same story went home of sickness, grave illness, or death. The "repetition grows almost wearisome, so that the edge of pity grows dulled through very monotony" (Thorp, p. 142). Writing on the remarkable contributions of these committed people to the development of Nigeria between 1850 and 1950, Ellen Thorp claims modern Africa has climbed *A Ladder of Bones* (London, 1956).

5. According to J. K. Giffen, *The Egyptian Sudan* (New York, 1905), p. 53, Gordon's "was a life and death of magnificent power." Gordon's epitaph read:

> MAJOR-GENERAL CHARLES GEORGE GORDON:
> Who at all times and everywhere
> Gave his strength to the weak,
> His substance to the poor,
> His sympathy to the suffering,
> His heart to God.

This is cited in Charles R. Watson, *The Sorrow and Hope of the Egyptian Sudan* (Philadelphia, 1913), facing p. 60. Winston S. Churchill, in "The River War" (1899; reprinted later in his *Frontiers and Wars* [London, 1962], p. 163), writes, "That one man, a European among Africans, a Christian among Mohammedans, should by his genius have inspired the efforts of 7,000 [native soldiers], and by his courage have sustained the hearts of 30,000 inhabitants of notorious timidity, and with such materials and encumbrances have offered a vigorous resistance to the increasing attacks of an enemy who, though cruel, would yet accept surrender, during a period of 317 days, is an event perhaps without parallel in history."

In 1875 the saintly Giffen joined the legendary John Hogg (1833–1885) itinerating along the Nile. See Rena L. Hogg, *A Master-Builder on the Nile* (Pittsburgh, 1914).

6. E. A. Wallis Budge, in *The Nile: Notes for Travellers in Egypt and The Egyptian Sudan* (London, 1912), p. 97, writes of Gordon: "His head was cut off and taken to the Mahdi, but his body was left in the garden for a whole day, and thousands of Dervishes came and plunged their spears into it; later the head was thrown into a well." Before being taken to the Mahdi, Gordon's head was exhibited to the Mahdi's most distinguished prisoner, Rudolf Karl Freiherr von Slatin (see his p. 340). Born near Vienna 7 June 1857, Slatin Pasha (governor or viceroy) spent nearly forty years in Sudan. He became governor of Darfur province in 1881 and converted to Islam to improve the morale of his Sudanese troops (pp. 214–17). Von Slatin was forced to surrender to the Mahdi's troops in 1883 and was held captive until his escape in 1895. See his *Fire and Sword in the Sudan: A Personal Narrative of Fighting and Serving the Dervishes 1879–95*, trans. by F. R. Wingate (London, 1896). Von Slatin served with Horatio Herbert Kitchener, who later reconquered Sudan. For the account of another prisoner, see Father Joseph Ohrwalder, *Ten Years' Captivity in the Mahdi's Camp 1882–1892*, ed. and trans. by F. R. Wingate (London, 1892).

The translator of these books, Francis Reginald Wingate, who became the sirdar of Sudan, was the chief intelligence officer in Kitchener's victorious Sudan campaigns. According to G. W. Steevens, in *With Kitchener to Khartum* (London, 1898), pp. 85–86,

> Whatever there was to know, Colonel Wingate surely knew it, for he makes it his business to know everything. . . . If he had not chosen to be chief of the Intelligence Department of the Egyptian army, he might have been Professor of Oriental Languages at Oxford. He will learn you any language you like to name in three months.

Sir Reginald was an older relation of Orde Wingate (note 41). His translations of von Slatin's and Ohrwalder's books powerfully influenced English public opinion about Sudan.

7. In a letter of 1 April 1932, the McClures' friend Minnie McKnight wrote,

> How quickly one can turn from rejoicing to sadness. Tuesday we went over to see Mrs. Giffen. She has been in bed and quite ill for nearly a month now, but she was looking so much better and Dr. Giffen was his own dear self. He has been with Mrs. Giffen constantly. Wednesday we were having the Reeds out for tea and supper, and about 4:30 P.M. a car stopped and Mary Jane came in. I thought she had brought news that the Reeds could not come, but instead she said that Dr. Giffen had just died. We could not believe it. We were expecting Mrs. Giffen's death at any time, but not his. He had gotten up, taken his bath, and was sitting in a chair sewing on a button. Sit. [Miss] Mary, the Syrian teacher who had been with them for many years, said, "Let me do that," and Dr. Giffen smiled and replied that he could certainly sew a button. Mrs. Giffen was teasing him about his sewing and they were both laughing.

The day before, Dr. Giffen had complained about a pain in his chest and Mrs. Giffen asked him if it still hurt. He put his hand up, remarked that he had no feeling in it, and the next instant his head hung down. Mrs. Giffen rang the bell for Sit. Mary, and she tried to get him to his bed, but he had collapsed. Then they ran for Frances Turk, our nurse, and she gave Dr. Giffen a hypodermic, but he had no pulse and when the doctor came, he was dead. He really died in just about five minutes. It was a lovely way of going, with no pain or suffering, and I am sure that it would have been the way he would have wanted to die. But poor Mrs. Giffen—they thought several times she was gone, too, and it would be a blessing. We are hoping that she can live until her daughter gets here from Assiut this Sabbath. If she does linger on, it will be a problem to know what to do. She cannot travel in her condition, and her daughter probably cannot stay here indefinitely, but then God knows best and His plan will be shown soon. I am writing this in detail so that if something should happen to one of us, you will be comforted in knowing just how nicely things can be done here. When Mary Jane brought the news, James went right along with her because if a person dies here, he must be buried the same day. We expected Dr. Giffen, although he died a little after three, would have to be buried before sunset, but they did wait until early the next morning.

Mrs. Giffen had an awful time at first, but after she received some morphine she quieted a bit. James helped dress Dr. Giffen in a nice black suit. The other men were all busy getting various permissions about burial, etc. Mary Jane and Miriam went to Khartoum and bought the black cloth to be put on the outside of the coffin and white silk to line it. They padded it up with lots of cotton and worked until after midnight. Two carpenters made the box and with a rolled-edge top. Usually a body is just put in a plain wooden box and draped with a flag or something while taking it for burial. The box is closed up immediately, too. Only a few of the folks, even of our own group, saw the coffin, but those who did said it was very nice. The outside really looked like a nice coffin from home. They had to take the body to the hospital for an examination. Death was caused by the arteries feeding the heart closing up, and Dr. Hill said it was the most painless death. The coffin was taken over to Khartoum North about midnight, and James stayed on to help put the body into it. Fortunately the heat of the day cooled a bit and a nice breeze was blowing during the night. James screwed down the lid around five in the morning, and he said that if the service had been at the house, the body was in such good condition that it might have been kept open a bit.

Then they had a little service at the house for Mrs. Giffen before leaving and got to the church just at seven yesterday morning. Esther Ganter and I went to the church early and decorated it with flowers. I had taken palm branches from here, and we tied them with purple ribbon and then we had lots of vincas that were white and rose purple. We got flowers from the palace, and they happened to be single carnations (pinks) in reddish purple and white. We tied them in sprays with white bows. Then the governor sent a beautiful wreath made up of these pinks with a border in the center and white on either side banked against greens. Also Dr. Malouf sent a nice wreath. The flowers that were not in sprays were in vases on tables banked around the coffin, and it really all looked very nice. The coffin was beautiful with a lovely coral spray of a dainty vine which Gail Reed and I scattered over the top.

I have always had such a fear of death out here, for everything must be done so quickly. But after seeing how nice everything was for Dr. Giffen—just like things at home—I have an altogether different feeling now. Everyone was busy doing something to help make things just right.

Later Dr. Giffen's son-in-law bought a large marble slab to be placed on the grave and level with the ground. The following inscription was cut into the marble and filled with molten copper:

JOHN KELLY GIFFEN
1853–1932
PIONEER MISSIONARY
Lover of God and All Things Fair
Friend to Little Children
He served All Men as His Brothers
With Love Unfeigned.

According to Ried F. Shields, in *Behind the Garden of Allah* (Philadelphia, 1937), p. 9, the day of Giffen's death was in the dry season and intensely hot. Suddenly the rain began, accompanied by thunder and lightning. A Sudanese woman remarked that the storm was a sign that a saint or a prince was dying. In this case it was both. Mrs. Giffen died three months later. Tom Lambie (not always the most generous of men, see note 38), in *A Doctor Without A Country*, p. 22, wrote, "Words can never express the high regard I have always had for Doctor and Mrs. Giffen. They were all that missionaries should be. . . . Ever kind-hearted and cheery, always unselfish, always willing by every way to make Christ known, there was nothing of sanctimoniousness about them—just pure goodness shone out of every word and act." Glenn Reed, who was the executor of Dr. Giffen's will, reported that several of the letters on the slab were later vandalized for the copper.

8. In addition to its work in India (from 1855), the American Mission established African outposts in Egypt (1854), Sudan (1900), and Ethiopia (1920). Describing the indigenous peoples of the latter regions, Edward Ullendorff, *The Ethiopians: An Introduction to Country and People* (London, 1960), says that the Abyssinians proper (which includes the Amharic ruling tribe), living in the central and northern highlands of Ethiopia, have a "medium stature, long face, and a fairly straight and thin nose. . . . The hair is curly or frizzy, lips are thinner and very much less protruding than is otherwise the case in Africa. The colour of the skin varies a good deal, but is generally rather light, somewhere between olive and light brown" (pp. 33–34).

The second large group, the Oromo or Galla, is divided into some two hundred tribes occupying "an enormous area which extends from the southern tip of the Tigrai to Harar in the east, thence as far south as the Tana River in Kenya and as far west as the tributaries of the Nile. . . . In appearance they are somewhat darker than the 'classical' Abyssinian type, but they are brown rather than black. They are strongly built, of tall stature; their lips are not very thick, nor their noses flat or broad" (p. 41).

The first work of the American Mission in Ethiopia was established at Dembi Dollo among the Oromo people by Tom Lambie (note 38) and continued by others after he moved to Addis Ababa.

Besides the Oromo, the American Mission served among the Nilotic peoples of south Sudan (and in Ethiopia when Don McClure crossed the border). At Doleib Hill they worked with the Shulla (Shilluk), the Anuak at Akobo, the Dinka at Abwong, and the Murle (Beir) at Pibor. There were three Nuer stations: among the eastern Nuer at Nasir, the central Nuer at Wanglel, and the western Nuer at Ler.

The third group, the Nilotic or negroid peoples, are very dark-skinned, often blue-black. Ullendorff describes them as "dolichocephalic [long-headed] and prognathous [jaws projecting beyond the upper part of the face] and their hair is woolly. They appear to be attuned to the severe tropical climate of the western lowlands, from which all true Abyssinians recoil by ascending the cool and salubrious highlands" (p. 45). In Ullendorff's judgment, the Nilotic people "form no integral part of the life and civilization of Ethiopia" (p. 44) and are dismissed. E. E. Evans-Pritchard, *The Nuer* (Oxford, 1940), divides the Nilotes into (1) a Nuer-Dinka group, and (2) a Shilluk-Luo group. The Nuers and Dinkas are tall, long-limbed, and narrow-headed, and "their languages and customs are too similar for any doubt to arise about their common origins, though the history of their divergence is unknown." The second Nilotic subdivision comprises the Shilluk and various peoples like the Luo and Anuak whose language resembles Shilluk (p. 31).

According to S. Robb McLaughlin, who lived in East Africa from 1947 to 1988, the Nuer are a proud, noble, and aggressive people. Therefore their relations with neighbors, especially the Anuaks, are often strained. Nuer self-esteem is unlimited. In their classic survey, C. G. and Brenda Z. Seligman, *Pagan Tribes of the Nilotic Sudan* (New York, 1950), p. 212, report, "The Nuer express supreme contempt for the fighting powers and prowess of the Dinka, and say that when they go out to raid Dinka they leave their shields at home." The name *Nuer* means "people who are real people." They believe that the first Nuer descended directly from heaven, and they know the exact location of this event (between Bentiu and Ler).

Among the Nilotics the Shullas are governed by a hereditary king and the Anuaks (who also have kings) are governed by councils of older men. Nuer political structure may be described as "ordered anarchy," because no Nuer will ever agree to another Nuer's telling him what to do or how to manage his affairs. Their chiefs are democratically elected and removed from office when they become unpopular. Even in office a Nuer chief can function only when requested to do so. One of the earliest European travelers in this region was Samuel W. Baker, whose fascinating *Exploration of the Nile Tributaries of Abyssinia* (Hartford, 1868) predicts that Upper Egypt and Abyssinia (Ethiopia) are capable of development because they are inhabited by races either Mohammedan or Christian "while Central Africa is peopled by a hopeless race of savages for whom there is no prospect of civilization" (p. x). Among these people, according to Baker, the Nuer is "one of the wildest savages of the White Nile" (p. 141). However, Baker was quite captivated by the Galla (Oromo) women of southern Ethiopia.

> On my return to camp, I visited the establishments of the various slave merchants: these were arranged under large tents formed of matting, and contained many young girls of extreme beauty, ranging from nine to seventeen years of age. These lovely captives, of a rich brown tint, with

delicately formed features, and eyes like those of the gazelle, were natives of the Galla, on the borders of Abyssinia, from which country they were brought by the Abyssinian traders to be sold for the Turkish harems. Although beautiful, these girls are useless for hard labor; they quickly fade away and die unless kindly treated. They are the Venuses of that country, and not only are their faces and figures perfection, but they become extremely attached to those who show them kindness, and they make good and faithful wives. There is something peculiarly captivating in the natural grace and softness of those young beauties, whose hearts quickly respond to those warmer feelings of love that are seldom known among the sterner and coarser tribes. Their forms are peculiarly elegant and graceful; the hands and feet are exquisitely delicate; the nose is generally slightly aquiline, the nostrils large and finely shaped; the hair is black and glossy, reaching to about the middle of the back, but rather coarse in texture (pp. 533–34).

9. According to Evelyn Baring—the Earl of Cromer—in *Modern Egypt*, 2 vols. (London, 1900), the authorized version of the conditions under which the true Mahdi was expected to appear include the belief that "[h]is advent shall coincide with that of Anti-Christ, after whom Jesus will descend and join himself to the Mahdi" (1:352). Steevens, in *With Kitchener to Khartum*, gives an enthralling eyewitness account of the movement, engagements, and the final battle of Kitchener's army with the Mahdi's forces at Omdurman. Likewise he gives a fascinating account of the funeral of Gordon fourteen years after his death. According to Steevens, the British had vindicated their honor and the Sudan had gained immunity from rape and torture and every extreme of misery. Then he bursts out:

> The poor Sudan! The wretched, dry Sudan! [I]t is not a country: it has neither nationality, not history, nor arts, not even natural features. Just the Nile—the niggard Nile refusing himself to the desert—and for the rest there is absolutely nothing to look at in the Sudan. . . . For beasts it has tarantulas and scorpions and serpents, devouring white ants, and every kind of loathsome bug that flies or crawls. Its people are naked and dirty, ignorant and besotted. It is a quarter of a continent of sheer squalor. Overhead the pitiless furnace of the sun, under foot the never-easing treadmill of the sand, dust in the throat, tuneless singing in the ears, searing flame in the eye—the Sudan is a God-accursed wilderness, an empty limbo of torment for ever and ever.

Steevens cites the Arab proverb that says, "Drink of Nile water and you will return to drink it again" and concludes, "I do not believe that any of us who come home whole will think, from our easy chairs, unkindly of the Sudan" (pp. 382–84). See also his sybaritic account of Sudan-induced thirst (pp. 242–49).

Horatio Herbert Kitchener, British secretary of state for war at the beginning of World War I, was lost at sea in 1916 when his ship was sunk by a German mine. In the cathedral at Khartoum there is a bronze effigy of the hero of Omdurman with this inscription: "The unrelenting giant, who above war's din, held his grave course and labored mightily, now beyond toil and clamor sleeps within the unresting bosom of the eternal sea" (reported by H. C. Jackson, *Pastor of the Nile—Llewellyn H. Gwynne* [London, 1960], p. 133). For a comprehensive account of the recapture of Sudan, including an astonishing grasp of the geopolitical situation, see Churchill, *The River War*. In the Battle of Omdurman, Churchill took part in the charge of the 21st Lancers.

10. On the history of Christianity in northern Sudan, see chapter 15 of E. A. Wallis Budge's massive and wonderful *Egyptian Sudan: Its History and Monuments*, 2 vols. (Philadelphia, 1907). Budge surveys the modern missionary enterprise in chapter 16, noting the sensational story of Alexandrine Tinne, the richest heiress in the Netherlands, who attempted at enormous expense to explore the White Nile and its tributaries including the Sobat. In 1869 this wealthy, beautiful, and adventurous young woman was hacked to death by Tuareg tribesmen who wrongly believed she was carrying gold hidden in her iron water-chests. For a dated account, see William Wells, *The Heroine of the White Nile, or What a Woman Did and Dared* (New York, 1871). A recent biography of this "capricious, self-opinionated, and dominating" woman is Penelope Gladstone's *Travels of Alexine: Alexine Tinne: 1835–1869* (London, 1970). See also Harry Johnston, *The Nile Quest* (London, 1903), pp. 192–99. This latter book and its author, lacking the perspective that only the passing of time provides and the benefits of the winnowing process that determines books based on other books, has the immense advantage of being contemporary or almost contemporary with the persons and events it describes. For example, on the basis of a personal letter from his aunt, John Tinne challenged the author's statement (repeated in other books) that Alexandrine went to Africa chiefly as the result of "a serious love disappointment" (p. 194). Moreover, in 1903 the great John Kirk (d. 1922) was still living. Kirk, later of Zanzibar, had served with David Livingstone in central Africa from 1858 to 1863.

Johnston, himself an African explorer, writes of other contemporaries, such as Lady Baker (d. 1916): "As already related, she was a Hungarian lady of great beauty, and possessed of extraordinary courage. Her fame as 'The Lady' ('Es-sitt') still lingers among the Nile negroes" (p. 182)—see note 24. Florence Baker's courage would be evident to anyone who read Samuel Baker's books, but presumably (and unlike Alan Moorehead, *The White Nile*) Johnston was an eye-witness to her beauty and an ear-witness to her fame. *The Nile Quest* also contains wonderful pictures, including one of Alexandrine Tinne (facing p. 193), Colonel J. B. Marchand (facing p. 286), and a sketch of J. H. Speke by the author.

11. Years later, Don and his daughter Marghi had tea with the grandson of the Mahdi. Since the men spoke Arabic, Marghi could not follow the conversation. Another time, riding a tram in Omdurman, when Don was explaining to his three children the events that had taken place there, a fellow passenger showed the children some bullets that had been fired in the battle and that he had recently dug up in his garden.

The prime minister of Sudan (1980–89) was the great-grandson of the Mahdi. Oxford-educated Sadiq al Mahdi (b. 1936) led the mediation mission to obtain the release of the American hostages from Iran in January 1980.

12. In the dark days of the late 1930s the McKnights returned to America. Minnie's mother was in failing health and needed constant care. Minnie herself had severe eye problems that were exacerbated by the fierce African sun. However, Jim was needed so badly at the J. Kelly Giffen Agricultural School in Gereif that he started back to Africa alone through a world at war. His ship, the *Zam Zam*, flying an Egyptian flag, was sunk by a German raider, but all the passengers were rescued.

Those holding British passports were sent to German internment camps, but the Egyptians and Americans—whose nations were still neutral at that time—were set ashore in Portugal. The McKnights at home heard on one day that Jim's ship had gone down and received word the next day that Jim was safe. Jim McKnight was not able to get through to Africa and returned to America for the rest of his life, leaving a large part of his heart in Africa—and as a result was another casualty of Hitler's war.

Don McClure wrote from Doleib Hill concerning the sinking of the *Zam Zam:*

> We greatly rejoice in the safety of the people, especially Jim McKnight, but his loss to our work here will be keenly felt, especially since we are already shorthanded in the Sudan. We have had no word from Jim directly, but I assume that all my ammunition is at the bottom of the sea and how I needed it! I have only thirty rounds left for the Winchester .405, and those I could fire off in a month at crocodiles. It will go against my grain to see the huge brutes swim past unmolested, but I must save the remaining ammunition to shoot our meat supply. We are sorry to have lost the other things that were sent out to us, too. We need some of them badly. I am almost out of shirts, and poor Lyda and the youngsters are running around in rags. We heard only yesterday from Mrs. Shields that parcel post has been resumed from America, so we are going to send off an order to Montgomery Ward immediately for some of the things we need most.

13. The anecdote regarding Don's trousers was related by the Reverend Myles W. MacDonald at a dinner inaugurating the annual W. Don McClure Lectures in World Missions and Evangelism at Pittsburgh Theological Seminary. Lyda McClure responded by noting that Don often added *her* jewelry to *his* giveaways.

14. In early manhood, Glenn Reed's heart and mind was fired by Samuel M. Zwemer's book *Raymund Lull: First Missionary to the Moslems* (New York, 1902). The overflowing love of God revealed in Jesus Christ impelled Lull (1235–1315) to Africa and Glenn Reed made the same commitment. Glenn, a college friend of Don's oldest brother, Bob, was the one who first suggested that Don McClure spend some time in Africa.

15. George Albert Sowash, D.D., was born in 1867 of French Huguenot stock. The original name "Sauvage" was changed when the family fled through Holland on their way to America. Of the branch that settled to farm in western Pennsylvania, George was the eldest son in a large family. Determined to get an education, Sowash entered Westminster College (New Wilmington, Pennsylvania) and later attended Pittsburgh Theological Seminary. After ordination in 1896 he went to Egypt as a missionary. In 1903 he married Kathleen Geraldine Spring, and they were soon transferred to Khartoum. All five of the Sowash children were born in Africa. About 1908 a mission station was opened in Omdurman, across the Nile where Sowash established a boys' school and a Christian church. During World War I, he was principal of the girls' school in Khartoum North. In 1924 Sowash spent a year alone at Doleib Hill, writing vivid descriptions of the rivers, birds, animals, plants, and trees that were so different from the arid, desert country around Khartoum. In 1926 he spent two furlough years building a house in New Wilmington where his children could live while attending college and where he and his wife could retire. In 1928 he returned to Sudan alone, to be joined a year later by his wife and the youngest children. In 1933 the youngest son became seriously ill, and Sowash rushed back to America to help in his care—never again to return to Africa. He spent the last nineteen years of his life serving various churches in western Pennsylvania. He died 26 May 1952 and is buried in New Wilmington.

Sowash had been blessed with a marvelous sense of humor. He advised all new missionaries to wear a pith helmet, drink two glasses of water every morning, take a siesta every afternoon, and practice a sport—his own being tennis and, in later years, golf. Sowash was a great student of classical Greek and Arabic, spending some time every day, even into his eighties, at his desk reading aloud in a low voice from his Greek or Arabic Bible. His wife, Kathleen Spring Sowash, was also an excellent linguist. She had an extraordinary knowledge of French and German and, of course, colloquial Arabic and to a lesser degree modern Greek and Italian. She died 10 May 1962 and is buried beside her husband.

George Sowash was a father figure to the Sudan missionaries of the American Mission, and his understanding of the ways of British diplomacy was especially helpful to Glenn Reed.

16. Theodore Roosevelt visited Doleib Hill on his way down the Nile. He was welcomed by Ralph W. Tidrick (note 26), and Mrs. McCreery (note 38) baked some bread for the former president. Later, in a public address at Khartoum, Roosevelt said, "I stopped a few days ago at the little Mission Station on the Sobat. One of the things that struck me there was what was being done by the medical side of that mission. . . . If you make it evident to a man that you are sincerely trying to better his body, he will be much more ready to believe that you are trying to better his soul." This is cited by Watson in *The Sorrow and Hope of the Egyptian Sudan*, p. 169.

17. According to Winston Churchill, *My African Journey* (1908; reprint, London, 1962), pp. 131–32, the sudd is a vast, appalling, dismal, horrible, and terrifying swamp into which the whole of the United Kingdom could be packed. "Rising fifteen feet above the level of the water, stretching its roots twenty or even thirty feet below, and so matted and tangled together that elephants can walk safely on its springy surface, papyrus is the beginning and end of this melancholy world. For hundreds of miles nothing else is to be perceived. . . . To travel through the *sudd* is to hate it forever." The White Nile flows some 1,800 miles from its source at Lake Victoria, and the Blue Nile some 1000 miles to the Mediterranean Sea. It is estimated that one-half the total flow of the mighty Nile, the longest river in the world, is lost to evaporation in the sudd, which defeated Nero's two centurions (Johnston, *The Nile Quest*, pp. 20–21). See also the immensely learned E. A. Wallis Budge's work *The Nile: Notes for Travellers in Egypt and in the Egyptian Sudan*. Working through this hefty, thousand-page handbook is a journey all of its own.

For an anthropological survey of the Shulla, Dinka, Nuer, and Anuak, see Seligman, *Pagan Tribes of the Nilotic Sudan*. During Mussolini's African war, Seligman's great student, Edward Evan Evans-Pritchard (professor of social anthropology at Oxford 1946–70), led a band of Anuak volunteers in resisting Italian incursions into southwest Ethiopia. During this time the warrior-scholar lived in the McClures' house at Akobo, and when he was not fighting, Evans-Pritchard spent his time compiling a dictionary of Anuak words that he left behind for Don McClure to use. In the Fontana Modern Masters series, Mary Douglas's book *Evans-Pritchard* (Glasgow, 1980) assesses his contribution. See E. E. Evans-Pritchard, *The Political System of the Anuak of the*

Anglo-Egyptian Sudan (London, 1940). Also his "Further Observations on the Political System of the Anuak," *Sudan Notes and Records,* 28 (1947), pp. 62–63, which offers a tribute to the loyalty and courage of the Anuak soldier. In addition, Evans-Pritchard wrote *The Nuer; Kinship and Marriage Among the Nuer* (Oxford, 1951); *Nuer Religion* (Oxford, 1956). *The Nuer* is dedicated to the staff of the American Mission at Nasir "not only as an expression of personal gratitude, but also as a tribute to their devoted service to the Nuer." Special mention is made of Blanche Soule (see note 70) who owned the white tablecloth that Don McClure used as a flag when he ran behind enemy lines (p. 176 of this book).

Divinity and Experience: The Religion of the Dinka (Oxford, 1961) is a splendid study of the Dinka done by Evans-Pritchard's good friend and close associate, Godfrey Lienhardt. According to one estimate, a million Dinka were taken away in slave raids. Ron Trudinger, M.D., an Australian who spent many years with the Sudan United Mission, was asked to come out of retirement when the American Mission began work at Abwong (1945). His task was to translate the New Testament into the Dinka language.

18. Don McClure wrote,

> I remembered the advice saintly W. B. Anderson tendered in the last letter I received from him and while he was on his deathbed. He wrote, ". . . and Don, when you are out looking for lions, don't stick your head into danger, because your first task in Africa is to save souls and not shoot lions. However, the next time you happen to see a lion, give me a thought. I sure would like to have the strength to join you in one of your adventures."

19. The Shullas are also known as Shilluks, a transliteration of the Arabic name for this tribe. See Diedrich Westermann, *The Shilluk People: Their Language and Folklore* (Philadelphia, 1912). Westermann (1875–1956), a missionary for a short time in Togo, was forced to return to Germany for health reasons. However, his brief experience in Africa revealed such phenomenal linguistic gifts that he was attached to the University of Berlin as Professor of African Languages and Director of the International Institute of African Languages and Cultures.

20. At the first outposts of the American Mission in south Sudan—Doleib Hill and Nasir—the rapid spread of infections made death from tropical disease an ever-present reality. On 12 December 1920 Mary Elizabeth was born to the David S. Oylers at Melut, Sudan. In a family diary her mother wrote,

> On 13 March 1921 we started home on furlough to America with our three children David II, John Henry and Betty. We had not traveled many miles on the White Nile steamer before it became evident that our curly, black-haired baby girl was desperately ill. Betty died at midnight on 16 March and was buried early the next morning at Renk about 150 miles north of Doleib Hill. She was three and one-half months old. The next year, as we were returning to Doleib Hill on another White Nile steamer, John Henry took sick, and in less than ten hours he too was gone (11 November 1922). John Henry lived three and one-half years. My little boy is buried under a big shady tree at Melut where Mary Elizabeth was born.

Late in 1924, Howard Buchanan, M.D., who was serving on the staff of the American Mission hospital in Assiut, Egypt, volunteered to go to Nasir for one year to replace a physician on furlough.

Older missionaries tried without success to dissuade Buchanan from taking his wife, Vera, and two children, Helen (age seven) and Rachael (three months), to such an isolated and primitive place. Nevertheless, the Buchanans set out from Assiut in high spirits even though the temperature was over one hundred degrees. From Aswan to Shellal they traveled by a narrow-gauge train and from Shellal to Wadi Halfa by riverboat. From Wadi Halfa to Khartoum, the Buchanans rode Sudan Railway through desolate country in which the crew was often required to stop and shovel sand off the track. In those days missionaries paid for second-class accommodations but traveled first class, since the British government did not want white people to travel any other way.

Arriving in Khartoum, the Buchanans were met by the bearded Dr. Giffen, who escorted them to the American Mission compound. There they made preparations for the twelve-day trip to Nasir. Boats only ran every two weeks, and the next one had a Sudanese captain who would not serve meals on board. Since women were not permitted into the hold of the boat to prepare food, Dr. Giffen hired an Arab cook for them.

The boat, a wood-burning paddle wheeler, stopped often for fuel at isolated stations where workmen could spend twelve hours loading wood. Turning into the Sobat, and after a short stop at Doleib Hill, the steamer made its way 180 miles farther up the Sobat to Nasir. At Nasir the Buchanans were welcomed by a party that included thirty or forty seven-foot and completely naked Nuers, each carrying a club and a spear. In honor of his arrival the Nuers presented Dr. Buchanan with a club and two spears. One was a spiked fishing spear and the other a fighting spear that had been made by Kogenbec, who had attacked the lion that had mauled Ralph Tidrick (see note 26).

The Buchanans moved into a house in which scorpions were so numerous that the family had to give up the practice of kneeling for prayer! Moreover, bats hung from the ceiling during the day and flew about at night. Once Vera Buchanan killed a cobra in her kitchen, and a viper was discovered in the folds of a bedquilt.

The meat they ate came largely from the men's game hunts: antelope, birds, gazelle, white-eared cob (waterbuck), and tiang (a species of small antelope). One day Dr. Buchanan brought down fourteen ducks with two shots. The mission feasted on these ducks and gave their servants all they could eat. The servants even chewed up the bones and licked the plates as they carried them from the table to the kitchen. In this part of Africa, flour had to be sifted *every week* to remove weevils and worms. In addition, for protection from white ants (termites), wooden table legs and bedsteads had to be placed in pans of water.

On 7 December 1924 Cuthbert B. Guthrie, who had served as an agriculturalist for sixteen years, died from an infection following malaria. On 25 January 1925 his daughter, Mary Catherine, was born to his widow. When Dr. Buchanan told Mrs. Guthrie that she had delivered a beautiful baby girl, she said, "But I don't have a husband to share her with." Less than a month later (17 February) Anna B. Guthrie died of malaria. Her last words were, "Oh, Cuthbert, I see you." In the space of two months at Doleib Hill, the Guthrie children lost both their parents.

A few months later, after experiencing excruciating pain, Dr. Buchanan saw his nine-month-old daughter for the last time. Dr. Buchanan went blind apparently because he caught an infection from a Shulla he had been treating. Buchanan was never able to practice medicine again and returned to America to earn his living selling life insurance. Buchanan was a member of the first class in America (1929) to learn to use a seeing-eye dog. "Gala," a German shepherd, was imported from Switzerland. The first dogs were trained not only as guides but as guards. Therefore the Buchanans had to buy new garments for the postman and the iceman when Gala, protecting her master, tore their clothing.

Dr. Buchanan's church, grateful for his sacrifice, refused to accept his resignation as a missionary and paid him a furlough salary as long as he lived. Both the Buchanans and the McLaughlins, his wife's family, had provided funds toward Howard's medical education with the understanding that the money was a contribution to world missions. Because his blindness prevented his serving as a missionary physician, Howard Buchanan, M.D., insisted on repaying every cent—completing his task shortly before he died. After suffering a heart attack, on 2 January 1945 Dr. Buchanan was sitting up in his hospital bed with his head resting on the pillows. "Suddenly," his wife writes, "Howard raised both his arms and looked upward. A beautiful smile came over his face. I knew at once that after twenty years of blindness he had seen a glimpse of the glories of heaven." For part of their story, see Vera and Howard Buchanan, *The Promise* (Nashville, 1929).

Traveling back to the United States, in addition to the four Buchanans, were the Heastys, who brought the three bewildered Guthrie children (Dorothy, Franklin, David) and baby Mary Catherine back with them. The children were scattered among relatives in Santa Ana (Calif.), Los Angeles, St. Louis, and Ithaca (N.Y.). It would be twenty years until they were together again.

Cuthbert and Anna Guthrie and J. Alfred Heasty (who died of a heart attack in 1951) are buried at Doleib Hill. In the hallway just outside my office is a small brass plaque that reads:

> Corridor in memory of
> Rev. J. A. Heasty, D.D.
> by Alfred R. Heasty, M.D.

I must have walked past this plaque hundreds of times without noticing it until I began to write this book.

The way the missionaries treated the Shullas was in marked contrast to how the Mahdists treated them. About 1890, the Mahdists, who had been buying grain from the Shullas to feed their armies, decided it would be cheaper to conquer and occupy Shulla territory. According to von Slatin,

> The Shilluks, however, who are the finest and bravest of the Sudanese Black tribes, collected both north and south of Fashoda, and defended their liberty and their homes with magnificent courage and resolution; but [the Mahdists] used to constant fighting, and armed with Remington rifles, were almost invariably victorious. It was not, however, until after many bloody fights, in which the Shilluks, armed only with their lances, frequently broke the squares and inflicted considerable loss on the soldiers that they had at last to admit they were beaten.

Dispersing through the country, the Shullas were pursued by the Mahdists, and large numbers of them were captured. The men were killed, but the women, young girls, and children were sent into slavery at Omdurman (*Fire and Sword in the Sudan,* pp. 471–72). Of the American missionaries in Sudan, an old Shulla once told his grandson, "The Arabs came through our land to take our people away and make slaves of them. These Christians came to live among us and to make us free. And they died here."

21. Since all the Shullas except royalty removed the four lower incisor teeth, it was difficult for missionaries who had these teeth to emulate the pronunciation of those who did not. Shulla royalty may have kept their teeth because they had no garment or document to demonstrate their status.

In order to translate the account of Jesus' death into the Shulla language, Heasty asked a native speaker for the word describing the group of stars that we call the Southern Cross. He used that term for "cross" until he discovered that the Shullas were being taught that Jesus was crucified on a fish! That is, the Shullas saw a fish rather than a cross in the heavenly constellation. Heasty had not yet finished translating the New Testament into the Shulla language when he died in 1951.

22. Watson, in *The Sorrow and Hope of the Egyptian Sudan,* pp. 112–13, describes the Shulla tribal marks as three, four, or five rows of dots across the forehead. "Most striking of all, however, are the head dresses of the men. The hair is woven or twisted into a solid felt, kept further in shape by mixtures of gum, mud or even cow-dung, and molded into the shape of a huge saucer, or of a single horn bent forward, or in separate points standing out like the spokes of a wheel. The hair of the face, even to the eyebrows, is ordinarily pulled out, heightening the weirdness of their appearance." To preserve the hairdresser's art during the hours of sleep (as well as to keep the face out of the dust), the men of various East African tribes use a small piece of wood in the shape of a *T* as a pillow to support the neck, leaving the coiffure unmussed. This pillow, standing about nine inches, doubles as a very small stool and, with the spear or club, is carried on all journeys.

23. All the Nilotic peoples, including the Nuer, Shulla, and Anuaks, are, to varying degrees, cattle people. Therefore cattle are the object of endless legal disputes. According to a Nuer fable, in the beginning all creatures had drums, but Man stole the drums of Buffalo and Cow so that they were no longer able to dance. In his fury Buffalo said, "Whenever I see Man I will attack him." Cow said, "Not I. I will go live with Man and make his life miserable with litigation."

24. For the nineteenth-century background, see Alan Moorehead's marvelous book *The White Nile* (New York, 1960). Samuel Baker and Major-General Gordon had done their best to stop the slave trade, which David Livingstone called the "open sore of the world" (p. 119). By one estimate, the slave trade cost 100 million African lives! Moorehead discusses Baker (see note 3) when he outlines the exploration of the African interior and the search for the source of the Nile. He judges that the explorers Speke and Grant were too bizarre and at the same time too pedestrian; Burton was too esoteric except for the sophisticated few; Dr. Livingstone lived on a high moral plane beyond the average reach.

But Baker's book *The Albert N'yanza* was just right; he and his wife had the sort of reactions that everyone could enjoy and understand. One suffered and lived vicariously with this couple in the terrible African jungle just as one lived with the characters in a novel. And how brave she was. How gallant and determined he was. [This book contains] the ingredients of almost all African adventure stories that have been written from that day to this. Here is Allan Quatermain in his broad-brimmed hat setting forth into the jungles with a young and lovely girl at his side, and they face every hazard with marvelous determination. When wild beasts charge, Baker with his deadly aim stops them in their tracks. At the outset of the journey he quells a mutiny among his own men by striking down the ringleader with his fist. Then, as they advance, all their baggage animals die and they are forced to ride oxen, their food supplies fail and they are reduced to eating grass, fever lays them prostrate for days and weeks on end, deceitful guides mislead them, hippopotamuses overturn their boats, the slave-traders cheat them, the tribes attack with poisoned arrows, and they are never for long out of sight and hearing of the war drums and savage dancing. Through it all Mrs. Baker never flinches. "She was not a *screamer*," her husband says. When she hears stealthy footsteps approaching their hut at night she quietly touches him on the sleeve and he reaches for his revolver to deal with the intruder (pp. 95, 87–88).

Samuel Baker truly loved and enjoyed the challenge of Africa. As he prepared to leave, he established his loyal African companion, Richarn, and his wife as private servants to the master of Shepheard's Hotel in Cairo. "I left my old servant with a heart too full to say good-bye; a warm squeeze of his rough, but honest black hand, and the whistle of the train sounded,—we were off!" And then this touching tribute,

> [T]he past appeared like a dream—the rushing sound of the train renewed ideas of civilization. Had I really come from the Nile sources? It was no dream. A witness sat before me; a face still young, but bronzed like an Arab by years of exposure to a burning sun; haggard and worn with toil and sickness, and shaded with cares, happily now past; the devoted companion of my pilgrimage, to whom I owed success and life—my wife (*The Albert N'yanza, Great Basin of the Nile and Explorations of the Nile Sources* [London, 1867], 2:338–39).

For a traditional biography, see Dorothy Middleton's *Baker of the Nile* (London, 1949). According to Richard Hall's racy *Lovers on the Nile: The Incredible African Journeys of Sam and Florence Baker* (New York, 1980), pp. 27–29, Florence, the frail, golden-haired girl, "the love of his life, his companion in adventures that would make his name familiar to millions," was *purchased* by Baker at a Turkish slave auction on the Danube.

On this trip to the Balkans, Baker traveled with the young Maharajah Duleep Singh, who had been retired to England on a pension when Great Britain took the country of his father, who was the last of the kings of the Punjab. Duleep Singh became a Christian at age twelve, partly under the influence of Bhajun Lal, a young Brahmin, who had been educated as part of the American Mission's work in India. In 1864, when the Maharajah decided to marry, he wrote to the American Mission in Egypt inquiring if they had under their care a young Christian girl, native to the East, who might be a suitable wife for him. Visiting Egypt, he fell in love with "a sweet face in the Mission Girls' School" (Charles R. Watson, *Egypt and the Christian Crusade* [Philadelphia, 1907], pp. 164–65). Bamba Müller (between fifteen and sixteen years of age) was the illegitimate, although adopted, daughter of a German father and an Abyssinian mother. After some soul-searching, the missionaries agreed to give their blessing to the marriage. In appreciation the Maharajah made an annual contribution to the American Mission on the anniversary of his wedding. Mrs. S. B. Lansing of the American Mission, Bamba's teacher and life-long friend, was at her bedside when she died in 1887 (Andrew Watson, *The American Mission in Egypt* [Pittsburgh, 1898], pp. 468–69). For a full account of the troubled life of the Maharajah and Maharani, see Michael Alexander and Sushila Anand, *Queen Victoria's Maharajah: Duleep Singh: 1838–93* (New York, 1980).

25. The tuga nut, which grows on the Doleib palm, is about the size of a grapefruit and has a strange strawberry-pineapple smell. Until the missionaries came to Doleib Hill, it was the Shullas' only fruit. According to John Dransfield in "Palmae," in *Flora of Tropical East Africa*, ed. by R. M. Polhill (Boston, 1986), p. 21, not only man and elephant, but lions are fond of this extremely fragrant fruit. For this reference I am indebted to Professor Carl R. Partanen.

26. Ralph W. Tidrick was a man of magnificent physique, an Iowa farm boy, and a veteran of the Spanish-American War who had spent many months in the Philippines. He had gained fame as a football player at Iowa State University. Tidrick was working with the American Mission as an agriculturalist when he was asked to shoot some lions that were stealing sheep and cows and terrorizing the people in a village near Malakal. Starting off early in the morning, Tidrick and his Shulla guides soon spotted three lions. With his Winchester .405, Tidrick quickly felled two lions and wounded the other, which ran off. When Tidrick approached the wounded lion, he thought to finish off the animal with a smaller-caliber bullet. However, while Tidrick was half-turned to reach for his smaller rifle, the lion sprang upon him with a roar, knocking the rifle from his hand. Tidrick tried to throttle the lion bare-handed, but was overcome by the snarling animal. Tidrick fell on a small stump and broke his ribs, one of which perforated the right lung.

The Shullas had run away, but because of Tidrick's repeated calls for help, one faithful friend returned. Kogenbec was unable to shoot the lion both because the man and animal were intertwined and because he did not know how to work the mechanism of the automatic shotgun. Therefore he tried to kill the lion with his spear, but his fear was so great and his aim so bad that he drove the spear into Tidrick's heel instead of the lion. Reaching down, Tidrick pulled the spear from his heel and cut the lion's throat with the spear edge. He was then able to stand and stagger to the shade of a tree, but he could go no further. Because Tidrick attempted to protect his head and neck during the struggle, both his hands had been severely mangled.

> Because of the intense heat and loss of blood, he was thirsty and sent the natives to the river for water. They were a long time in returning, and when they came at last he spoke of the delay. They told him that beneath a clump of trees a few hundred yards away they had seen three other lions and they had to make a circuit to go around them. At this Tidrick looked at his

mangled hands and said, "I believe I could crawl to those trees, if only I could shoot."

Tidrick was carried to the river, and a passing steamer took him to Khartoum, where he died and was buried two days later on 21 April 1914. See Lambie's *Doctor Without a Country*, pp. 28, 52–53. Ralph W. Tidrick was the first member of the American Mission to be buried in Sudan. In Khartoum in 1977, Eathel Tidrick Mendenhall's son, Gordon, tried to locate his grandfather's grave without success.

27. Jesse Owens (1913–1980) was known as "the world's fastest human." Born in Alabama and educated at Ohio State University, Owens won four gold medals in the 1936 Olympic games at Munich. Adolf Hitler regarded these record-setting and record-tying victories by a black American as a threat to his Nazi theory of the Aryan master race. So Hitler walked out of the stadium to avoid congratulating the Olympic champion.

28. Some of Don McClure's letters, including this one, were compiled by Marion Fairman under the title *Redheaded, Rash, and Religious* (Philadelphia, 1954).

29. Exactly one year later (23 October 1937), which he had forgotten was the first anniversary of John's death, Don woke up in terror while it was still dark. He was afraid that something awful had happened to his wife and daughter, but was reassured by their quiet breathing.

> Then I wondered why I was experiencing such coldness in my soul and panic in my breast. Suddenly John spoke to me, and I heard his voice say, "Quiet your fears, I am not dead but alive." The next hour was the richest of my life. Johnny and I talked as we never talked before. I longed to go over and be with him. I know he is happy, and his prayers for us are messengers of light and strength.

30. In the old days the Shulla priest-king was not allowed to die naturally, but was put to death along with at least four of his wives. The king was strangled, and his body was robed and laid on a bed in one of the royal huts. Two of his wives were placed as guardians of his body and given pipes, tobacco, and water, but no food. Then the doors and windows were sealed shut so that escape was impossible. No one was permitted to say, "The king is dead," but they could say, "The great one is missing." After a month, when the termites had worked through the roof, demonstrating that no one was left alive, the bodies were removed and put in a canoe. Two more of the king's wives were bound with rope and also placed in the canoe, which was sunk in the middle of the river as a sacrifice to the crocodile god. The British stopped this practice when they occupied the Sudan in 1898. See Lambie's *Doctor Without a Country*, p. 31.

31. In July 1898, six weeks before the battle of Omdurman, Captain Jean-Baptiste Marchand and a handful of French soldiers arrived at Fashoda, completing a two-year, three-thousand-mile march across Africa. His purpose was to seize the valley of the Upper Nile in the name of France, make an alliance with Menelik in Abyssinia, and forestall the British influence in Sudan that was advancing up the river with Kitchener's great army. According to Moorehead in *The White Nile*, p. 340, "[H]ardly anything more provocative, more hopeless of accomplishment or more audacious could have been imagined." In addition, it was unintelligible that Marchand chose Fashoda, because it was a miserable and pestilential place whose "only claim to fame was that it was the headquarters of the priest-king of the Shilluk tribe" (p. 341). Churchill devotes a chapter to "The Fashoda Incident" in *The River War*.

32. Because of rampant tropical diseases, the British government did not want women to go south of Khartoum and believed that the Akobo area was not safe for women and children. They especially did not want to allow Don to bring his family to Akobo to live in a native hut. Permission was finally granted, but only on the condition that Lyda could keep the children healthy. This involved keeping them in the house after dark and away from the swarms of mosquitoes. When the children protested their father's going out after dark, Lyda explained that mosquitoes could not bite Don because of all the hair on his body. Thus the McClure children sat down and waited impatiently for hair to grow on their arms.

33. The Nuers, except for married women, are naked. Men cover their bodies with ashes until they are a grayish-white. Their hair grows long and makes a flowing mane, which is bleached yellow by the application of cow-dung ashes. Girls pierce a hole in their upper lip in which, for decoration, they may wear a flower or a nail with the sharp point sticking out. See Shields, *Behind the Garden of Allah*, p. 158.

For an early account of the Nuer by a nurse who spent her long career with the American Mission in Sudan, see Ray Huffman, *Nuer Customs and Folklore* (Oxford, 1931; repr. 1970). The Nasir station is pictured facing page 65. A recent children's book, *What's So Funny, Ketu? A Nuer Tale*, retold by Verna Aardema with pictures by Marc Brown (New York, 1982) is based on Huffman. Apparently the artist had not read, or chose to ignore, Huffman's descriptions of the forehead scarring of all Nuer men and of the married women wearing white beads (not gold hoops) in their ears.

34. This citation is a paraphrase from Langdon Gilkey's fascinating account of life in a Chinese internment camp, *Shantung Compound* (New York, 1966), p. 177.

35. "The first principle of Protestant missions has been that Christians should have the Bible in their hands in their own language at the earliest possible date," according to Stephen Neill in *A History of Christian Missions* (New York, 1964), p. 209. Don wrote,

> Two weeks ago I received the greatest Christmas gift ever—the first complete printed copy of the Anuak New Testament. I had started to translate the New Testament into Anuak way back in 1944 and worked on it sporadically until 1950, when Harvey Hoekstra [see note 44] joined us to do translation work. He revised what I had done and then during the next ten years completed a draft of the entire New Testament. It went through four or five revisions and was finally accepted by the American Bible Society about a year ago. They completed the printing and binding in November 1962 and sent some copies out to us. Those copies that were sent to the Sudan were confiscated by the government, and Harvey was given seven days to leave the country! This eviction does not make any sense at all. The Sudan government knew that Harvey was doing this translation and had seen copies of the various books as they were completed. In addition, a copy of the complete manuscript had been sent to the government at the same time

it was sent to the Bible Society. At least we are glad that the Sudan waited until the translation was finished before they kicked the Hoekstras out.

I feel the New Testament is the greatest gift we can give the Anuak people. By having the whole New Testament in their own language, the Anuak church has come to age. They will never slip back into paganism again, nor will pagan practices creep into the church even if we must all leave. Now the Anuaks have the Word of God to guide them, and thousands can already read it. We still have a tremendous task to complete the transliteration of the Roman script into the Amharic script, but Jim and Aurelia Keefer are working on that and making good progress. Still, it will be three years before they finish. Then we will have the Anuak Bible in two different scripts—the Roman for the Sudan (until they insist that we change it to Arabic script) and the Amharic for Ethiopia. We have the distinction of the only complete native-tongue New Testament in all of Ethiopia—except for the Amharic Bible. This is the culmination of my fondest dreams for the Anuak people, and I feel the major part of our work is finished.

36. This exposition of the Anuak plan is greatly indebted to Carl H. Templin, who worked in the Anuak project for twelve years. The Anuak plan has much in common with the Nevius plan, first published in China in 1885. See John L. Nevius, *The Planting and Development of Missionary Churches* (Grand Rapids, 1958). Also Roland Allen, *Missionary Methods: St. Paul's or Ours* (New York, 1913).

37. One morning while on furlough at home in America, Don received a letter from Ethiopia informing him that his old truck had finally died and could not be brought back to life. When his father asked him at lunch what he was going to do without a truck, Don replied that he would commit the problem to the Lord. If God wanted him to have a truck, he would provide one; otherwise, Don would get along without a truck. In a few minutes the telephone rang and a farmer friend, who could not work that day because of the rain, asked Don to come out to his house for a visit. During the conversation the farmer asked Don if he had any special needs. Don mentioned the truck and was asked what a replacement would cost. When Don quoted a figure, the farmer smiled and pulled a sealed envelope out of his pocket that contained a check for that exact amount!

38. The most famous loose cannon on the deck of the American Mission ship in Africa during these years was Thomas A. Lambie, M.D. Born in 1885, Lambie earned his medical degree from the University of Pittsburgh in 1907. Later that year he was at Doleib Hill among the Shullas, and then he and the Reverend Elbert McCreery opened the mission at Nasir among the Nuers. The first Nuer Christian was named Pok Jok. In 1918, on the wave of a devastating influenza epidemic, the governor of Wollego province asked Dr. Lambie to come over into Ethiopia.

Accompanied by Dr. and Mrs. Giffen, Lambie, with his wife, Charlotte, and their children, Betty (age eight) and Wallace (age nine), traveled seventeen days from Nasir to Gambela on an empty Nile steamer that would be loaded with Ethiopian coffee for the return journey. From Gambela to Dembi Dollo, Lambie traveled by horse. Because of the tsetse fly, a horse never survived more than one trip, although a mule or donkey might make that journey nine or ten times before it died. When Lambie entered Ethiopia, there was only one foreign Christian missionary—the Rev. Dr. Karl

Cedarquist, a Swede, who operated a school in Addis Ababa. At Dembi Dollo, Lambie worked with Gidada Solon (note 53). On one of his trips to America, Lambie spoke to a Junior Missionary League meeting attended by a young Lyda Boyd.

While in the Dembi Dollo area, Dr. Lambie removed a small beetle that had crawled into Governor Ras Nado's ear and was causing great pain. Ras Nado's followers identified this insect as a wood-boring beetle and were convinced, in spite of Lambie's assurances to the contrary, that it would have drilled right through the governor's head and killed him. Ras Nado's gratitude for saving his life resulted in a letter of commendation for Dr. Lambie and an introduction to the prince regent, Ras Tafari Makonnen (later Haile Selassie I).

After meeting Ras Tafari Makonnen and with money he had raised in America, Lambie built George Memorial Hospital in Addis Ababa (see Lambie, *A Doctor's Great Commission*, pp. 150–61), receiving Ethiopian citizenship in 1934 so that he could hold title to the property. Early in the Italian war Lambie became the executive secretary of the Ethiopian Red Cross. During this time he met a young aviator, Count Carl Gustav von Rosen, who, like Don McClure, was killed at Gode (13 July 1977) by Somali raiders.

Born near Stockholm (19 August 1909), von Rosen received his pilot's license in 1929. In 1935 he attended a lecture by Gunnar Agge, a missionary doctor in Ethiopia, who attempted to mobilize Swedish public opinion against the Italian invasion of that African nation. In response, von Rosen placed himself and his plane, a Heinkel, at the disposal of the Red Cross in Ethiopia. After World War II von Rosen was asked to build the Ethiopian air force and served as principal instructor with the rank of colonel from 1945 to 1956. In 1974 he returned to Ethiopia to aid in airlifting relief supplies to famine and drought victims in villages inaccessible to surface transport. Survived by his wife and six children, two of whom were born in Ethiopia, Count Carl Gustav von Rosen asked in his will that his body be buried in Ethiopia—a request that was honored by that grateful nation. For more information, see Ralph Herrmanns's *Carl Gustav von Rosen* (Stockholm, 1975).

According to John H. Spencer in *Ethiopia at Bay: A Personal Account of the Haile Selassie Years* (Algonac, Michigan, 1984), p. 85, in order to continue his missionary work, Lambie willingly submitted to the Italian conquest of Ethiopia and made widely publicized retractions of his earlier reports of Italian attacks on Red Cross ambulances and the Italian use of poison gas. Yet, see Lambie's account of the Italian bombing of the defenseless Doro Mission station in *A Doctor Carries On*, pp. 59–72. In any case, Lambie, who had transferred from the American Mission to the Sudan Interior Mission, lost the confidence of Haile Selassie and consequently his Ethiopian citizenship. He became stateless until a special act of the 76th Congress (11 July 1940) restored his American citizenship.

In Khartoum, April 1941, the McClures were with the Ried Shieldses, but visited the Lambies alone, since the Lambies and the Shieldses (Shields's book is mentioned in note 7) were not on speaking terms. Of that situation Lyda wrote,

> Imagine two missionary families in the heart of Africa acting like that! Anyway, we had a wonderful time. When we left, the Lambies asked us to take their small puppy, a delightful fox terrier about two months old. Our youngsters are crazy about him. For a while we called him "Typhoon" (as the Lambies did), but that was too difficult for the kids to say, so Marghi

suggested "Calico Pup." The name stuck for a few days until Donnie began calling him "Tim."

After the death of his first wife in 1945 (buried in the British cemetery in Port Said), Lambie founded and served as director of the Berachah Tuberculosis Sanatorium in Bethlehem (Hashemite Kingdom of Jordan). While there, Dr. Lambie was invited to bring the message at the sunrise service under the brow of Calvary's hill. A few days before Easter he went with friends to make preparations for this service, and as he was stating the substance of the address he planned to give, his voice faltered and he died. Thomas A. Lambie, M.D., died on 14 April 1954 and is buried in Allegheny Cemetery, Pittsburgh. Lambie tells his own story in *A Doctor Without a Country* (New York, 1939); *A Doctor Carries On* (New York, 1942); *Boot and Saddle in Africa* (New York, 1943); and *A Doctor's Great Commission* (Wheaton, Illinois, 1954).

39. Later Don wrote,

> I really do not know what we should do about polygamy in this culture. What is ideal and what is practical are not always the same. Not long ago one of our best evangelists inherited a wife and then married another and refused to give up either woman. According to our long-established rules, a man with more than one wife cannot be an evangelist, so we had to let him go. But Garby did not stop teaching and preaching, and now he has gathered a fine Christian group in his village who want baptism and are building a church and school. Within the next several weeks I will go up to baptize these new Christians and dedicate the church, and I am inclined to restore Garby to his place as an evangelist. If having two wives makes him so zealous, I wish some more of our evangelists would hurry and marry a couple of times or whatever it takes to warm them up. Maybe Garby has something to teach us!

40. Some evil medicine men are identified at birth by their "deformities." The three classes of witchdoctors include those born with one testicle showing in the scrotum, those with two very small testicles, and those with none.

Often these boys are not allowed to grow up to become witchdoctors because the fathers usually decide that such babies must be killed. In these cases the child is placed in a little basket, the top is woven shut, and the basket is abandoned in the middle of the river. If the mother weeps for the death of her baby boy, her next son will be deformed in the same way (see D. S. Oyler, "The Shilluk's Belief in the Evil Eye," in *Sudan Notes and Records* 2, no. 2 [1919]: 122–37).

Oyler (see note 20) records how the Shullas believe that the witchdoctors can cast the evil eye on others. He notes that a Shulla with a fine head of hair weaved into a fantastic shape will place a few thorns in it to ward off the evil eye. Otherwise his head would break out in sores (p. 127).

41. For the horrifying, detailed, and moving story of an eyewitness to the Italian invasion of Ethiopia, see G. L. Steer, *Caesar in Abyssinia* (London, 1936). The brave Ethiopians, defending their land with nineteenth-century weapons, were no match for Mussolini's troops, who strafed defenseless villages, bombed Red Cross hospitals and transports, and sprayed poison gas. On Wingate, see Leonard Mosley's *Gideon*

Goes to War (New York, 1955) and Christopher Sykes's *Orde Wingate: A Biography* (Cleveland, 1959). The toothbrush bath is mentioned in Leonard Mosley's *Haile Selassie: The Conquering Lion* (London, 1964), p. 257.

42. In his book *Ismailia* (London, 1879), Samuel W. Baker (see notes 4, 10, and 24) let the reader know that he was a practical man: "I do not love to dwell upon geographical theories, as I believe in nothing but actual observation" (p. 469). In his view, Africa could only be civilized by commerce that required, first of all, the suppression of the slave trade. Until then,

> [D]ifficult and almost impossible is the task before the missionary. The Austrian mission has failed, and their stations have been forsaken; their pious labor was hopeless, and the devoted priests died on their barren fields. . . . It is my opinion that the time has not yet arrived for missionary enterprise . . . but at the same time a sensible man might do good service by living among the natives, and proving to their material minds that persons do exist whose happiness consists in doing good to others.

The description of this "sensible man" sounds remarkably like Samuel Baker himself. Such a person, Baker reasoned, should avoid theological teaching until he has gained ascendancy over the minds of the natives by the means he sets forth as follows:

> If he wished to secure their attention and admiration, he should excel as a rifle shot and sportsman. If musical, he should play the Highland bagpipes. He should be clever as a conjurer, and be well provided with conjuring tricks, together with a magic lantern, magnetic battery, dissolving views, photographic apparatus, colored pictorial illustrations, etc. etc. He should be a good surgeon and general doctor, etc., and be well supplied with drugs, remembering that natives have a profound admiration for medical skill. A man who in full Highland dress could at any time collect an audience by playing a lively air with the bagpipes, would be regarded with great veneration by the natives, and would be listened to when an archbishop by his side would be totally ignored. He should set all psalms to lively tunes, and the natives would learn to sing them immediately. Devotional exercises should be chiefly musical. In this manner a man would become a general favorite; and if he had a never-failing supply of beads, copper rods, brass rings for arms, fingers, and ears, gaudy cotton handkerchiefs, red or blue blankets, zinc mirrors, red cotton shirts, etc., to give to his parishioners, and expected nothing in return, he would be considered a great man, whose opinion would carry considerable weight, provided he only spoke of subjects which he thoroughly understood. A knowledge of agriculture, with a good stock of seeds of useful vegetables and cereals, iron hoes, carpenter's and blacksmith's tools, and the power of instructing others in their use, together with a plentiful supply of very small axes, would be an immense recommendation to a lay missionary who should determine to devote some years of his life to the improvement of the natives" (pp. 467–68).

43. Richard Lyth returned to England and became an Anglican priest and was later appointed a bishop in Uganda. Because he felt that an indigenous Ugandan should hold this office, Lyth eventually resigned and went back to England.

44. Harvey Hoekstra (see note 35) later translated the New Testament into the Murle language with Lado's help. In 1952 the American Mission began work among the Murle people at Pibor, by river 120 miles south of Akobo. In the early days it was a nine-day boat trip just from Malakal to Akobo. When the Missionary Aviation Fellowship was established after World War II, it cut the travel time to one and a half hours.

45. As an indication of the medical staffing in Africa at that time, there were *no* indigenous medical doctors in Ethiopia, to which Haile Selassie returned in 1941. Therefore Ethiopia had to rely on foreign, and especially missionary, physicians. In 1947 there were 47 hospitals with 3,400 beds (one-third in Addis Ababa) and 110 doctors (65 in the capital). This is reported by J. Spencer Trimingham in *The Christian Church and Mission in Ethiopia* (London, 1950), p. 13. Donald N. Levine in *Wax and Gold: Tradition and Innovation in Ethiopian Culture* (Chicago, 1965), p. 190, points out that in 1965 the number of those who had completed elementary school in Ethiopia was still under one percent of the national population.

46. See Darrell Bates, *The Abyssinian Difficulty: The Emperor Theodorus and the Magdala Campaign 1867–68* (New York, 1979), pp. 2–3. Levine, in *Wax and Gold*, p. 78, writes that "the Amhara consider themselves distinctly more handsome than both the white man and the Negro man." For a scholarly discussion of the Queen of Sheba legend, see Edward Ullendorff, *Ethiopia and the Bible* (London, 1968), pp. 131–45. In the Arabic version, Makeda is called Bilkis. Ullendorff's *Ethiopians: An Introduction to Country and People* (see note 8) is a fine one-volume survey.

47. The ark of the covenant, called the Tabot, is found in every Ethiopian church. According to tradition, Eleazer, the oldest son of Solomon's high priest, stole the original tablets on which the Ten Commandments were written, and Menelik (in Hebrew, Ben-Melek means "son of the king") brought them with the original ark to Ethiopia (p. 48). Ethiopian Christians also observe the food laws of the Pentateuch, including the statement (Genesis 32:32) concerning the forbidden sinew (p. 46). For additional information see Ephraim Isaac, *The Ethiopian Church* (Boston, 1968). Numerous biblical references to Ethiopia are discussed in Ullendorff, *Ethiopia and the Bible*, pp. 1–15.

The Hebrew word *Cush* is translated in the Septuagint as "Aithiopia" (p. 5). The principal New Testament reference (Acts 8:27) refers to an Ethiopian eunuch having great authority under Candace, queen of the Ethiopians, who is identified by them with the Queen of Sheba. Then Candace and the Queen of the South (cf. Matthew 12:42 and Luke 11:31) are fused into one person (p. 5). The Greeks called all those who lived south of Egypt "Ethiopians," or "people with burnt faces." For the Greek etymology, see Ernst Hammerschmidt, "Die Anfänge des Christentums in 'Äthiopien,'" *Zeitschrift für Missionswissenschaft und Religionswissenschaft* 38 (1954): 281. Hammerschmidt says that in the Greek and Roman periods, not only was all of Africa south of Egypt called Ethiopia, but eastern Persia and India were included (p. 282). Homer in *Odyssey*, I, 22, writes of Neptune going off to the Ethiopians, who are at the end of the world.

One of the most interesting, endangered, and isolated minorities is the Falashas, the black Jews of Ethiopia, who once numbered 1,000,000 and now number about 28,000 and claim descent from Menelik I. In 1984–85, during a time of drought, the

State of Israel in its "Operation Moses" airlifted about 8000 Falashas from Ethiopia to the "Promised Land." See Louis Rapoport's *Redemption Song: The Story of Operation Moses* (San Diego, 1986) and his passionate and moving *Lost Jews: Last of the Ethiopian Falashas* (New York, 1980).

48. For a fascinating insider's account of the reign of Haile Selassie, see John H. Spencer's *Ethiopia at Bay: A Personal Account of the Haile Selassie Years.* Peter Schwab's *Haile Selassie I: Ethiopia's Lion of Judah* (Chicago, 1979), written after the emperor's fall, is almost wholly unsympathetic to its subject. It is flawed, in my judgment, by the attempt to provide a cross-cultural, psychological account of Haile Selassie (attributing the emperor's behavior to parental neglect).

Before ascending the throne of Ethiopia, Haile Selassie was named Ras Tafari Makonnen. As an orthodox Ethiopian Christian, Haile Selassie (who visited Jamaica in 1966) was embarrassed by the millenarian-messianic Jamaican cult called the Rastifarians, who believe that he was the returned Messiah and that Ethiopia is the promised land of all black people exiled in a world of white oppressors. For more information, see Leonard E. Barrett, *The Rastifarians: Sounds of Cultural Dissonance* (Boston, 1977). See also G. Shepperson, "Ethiopianism: Past and Present," in *Christianity in Tropical Africa*, ed. by C. G. Bäeta (Oxford, 1968), pp. 259–68.

49. At the World Missionary Conference (Edinburgh, 1910) a letter was read from the influential professor of missions, Gustav Warneck, who claimed that the first missionary priority was the race against Islam to convert the animist people of the world. Cited from Ronald Oliver, *The Missionary Factor in East Africa* (New York, 1952), p. 205. Oliver is concerned with East Africa *south* of Sudan and Ethiopia. Gustav Warneck's *Outline of a History of Protestant Missions*, ed. by George Robson (New York, 1901), deals with Africa on pp. 188–236.

50. Emperor Menelik II once said, "Ethiopia is an island of Christians in a sea of Muslims" (quoted by Trimingham, in *The Christian Church and Missions in Ethiopia*, p. 7).

51. Don McClure wrote from Pokwo,

> You will notice that our mailing address is Gambela, the Anglo-Egyptian Sudan, but this town is actually more than a hundred miles within the borders of Ethiopia. Gambela is an area one mile square that was given to the British government of Sudan many years ago by the then emperor of Ethiopia, Menelik II. Thus it is still considered to be a part of the Sudan.

According to Lambie in *Boot and Saddle in Africa*, p. 25, Gambela is one of the most pestilential places in the world.

52. In spite of Don's praise, the Oromo (or Galla) people were not everywhere advanced or civilized. According to Mosley in *Haile Selassie*, p. 29, "Until recent times, it has been mandatory evidence of the manliness of certain Galla tribesmen to prove they have killed a man by presenting his testicles to the killer's bride-to-be. Nowadays [1964] to slay and emasculate a wild beast is considered sufficient." For an ethnographical survey, see G. W. B. Huntingford, *The Galla of Ethiopia* (London, 1955). Among the Galla, a man is not considered a full man until he has killed a human being. "Only after such a murder may a man wear a copper ring in his ear"

(Huntingford, p. 64). See also John Buchholzer, *The Land of Burnt Faces*, trans. by Maurice Michael (London, 1955), pp. 108–113, on "The Testicle Gatherers of the Savanna."

53. The story *Keis Gidada Solon: The Other Side of Darkness* was told to and recorded by Ruth McCreery and Martha M. Vandevort, ed. by Marion Fairman (New York, 1972). Gidada Solon was born in 1902. His six siblings all died from smallpox in 1906, and he was blinded by the disease. When the American Mission opened work at Dembi Dollo, Gidada became a Christian. During the Italian occupation (1936–41), Keis Gidada and Keis Mamo Chorka continued to proclaim the gospel. When the foreign missionaries were expelled from Ethiopia, they left behind a handful of Oromo Christians; when they returned, there were thousands. Keis Gidada Solon died 24 February 1977 in the confidence that the eyes of the blind shall be opened.

54. Lyda McClure wrote,

Donnie came in just now with two ducks and was boasting about how good a shot he is. He bet me that I could not do better. I took the .22 Hornet rifle and with my first shot hit the inch and a half target-center almost in the middle! Donnie was surprised, because I never shoot unless I have to. I would do more shooting, but when I am out, both Don and Donnie are there, so why should I bother? Don had the same idea that I could not hit anything until he insisted that I shoot at an animal. I killed it with my first shot. Don had seen me shoot geese, but there were always a lot of geese around and Don thought that I never got the one at which I was aiming. He knows better now. I like to show that I can shoot, too, and well, especially since I am so often here alone. If people know that I can shoot and have the gun, I will have no trouble from strangers. Of course, our Anuak people give me no trouble at any time.

55. On one occasion, when the Oylers (notes 20 and 40) were heading downriver to Egypt, their steamer was towing six open-air barges containing about fifty officers and men of a Scottish Highland regiment returning from a peace-keeping mission in south Sudan. Since the barges were not screened from mosquitoes, the soldiers unrolled nets over their cots each night. When the unwieldy steamer swung wide to avoid a sandbar, the lead barge brushed against an enormous old thorn tree and dislodged a huge swarm of vicious African bees that immediately laid siege to the hapless Scots. An officer quickly ordered the soldiers to get on their cots and drop the mosquito nets. This was a splendid idea except for the fact that the attacking bees were moving faster than the retreating men, who, wearing their regimental kilts, were not as protected on certain sensitive parts of their bodies as they would have preferred. For a few moments there was absolute and profane pandemonium. Afterward, Mrs. Lillian Oyler made certain that young David would never attempt to memorize or use any part of his newly augmented vocabulary.

56. The proclamation's text is printed in appendix B of Trimingham's *Christian Church and Missions in Ethiopia*, pp. 68–71. The "Open Areas" in which Christian missionary activity was permitted were chiefly in the south and west of Ethiopia. According to Don McClure, when a mission became successful, the Ethiopian Orthodox Church moved in, distributed a few religious trinkets, sprinkled some holy water, and declared the area closed. The various missions were afraid to protest this high-handed procedure for fear of being expelled entirely from Ethiopia. Levine in *Wax and God*, p. 3, points out that "Ethiopia is the only country in Africa with a large number of ethnic groups where one of these groups [the Amhara] has imposed its rule and its language over the rest and has preserved indigenous national institutions, elites, and culture patterns from displacement by Western forms and authorities."

57. A masterful picture of a detribalized African is presented by Joyce Cary in *Mister Johnson* (1939; reprint, New York, 1989). This classic book is far superior to the African work of Isak Dinesen and of Graham Greene, *A Burnt-Out Case* (New York, 1961). For a deeply sensitive, troubled, and troubling description of the difficulties and dislocations resulting from the introduction of the Christian faith among the Nuers, see Eleanor Vandevort, *A Leopard Tamed* (New York, 1968). This is an account of the first seminary-trained Nuer pastor.

58. Don's volunteers in Africa grew accustomed to hearing leopards and lions, seeing waterbucks and a fantastic assortment of birds. They learned to eat bushbucks, reedbucks, antelopes, tiangs (a species of small antelope), wild pigs, and the great bustard (a kind of African wild turkey). In Don's first days at Gilo, one volunteer killed two cobras, seven puff adders, and a python. One night when the volunteer lay down to sleep, he heard a hissing noise a few inches from his head, and thinking that the nozzle of insect repellent was spraying, he shined a flashlight on a puff adder under his bed.

On another occasion four of Don's volunteers decided they wanted to shoot a buffalo or two, so they went hunting out behind the mountains at Pokwo.

> However, the grass was too high for good hunting, and after a couple of days they gave it up and started back. Still in hopes of getting some meat, they split up; two came in by tractor and two started to walk. The chaps on the tractor followed the tracks they had made going out, so they arrived home about four in the afternoon on Wednesday. They thought the other two would beat them in because they started ahead and the tractor moves very slowly through the grass and elephant tracks.
>
> As it became dark, I got uneasy and suggested to a couple of Anuaks that they go back and let out a few yells. Later I sent a chap out with my shotgun to signal them, but still no reply. We had a prayer meeting scheduled that night, so we made it short and to the point, and then I organized a search party because I did not want the two fellows to spend a night out without food, water, or mosquito nets. They had not taken any water with them and thus had been without water for twelve hours, and that is very dangerous in this heat. I sent some Anuaks in one direction, and I took the Jeep and the other two chaps and we started back for the mountains. The grass was twelve feet high, so we could see nothing at all but that little moon in the sky. About midnight I stood on top of the Jeep and could see a fire a long way off, and we started for it. A mile or so later, we again looked and as we stood there, we heard a shout in the opposite direction. We fired our guns, and they replied with one shot. So we turned back and pushed on through the grass. A half-hour later we again shouted and shot. We heard an answering shout, but no shot so we kept on. At 1:00, we found them lying

under a tree by a small fire, completely surrounded by grass and nearly dead from thirst and fatigue.

Their story was fantastic. They had seen a Roan antelope, and in following it they had become lost. So they climbed a tree to sight the big mountain near the mission. They got to the mountain and from a tree could see the mission, but when they got down and started to walk through the grass, they were lost in ten minutes and had to go back to the mountain for their direction. After they had done this three or four times, they found their strength draining away and thirst getting them down. Soon they were worn out and could not walk. They tried crawling and must have crawled a half-mile through the tall, thick grass until they found a tree, but they did not have the strength to climb it and see where they were. Nor could they have gone on even if they had known where they were. So they built a small fire and waited until darkness. But darkness brought millions of mosquitoes, and they fought them like mad until their strength was so sapped they could not even swat at the mosquitoes. So they just lay down and waited. Then they thought of their guns and started to shoot them in the air. They had no idea how many shots were fired, but I found a couple of boxes of empty cartridges lying on the ground, and of course, I did not find them all. So they must have shot at least fifty times wildly and with no purpose. They suddenly realized that only one round remained, so they saved it until they might hear us. And it is a good thing they did, or we never would have found them in all that grass.

They were so weak that they could not climb into the Jeep, and both of them looked like old men with mouths drawn in and eyes sunken in their heads. We were only four miles from home, but could not follow our trail back because we had wandered all over the place looking for them. So we struck out in the direction I thought the mission ought to be, traveling in the lowest gear all the time because of the difficulty of pushing through the grass and the necessity of going slow. Our motor started to boil because there was no air, and our radiator was full of grass seed. We stopped to cool it off and could not get started again. We tried and tried until the battery was dead, and then all of us were stuck! So we built another fire and lay down to sleep. Needless to say, we did not get much sleep with millions of mosquitoes attacking us. They nearly drove us mad, and we slapped and waved until daylight. When daylight came, I climbed a tree and saw that we were just about a mile from the mission, although we would have to travel at least three miles around the swamps. We could have made it home very easily the night before if the Jeep had not died. The grass was too green to burn, so we tramped it down for twenty feet ahead of the Jeep, pushing the Jeep over it a couple of times to wear down a path. Finally, we gave a mighty push and got up enough speed to turn the motor over and the Jeep started. We got home in time for breakfast. Being lost in high grass can be terrifying. It was a lesson to them, and they will not be quite so sure of themselves hereafter. They thought they could not get lost in flat country with the two or three mountains for landmarks.

59. The McClures received one of their tools for the Anuak work as a direct result of President Eisenhower's projected visit to the Soviet Union in 1960. The visit was canceled in the wake of the U-2 incident, when U.S. pilot Francis Gary Powers was shot down. As part of that visit, the American president had planned to give Premier Nikita Khrushchev a water-jet boat with a 185-horsepower Ford Marine Interceptor engine—so new that the Russians could not claim to have invented it. This boat sat on the lawn of the American Embassy in Moscow for five months before being returned to the builder in Indianapolis.

Pastor R. Byron Crozier, one of Don McClure's most loyal supporters, persuaded his Wisconsin congregation to purchase this boat for the Anuak project. To fulfill the builder's requirement of fifty hours on Lake Michigan, the boat—now named the *Dove*—was taken by trailer from Indianapolis to Milwaukee. Then it was shipped through the Great Lakes and the St. Lawrence Seaway across the Atlantic Ocean through the Mediterranean Sea and Suez Canal to be unloaded at Port Sudan on the Red Sea. From there it was to go overland to Khartoum, where Crozier himself and Dr. Allan Fidler, a radiologist, were waiting to run the *Dove* eight hundred miles up the White Nile River system to the Gilo River station. However, heavy rains washed out the railroad from Port Sudan, and the boat was landed in Eritrea instead, taken by truck to Addis Ababa and down the mountains over nearly impassable roads to Pokwo.

The *Dove*, being jet-propelled, had no rudder and no propeller. Thus, when on plane, it required only three inches of water. However, it chewed up water hyacinths and spewed them out like a thick spinach soup. It also required the high-test gasoline used by airplanes, which was very expensive to import into a primitive area of Ethiopia. The *Dove* turned out to be too sophisticated for long-term use on African rivers because sand wore down the blades in the turbine. Nevertheless, this endeavor was given wide publicity in American newspapers, and Crozier's congregation had a deep, costly, and personal stake in the work of a Christian missionary named Don McClure.

The *Dove* plied the rivers of Anuak territory for some years with the brass plaque still affixed to the dash that read:

A Gift
from
Dwight D. Eisenhower, President of the United States of America
to
Premier Nikita Khrushchev, First Secretary of the Communist Party
1960

60. The Monophysites held that the divine nature and the human nature of Christ mixed like wine and water to form a single and unique nature. The Nestorians thought of the two natures as remaining unmixed, like oil and water. The Council of Chalcedon tried to avoid both views, but the Ethiopian Church preferred the former. These similes are found in Neill, *A History of Christian Missions*, p. 64.

61. "Encompassed on all sides by the enemies of their religion, the Ethiopians slept near a thousand years, forgetful of the world, by whom they were forgotten." This citation of the rounded prose of Edward Gibbon in *The Decline and Fall of the Roman Empire* (Chicago, 1952), 2:159–60, is to be found in nearly every book on

Ethiopia. Gibbon, for whom Christianity was beneath contempt (see his chapter 15), continues, "The Abyssinians still adhered with unshaken constancy to the Monophysite faith; their languid belief was inflamed by the exercise of dispute; they branded the Latins with the names of Arians and Nestorians, and imputed the adoration of *four* gods to those who separated the two natures of Christ" (p. 160).

Johann Ludwig Krapf (1810–81) was driven out of Ethiopia in 1838. In 1844 he established a station at Mombasa, the seaport of Kenya. Two months later, on 6 July 1844, Mrs. Krapf delivered a healthy daughter. After three days she became delirious with fever and died. The baby died of the same disease on 15 July. In his *Travels, Researches, amd Missionary Labors* (London, 1867), p. 132, Krapf says, "I was obliged by the climate to conduct this second victim of the king of terrors to the grave of my beloved Rosine as soon as possible." He continues, "Afterwards Mr. Waters and his friends in Bombay erected a stone monument over the grave, so that it might always remind the wandering Suahilis and Wanika, that here rested a Christian woman who had left father, mother, and home to labor for the salvation of Africa." In famous words, Krapf wrote to the Church Missionary Society: "Tell our friends that in a lonely grave on the African coast there rests a member of the Mission. This is a sign that they have begun to struggle with this part of the world; and since the victories of the Church lead over the graves of many of her members, they may be the more convinced that the hour is approaching when you will be called to convert Africa, beginning from the East Coast" (quoted in Neill, *A History of Christian Missions*, p. 317).

62. The history of Ethiopia is recounted by J. Doresse, in *L'Empire du Prêtre-Jean*, 2 vols. (Paris, 1957). Apparently Doresse found Ato (Mr.) Kebede Michael more helpful than Don McClure did (see p. 301 of this book). Medieval mapmakers knew three Indias: Nearer India, Farther India, and Middle India, which was later known as Ethiopia. The king-priest, Iohannes Presbyter or Prester John (John the Elder), was supposed to be a direct descendant of one of the three Magi who visited the infant Jesus (see Reader's Digest editors, *Quest for the Past* [Pleasantville, 1984], p. 238).

For the heroic story of the Portuguese connection with Prester John and Ethiopia, see Elaine Sanceau's *The Land of Prester John: A Chronicle of Portuguese Exploration* (New York, 1944). Sanceau concludes that the quest for Prester John was one of the blind alleys of history and vanished into the junk heap of lost causes. "Yet what enthusiasm had gone into it! For a hundred years Portugal sought Prester John." And when the Portuguese rescued the Ethiopian from the Turk "only to find that he was not what they imagined, they simply set to work once more and tried to make him what they thought he ought to be. Four hundred of the nation's finest manhood [including the incredibly brave son of Vasco da Gama] were lost forever, and a band of earnest missionaries threw their lives upon a work that had no continuity" (pp. 230–31).

63. See Levine, *Wax and Gold*, p. 232.

64. For descriptions of Maskal and Timkat, see Stuart Bergsma's chatty *Rainbow Empire: Ethiopia Stretches Out Her Hands* (Grand Rapids, 1932), pp. 57–64; also Levine's *Wax and Gold*, pp. 62–63.

65. According to the "Friends of Ethiopia Newsletter" (September 1989), Crown Prince Asfa Wossen announced in London on 6 April 1989 that he had acceded to the throne and assumed the name Amha Selassie I, Emperor of Ethiopia. His only sister, Princess Tenagnework, who lives in Addis Ababa, was released in May 1988 after fourteen years in prison. The grandsons of the late Emperor Haile Selassie— Beidemariam, Mikael, and Wossen Seged—were recently freed after fifteen years in jail.

66. In 1924 Dr. Mary Smith was a little girl in the welcoming party that greeted the Buchanans at Nasir (note 20).

67. For the story of Bishop Gwynne (1863–1957), see Jackson, *Pastor on the Nile— Llewellyn H. Gwynne*. In 1902 Gwynne visited Doleib Hill, remarking, "Here in the midst of perhaps the most primitive savages in existence [the American Mission is] attempting, by the strength of Christ, for His sake, a most heroic work. . . . It was wonderful to see how in so short a space of time they had won the confidence of the honest, simple, finely built, naked Shilluk who had already learnt to trust and love the stranger in their midst—perhaps the only friends they had ever known" (pp. 54– 55).

68. The exception to the worthlessness of the Ogaden desert, contested between Ethiopia and Somalia, "was the well-known fact that the geological formations of the oil-rich Persian Gulf curve in a vast semicircle through the Arabian Sea to the Horn of Africa, including the Ogaden" (Spencer, *Ethiopia at Bay*, p. 106).
    According to Schwab in *Haile Selassie I*, p. 99, "Not until 1977 [the year of Don McClure's death], with huge support from the Soviet Union, did Somalia temporarily occupy the Ogaden." In early 1978 the Somalis were thrown out by the Ethiopians, and the Soviets switched allegiance from the Somalis to the Ethiopians. In a reverse response, in 1977 the United States (under President Jimmy Carter) switched from its long alliance with Ethiopia (under Haile Selassie) to closer political ties with Somalia.

69. In her account of the rescue of the royal grandchildren of Haile Selassie from Ethiopia, Jodie Collins, in *Code Word: Catherine* (Wheaton, Illinois, 1984), p. 172, reports that the crown princess (then in London) mentioned that Dr. McClure had an airplane. "I am wondering about asking him to help us get the children out of Ethiopia. Do you think your husband could contact him?" A few days later Don McClure was killed at Gode.

70. On cicatrization, or the forehead scarring called "gar," see Pasquale Crazzolara, "Die Gar-Zeremonie bei den Nuer," *Africa* 5 (1932): 23–39. A summary is found in Seligman's *Pagan Tribes of the Nilotic Sudan*, pp. 223–26, and also in Shields, *Behind the Garden of Allah*, pp. 158–61. Since the Anuaks mark their bodies but not their foreheads, according to Blanche Soule of the American Mission (as reported by Seligman, p. 223), the Nuers feel a profound contempt for the Anuaks.

71. Many Nuers had become very familiar with Scripture once the New Testament in the Nuer language was published in 1968. Various members of the American Mission, including S. Robb McLaughlin (note 8) and Eleanor Vandevort (note 57), were involved, but the work was completed by Mac Roy in Kenya after the Roys were expelled from the south Sudan.

72. In the small notebook that he always carried, Don had copied these words ascribed to A. S. Cripps:

> To me
> He hath revealed Himself,
> Not as to Paul,
> Christ throned and crowned;
> But marred,
>   despised,
>   rejected.
> The Divine Outcast of a terrible land,
> The Black Christ with parched lips and empty hand.

73. A picture of this animal-type is found in Evans-Pritchard, *The Nuer* p. 42, fig. 8, no. 2.

74. For a careful, theological articulation of this position see "The Frankfurt Declaration" in *Creeds of the Churches,* ed. by John H. Leith (Atlanta, 1982), pp. 683–91.

75. An evaluation of the Christian world mission that varies considerably from Don McClure's view is expressed by Paul A. Hopkins in *What Next in Mission?* (Philadelphia, 1977). One might almost think that Hopkins's strictures against certain types of missions and missionaries have someone like Don McClure in mind.

76. This film, *The Nuer,* was produced in 1981 by Robert Gardner and Hilary Harris, with McGraw-Hill Films, for the Film Study Center of the Peabody Museum at Harvard University. It is available as a 16mm. movie and on videotape. A videotape copy is in the Clifford E. Barbour Library of Pittsburgh Theological Seminary.

77. For a personal experience of the troubles in Eritrea, see Karl and Debbie Dortzbach's *Kidnapped* (New York, 1975). Debbie's ordeal was widely reported in the American press. Her mother was our son's first-grade teacher.

78. This unhappy story is related here with the names of the persons involved and the places changed in order to disguise completely their true identities.

79. François Coillard, who served in Africa from 1857 to 1904, once wrote to a friend, "My great, *great* desire is not to live a day longer than I can work" (cited in J. H. Morrison's *Missionary Heroes of Africa* [New York, 1922], p. 241).

80. These events at Gode are narrated from a strikingly different perspective by Pam Smith in her book *If God Be for Us* (Hong Kong, 1985). Of course, the Smiths tell the Gode story as *they* experienced it and therefore as a miracle of *their* deliverance.

▼ Person Index

Place Index

Subject Index